THE DARK AGES
476-918

CHARLES OMAN, M.A, F.S.A.
FELLOW OF ALL SOULS COLLEGE AND LECTURER AT NEW COLLEGE, OXFORD

First published by Rivingtons in 1898.

Copyright © Charles Oman.

This edition published in 2017.

TABLE OF CONTENTS

AUTHOR'S PREFACE

In spite of the very modest scale on which this book has been written, I trust that it may be of some use to students of European History. Though there are several excellent monographs in existence dealing with various sections of the period 476-918, there is no continuous general sketch in English which covers the whole of it. Gibbon's immortal work is popularly supposed to do so, but those who have read it most carefully are best aware that it does not. I am not acquainted with any modern English book where the inquirer can find an account of the Lombard kings, or of the Mohammedan invasions of Italy and Sicily in the ninth century, or of several other not unimportant chapters in the early history of Europe. I am in hopes, therefore, that my attempt to cover the whole field between 476 and 918 may not be entirely useless to the reading public.

I must acknowledge my indebtedness to two living authors, whose works have been of the greatest possible help to me in dealing with two great sections of this period, Doctor Gustav Richter, whose admirable collection of original authorities in his Annalen des Frankischen Reichs makes such an excellent introduction to the study of Merovingian and Carolingian times, and Professor Bury of Dublin, whose History of the Later Roman Empire has done so much for the knowledge of East-Roman affairs between 476 and 800.

A word ought, perhaps, to be added on the vexed question of the spelling of proper names. I have always chosen the most modern form in speaking of places, but in speaking of individuals I have employed that used by contemporary authorities, save in the case of a few very well known names, such as Charles, Henry, Gregory, Lewis, where archaism would savour of pedantry.

Oxford, November 1893.

BOOK I

CHAPTER I: ODOACER AND THEODORIC — 476-493

Importance of the year 476 — The Emperor Zeno recognises Odoacer as
Patrician in Italy — Odoacer's position — Divisions of Europe in 476 —
The Vandals in Africa and King Gaiseric — Rule of Odoacer in Italy —
His war with Theodoric, and fall.

In the summer of 477 A.D. a band of ambassadors, who claimed to speak
the will of the decayed body which still called itself the Roman senate,
appeared before the judgment-seat of the emperor Zeno, the ruler of
Constantinople and the Eastern Empire. They came to announce to him
that the army of the West had slain the patrician Orestes, and deposed from
his throne the son of Orestes, the boy-emperor Romulus. But they did not
then proceed to inform Zeno that another Caesar had been duly elected to
replace their late sovereign. Embassies with such news had been common
of late years, but this particular deputation, unlike any other which had yet
visited the Bosphorus, came to announce to the Eastern emperor that his
own mighty name sufficed for the protection of both East and West. They
laid at his feet the diadem and purple robe of Romulus, and professed to
transfer their homage and loyalty to his august person. Then, as if by way
of supplement and addendum, they informed Zeno that they had chosen
Flavius Odoacer for their governor, and trusted that their august master
would deign to ratify the choice, and confer on Odoacer the title of
Patrician.

It has often been repeated of late years that this date, 476 A.D., does not
form a very notable landmark in the history of the world, that its sole event
was the transfer of the nominal supremacy of the Western World from a
powerless Caesar who lived at Ravenna to a powerless Caesar who lived at
Constantinople. We are reminded that the patrician Odoacer and the
deputies of the Roman Senate assured the Eastern Emperor not that they
had cast off allegiance to the imperial name, but that Italy no longer needed
a separate Augustus, and that a single ruler might once more rule East and
West, as in the days of Constantine and Theodosius. And if the
representatives of the western realm then proceeded to recommend Zeno to
appoint as his vicegerent among them 'Odoacer, a mighty man of war, and

a person well skilled in political matters, whom they had selected to defend their interests,' they were, in truth, making no new or startling proposition; for similar embassies had often arrived at Constantinople to announce, not the choice of a mere patrician, but the election of an independent emperor.

In a purely formal way all this is true enough, and we must concede that the permanent establishment of a Teutonic ruler in Italy was only another instance of what had already occurred in Spain and Africa. As yet nobody in either of the three countries had asserted that the Roman Empire had died out and been replaced for all purposes by a Teutonic kingship. Documents were still dated and coins still struck with the name of a Roman Emperor upon them alike in Spain, Africa, and Italy. After 476 the subjects of the Visigoth Euric, no less than those of the Scyrrian Odoacer, proceeded to grave a rude portrait of Zeno on their moneys, just as they had done a few years earlier with a rude portrait of Valentinian III. What mattered it to them that the one dwelt east of the Adriatic and the other west?

But if the historians of the last century were too neglectful of the constitutional and theoretical aspect of affairs, when they bluntly asserted that the Roman Empire ceased in the West in 476, there is a danger that our own generation may become too much imbued with the formal aspect of things, and too little conscious of the real change which took place in that obscure year. The disappearance of the Roman Empire of the West was, in truth, a long process, which began as early as 411 when Britain — first of all the Occidental 'dioceses' — was abandoned to the barbarian, and did not, perhaps, end till Francis II. of Austria laid down the title of Emperor in the year 1806. Yet if we must choose a point at which, rather than at any other, we are to put the breach between the old and the new, if we must select any year as the dividing-line between ancient history and the Middle Ages, it is impossible to choose a better date than 476.

Down to the day on which Flavins Odoacer deposed Augustulus there was always at Rome or Ravenna a prince who represented in clear heritage the imperial succession that descended from Octavian and Trajan and Constantino. His crown might be fragile, his life in constant danger; his word might be less powerful in Italy than that of some barbarian Ricimer or Gundobad who stood behind the throne. Nevertheless, he was brought into real contact with his subjects, and was a visible, tangible personage whose will and character still made some difference in the governance of the state. The weakest Glycerius or Olybrius never sank into being a mere puppet, like an eighth century king of the Franks, or a seventeenth century Mikado. Moreover, there was till the last a possibility — even, perchance, a probability — that there would arise some strong emperor who would free himself from the power of his German prime minister. Majorian nearly succeeded in doing so; and the stories of the falls of the Goths, Gainas and Aspar, in the East show that such an attempt was not a hopeless undertaking.

But when Odoacer seized the throne from the boy Augustulus, and became with the consent, if not the good-will, of the Constantinopolitan Caesar, the sole representative in the West of the imperial system, a very grave change took place in the status of the empire. Flavins Odoacer was something far more than a patrician ruling as the representative of an absentee emperor. He was not only the successor of Ricimer, but the predecessor of Theodoric and Alboin. For, besides being a Roman official, he was a German king, raised on the shield and hailed as 'Thiudans' by the whole Teutonic horde who now represented the old legions of the West. If he never took the title of 'king of Italy,' it was because territorial appellations of the kind were not yet known. Euric and Gaiseric, his contemporaries, called themselves Kings of the Visigoths and Vandals, not of Spain and Africa. And so Odoacer being king of a land and an array, but not of a nation, may have been somewhat at a loss how to set forth his royal appellation. He would not have deigned to call himself 'king of the Italians;' to call himself king of the Scyrri or Turcilingi, or any other of the tribes who furnished part of his host, would have been to assume an inadequate name. Puzzled contemporary chroniclers sometimes called him king of the Goths, though he himself never used such a title.

Still he was a king, and a king with a settled territory and an organised host; not a migratory invader of Italy, as Alaric had been, but a permanent ruler of the land. In this way he was undoubtedly the forerunner of the Ostrogoths and Lombards who took his place, and, though the title would have sounded strange in his own ears, we may fairly style him king of Italy, as we so style Theodoric, or Berengar, or Victor Emmanuel. For it was the will of Odoacer that was obeyed in the land, and not the will of his titular superior at Constantinople. It was Odoacer who appointed taxes and chose officials, and interfered in the election of bishops of Rome, and declared war on the Rugians or the Vandals. In the few documents of his time that have survived, the name of Zeno is seldom mentioned, and in signing grants he styles himself Odovacar Rex, and not Odovacar Patricius, as strict Roman usage should have prescribed. Similarly, an Italian official acknowledges his regia largitas, not his patricia magnitudo. It is, then, in every way correct, as well as convenient, to style him the first German king of Italy, and to treat his reign as the commencement of a new era. If we hesitate to do this, we are logically bound to refuse to recognise the Visigothic or Frankish kings in Spain and Gaul as independent sovereigns till the middle of the sixth century, and to protract the Roman Empire of the West till Leovigild and Theudebert formally disclaimed the imperial supremacy (540-70).

In the year 476 the greater parts of the lands which had formerly composed the Roman Empire of the West had taken new forms in the shape of six large Teutonic kingdoms. Italy and Noricum formed the kingdom of Odoacer; North Africa the dominions of the Vandal Gaiseric. The Visigothic realm of Euric extended from the Loire to the Straits of Gibraltar. King Gundobad the Burgundian occupied the valleys of the Rhone and Saone, as far as their extreme head-waters. The Princes of the Franks reigned on the Meuse, Moselle, and lower Rhine. Last and smallest of the six Teutonic States was the kingdom of the Suevi in what would now be called north Portugal and Galicia. Interspersed among these German kingdoms were three or four remnants of the old Roman Empire, which had not yet been submerged by the rising flood of Teutonism, though they were destined ere long to disappear beneath its surface. The province of Britain had become a group of small and unhappy Celtic kingdoms, on whose borders the Angle and Saxon had not yet made any appreciable encroachment. Armorica, the modern Brittany, was also a rough confederacy of Celtic states. The Seine valley and the middle Loire formed a Romano-Gallic kingdom under Syagrius, the last governor who had acknowledged the supremacy of the empire beyond the Alps. The Cantabrians and Basques in their hills above the Bay of Biscay had preserved their independence against the Visigoths, just as their ancestors, five centuries before, had held out against the Roman conquerors of Spain. Lastly, there was still a fragment of territory on the Adriatic which claimed to represent the legitimate Empire of the West. The emperor Julius Nepos, when driven from Rome and Ravenna, had fled to Dalmatia, where he contrived to keep together a small kingdom around his capital of Salona. Of these five scattered remnants of territory which had not yet fallen into the hands of the Germans, there were two, the kingdoms of Syagrius and

Nepos, which were doomed to a speedy fall; for the other three a longer and more chequered career was reserved.

Around the solid block of land, which had once formed the Western Empire, were lying a ring of German tribes, who had worked forward from the North and East into the deserted dwellings of the races who had already passed on within the Roman border. The Frisians lay about the mouths of the Waal and Lech, north of the land lately won by the Franks. The Alamanni, a confederacy of Suevian tribes, had possession of the valleys of the Main and Neckar, the Black Forest, and the banks of the upper Danube. East of them again lay the Thuringians and Rugians, in the lands which we should now call northern Bavaria and Bohemia. Beyond them came the Lombards in Moravia and northern Hungary, and the Herules and Gepidae on the middle Danube and the Theiss. All these tribes, like their brethren who had gone before them, were showing a general tendency to press West and South, and take their share in the plunder of the dismembered Empire.

The history of the Teutonic kingdoms of the later fifth and earlier sixth century falls into two distinct halves. The tale of the doings of Frank, Visigoth, Burgundian, and Suevian in the West forms one. Very slightly connected with it do we find the other, the story of the doings of Odoacer in Italy, and of the Vandal kings in Africa, whose connections and interests are far more with the Eastern Empire than with the Transalpine kingdoms. It is with these two states that we shall first have to deal, leaving the discussion of the affairs of the Teutons of Gaul and Spain for another chapter.

Gaiseric, or Genseric as the Romans sometimes called him, first of the Vandal kings of Africa, was still reigning at Carthage in the year when Odoacer became ruler of Italy. For forty-eight years did this first of the Teutonic sea-kings bear sway in the land which he had won, and hold the naval supremacy in the central Mediterranean. The creation of the Vandal kingdom had been one of the most extraordinary feats of the time of the great migrations, and must be attributed entirely to the personal energy of their long-lived king. His tribe was one of the least numerous of the many wandering hordes which had trespassed within the bounds of the empire, no more than 80,000 souls, men, women, and children all counted, when they first invaded Africa. That such a small army should have overrun a province a thousand miles long, and should have become the terror of the whole seaboard of the Western Empire was the triumph of Gaiseric's ability. He was not one of the stalwart, hard-fighting, brainless chiefs who were generally to be found at the head of a German horde, but a man of very moderate stature, limping all his life through from a kick that he got from a horse in early youth. His mental powers alone made him formidable, for he was not only a general of note, but a wily politician, faithless not with the light and heady fickleness of a savage, but with the deliberate and malicious treachery of a professional intriguer. He was one of those not uncommon instances of a Teuton, who, when brought into contact with the empire, picked up all the vices of its decaying civilisation without losing those of his original barbarism. It is not without some reason that the doings of Gaiseric have left their mark on the history of language in the shape of the modern word 'Vandalism.' The sufferings of Italy and Africa at his hands were felt more deeply than the woes they had endured at the hands of other invaders, because of the treachery and malice which inspired them. Compared with Gaiseric, Alaric the Goth seemed a model of knightly courtesy, and Attila the Hun a straightforward, if a brutal, enemy. The Vandal king's special foibles were the conclusion of treaties and armistices which he did not intend to keep, and a large piratical disregard for the need of any pretext or justification for his raids, save indeed the single plea that the city or district that he attacked was at that particular moment not in a good position to defend itself.

From his contact with the empire, Gaiseric had picked up the characteristics of the two most odious types of the day — the tax-collector and the persecuting ecclesiastical bigot. There was more systematic financial oppression in Africa than in any of the other new Germanic kingdoms, and far more spiteful persecution of religious enemies.

The system on which the Vandal organised his realm was not the comparatively merciful 'thirding of the land' that Odoacer and Theodoric introduced into Italy. He confiscated all the large estates of the great African landowners, and turned them into royal domains, worked by his bailiffs. Of the smaller estates, tilled by the provincials who owned them, he made two parts; those in the province of Africa proper and the best of those beyond it, were appropriated and made into military fiefs for his Teutonic followers. These sortes Vandalorum, as they were called, were hereditary and free from all manner of taxation. The royal revenue was raised entirely from those of the poorer and more remote provincial proprietors, who had not been expropriated, and from them Gaiseric, by pitiless taxation, drew a very large revenue.

But it was for his persecution, far more than his fiscal oppression, that Gaiseric was hated. The Vandals, like most of the other Teutons, had embraced Arianism when they were converted, and Gaiseric — evil-liver as he was — had set his mind on forcing his subjects to conform to the religion of their masters. He confiscated all the Catholic churches in Africa, and either handed them over to the Arians or destroyed them. He forbade the consecration of new Catholic bishops, and banished or imprisoned all whom he found already existing in his dominions. Occasionally he put to death, and frequently he imprisoned or sold as slaves, prominent supporters of the orthodox faith. If martyrdoms were few, 'Dragonnades' were many, and, by their systematic cruelty, the Vandal king and people have gained for themselves an ill name for ever in the pages of history.

Their hateful oppression of the provincials made the Vandals' power in Africa very precarious. They were far too few for the mighty land they had conquered, even when Gaiseric had attracted adventurers of all sorts to his banner, and had even enlisted the savage Moors of Atlas to serve on his fleet. The fanatical Africans, the race who had produced the turbulent Donatist sectaries and the wild Circumcelliones, were not likely to submit with meekness to their new masters. They only waited for a deliverer in order to rise against the Vandals, and twice, during the reign of Gaiseric, it seemed as if the deliverer were at hand. On each occasion, the Vandal snatched a success by his cunning and promptitude, when all the probabilities of success were against him. In 460, the Emperor Majorian had collected a fleet of overwhelming strength at Carthagena, and was already gathering the army that was to be conveyed in it. But warned and helped by traitors, Gaiseric came down on the ships before they were manned or equipped, and carried off or burnt them all. In 468, a still greater danger had threatened the Vandal; the Emperors of East and West, Leo and Anthemius, had joined their forces to crush the nest of pirates at Carthage. They actually sent to Africa an army that is said to have amounted to nearly 100,000 men, and overran the whole country from Tripoli to the gates of Carthage. In the hour of danger Gaiseric's courage and treachery were both conspicuous. After deluding the imbecile Roman general Basiliscus, by asking and gaining a five days' truce for settling terms of submission, he sent fire-ships by night against the hostile fleet, and, while the Roman troops were endeavouring to save their vessels, attacked their unguarded camp. After suffering a defeat, the coward

Basiliscus drew off his armament, and the Vandal, saved as by a miracle, could breathe again.

The last ten years of Gaiseric's reign were filled with countless pirate raids on Italy and Sicily, unopposed by the five puppet-emperors who ruled at Rome and Ravenna in those evil days. Gaiseric survived the fall of Romulus Augustulus just long enough to enable him to make a treaty with Odoacer. By this agreement the Vandal, always more greedy for money than for land, gave up his not inconsiderable conquests in Sicily in return for an annual payment from the newly-enthroned king of Italy.

Gaiseric died in 477, and with him the greatness of the Vandals, though their kingdom was to endure fifty years more. He left behind him a fine fleet and a full treasury, and a palace resplendent with the spoils taken at the great sack of Rome in 455. But the dominion of his handful of Vandal followers in Africa was still as precarious as ever; their one security had been the cunning and courage of their aged king, and when he was gone there was no defence left to prevent the Vandal dominion from falling, the moment that it should be attacked. Dreading rebellion among the provincials, Gaiseric had dismantled the walls and gates of every African town save Carthage. One battle lost would place the whole country-side in the hands of an assailant, and at no very distant day the assailant was to come, to avenge the sufferings of three unhappy generations of the oppressed subjects of the Vandals.

Gaiseric was succeeded by his son, Hunneric, a man already advanced in years, who was, like his father, an Arian and a bitter persecutor. He was married to Eudocia, the daughter of the emperor Valentinian III., a prisoner of the sack of Rome in 455. But his wife did not much influence him; he drew from her no tincture of Roman civilisation, nor did her persistent orthodoxy wean him from his Arianism. After living with him for sixteen unhappy years and bearing him two sons, she at last contrived to escape secretly from Carthage, fled to Jerusalem, and died there enjoying once more the Catholic communion of which she had been so long deprived.

Hunneric was a tyrant of the worst type. His dealings with his family are a sufficient proof of his character. Gaiseric, to avoid the danger of a minority — a contingency which would have been fatal to his precarious monarchy — had prescribed that each Vandal king should be succeeded, not by his next-of-kin, but by his eldest relative. Such successions were very usual among the Teutonic tribes, though they had never before been formally made into a rule. Now Hunneric had a grown-up son, Hildecat, whom he destined for his successor; but the prince was, of course, younger than the king's own brothers. Instead of cancelling his father's law, Hunneric set to work to exterminate his brothers, and slew them with all their children, save two youths, the sons of his next brother, Genzo, who saved themselves by timely flight.

During the seven years of his reign (477-484) Hunneric waged no wars; his fleet could no longer prey on the dying carcase of the Western Empire. The two formidable kingdoms of the Visigoth Euric and the Scyrrian Odoacer could not be ravaged like the realm of a Maximus or a Glycerins. They were left alone, while the energies of Hunneric were devoted to persecution of the Catholics in his own realm. The orthodox declared that he from first to last caused the death of 40,000 persons, a hyperbolical exaggeration which half causes us to doubt the reality of what was in truth a very cruel and severe persecution. Hunneric delighted more in mutilation of hands and eyes and tongues than in death given by the sword and the rope, but there is no doubt that, in a considerable number of cases, he punished Catholics with the extreme penalty.

While Hunneric was thus employed it is not strange to hear that he was vexed by rebellions. The Moors of Mount Atlas rose against him, and, by no means to the grief of the Latin speaking provincials, encroached on the Southern border of the Vandal kingdom, and pushed their incursions as far as the Mons Aurasius in Numidia. While preparing to attack them the king died, smitten, if the Catholic chroniclers are to be believed, by the same horrid disease which made an end of Herod Agrippa. His eldest and only grown-up son, Hildecat, had died before him, and the Vandals at once placed on the throne Gunthamund, the eldest of his two surviving nephews, a prince who showed great forbearance, when the circumstances are considered, in imprisoning instead of murdering Hunneric's two younger children.

While we turn from the Vandal kingdom in Africa to the dominions of Odoacer in Italy, we are struck at once by the contrast between the methods of government employed in the two countries. While Gaiseric and Hunneric ruled as mere barbarians, and cast away all the ancient Roman machinery of administration, king Odoacer kept up the whole system as he found it. He appointed praetorian praefects, and magistri militum, and counts of the sacred largesses, just as the Emperors before him had done. The senate still sat at Rome and passed otiose decrees, the consuls still gave their names to the year. But his great scheme of expropriation, by which one-third of the land of each of the richer proprietors of Italy was confiscated for the benefit of his mercenary troops, must have caused much trouble and heart-burning. It is curious that we find so little complaint made about it in the historians of the time. Probably Odoacer's wisdom in letting the smaller proprietors alone has preserved his name from the abuse which still clings to the reputations of many of the Teutonic conquerors of the empire.

On the whole the provincials of Italy must have felt comparatively little change, when they began to be governed by a barbarian king, instead of by a barbarian patrician, such as Ricimer or Gundobad had been. Odoacer appears to have been one of those wise men who can let well alone. Though an Arian himself, he refrained from all religious persecution; and, if he firmly asserted his right to confirm the election of bishops of Rome, we do not find that he ever forced his own nominees on the clergy and people. Indeed, he was noted as a repressor of the alienation of church lands and of simony.

Odoacer's foreign policy seems to have been limited in its scope to the design of keeping together the old 'Diocese of Italy,' that is, the peninsula with its mainland appendages of Noricum and north Illyria. He ceded to the Visigoth Euric the coastland of Provence, which he had found still in Roman hands, and made no attempt to establish relations with the Romano-Gallic governor Syagrius, who held Mid-Gaul, pressed in between Visigoth and Frank. On the other hand, he pursued a firm policy on his north-east frontier. When Julius Nepos was murdered by rebels in 480, Odoacer at once invaded and subdued the Dalmatian kingdom, which the ex-emperor had till the last contrived to retain. Further north, in Noricum, the Rugians had for many years been molesting the Roman provincials and pushing across the Danube. Odoacer sent against them his brother Hunwulf, who drove them back over the river, and took prisoner Feva their king. But, when freed for a moment from their Rugian oppressors, the Roman provincials took the opportunity, not of repairing their ruined cities, but of migrating en masse to Italy. Protected by the army of Hunwulf, the whole population of Noricum, bearing all their goods and chattels, their treasures, and even the exhumed bodies of their saints, poured southward over the Alps, and obtained from Odoacer a settlement on the waste lands of Italy, which the Vandals had ruined. Only in the Rhaetian valleys did some remnants of the Latin-speaking population linger behind. Hence it comes that south Bavaria and archducal

Austria are not at this day speaking Roumansh, like the Engadine, but the German tongue of the Rugians and Herules who passed into the deserted province of Noricum, when it was abandoned a few years later by the armies of Odoacer.

For thirteen years, 476-489, the Scyrrian king bore rule over Italy, Noricum, and Dalmatia with very considerable success. As the years rolled on without any disaster, with the army in good temper, and the Italians fairly content at being at last freed from Vandal and Gothic raids, Odoacer must have begun to believe that he had established a kingdom as well founded as those of his Burgundian or Visigothic neighbours. But there was one fatal weakness in his position: he depended not on the loyalty of a single compact tribe, but on the fidelity of a purely mercenary army, made up of the remnants of a dozen broken Teutonic clans, which looked upon him as a general and a paymaster, and not as a legitimate hereditary prince, descended from the gods and heroes. The regiments of Foederati, who had proclaimed him king, were in no sense a nation; it would have taken many generations to weld them into one, and the fabric of the new kingdom was to be tried by the roughest of shocks before it was even half a generation old.

In 489 there came against Odoacer from the Danube and the Illyrian Alps, Theodoric, son of Theodemir, the king of the Ostrogoths, with all the people of his race behind him — a vast host with their wives and children, their slaves and their cattle, blocking all the mountain-passes of the north-east with the twenty thousand ox-waggons that bore their worldly goods.

Theodoric, the king of that half of the Gothic race which had lingered behind in the Balkan peninsula, when Alaric led the other half westward, was just at the end of a long series of rebellions and ravages by which he had reduced Thrace and Moesia to a condition even more miserable than that in which they had been left by the hordes of Attila. Having failed, like all his forerunners, to take Constantinople, and having concluded his fourth peace with the emperor Zeno, he found himself left with a half-starved army in a land which had been harried quite bare. He had tried his best to reduce the Eastern empire to the condition to which Ricimer had brought the Western, but the impregnable walls of Byzantium had foiled him. Young, capable, and ambitious, he was yearning for new and more profitable fields to conquer; while, at the same time, the emperor of the East was casting about for all possible means to get the Goths as far away from his gates as could be managed. Both Zeno and Theodoric had their reasons for wishing ill to Odoacer: the emperor believed him to have fostered or favoured a late rebellion in Asia which had shaken his throne; the Ostrogothic king was being stirred up by Rugian exiles who had fled before the conquering arm of the king of Italy.

Neither party then needed much persuasion when a scheme was broached for an invasion of Odoacer's realm by the Ostrogoths. Zeno, taking the formal ground that, by the admission of Odoacer and the Italians, he was emperor as well of West as of East, proceeded to decree the deposition of the patrician who now ruled at Rome, and his supersession by a new patrician, the king of the Ostrogoths. Theodoric, in return for his investiture with his new title, and the grant of the dominion of Italy, made a loosely-worded promise to hold his future conquests as the emperor's representative. How far such homage would extend neither party much cared; the emperor only wanted to get rid of the king of the Goths; the king of the Goths knew that once master of Italy he could pay the emperor just as much or as little deference as he might choose.

In the autumn of 488 Theodoric called together the whole Ostrogothic people to a camp on the middle Danube, and bade them prepare for instant migration. The inclement season of the year that he chose for this march seems to have been dictated by fear of famine, for the war had so ravaged Moesia that the Goths had not provisions enough to last till next spring. So, in the October of 488, the Ostrogoths, a great multitude of 200,000 or 300,000 souls, followed the Roman road along the Danube, crossed at Singidunum and set out to march across Pannonia. But they soon met with opposition; Traustila, king of the Gepidae, who now occupied both banks of the mid-Danube, came out against them with his host to prevent them from passing through his land. Theodoric defeated him, but found such difficulty in pressing on through the hostile country that he had to winter on the Save, supporting all his host on the plunder of the farms of Gepidae. In the spring of 489 he moved on, and pressing through the passes of the Julian Alps, without meeting any opposition from the

troops of the king of Italy, came out at last to the spot where the gorge of Schonpass leads down into the plain of Venetia. Here, on the banks of the Isonzo, Odoacer was waiting for him with all his host of Foederati, and there was a mighty battle. The result was not doubtful; the Ostrogoths, a single people, fighting for their wives and families, who lay behind them in the crowded pass, led by their hereditary king, the heaven-born Amal, and knowing that defeat meant destruction, were too desperately fierce to be stopped by the mixed multitude of mercenaries that followed Odoacer. The king of Italy was routed, his camp stormed, his army scattered. It was only beneath the walls of Verona that he could rally it for a second stand. Just a month after the battle of the Isonzo, Theodoric appeared again in front of his enemy, and again won a prompt victory. Here perished most of the old regiments of Foederati that had been wont to defend Italy, for Odoacer had fought with the rapid Adige behind him, and the greater part of his army was rolled back into the fierce stream.

Abandoning north Italy Odoacer now fell back on the marsh-girt fortress of Ravenna, which had baffled so many invaders of the peninsula. Theodoric meanwhile pressed forward and occupied Milan and all the valley of the Po; his triumph was apparently made complete by the surrender of Tufa, the Magister militum of Odoacer's host, who submitted to the Ostrogoth with the wreck of the Italian army. (Autumn, 489.)

But the war was destined to endure for three years more: Ravenna was impregnable and Theodoric was thrice diverted from its siege by disturbances from outside. First Tufa, with the remnant of the Foederati, broke faith and rejoined his old master Odoacer. Then, in the next year, Gundobad, king of the Burgundians, came over the Alps and had to be turned back. Last Frederic, king of the Rugians, the first of the many Frederics of German history, took arms in favour of Odoacer, though Theodoric had sheltered him three years before, when he had fled from the armies of the king of Italy. It was not till July 491 that Odoacer was for the last time driven back within the shelter of the marshes of Ravenna. For twenty months more he maintained himself within its impregnable walls, till sheer famine drove him to ask for peace in February 493.

Theodoric proffered his vanquished enemy far better terms than he could have expected — that he should retain his kingly title and a share in the rule of Italy. But, when Odoacer had laid down his arms and came to his conqueror's camp, he was treacherously slain at a banquet, only ten days after Ravenna fell. This was almost the only base and mean crime in Theodoric's long and otherwise glorious career: his whole conduct at the time of the surrender seems to prove that he deliberately lured his rival to visit him, with the fixed intention of putting him to death. (March, 493.)

So died Odoacer in the sixtieth year of his age; seventeen years after he had slain Orestes, he met the same fate that he had inflicted on his predecessor.

CHAPTER II: THEODORIC KING OF ITALY — 493-526

The Ostrogothic race — Character of Theodoric — His Administration of Italy — Theodoric in Rome — Foreign Policy of Theodoric — His wars with the Franks and Burgundians — His supremacy in Western Europe — Misfortunes of his later years — Death of Boethius — Failure of Theodoric's great schemes.

From the formal and constitutional point of view the substitution of king Theodoric for king Odoacer, as ruler in Italy, made no change in the position of affairs. From the practical point of view the change was important, for the new Teutonic kingdom was very much stronger than the old. Its ruler was a younger and a far abler man, the wisest and most far-sighted of all the Germans of the fifth and sixth centuries. Moreover, the military power of the Ostrogoths was far greater than that of the mixed multitude of Foederati who had followed Odoacer. They were a numerous tribe, confident of their own valour after a century of successful war, and devotedly attached to the king, who, for the last twenty years, had never failed to lead them to victory. While they preserved their ancient courage, they had acquired, by a stay of three generations within the bounds of the empire, a higher level of civilisation than any other of the Teutonic tribes. Their dress, their armour, their manner of life, showed traces of their intercourse with Rome; they had been Christians for a century, and had forgotten many of the old heathen and barbarous customs of their ancestors. They possessed, too, first of all Teutonic peoples, the germ of a written literature in the famous Gothic Bible of Ulfilas. There are documents surviving, written in the character which Ulfilas had devised for his people, which show that there were Gothic clergy and even laymen who could commit their contracts to paper in their own tongue. Theodoric himself never learnt to write, but there must have been many among his subjects who could do so. Though the king actually discouraged the Goths from giving themselves up to book-learnings yet in the generation which followed him there were Goths skilled both in Roman and Greek literature, — some even who called themselves philosophers and claimed to follow Plato.

Of all the German nations it seemed that the Ostrogoths were the most suited to form the nucleus for a new kingdom, which should grow up a young and strong yet civilised state on the ruins of the Roman empire. And if any one man could have brought such a consummation to pass, Theodoric was certainly the most fitted for the task. Ten years spent as a hostage at Constantinople had shown him the strong and the weak points in the Roman system of administration; twenty years Spent in the field at the head of his tribesmen had won him an experience in war, both with Roman and barbarian, that made him unequalled as a general. Italian statesmen found him a master-mind who could comprehend all difficulties of the administration of an empire. Gothic warriors looked up to him not only as the most skilful marshaller of a host, but also as the stoutest lance in his own army. Alike when he smote the Gepidae by the Danube, and when he drove the Foederati of Odoacer into the Adige, the king had himself headed the final and decisive charge that broke the shield-wall of the enemy. But Theodoric was even more than a great statesman and warrior: he was a man of wide mind and deep thought. His practical wisdom took shape in numerous proverbs which his subjects long treasured. And, in spite of one or two deep stains on his character, we may say that his brain was inspired by a sound and righteous heart. The essential justice and fairness of his mind shines out in his official correspondence, even when enveloped in the obscure and grandiloquent verbiage of his secretary Cassiodorus. Among all the Teutonic kings he was the justissimus unus et servantissimus aequi, who set himself to curb the violence of the Goth, no less than the chicanery of the Roman, and taught both that he was no respecter of persons, but a judge set upon the throne to deal out even-handed justice. Alone among all rulers, Roman or German, in his day, he was a believer without tending in the least to become a persecutor. No monarch for a thousand years to come could have been found to echo Theodoric's magnificent declaration that 'religion is a thing which the king cannot command, because no man can be compelled to believe against his will.' Though an Arian himself he employed Catholics, Gothic and Roman, as freely as those of his own sect. Even the Jews got strict justice from him, when every other state in the world dealt hardly with them. The abuse which he won from fanatical Christians for resenting the mobbing of a Rabbi, or the profanation of a synagogue, is one of the highest testimonies in his praise. 'The benefits of justice,' he said, 'must not be denied even to those who err from the faith.' Yet he was not, as were some others who tolerated Jews, a semi-pagan or an agnostic; the very rescripts which grant temporal justice to the oppressed Hebrews end with an appeal to them to leave their hardheartedness and flee from the wrath to come.

In managing the settlement of his victorious tribesmen on the soil of Italy, Theodoric showed much ability. The third of the land, which Odoacer had confiscated seventeen years before, seems to have sufficed for their establishment. The greater part of the Foederati who had been holding this third, had fallen in battle, and those who escaped the Gothic sword seem mostly to have perished in a simultaneous outbreak of riot and murder, by which the Italians celebrated the downfall of Odoacer, when they heard that he had finally been shut up in Ravenna. Hence Theodoric was able to provide for his countrymen without further spoliation of the native proprietors. He threatened

indeed for a moment to deprive of their lands and rights those Italians who adhered too long to Odoacer, but better counsel prevailed, and even those men were spared. So the Goths settled down with little friction among their new subjects: they lay thickly along the valley of the Po, and in Picenum, more sparsely scattered in Tuscany and central Italy; into the south few seem to have penetrated. Nearly all settled down to farm the country-side; only in the royal towns of Ravenna, Pavia, and Verona did the Goths become an appreciable element in the urban population.

Theodoric's plan for dealing with the government of conquered Italy deserves careful study. He did not abolish the remains of the Roman administrative system which he found still existing, nor did he, on the other hand, endeavour to subject the Goths to Roman law. He was content that, for a time, two systems of administration should go on side by side. The Goths were to be ruled and judged by his 'counts,' the Gothic governors whom he set over each Italian province, his ealdormen, as an Anglo-Saxon would have called them, according to the traditional folk-right of their tribe. The Romans looked for justice to magistrates of their own race. If a Goth and a Roman went to law, the case was heard before the count and the Italian judge, sitting together on the same bench.

In the central administration the same mixture of systems was seen. Theodoric's court was like that of another German king in many ways; he had about him his personal retinue of military retainers, the king's men, whom the Goths called by the name of Saiones, but whom, in writing our own English history we should call thegns or gesiths. The Saiones went on the king's errands, served him in bower and hall, and acted as his body-guard on the battle-field. Above their rank and file rose two or three more prominent followers who seem to represent the great officers of the household of the later Middle Ages; such were the chamberlain, regiae praepositus domus, and the great captains who in Roman usage were styled magistri militum, and the king's high-butler and steward.

But beside his Teutonic court — 'the hounds of the royal hall,' as Boethius called them — Theodoric kept up a full establishment of Roman officials, bearing the old titles that had been used under the empire — praetorian praefects, masters of the offices, quaestors, and notaries. He showed great skill and discretion in choosing the most honest among his Italian subjects for these posts, so that his courtiers never became an oppressive official clique, as had habitually been the case under the later emperors. He even chose as his praetorian praefect Liberius, who had adhered to Odoacer to the last, and told him that he esteemed him all the more for his fidelity to his first master. The best men in Italy were undoubtedly set to administer the central government; but it was Theodoric's misfortune that the better the man the more likely he was to indulge in vain dreams of old Roman glory, and to resent in his heart the wise rule of the Ostrogoth. Boethius, the last of the Romans as he may be called, served Theodoric all his life without learning true loyalty to him.

We have not space to notice half of Theodoric's reforms in the administration of Italy. Most wise among them was the careful restoration of the old roads, aqueducts, and drainage canals, which had been the glory of the early empire. He was himself a great builder, and erected royal palaces at Verona and Ravenna, of which, alas! only the smallest fragments survive. But he spent even greater care in keeping up ancient edifices. In Rome he set apart every year two hundred pounds weight of gold pieces for the repair of palaces and public buildings. He took under his protection even statues and monuments, and added representations of himself to the crowd of effigies which adorned Rome. So thoroughly did he put himself in the place of the Caesars that he even took care to celebrate games in the circus, and harangued the assembled people in the Forum. He attended and took part in the debates of the Senate, and endeavoured to strengthen it by the appointment of a few Gothic senators. If he showed some unwisdom in arranging for the resumption of the bread-dole, which had been such a curse to Rome, he atoned for it by a liberal scheme for the rearrangement of taxes, which at once relieved the people and filled the treasury. At his death the royal hoard at Ravenna amounted to no less than 40,000 pounds weight of gold, £1,600,000 in hard cash.

Theodoric's wise administration at home was accompanied by an equally firm and able foreign policy. His first care was to establish friendly relations with the Eastern Empire. Even before Odoacer had met his death, he despatched an embassy to report to Zeno that he had carried out his commission of conquering Italy, and claimed an imperial confirmation of his title. But the embassy found Zeno just dead, and his successor, Anastasius, engrossed in the suppression of riots and rebellions. It was not till 497 that the emperor recognised the king of the Goths as ruler in Italy. Then, however, Anastasius made up for his tardy recognition by sending to Theodoric the regalia which Odoacer had forwarded to Zeno twenty years before, the robes and palace ornaments, which had last been used by the boy Romulus Augustulus.

During the thirty-three years of the Amal's reign in Italy he had only one dispute with the emperor: this was a frontier quarrel in 505, caused by troubles in Illyricum. Theodoric had taken in hand the restoration of the bounds of the Western Empire towards the East, and his generals, having subdued Pannonia as far as Sirmium and Singidunum, trespassed on to Moesian soil, and came into contact with the East-Roman armies. There was some trouble for three years, but no great war, though in 508 two of Anastasius' generals made a destructive raid on Apulia. But peace was ultimately made on the terms that the boundary should be drawn, as in the days of the Western Empire, at the Save and Danube.

Much more important were Theodoric's dealings with his neighbours to west and north. He took over the task of Odoacer in guarding the old Roman districts beyond the Alps, which had once composed the provinces of Rhaetia and Noricum. Both were now becoming Teutonic rather than Latin-speaking lands. Into Rhaetia had fled many of the Alamanni, or Suabians, when Chlodovech the Frank in 496 drove them out of their lands on the Main and Neckar. This people gladly acknowledged Theodoric as over-lord, in return for his protection against the pursuing Franks, whom the Ostrogoth bade halt at the line of the upper Rhine, between Basel and Constanz. Farther east, in Noricum, the place of the emigrant Roman provincials had now been taken by a mixed Teutonic population, the remnant of the broken clans of the Rugians, Scyrri, and Turcilingi, who were just beginning to call themselves by the common name of Bavarians, under which we know them so well a few years later. They, too, like the

Alamanni, were glad to acknowledge Theodoric as suzerain, and pay him tribute.

To the west, Theodoric at his accession found his kingdom bounded by the Alps, for Odoacer had given up to the Visigoths Marseilles, and the other towns which had obeyed the emperor down to the year 476. Beyond the Alps, Alaric the Visigoth now held the mouths of the Rhone and the Provencal Coast, while Gundobad the Burgundian ruled on the middle and upper Rhone, from Avignon as far as Besancon and Langres. North of both Burgundian and Visigoth, and far from the Alpine borders of Theodoric, lay the new Frankish kingdom of Chlodovech, now reaching as far as the Loire and the upper Seine.

With all these three monarchs the king of the Ostrogoths had many dealings. At the very beginning of his reign he asked for the hand of Augofleda, the sister of Chlodovech, and hoped that by this alliance he had bound the clever and unscrupulous Frank to himself. By Augofleda he became the father of Amalaswintha, the only child born to him in lawful wedlock, though he had two elder daughters by a concubine ere he came to Italy. Soon after his own marriage with the Frankish princess, Theodoric wedded one of these natural children to Sigismund, the son and heir of the Burgundian Gundobad, and the other to Alaric the Visigoth. Thus all his neighbours became his relatives.

But this did not secure peace between the new kinsmen of Theodoric. In 499 Chlodovech fell on Gundobad, to strip him of his realm, routed him, and shut him up in Avignon, the southernmost of his strongholds; but after many successes the Frank lost all that he had gained, and turned instead to attack the king of the Visigoths. Theodoric strove unsuccessfully to prevent both wars, and was not a little displeased when, in 507, his brother-in-law Chlodovech overran southern Gaul, and slew his son-in-law Alaric in battle. Burgundian and Frank then united to destroy the Visigoths, and might have done so had not Theodoric intervened. The heir of the Visigothic throne was now Amalric, the son of Alaric and of the king of Italy's daughter. To defend his grandson's realm Theodoric declared war both on Chlodovech and on Gundobad, and sent his armies over the Alps to save the remnants of the Visigothic possessions in Gaul. One host crossed the Cottian Alps, and fell on Burgundy; another entered Provence, and smote the Frank and Burgundian besiegers of Aries. With his usual good fortune, Theodoric recovered all Gaul south of the Durance and the Cevennes (509), so that the conquests of Chlodovech were confined to

Aquitaine. The way was now clear for the Ostrogothic armies to march into Spain, to support the claims of the child Amalric against Gesalic, a bastard son of Alaric II., who had been proclaimed king of the Visigoths at Barcelona. After two years of guerrilla fighting, the pretender was hunted down and slain, though he had sought and obtained some help from the Vandal king Thrasamund (511).

For the next fourteen years, till Amalric reached manhood, Theodoric ruled Spain in his grandson's behalf. He was recognised as king of the Visigoths, in common with Amalric, and ruled both halves of the Gothic race — reunited after an interval of two hundred years — with equal authority, and his royal mandates ran in Spain as well as in Italy. His delegate was Count Theudis, an Ostrogothic noble, who was made regent, and ruled at Narbonne over all the Visigothic realm west of the Rhone; while the Roman Liberius, named praetorian praefect of Gaul, administered Visigothic Provence from the ancient city of Aries.

Theodoric's power was now supreme from Sirmium to Cadiz, and from the upper Danube to Sicily. He ruled the larger half of the old Roman Empire of the West, and exercised much influence in Gaul and Africa, the two parts of it that were not absolutely in his hands. After the war of 507-10 Clodovech the Frank had died, and his four sons, who parted his realm, made peace with the Ostrogoth; while Gundobad, the Burgundian king, had been fain to follow their example even earlier.

Twelve years of peace followed (511-523) before Theodoric, now in extreme old age, had occasion to interfere in Gaul. Sigismund, the husband of Theodoric's elder natural daughter, was now king of the Burgundians. He was a gloomy and suspicious tyrant, and drew down the wrath of Theodoric by murdering his own heir, Sigeric, who was the Gothic king's eldest grandson. To punish this crime Theodoric leagued himself with the Franks, and attacked Burgundy. He conquered, and took as his share of the spoil the lands between Durance and Drome, with the cities of Avignon, Orange, and Viviers, the farthest extension to the north-west of the Ostrogothic empire.

The circle of family alliances which Theodoric had made with his European neighbours was extended even beyond the Mediterranean. He married his sister, Amalafrida, a widowed princess, no longer in her first youth, to Thrasamund, the old king of the Vandals. In virtue of this connection he seems to have treated Thrasamund as a younger brother, if not as a vassal. When the Vandal dared to help the usurper Gesalic in

Spain, Theodoric imposed a tribute on him, and bade him for the future do nothing without the counsel of his wife Amalafrida. Thrasamund did not resent this treatment, and for the future did all he could to propitiate his brother-in-law. The Vandal state, indeed, was not in a condition to risk a quarrel with Theodoric. Ever since the death of Hunneric it had been steadily on the decline. In the reigns of Gunthamund (484-496) and Thrasamund himself (496-523) it was continually losing ground to the insurgent Moors of Atlas. Gunthamund, who was not a persecutor like his predecessor Hunneric, had endeavoured to win the favour of the Catholics by allowing them to recall their exiled bishops and open their churches. But these boons did not check the falling away of his subjects, and during his reign the Moors conquered from him the whole sea-coast from Tangiers to the gates of Caesarea. His brother Thrasamund tried the opposite policy, resumed the persecutions, deported two hundred Catholic bishops to Sardinia, and renewed the horrors of the days of Hunneric. Naturally, he was no more fortunate in dealing with the native rebels than his brother had been. A quarrel with Theodoric would have meant ruin, so he kept himself from all foreign war. He died in 523 at a great age, killed, it is said, by the news of a great defeat which his armies had suffered at the hands of the Moors. His successor was his cousin Hilderic, the son of Hunneric and the Roman princess Eudocia, the last scion of the house of Theodosius the Great. Educated by a Catholic mother, Hilderic was himself the first orthodox Vandal king, and ended the long African persecutions. But his reign was not happier than those of his two cousins. His enthusiastic championship of the Catholic cause brought him into collision with the bulk of his Vandal subjects, and he was attacked by a rebellious party, headed by Theodoric's sister, the queen-dowager Amalafrida, who wished to proclaim as king of Africa one of her late husband's nephews. Hilderic had the better of the fighting, defeated the rebels, and captured Amalafrida, whom he consigned to a dungeon, to the great wrath of her brother, the king of the Goths (523). As long as Theodoric lived he merely kept her in close confinement, but the moment he heard of the old man's death, in 526, he had the cruelty to slay the aged queen, a deed which alienated for ever the Vandals and the Ostrogoths.

The captivity of his sister was not the only sorrow which clouded the last few years of Theodoric s long life. He was left in some trouble as to the succession to his crown. He had married his only legitimate child, Amalaswintha, to a Visigothic prince named Eutharic, of whose prudence and valour much was expected. Theodoric intended him to reign with his daughter as colleague and king-consort, but in 522 Eutharic died, leaving as his heir a boy of only five years of age. Theodoric could not but see that on his death the accession of a woman and a child to the throne would be fraught with the gravest danger, more especially as his nephew Theodahat, the nearest male heir of the Amal house, was known to be an unscrupulous intriguer.

It was perhaps owing to a temper embittered by these family troubles that Theodoric was led, during the last few years of his life, into an unhappy quarrel with some of the best of his Italian subjects. Rightly or wrongly, he had imbibed a notion that the Italians would take advantage of his death to stir up the emperor at Constantinople against his infant heir. The idea was very justifiable; for, in spite of all Theodoric's wisdom and goodness, most of his Roman subjects never learnt to look kindly upon a ruler who was at once an Arian and a Goth, and it seems that some, at least, of the Senate were secretly corresponding with the emperor Justin. That monarch, the first Eastern Emperor for fifty years who was undisputedly orthodox, had fired the enthusiasm of Catholics all over the world by his attempts to suppress Arianism, and the faithful in Italy were undoubtedly contrasting his action with the strict impartiality of Theodoric, to the latter's disadvantage. In 524 the patrician Albinus was accused by Cyprian, the magister officiorum, of sending disloyal letters to Constantinople. At his trial he was defended by the Consular Boethius, at once a great official and the best-known author of the day, noted as philosopher, theologian, astronomer, and mechanist — in short, the chief representative of the intellect of Italy. Boethius resented the impeachment of Albinus in the most fiery terms. 'If this man is guilty,' he cried, 'then both I and all the Senate are guilty too.' The accuser, Cyprian, proceeded to take him at his word, and brought forward further evidence to prove that Boethius himself had been one of the senators in correspondence with Justin, or had, at least, done his best to suppress evidence against those who actually were so engaged. Such an accusation, even if not fully proved, seems to have fired the anger of the old king. He could not tolerate disloyalty in a man whom he had always distinguished by his favour, and preferred to the highest offices. By his orders Boethius was put on his trial before the Senate, and there condemned. For a year Theodoric kept him in prison — a year invaluable to future ages, for in it the captive composed his Consolation of Philosophy , a work which was to be the comfort of many a noble but unhappy soul in the Middle Ages, and to find countless readers from King Alfred down to Sir Thomas More. At the end of a year's confinement Boethius was tortured and put to death. Possibly he was altogether innocent of the charge laid to his account, that of secret correspondence with Constantinople; but more probably he had actually written harmless letters into which a treasonable purpose was read by the malice of his accusers and the fears of the king.

The death of Boethius was followed by another execution, that of his aged father-in-law, Symmachus, the chief of the senate, whom Theodoric put to death on the mere suspicion that he resented his son-in-law's cruel end. There seems to have been no further charge laid against him, and no formal trial, so that this action ranks with the murder of Odoacer as the second unpardonable sin of Theodoric's life (525),

Others also suffered during the last two years of the old king's reign. In anger at Justin's persecution of the Arians, he threatened reprisals against the Catholics of Italy, and charged John the bishop of Rome to sail at once to Constantinople, and inform the emperor that further persecution would mean war with the Goths, and involve an attack on the orthodox throughout the Ostrogothic dominions. Moved by these threats, Justin suspended his harrying of the Arians, and treated the Pope with such respect and distinction that he roused the suspicions of the king of Italy. Theodoric thought that John had been too friendly with the emperor, and suspected that the honours and reverence shown him at Constantinople were part of a plan for seducing away the allegiance of his Roman subjects. When the Pope returned he was thrown into prison, where, being already in ill-health, he soon died. He was at once hailed as a martyr by all the Western Church (526).

The Italians thought that the execution of Symmachus and the imprisonment of Pope John foreboded a general persecution throughout Italy. It was rumoured that the Arians had won from the king his consent to an edict closing the Catholic Churches, and that the Goths were to take arras against their fellow-subjects. Considering the tenor of the whole of Theodoric's previous life, it is most improbable that he had any such wild scheme of intolerance in hand. But he had certainly grown gloomy, suspicious, and hard in his declining days, and it was well for his own fame, as well as for his subjects, that he was carried off by dysentery not long after the death of Pope John. It would have been still better, both for king and people, had the end come three years earlier, before his first harsh dealings with Boethius. His unpopularity at the moment of his death is shown by the survival of several curious legends, which tell how holy hermits saw his soul dragged down to hell by the injured ghosts of John and Symmachus, or carried off by the fiend himself.

So, after reigning thirty-three years over Italy, and twelve years over Spain, Theodoric died, aged seventy-two, and was buried by the Goths in the round mausoleum outside the gate of Ravenna, which he had built for himself many years before. His body has long disappeared, but his empty tomb still survives, well-nigh the only perfect and unbroken monument that recalls the sixty years of Gothic dominion in Italy.

CHAPTER III: THE EMPERORS AT CONSTANTINOPLE — 476-527

Contrast between the fates of the Eastern and Western Empires — The East recovers its strength — Leo I. and the Isaurians — The Emperor Zeno and the rebellion against him — Wars of Zeno with the two Theodorics, 478-483 — The 'Henoticon' — Character of the Emperor Anastasius — Rebellion of the Isaurians — War with Persia, 503-5 — The 'Blue and Green' Factions — Rebellion of Vitalian — Accession of Justin I.

At Rome the emperors of the third quarter of the fifth century — all the ephemeral Caesars whose blood-stained annals fill the space between the death of Valentinian III. and the usurpation of Odoacer — had been the mere creatures of the barbarian, or semi-barbarian, 'patricians' and 'masters of the soldiers,' to whom they owed alike their elevations and their untimely ends. The history of those troubled years would be more logically arranged under the names of the Caesar-makers, Ricimer, Gundobad, Orestes, than under those of the unhappy puppets whom they manipulated.

But, when we turn our eyes eastward to Constantinople, we are surprised to find how entirely different was the aspect of affairs. The Western Empire was rapidly falling to pieces, province after province dropping out of the power of the emperor, and becoming part of the realm of some Gothic, Burgundian, or Vandal prince, who paid the most shadowy homage, or no homage at all, to the ephemeral Caesar at Rome. The Eastern Empire, on the other hand, maintained its boundaries intact, and was slowly building up its strength for renewed activity in the next century. While nine emperors' reigns filled no more than twenty-one years at Rome (455-476), two emperors were reigning for thirty-four years (457-491) on the Bosphorus. And the character of the rulers of East and West was as different as their fates: the short-lived Roman Caesars were either impotent nobodies raised to the throne by the caprice of the barbarian, or ambitious young soldiers who vainly dreamed that they might yet redeem the evil day, and save the State. Their contemporaries in the East, Leo, Zeno, and Anastasius, were three elderly officials, men of experience, if not of great ability, who followed each other in peaceable succession, and devoted their declining years to a cautious defensive policy, with the result that they left a full treasury, a strong and loyal army, and an intact realm behind them.

At the beginning of the fifth century the eastern half of the Empire had seemed no less likely than the western to fall under the dominion of the barbarian, and crumble to pieces. The Goths were cantoned all over Thrace, Moesia, and Asia Minor, and the Gothic general Gainas had taken possession of the person and authority of the Emperor Arcadius. Had he been a man of greater ability he might have made and unmade emperors, as Ricimer afterwards did in the West. But the schemes of Gainas were wrecked, and the Empire saved by the great riot at Constantinople in 401, when the Gothic foederati were massacred, and their leader chased away by the infuriated populace, who thus saved not only their own homes, but the whole East, from the danger of Gothic domination.

Though the European provinces of the Eastern Empire suffered grievously from Teutonic ravages during the first eighty years of the century, there was never again any danger that the barbarians would get hold of the machinery of government, and subvert the Empire from within. In the long reign of Theodosius II. (406-450), if no progress was made in strengthening the realm, at least no ground was lost.

Two external causes were, during this time, operating in favour of the Eastern Empire. The first was the absolute impregnability of Constantinople against any invader who could only assault it from the land side: the town could not be starved out, — as Rome was starved by Alaric, — and its walls could laugh to scorn all such siege appliances as that age knew. Though Goth and Hun pushed their ravages far and wide in the Balkan peninsula, they never seriously attempted to molest the great central place of arms on which the East-Roman power based itself. The Western Empire had no such stronghold — capital, arsenal, harbour, and centre of commerce all in one. Ravenna, where the Western Caesars took refuge in times of storm and stress, was in every way inferior to Constantinople as a base of armed resistance to the invader. Though its marshes made it strong, it did not cover or protect any considerable tract of country, and it was just far enough from its harbour to allow of an enemy cutting off its supplies.

The second great factor in the vitality of the Eastern Empire was the prolonged freedom from foreign war enjoyed by its Asiatic provinces.

After the revolt of Gainas in 401, the Goths disappeared from Asia Minor, and no other invaders made any serious breach into that peninsula, into Syria, or into Egypt, for a hundred and forty years. Two short Persian wars, in 420-421 and 502-505, led to nothing worse than partial ravages on the Mesopotamian frontier. It is true that the Asiatic provinces of the empire were not altogether spared by the sword in the fifth century, but such troubles as they suffered were due to native revolts, chiefly of the Isaurians among the mountains of southern Asia Minor. These risings were local, and led to no very widespread damage, nor was the fighting caused by the revolts of the rebel-emperors Basiliscus and Leontius, in the reign of Zeno, much more destructive. On the whole, the four oriental 'dioceses' of the Eastern Empire must have enjoyed in the fifth century a far greater measure of peace and prosperity than they had known, or were to know, in the previous and the succeeding ages. It was their wealth, duly garnered into the imperial treasury, that made the emperors strong to defend their European possessions. We shall soon see that their military resources also were to count in a most effective way in the reorganisation of the East-Roman army.

But the strength of Constantinople and the wealth of Asia might have proved of no avail had they fallen into the hands of a series of emperors like Honorius or Valentinian III. We must in common fairness grant that the personal characters of the Emperors Leo I., Zeno, and Anastasius I. had also the most important influence on the empire. These three cautious, persistent, and careful princes, who neither endangered the empire by over-great enterprise and ambition, nor let it fall to pieces by want of energy, were exactly the men most fitted to tide over a time of transition.

Leo, the first of these three emperors, was already dead when Romulus Augustulus was deposed in the West. He had left his mark on Constantinopolitan history by his summary execution of Aspar, the last of the great barbarian 'masters of the soldiers,' who rose to a dangerous height of power in the East; and still more by his very important scheme for reorganising the army, by enrolling a large proportion of native-born subjects of the empire in its ranks. Recognising the peril of trusting entirely to Teutonic mercenaries, — the fatal error that had ruined the Western Empire, — Leo had enlisted, in as great numbers as he could obtain, the hardy the mountaineers of Asia Minor, more especially the Isaurians. His predecessors had distrusted their unruly and predatory habits, but Leo saw that they supplied good and trustworthy fighting material, and dealt with them as the elder Pitt dealt with the Highlanders after the rebellion of 1745, teaching them to use in the service of the government the wild courage that had so often been turned against it. Leo had indeed done all that he could for the Isaurians, and had at last married his elder daughter Ariadne to Zeno, an Isaurian by birth, and one of the chief officers of his court.

It was this Zeno who was seated on the throne of the Eastern realm at the moment that Odoacer made himself ruler of Italy, and to him was addressed the celebrated petition of the Roman Senate which besought him to allow East and West alike to repose under the shadow of his name, but to confide the practical governance of Italy to the patrician Odoacer. Zeno was neither so able nor so respectable a sovereign as his father-in-law: two faults, a caution which verged on actual cowardice and a taste for low debauchery, have blasted his reputation. His enemies were never tired of taunting him with his Isaurian birth, and recalling to memory that his real name was Tarakodissa, the son of Rusumbladeotus, for he had only taken the Greek appellation of Zeno when he came to court. But though he was by birth an obscure provincial, and by nature something of a coward and a free liver, Zeno had his merits. He was a mild and not an extortionate administrator, had a liberal hand, a good eye for picking out able servants, was sanguine and persevering in all that he undertook, and pursued in Church matters a policy of moderation and conciliation, which may bring him credit now, though in his own time it provoked many strictures from the orthodox. The worst charges that can be laid to his account were acts that were prompted by his timidity rather than by any other motive, — two or three arbitrary executions of officers whom he rightly or wrongly suspected of plotting against his life. After three rebellions which came within an ace of success, it is not unnatural that he grew somewhat nervous about his own safety.

Zeno's reign was more troubled in this way than those of his predecessor and successor. His well-known lack of daring tempted men to conspire against him, but they reckoned without his cunning and his perseverance, and in every case came to an evil end. Zeno could count on the active support of his countrymen the Isaurians, who now formed the most trustworthy part of the army, and on the passive obedience, or at worst the neutrality, of the mercantile classes and the bureaucracy, who disliked all change and disorder. Hence it came to pass that court conspiracies, or local revolts of divisions of the army, were not enough to shake his throne.

The first half of Zeno's reign may be divided into three parts by these three conspiracies. The emperor had hardly ascended the throne when the first of them broke out: it was a palace intrigue hatched by the Empress-Dowager Verina, who detested her son-in-law. The conspirators took Zeno quite by surprise, they failed to catch him, for he fled from Constantinople at the first alarm, but they got possession of the capital, and proclaimed Basiliscus, the brother of Verina, as Augustus. The mob of the city, with whom Zeno was very unpopular, joined the rising, and massacred the Isaurian troops who were within the walls; their leader's absence seems to have paralysed the resistance of the soldiery, Zeno meanwhile escaped to his native country, and raised an Isaurian army: Syria and the greater part of Asia Minor remained faithful to him, and he prepared to make a fight for his throne. Luckily for him, Basiliscus was a despicable creature, — it was he who had wrecked the great expedition against the Vandals which Leo I. had sent out seven years before. He soon became far more hated by the Constantinopolitans than Zeno had ever been; it is doubtful whether his arrogance, his financial extortions, or his addiction to the Monophysite heresy made him most detested. The army which he sent out against Zeno was intrusted — very unwisely — to a general of Isaurian birth, the magister militum Illus, who allowed himself to be moved by the prayers and bribes of the legitimate emperor, and finally went over to him. Having recovered all Asia Minor, Zeno then stirred up in Europe Theodoric the Amal against his rival, and induced the Goth to beset Constantinople from the West, while he himself blockaded it on the Eastern side. The town threw open its gates, and Basiliscus, after a reign of twenty months, was dragged from sanctuary and brought before his nephew's tribunal. Zeno promised him that his blood should not be shed, but sent him and his sons to a desolate castle in Cappadocia among the mountain-snows, where they were given such scanty food and raiment in their solitary confinement, that ere long they died of privation (477).

It was just after his triumph over Basiliscus that Zeno received the ambassadors of Odoacer, and was saluted as Emperor of West and East alike, in spite of his advice to the Romans to take back as their Caesar their old ruler, Julius Nepos, who was still in possession of part of Dalmatia, though he had lost Italy three years before. Perhaps Zeno might have been tempted to interfere with something more than advice in the affairs of the West, if his second batch of troubles had not fallen upon him, in the form of his long Gothic war with the two Theodorics — the sons of Theodemir and Triarius — which began in the year following his restoration.

The Ostrogoths had never gone westward, like their kinsmen the Visigoths. They had lingered on the Danube, first as members of the vast empire of Attila the Hun, then as occupying Pannonia in their own right. But, in the reign of Leo I., they had moved across the Save into the territory of the Eastern Emperors, and had permanently established themselves in Moesia. There they had settled down and made terms with the Constantinopolitan Government. But they were most unruly vassals, and, even in full time of peace, could never be trusted to refrain from raids into Thrace and Macedonia. The main body of their tribe now acknowledged as its chief Theodoric the son of Theodemir, the representative of the heaven-born race of the Amals, the kings of the Goths from time immemorial. Theodoric was now a young man of twenty-three, stirring and ambitious, who had already won a great military reputation by victories over the Bulgarians, the Sarmatians, and other tribes who dwelt across the Danube. He had spent ten years of his boyhood as a hostage at Constantinople, where he had learnt only too well the weak as well as the strong points of the East-Roman Empire. His after-life showed that he had there imbibed a deep respect for Roman law, order, and administrative unity; but he had also come to entertain a contempt for the timid Zeno, and a conviction that his bold tribesmen were more than a match for the motley mercenary army of the emperor, of which so large a proportion was still composed of Goths and other Teutons, who could not be trusted to fight with a good heart against their Ostrogothic kinsmen.

But Theodoric the Amal was not the only chief of his race in the Balkan peninsula. He had a namesake, Theodoric the son of Triarius, better known as Theodoric the One-eyed, who had long served as a mercenary captain in the imperial army, and had headed the Teutonic auxiliaries in the camp of the usurper Basiliscus. When Basiliscus fell, Theodoric the One-eyed collected the wrecks of the rebel forces, strengthened them with broken bands of various races, many of whom were Ostrogoths, and kept the field against Zeno. He retired into the Balkans, and occasionally descended to ravage the Thracian plains; but meanwhile he sent an embassy to Zeno, offering to submit if he were given the title of magister militum, which he had held under Basiliscus, and taken with all his army into the imperial pay.

Zeno indignantly refused to entertain such terms, and resolved to take in hand the destruction of the rebel. He sent an Asiatic army into Thrace to beset the son of Triarius from the south, and bade his warlike vassal the son of Theodemir to attack his namesake from the north, on the Moesian side. The younger Theodoric eagerly consented, for he grudged to see any other Gothic chief than himself powerful in the peninsula, and looked down on the son of Triarius as a low-born upstart, because he did not come like himself from the royal blood of the Amals.

The campaign against Theodoric the One-eyed turned out disastrously for the imperial forces. The Roman army in the south missed the track of the rebel, whether by accident or design, while Theodoric the Amal with his forces got entangled in the defiles of the Balkans, and surrounded by the army of his rival. He had been promised the co-operation of the army of Thrace, but no Romans appeared, and his projects began to look dark. His one-eyed rival, riding to within earshot of his camp, taunted him with his folly in listening to the orders and promises of the emperor. 'Madman,' he cried, 'betrayer of your own race, do you not see that the Roman plan is always to destroy Goths by Goths? Whichever of us falls, they, not we, will be the stronger. They never will give you real help, but send you out against me to perish here in the desert.' Then all the warriors of the Amal shouted that the One-eyed was right, and that they would not fight against their brethren in the other camp. The son of Theodemir bowed to their will and joined himself to the son of Triarius. Uniting their armies, they moved down into the valley of the Hebrus, and advanced toward Constantinople. They sent Zeno an ultimatum, in which the Amal demanded more territory for his tribe, and a supply of corn and money, while the One-eyed stipulated for the post of magister militum, and an annual payment of 2000 pounds of gold. Zeno, who was very anxious to keep the younger Theodoric on his side, proffered him a great sum of money, and the hand of the daughter of the patrician Olybrius, if he would abandon his namesake the rebel. But the Amal refused to break the oath that he had sworn to his ally, and marched westward to ravage Macedonia up to the very gates of Thessalonica. Zeno sent his troops into winter-quarters, as the season was late, and made one final attempt to stave off the impending danger by offering terms to Theodoric the One-eyed. Less true to his word than the Amal, the elder Theodoric listened to the emperor's offer, and, on being promised the title of magister militum and all the revenues that he had enjoyed under Basiliscus, led his troops over into the imperial camp (479).

For the next two years the son of Theodemir ranged over the whole Balkan peninsula from Dyrrhachium to the gates of Constantinople, plundering and burning those parts of Macedonia and Thrace which had hitherto escaped the ravages of the Huns of Attila and the Ostrogoths of the previous generation. The generals of Zeno met with little good fortune in their attempts to check him, the only success they obtained being a victory won by a certain Sabinianus in 480, who cut off the rear-guard of Theodoric as it was crossing the Albanian mountains, and captured 2000 waggons and 5000 Gothic warriors. But Sabinianus made himself too much feared by Zeno, who, on a suspicion of treachery, had him executed in the following year. It was not till 483 that the Amal, having wasted Thrace and Macedon so fiercely that even his own army could no longer find food, at last came to terms with Zeno, on being made magister militum, and granted additional lands in Moesia and Dacia for his tribesmen. The son of Triarius had died a year earlier: he had again burst out into insurrection against the emperor, and was mustering an army on the Thracian coast when he was slain in a strange manner. A restive horse threw him against a spear which was standing by the door of his tent, and he was pierced to the heart. His son Recitach continued his rebellion, but Theodoric the Amal, who wished to see no other Gothic chief but himself in the Balkan peninsula, slew the young man, and incorporated his warriors with the main body of the Ostrogoths.

The utter helplessness which Zeno showed in dealing with the two Theodorics may be attributed in a large measure to his troubles at home. In 479, the year when he had failed to support Theodoric the Amal in the Balkans, his throne had nearly been overturned by a rising in Constantinople. Marcianus and Procopius, the two sons of Anthemius, the late emperor of the West, who were popular with the citizens of the capital, formed a plot for overthrowing the emperor, in which they enlisted many men of importance. They surprised the palace and massacred the body-guard, but Zeno escaped, brought over his faithful Isaurians from Asia, and crushed the rebellion after a vigorous street fight. In 482-3 he had a prolonged misunderstanding with his commander-in-chief Illus, the Isaurian general who had put down the rebellion of Basiliscus five years before. Zeno neither banished nor fully trusted him. He left him in office, but was nervously on his guard, and always thwarting his Minister. It is said that, with or without his consent, the Empress Ariadne endeavoured to procure the assassination of Illus.

In 483, the year in which Theodoric the Amal made his peace with Zeno, a certain Leontius raised a rebellion in Syria. Illus, who was sent to put him down, had grown tired of serving his suspicious and ungrateful master, and joined in the revolt. He and Leontius seized Antioch, where the latter was proclaimed emperor, and got possession of Cappadocia, Cilicia, and north Syria. It is said that they designed to re-establish paganism, a project which seems absolutely incredible in the very end of the fifth century, when the heathen were no more than a forlorn remnant scattered among a zealous Christian population. The empress-dowager Verina, who was living in exile in Cappadocia, joined herself to them, and adopted Leontius as her son. But the rebels took more practical measures to support their cause when they applied for aid to Odoacer the king in Italy, and to the Persian monarch Balas. Both promised aid, but, before they could send it, Zeno had put the rebellion down. He induced his late enemy Theodoric to join his army, and the Goths and Isaurians combined easily got the better of Leontius. Syria submitted, and the rebel emperor and Illus, after a long and desperate defence in a castle in Cappadocia, were taken and slain.

Zeno enjoyed comparative peace after Leontius' rebellion had been crushed, and was still more fortunate when, in 488, he induced Theodoric the Amal to move his Ostrogoths out of Moesia and go forth to conquer Italy. How Theodoric fared in Italy we have already related. His departure was of enormous benefit to the empire, and, for the first time since his accession, Zeno was now able to exercise a real authority over his European provinces. They were left to him in a most fearful state of desolation: ten years of war, ranging over the whole tract south of the Danube and north of Mount Olympus, had reduced the land to a wilderness. Whole districts were stripped bare of their inhabitants, and great gaps of waste territory were inviting new enemies to enter the Balkan peninsula, and occupy the deserted country-side.

North of the Balkans the whole provincial population seems to have been well-nigh exterminated. When the Ostrogoths abandoned the country there was nothing left between the mountains and the Danube but a few military posts and their garrisons, nor was the country replenished with inhabitants till the Slavs spread over the land in the succeeding age. Illyria and Macedonia had not fared so badly, but the net result of the century of Gothic occupation in the Balkan peninsula had been to thin down to a fearful extent the Latin-speaking population of the Eastern Empire. All the inland of Thrace, Moesia, and Illyricum had hitherto employed the Latin tongue: with the thinning out of its inhabitants the empire became far more Asiatic and Greek than it had before been.

When the Ostrogoths migrated to Italy, the empire acquired a new set of neighbours on its northern frontier, the nomad Ugrian horde of the Bulgarians on the lower Danube, and the Teutonic tribes of the Gepidae, Heruli, and Lombards on the middle Danube and the Theiss and Save. Contrary to what might have been expected, none of these races pushed past the barrier of Roman forts along the river to occupy Moesia. They vexed the empire with nothing worse than occasional raids, and did not come to settle within its limits.

Zeno's ecclesiastical policy demands a word of notice. He was himself orthodox, but not fanatical: the Church being at the moment grievously divided by the Monophysite schism, to which the Churches of Egypt and Palestine had attached themselves, he thought it would be possible and expedient to lure the heretics back within the fold by slightly modifying the Catholic statement of. doctrine. In 482, though he was in the midst of his struggle with Theodoric the Amal, he found time to draft his 'Henoticon,' or Edict of Comprehension. The Monophysites held that there was but one nature in our Lord, as opposed to the orthodox view, that both the human and the divine element were fully present in His person. Zeno put into his 'Henoticon' a distinct statement that Christ was both God and man, but did not insert the words 'two natures,' which formed the orthodox shibboleth. But his well-meant scheme fell utterly flat. The heretics were not satisfied, and refused to conform, while the Catholics held that it was a weak concession to heterodoxy, and condemned Zeno for playing with schism. The patriarch, Acacius, who had assisted him to draft the 'Henoticon,' was excommunicated by the Bishop of Rome, and the churches of Italy and Constantinople were out of communion for more than thirty years, owing to an edict that had been intended to unite and not to divide.

The last years of Zeno's reign were far more undisturbed by war and rebellion than its earlier part. He survived till 491, when he died of epilepsy, leaving no heir to inherit his throne. He had had two sons, named Leo and Zeno: the first had died, while still a child, in 474; the second killed himself by evil living, when on the threshold of manhood, long ere his father's death.

The right of choosing Zeno's successor fell nominally into the hands of the Senate and people, really into those of the widowed Empress Ariadne and the Imperial Guard. The daughter of Leo made a wise choice in recommending to the suffrages of the army and people Anastasius of Dyrrhachium, an officer of the silentiarii, who was universally esteemed for his piety and virtue.

Anastasius was a man of fifty-two or fifty-three, who had spent most of his life in official work in the capital, and was specially well known as an able and economical financier. He was sincerely religious, and spent many of his leisure hours as a lay preacher in the church of St. Sophia, till he was inhibited from giving instruction by the Patriarch Euphemius, who detected Monophysitism in his sermons. He had once proposed to take orders, and had been spoken of as a candidate for the bishopric of Antioch. Yet, in spite of his religious fervour, he was never accused of being unworldly or unpractical. Anastasius was a man of blameless life, learned and laborious, slow to anger, a kind and liberal master, and absolutely just in all his dealings. 'Reign as you have lived,' was the cry of the people when he first presented himself to them clad in the imperial purple. Only two objections were ever made to him — the first, that he leaned towards the Monophysite heresy; the second, that his court was too staid and puritanical for the taste of the multitude, who had loved the pomp and orgies of the dissolute Zeno. He earned unpopularity by suppressing gladiatorial combats with wild beasts, and licentious dances.

Six weeks after his accession the new emperor married the Empress-Dowager Ariadne, who had been the chief instrument in his election. She was a princess of blameless life, and had done much in the previous reign to redeem the ill-repute of her first husband. It was a great misfortune for the empire that she bore her second spouse no heir to inherit his throne.

The commencement of the reign of Anastasius was troubled by a rebellion of the Isaurians. Zeno had not only formed an Imperial Guard of his countrymen, but had filled the civil service with them, and encouraged them to settle as merchants and traders in Constantinople. They had been much vexed when the sceptre passed to the Illyrian Anastasius, and entered into a conspiracy to seize his person, and proclaim Zeno's brother, Longinus, as emperor. A few months after his accession they rose in the capital and obtained possession of part of the city near the palace, but the majority of the people and array were against them, and they were put down after a sharp street fight, in which the great Hippodrome was burnt.

Longinus was captured, and compelled to take orders. He died long after as a priest in Egypt. Anastasius, after this riot, dismissed all the Isaurian officers from the public service. They returned to their homes in Asia Minor, and organised a rebellion in their native hills. A second Longinus, who had been magister militum in Thrace, put himself at the head of the insurrection, which lingered on for five years (491-496), but was never a serious danger to the empire. The rebels were beaten whenever they ventured into the plains, and only maintained themselves so long by the aid of the mountain-castles with which their rugged land was studded. In 496 their last fastnesses were stormed, and their chief, the ex-magister, taken and executed. Anastasius punished the communities which had been most obstinate in the rebellion by transferring them to Thrace, and settling them on the wasted lands under the Balkans, where he trusted that these fearless mountaineers would prove an efficient guard to keep the passes against the barbarians from beyond the Danube.

The Asiatic provinces of the empire had no further troubles till 502, when a war broke out between Anastasius and Kobad king of Persia. The Mesopotamian frontier had been singularly quiet for the last century; there had been no serious war with the great Oriental monarchy to the East since Julian's unfortunate expedition in 362. The same age which had seen the Teutonic migrations in Europe had been marked in inner Asia by a great stirring of the Huns and other Turanian tribes beyond the Caspian, and while the Roman emperors had been busy on the Danube, the Sassanian kings had been hard at work defending the frontier of the Oxus. In a respite from his Eastern troubles Kobad made some demands for money on Anastasius, which the emperor refused, and war soon followed. It began with several disasters for the Romans, and Amida, the chief fortress of Mesopotamia, was stormed in 503. Nisibis fell later in the same year, and when Anastasius sent reinforcements to the East he appointed so many generals with independent authority that the whole Roman army could never be united, and the commanders allowed themselves to be taken in detail and defeated in succession. In 504, however, the fortune of war turned, when the supreme authority in the field was bestowed on Celer, the magister officiorum; he recovered Amida after a long siege, and began to press forward beyond the Persian frontier. Kobad was at the same time assailed by the Huns from beyond the Oxus, and gladly made peace, on terms which restored the frontier of both parties to the line it had occupied in 502. Anastasius provided against future wars by building two new fortresses of the first class on the Persian frontier, Daras in Mesopotamia, and Theodosiopolis farther north on the borders of Armenia. These places served to break the force of the Persian attack thirty years later, when the successors of Kobad and Anastasius again fell to blows. The Persian war, like the Isaurian, had only afflicted a very limited district, — the province beyond the Euphrates, — and no raids had penetrated so far as Syria. Indeed, during the whole reign of Anastasius, the only serious trouble to which the Asiatic half of the empire was exposed was a Hunnish raid from beyond the Caucasus, which in 515 caused grave damage in Pontus, Cappadocia, and Lycaonia. This invasion, however, was an isolated misfortune, followed by no further incursions of the nomads of the Northern Steppes.

The European provinces — now as in the time of Zeno — had a far harder lot. The Slavs and Bulgarians repeatedly crossed the Danube and pressed over the desolated plains of Moesia to assail Thrace. More than once the Bulgarians defeated a Roman army in the field, and their ravages were at last pushed so far southward that Anastasius built in 512 the celebrated wall which bears his name, running from the Black Sea to Propontis, thirty-five miles west of Constantinople. These lines, extending for more than fifty miles across the eastern projection of Thrace, served to defend at least the immediate neighbourhood of the capital against the restless horsemen from beyond the Danube. Macedonia and Illyricum seem to have suffered much less than Thrace during this period; the Slavs who bordered on them were as yet not nearly such a dangerous enemy as the Bulgarians, while the Ostrogoths of Italy, on reconquering Pannonia, proved more restful neighbours to the north-western provinces of the empire than they had been in the previous century.

It was in the reign of Anastasius that one of the most characteristic features in the social life of Constantinople is brought forward into prominence for the first time. This was the growing turbulence of the 'Blues and Greens,' the factions of the Circus. From the very beginning of the Roman Empire these clubs had existed, but it was only at Constantinople that they became institutions of high political importance. There the rivalry of the Blues and Greens was not confined to the races of the Circus, but was carried into every sphere of life. Nor was it any longer only the young men of sporting and fashionable proclivities that joined the 'factions.' They served as clubs or political associations for all classes, from the ministers of state down to the poorest mechanics, and formed bonds of union between bodies of churchmen or supporters of dynastic claims. It is hard for an Englishman to realise this extraordinary development of what had once been a mere rivalry of the Hippodrome. To make a parallel to it we should have to suppose that all who mount the light or the dark blue on the day of the Oxford and Cambridge boat race were bitterly jealous of each other — let us say, for example, that all Dark Blues were Conservatives and Anglicans, and all Light Blues were Radicals and Dissenters. If this were so, we can imagine that in times of political stress every boat race might be followed by a gigantic free-fight. This, however, was exactly what occurred at Constantinople; the 'Blue' faction had become identified with Orthodoxy, and with a dislike for the family of Anastasius. The 'Green' faction included all the Monophysites and other heterodox sects, and was devoted to the person and dynasty of Anastasius. In any time of trouble the celebration of games in the Hippodrome ended with a fierce riot of the two factions. No wonder that the just and peaceable emperor strove to suppress shows of all sorts, and in especial showed a dislike for the disloyal 'Blue' faction.

The worst of Anastasius' domestic troubles were due to the suspicion of heterodoxy that clung to him. In 511 when he added to the hymn called the Trisagion a line in a context which seemed to refer to the whole Trinity, the orthodox populace of Constantinople headed by the Blue faction burst out into sedition. It was only quelled by the old Emperor presenting himself before the people in the Hippodrome, without crown or robe, and announcing his intention of abdicating. So great was the confidence which his justice and moderation had inspired in all ranks and classes, that the proposal filled the whole multitude with dismay, and they rose unanimously to bid him resume his diadem.

But the grievance against the Monophysite tendencies of Anastasius was not destined to be forgotten. In 514 an ambitious general named Vitalian, who held a command in Moesia, rose in arms, alleging as the cause of his rebellion, not only certain misdeeds committed in that province by the emperor's nephew Hypatius, but also the dangerous heterodoxy of Anastasius' religious opinions. When Hypatius was removed from his office the greater part of Vitalian's army returned to its allegiance, and the rebel then shewed how much importance was to be attached to his religious scruples, by calling in the heathen Bulgarians and Huns to his aid. At the head of an army composed of these barbarians he maintained himself in Moesia for some time. The emperor, somewhat unwisely, replaced his nephew Hypatius in command, and sent him with a large army to put down the rebel; but, while the Romans lay encamped on the sea-shore near Varna, they were surprised by a night attack of the enemy and completely scattered. Many thousand men were driven over the cliffs into the sea and crushed or drowned, while Hypatius himself was taken prisoner (514). The old emperor was driven, by concern for his nephew's life, to make peace. He ransomed Hypatius for 15,000 lbs. of gold, and granted Vitalian the post of magister militum in Thrace. The pardoned rebel for the remainder of Anastasius' reign occupied himself in strengthening his position on the Danube, being determined to make a bold stroke for the imperial throne when old age should remove the octogenarian ruler of Constantinople.

In spite of all his troubles with the two Longini, king Kobad and Vitalian, Anastasius may be called a successful and prosperous ruler. All these rebellions had been of mere local import, and for the whole twenty-seven years of his reign the greater part of the empire had enjoyed peace and plenty. The best testimony to his good administration is the fact that at his accession he found the treasury emptied by the wasteful Zeno, and that at his death he left it filled with 320,000 lbs. weight of gold, or £15,000,000 in hard cash. This was in spite of the fact that he was a merciful and lenient administrator, and had actually abolished several imports including the odious Chrysargyron or income-tax. Nor was the money collected at the cost of neglecting proper expenditure. Anastasius had erected many military works, — in especial his great wall in Thrace, and the strong fortress of Daras — and restored many ruined cities. 'He never sent away petitioners empty, whether they represented a city, a fortress, or a seaport.' He left an army of 150,000 men in a good state of discipline and composed for its larger half of native troops, with a frontier intact alike on east and west and north.

The good old man died in 518; his wife Ariadne had preceded him to the grave three years before. He had refrained from appointing as his colleague his nephew Hypatius, whom many had expected him to adopt, and the empire was left absolutely masterless. The great State officials, the Imperial Guard, and the Senate had the election of a new Caesar thrown upon their hands. The most obvious candidates for the throne were Hypatius, whom the Green faction should have supported, and the magister militum Vitalian, who at once to okarms to march on the capital. But neither of them was destined to succeed. The sinews of war lay in the hands of the treasurer Amantius; he himself could not hope to reign, for he was a eunuch, but he had a friend whom he wished to crown. Accordingly he sent for Justinus, the commander of the Imperial Guard, and made over to him a great sum to buy the aid of the soldiery. Justinus, an elderly and respectable personage whom no one suspected of ambition, quietly took the gold, distributed it in his own name, and was saluted as Augustus by his delighted guardsmen. The Senate acquiesced in the nomination, and he mounted the throne without a blow being struck.

Justinus was an Illyrian by birth, and had spent fifty years in the imperial army; he had won his promotion by good service in the Isaurian and Persian wars. He was very illiterate — we are told that he could barely sign his own name — and knew nothing outside his tactics and his drill-book. He had the reputation of being quiet, well-behaved, and upright; no one had anything to say against him, and he was rigidly orthodox in matters of faith. He was sixty-eight years of age, fifteen years older than even the elderly Anastasius had been at the moment of his accession.

Justinus seated himself firmly on the throne; he executed the treasurer Amantius, but made terms with the two men who might have been his rivals. Hypatius remained a simple senator; Vitalian was confirmed in his command in Moesia and given a consulship. While holding this office and dwelling in the capital he was assassinated; rumour ascribed the crime to the emperor's nephew Justinian, who thought the turbulent magister too near the throne.

There is very little to record of the nine years of Justinus' reign, save that he healed the forty years' schism which had separated the churches of Rome and Constantinople since the publication of Zeno's 'Henoticon.' Being undisputedly orthodox, he withdrew that document, and the schism disappeared with its cause. The only real importance of Justinus is that he prepared the way for his famous nephew and successor, Justinian, whom he adopted as colleague, and intrusted with those matters of civil administration with which he was himself incompetent to deal. He died and left the throne to Justinian in A.D. 528.

CHAPTER IV: CHLODOVECH AND THE FRANKS IN GAUL — 481-511

The Franks in Northern Gaul — Their early conquests — State of Gaul in 481 — Chlodovech conquers Northern Gaul, 486 — He subdues the Alamanni, 495-6 — Conversion of Chlodovech, 496 — He conquers Aquitaine from the Visigoths, 507 — He unites all the Frankish Kingdoms, 511.

While Odoacer was still reigning in Italy, and Theodoric the Amal had not yet left the Balkans, or the banks of the Danube, the foundations of a great kingdom were being laid upon the Scheldt and the Meuse. Early in the fifth century the confederacy of marsh-tribes on the Yssel and Lech who had taken the common name of Franks, had moved southward into the territory of the Empire, and found themselves new homes in the provinces which the Romans called Belgica and Germania Inferior. For many years the hold of the legions on this land had been growing weaker; and, long ere it became a Frankish kingdom, it had been largely sprinkled with Frankish colonists, whom the emperors had admitted as military settlers on the waste lands within their border. In the lowlands of Toxandria, which after-ages called Brabant and Guelders, there were no large cities to be protected, no great fortresses to be maintained, and, while the Romans still exerted themselves to hold Treveri and Colonia Agrippina and Moguntiacum, they allowed the plains more to the north and west to slip out of their hands. By the second quarter of the fifth century the Franks were firmly established on the Scheldt and Meuse and lower Rhine, where the Roman garrisons never reappeared after the usurper Constantine had carried off the northern frontier legions to aid him in his attack on Italy (406). By this time, too, Colonia Agrippina, first of the great Roman cities of the Rhineland, seems to have already fallen into the hands of the Franks. Between 430 and 450 they continued to push forward as far as the Somme and the Moselle, and, when, at the time of Attila's great invasion of Gaul, the last imperial garrisons in the Rhineland were exterminated; and the last governors driven forth by the Huns from Treveri and Moguntiacum and Mettis, it was the Franks who profited. After the Huns had rolled back again to the East, Frankish kings, not Roman officials, took possession of the ravaged land along the Moselle and Rhine, and the surviving provincials had for the future to obey a Teutonic master near home, not a governor despatched from distant Ravenna.

The Franks were now divided into two main hordes; the Salians — who took their name from Sala, the old name of the river Yssel — dwelt from the Scheldt-mouth to the Somme, and from the Straits of Dover to the Meuse. The Ripuarians, whose name is drawn from the fact that they inhabited the bank (ripa) of the Rhine, lay along both sides of the great river from its junction with the Lippe to its junction with the Lahn, and extended as far east as the Meuse. Each of these two tribes was ruled by many kings, all of whom claimed to descend from the house of the Merovings, a line lost in obscurity, whose original head may, perhaps, have been the chief who in the third century first taught union to the various tribes who formed the Frankish confederacy.

The Franks were one of the more backward of the Teutonic races, in spite of their long contact with Roman civilisation along the Rhine. Kings and people were still heathens. They had not learnt like the Goths to wear armour or fight on horseback, but went to war half-naked, armed only with a barbed javelin, a sword, and a casting-axe or tomahawk, called the Francisca after the name of its users. Unlike Goth and Vandal they had not learnt the advantages of political union, but obeyed many petty princes instead of one great lord. All Roman writers reproach them for a perfidy which exceeded that of the other barbarians. The Saxons, we are told, were cruel, the Alamanni drunken, the Alans rapacious, the Huns unchaste, but the special sin of the Frank was treachery and perjury.

At the time of the deposition of Romulus Augustulus by Odoacer, the Salian Franks held the old Roman towns of Cambrai, Arras, Tournay, and Tongern, while the Ripuarians occupied Koln, Trier, Mainz, and Metz. South of the Ripuarians lay the new Burgundian kingdom which Gundobad had founded in the valleys of the Rhone and Saone. South of the Salians was a district of Roman Gaul which had to the last acknowledged the supremacy of the ephemeral emperors of the West, and kept itself free from barbarian invaders under the patrician Aegidius. After his death in 463 his son Syagrius succeeded to his power, and ruled at Suessiones (Soissons) over the whole Seine valley, and the plain of central Gaul as far as Troyes and Orleans. After the disappearance of the last Western Emperor, Syagrius had no over-lord, but was so much his own master that the Franks called him 'king of the Romans,' though he himself took no title but that of patrician. South of the realm of Syagrius lay the Visigothic kingdom of Euric, a vast state extending from the Loire to Gibraltar, and from the Bay of Biscay to the Maritime Alps. Its king dwelt at Toulouse, and the Gaulish rather than the Spanish half of his dominion was considered the more important. Indeed his rule in Spain was still incomplete, as the Suevi held its north-western corner, the land which we now call Galicia and north Portugal, and the Basques maintained their independence in the western Pyrenees. In the third quarter of the fifth century the most important of the Frankish chiefs of the Merovingian line was a prince of the Salians, named Childerich, who dwelt at Tournay, and ruled in the valley of the upper Scheldt. He died in 481, leaving his throne to his sixteen-year-old son and heir, a prince named Chlodovech or Chlodwig, who was destined to found the great Frankish kingdom, by extinguishing the other Frankish principalities, and conquering southern and central Gaul.

Such an event seemed most unlikely at the time of Chlodovech's accession, when the dominant power in the land was that of the fierce and able king Euric the Visigoth. It was Euric who had brought the Visigothic kingdom up to its largest extent, by driving the Sueves into a corner of Spain, conquering the last Roman provinces in central Gaul, and receiving Provence from the hands of Odoacer, king of Italy. He was the first Visigothic king to publish a code of laws, and would have left a good name in history but for his assassination of his brother Theodoric, and his persecutions of the Catholics. Though not such an oppressor as the Vandals Gaiseric and Hunneric, he had made himself hated by refusing to allow the election of Catholic bishops, and by closing or handing over to his favourites, the Arians, many of the churches of the orthodox. Euric died in 485, just as Chlodovech was about to commence his conquering career in northern Gaul, a career which the Visigoth would probably have checked if a longer life had been granted him. He was succeeded by his son Alaric, a boy of only sixteen or seventeen years.

It was in the very year of Euric's death that Chlodovech, now aged twenty-one, set out on the first of his warlike expeditions. In company with his kinsman Ragnachar, king of Cambrai, he invaded the realm of the Roman patrician Syagrius. The Gaulish troops were unable to resist the onset of the Franks, and their leader, after a short struggle, abandoned his home, and fled for safety to the court of Alaric the Visigoth. The councillors of Alaric, either wishing to gratify their Teutonic neighbours, or fearing the event of a war while their king was yet so young, threw the patrician into bonds, and sent him back to Chlodovech, who promptly put him to death. The Seine valley and the great towns of Soissons, Paris, Rouen, and Rheims now fell into the hands of the Frankish king, and, in the course of the next three years, he extended his power up to the Loire and boundary of Armorica, where the Romano-Celts of the extreme west still succeeded in holding out. Chlodovech took all the spoils for himself, none fell to his neighbours, the other kings of the Salian Franks. It was these princes who were next to feel the force of his arm. He picked quarrels with his kinsmen the kings of Cambrai and Terouanne, the one for not helping him against Syagrius, the other for claiming part of the spoil of the Roman, and slew them both, the one by treachery, the other in open battle. The remaining Merovingian princes of the Belgic plains soon shared their fate; then Chlodovech pressed eastward against the Ripuarian Franks, and conquered the Thoringi, their chief tribe, in the year 491 In a short time he had won all the Frankish kingdoms save that of his ally Sigebert the Lame, king of Koln. He remorselessly slew every prince of Meroving blood who fell into his hands, and did his best to exterminate all the rival lines. When he could find no more to kill, he is said to have made open lamentation that he was left alone in the world, and that the royal house of the Franks was threatened with extinction; he then bade any kinsman who might yet survive come to him without fear. But it was cruelty, not remorse, that moved him, for his only object was to catch and slay any Meroving who might yet survive.

His conquests in Ripuaria brought Chlodovech into touch with new neighbours, the Burgundians to the south, and the confederacy of the Alamanni to the east, along the Main and Neckar. With the first named he entered into friendly relations, and married Chrotechildis (Clotilde), niece of King Gundobad, in 492. The princess, unlike her uncle and most of her tribe, was a devout Catholic, and much was destined to follow from her alliance with the pagan Frank, With the Alamanni the relations of Chlodovech were from the first hostile; in fact, when he brought his frontier up to the middle Rhine, he was constrained to take up an already existing feud between the Ripuarians and their eastern neighbours. For several years he was engaged in a struggle with this confederacy, who held the east bank of the Rhine from Coblenz upwards, the valleys of the Main and Neckar, and all the Black Forest. At last, in 496, he got the better of them in a decisive battle — apparently near Strasburg — and forced the main body of the confederacy to do him homage and acknowledge him as over-lord. An obstinate remnant retired over the Rhine, and took refuge in Rhaetia under the protection of the great Theodoric, but all the rest became Frankish vassals. As a result of this war the Alamanni were driven southward out of the Main valley, which was seized and settled by Ripuarian settlers, and became a Frankish country under the name of East Francia, or Franconia.

A suggestive legend and an important fact are connected with these campaigns of Chlodovech against the Alamanni. The ecclesiastic writers of the next century state that, in his decisive battle with the confederates, Chlodovech was driven back and almost routed. Then, recalling the words of his wife Chrotechildis, 'who never ceased to persuade him that he should serve the true God.' that the Lord was the Lord of Hosts and the arbiter of battles, he cried aloud, 'O Christ Jesu, I crave as a suppliant Thy glorious aid; and if Thou grantest me victory over these enemies I will believe in Thee, and be baptized in Thy name.' At once the Alamanni began to give back, and the king obtained a complete triumph.

Whether this was the manner of his conversion or not, it is at any rate certain that Chlodovech, on returning from his Alamannic campaign, had himself baptized at Rheims on Christmas Day, 496. His sister and 3000 of his warriors followed him to the font. Every reader of history knows the famous tale how Archbishop Remigius hailed the king with the words, 'Bow thy neck Sigambrian, adore that which thou hast burnt, and burn that which thou hast adored.' First among the converted Teutonic kings Chlodovech was received into the Catholic Church, and did not become an Arian like his neighbours. In this we may, no doubt, trace the influence of his orthodox queen Chrotechildis. The consequences of his conversion to the orthodox faith were most important; he was the only Teutonic king who adopted the faith of his Roman subjects, and was therefore served by them, and more especially by their clergy, with a loyalty which no Goth, Vandal, or Burgundian prince could ever win. Not least among the causes of Chlodovech's easy triumphs and of the permanence of his kingdom may be reckoned his adherence to Catholicism.

It cannot be said that the king's conversion made any favourable change in his character or his conduct. He still remained the cruel, unscrupulous, treacherous tyrant that he had always been. It will be seen that his last recorded action was an elaborate incitement to parricide followed by a horrid murder. Yet he was granted a measure of success that was refused to kings of far better disposition and far stronger intellect, such as Theodoric the Ostrogoth, or Ataulf the Visigoth.

After their king's conversion the Franks, both Salian and Ripuarian, hastened to follow him to the fold of the Church, and in a single generation the old Frankish paganism disappeared. But, as with king so with people, the change was almost entirely superficial; it is long before we trace the influence of any Christian graces on the ungodly and perfidious race of the Franks.

After subduing the Alamanni, Chlodovech's next war was with the people of his wife's uncle, Gundobad, the king of Burgundy. He made a secret agreement with Godegisl, Gundobad's younger brother, to invade and divide the Burgundian realm. While the treacherous brother raised war in Helvetia, where he possessed an appanage, the king of the Franks attacked Gundobad from the front, and invaded the valley of the Saone. It appeared as if here, as well as in the lands farther north, Chlodovech would sweep all before him. The Burgundian king was beaten and driven out of Dijon, Lyons, and Valence into Avignon, the southernmost fortress of his realm, while his brother was made king by the Frank, and became his vassal. But, in the next year, Gundobad recovered all he had lost, slew Godegisl at Vienne, and drove the Franks out of Burgundy with such success that Chlodovech ere long made peace with him (501).

But the next campaign of the Frankish king was one of far greater importance and success. He was set on trying his fortune against the young king of the Visigoths, whose personal weakness and unpopularity with his Roman subjects tempted him to an invasion of Aquitaine. It would seem that Chlodovech carefully chose as a casus belli the Arian persecutions of Alaric, who, like his father Euric, was a bad master to his Catholic subjects. A first quarrel in 504 was composed by the great Theodoric, who, as father-in-law of the Visigoth and brother-in-law of the Frank, could appeal with authority to each of the rivals. But in 507 Chlodovech declared war on the Visigoths. 'I cannot bear,' he said, 'that those Arians should hold any part of Gaul. With God's aid we will go against them, and subdue their land beneath our sway.' Knowing the strength of the Visigothic realm, Chlodovech allied to himself for the struggle his old enemy Gundobad the Burgundian, and Sigebert of Koln, the last surviving Ripuarian king.

Advancing from Paris Chlodovech crossed the Loire, and met the Visigoths and their king on the Campus Vocladensis, the plain of Vougle, near Poictiers. Whether from cowardice, or from distrust of his own generalship, Alaric held back from fighting, but his army forced him to give battle. He attacked the Franks, was utterly defeated, and fell with the greater part of his men. So crushed were the Visigoths by the disaster that Chlodovech was able to overrun all the provinces between the Loire and the Garonne without striking another blow. He entered Bordeaux in triumph, and there spent the winter. Next spring he marched against Toulouse, the Gothic capital, and took it, and with it the great hoard of the Visigothic kings, including many of the Roman trophies that Alaric and Ataulf had carried off from Italy a hundred years before. Meanwhile, Chlodovech's Burgundian allies overran Provence, and captured all its cities save Aries. To add to the troubles of the Visigoths they were distracted by civil strife; one party recognised as king Amalric, the infant son of Alaric, by Theodoric's daughter, his lawful queen; the other elected Gesalic, a bastard son of Alaric, who had fortified himself in Narbonne and Barcelona. But the Franks and Burgundians drove Gesalic over the Pyrenees, and it appeared as if there was about to be an end of all Visigothic power north of those mountains.

Meanwhile, Chlodovech returned from Toulouse to Tours, where he found awaiting him ambassadors from the Emperor Anastasius, who saluted him by their master's command with the titles of proconsul and patrician, and presented him with a diadem and purple robe. Anastasius sought by these honours to win an ally against Theodoric the Ostrogoth, with whom he had lately quarrelled. Chlodovech accepted them with alacrity, because of the prestige they gave him in the eyes of his Roman subjects, who saw his power over them formally legalised by the grant of the Emperor.

This was the culminating scene of Chlodovech's life; for, in the next year, fortune turned somewhat against him. The great Theodoric interfered in the Gothic War as the guardian and protector of his grandson, Amalric. His armies routed the united Franks and Burgundians near Aries, where they are said to have slain 30,000 men. They then reconquered Narbonne and all the Mediterranean coast as far as Spain. Chlodovech's conquests were thus restricted to the land west of the Cevennes, but still comprised the greater bulk of Visigothic Gaul, with the three great cities of Poictiers, Bordeaux, and Toulouse (510). Only the Narbonensis and Provence were saved from him by Theodoric, who now chased away the usurper Gesalic, and ruled all Spain and south Gaul till his grandson Amalric came of age.

Checked on the south by the great Ostrogoth, Chlodovech turned north to round off his dominions by the acquisition of the last independent Frankish state. Sigebert of Koln was now very old, and his ambitious son Chloderich was persuaded by Chlodovech not only to dethrone, but to slay his father. When he had seized the kingdom Chlodovech affected great wrath and indignation against him, procured his death at the hands of assassins, and then annexed his kingdom. All the Frankish states were now united under one hand, but Chlodovech did not long survive this last success, though, according to the strange words of his admirer, Bishop Gregory of Tours, 'The Lord cast his enemies under his power day after day, and increased his kingdom, because he walked with a right heart before Him, and did that which was pleasing in His sight!'

In 511 this sanguinary ruffian, murderer, and traitor died, just after he had presided at Orleans over a synod of thirty-two Gaulish bishops who were anxious to repress Arianism, and gladly called in the secular arm of their orthodox lord to their aid. Chlodovech was morally far the worst of all the Teutonic founders of kingdoms: even Gaiseric the Vandal compares favourably with him. Yet his work alone was destined to stand, not so much from his own abilities, though these were considerable enough, as from the happy chance which put his successors in religious sympathy with their subjects, and preserved the young kingdom, during the following generation, from any conflict with such powerful foes as those who were destined to overthrow the monarchies of the Ostrogoths, the Visigoths, and the Vandals.

CHAPTER V: JUSTINIAN AND HIS WARS — A.D. 528-540

Character of Justinian — His marriage with Theodora — His first War with Persia, 528-31 — Rise of Belisarius — Justinian suppresses the 'Nika' sedition, 532 — His foreign policy — Belisarius conquers the Vandals, 533-4 — Decay of the Ostrogoths in Italy — Justinian attacks Theodahat — Belisarius conquers Sicily, Naples, and Rome — Siege of Rome by the Ostrogoths [537-8] — Belisarius defeats the Ostrogoths and captures Ravenna [540].

For three quarters of a century, during the reigns of the four cautious and elderly Caesars, whose annals fill the space between 457 and 527, the East-Roman Empire had been recovering its strength, and storing up new energy for a sudden outburst of vigour under the able, restless, and ambitious sovereign who followed the aged Justinus I. Justinian — the son of Sabatius the brother of Justinus — was nearly forty years old when he became, by his uncle's death, sole ruler of the empire. He was no mere uncultured soldier like his predecessor; when he obtained promotion in the army, Justinus sent for his nephew from the Dardanian village where his family dwelt, and had him reared in the capital in all the accomplishments which befitted the heir of a great fortune. By the acknowledgment of his bitterest enemies Justinian had an extraordinary power of assimilating knowledge of all kinds: he took a keen interest alike in statecraft and architecture, in theology and law, in finance and music. When his uncle came to the throne, the student soon developed into the practical administrator, for Justinus trusted him with all those details of civil government which he himself was unable to understand or to manage. It soon became known that the heir of Justinus was a man of extraordinary ability and untiring thirst for work. At an age when most young men would have been tempted by their sudden elevation to plunge into the enjoyments that lay open to an imperial prince, Justinian applied himself to mastering all the tiresome details of the administration of the empire. Men noted with surprise that he never seemed happy save when he was in his cabinet, surrounded by his secretaries, his registers, his files of reports, and despatches. He was like the Aristotelian character who was 'too indifferent to things pleasurable,' for nothing save work appeared to have any attraction for him. He rose early, spent his day in administrative duties, and his night in reading and writing. As he grew older he seemed to dispense with sleep altogether, as if he had become free from the common necessities of man's nature. There was something strange and horrible in his cold-blooded, untiring energy; superstitious men whispered that he was inspired by a restless demon who gave him no peace, or that he was actually a demon himself Had not a belated courtier met him after midnight pacing the dark corridors of the palace with a fearful and changed countenance that was no longer human, or even — as the story grew — with no face at all, a shapeless monstrous shadow?

But that Justinian was a man, with all a man's waywardness and recklessness, was proved ere long. To the surprise of the whole population of the empire, and the utter horror and confusion of all respectable persons, it was suddenly noised abroad that the heir of the empire had announced his intention of marrying Theodora the dancer, the chief star of the Byzantine comic stage. The staid passionless bureaucrat was contemplating a step from which Nero or Heliogabalus would have shrunk with dismay.

We have elaborate but untrustworthy details of the scandalous early life of Theodora in a book — the 'Secret History' — which bears the name of the historian Procopius, but was in all probability no work of his. She was the daughter of Acacius the Cypriot, an employe of the 'Green Faction' at the Hippodrome, and had for some years appeared on the stage as an actress and dancer. So much we may take for truth; knowing the general character of Roman actresses we may assume that there was some foundation for the stories over which the 'Secret History' gloats. As to the particular facts alleged, we may conclude that they are untrustworthy — among those which the 'Secret History' gives as most certain are the statements that she was a vampire, and often held intercourse with evil spirits; the rest is written in the same spirit of silly and superstitious malignity. But we may fairly conclude that the marriage of Justinian was a scandal and a wonder. His mother and his aunt the Empress Euphemia, as we know, set their faces against it; but he went on in his usual steady persistence, gradually warred down the will of his old uncle Justinus, and formally took Theodora to wife. The emperor was even induced to bestow upon her the high title of Patrician.

In brains and power of will Theodora was a fit enough occupant for the imperial throne, whatever her past history may have been. She was as ambitious, restless, and capable as her husband, and acted as much as his colleague as his consort. We shall see how on one occasion of crisis she stood boldly forward and interposed between him and destruction. Her worst enemies do not suggest that she was an unfaithful or profitless spouse to him; the 'Secret History' itself calls her after her marriage luxurious, cruel, capricious, arrogant, but does not accuse her of evil-living or folly. Against this we may set the well-ascertained facts that she was devoted to the exercises of religion, and founded many charitable institutions. Remembering the dangers of her own youth, she built a great institution for the reclaiming of fallen women — the first of the kind known in Christendom. She was zealous in buying and freeing slaves, and in caring for the bringing up of orphans and the marriage of dowerless girls.

Theodora was by all accounts the most beautiful woman of her age. Even the 'Secret History' allows this, adding only that she was rather below the middle stature, that her complexion was somewhat pale, and that she devoted untold hours to the mysteries of the toilet. Two portraits of her have survived, one at the monastery on Mount Sinai, the other in the Church of San Vitale at Ravenna — two spots so far apart as to call up vividly to our memory the wide extent of her influence. Unfortunately the hieratic style of art into which Roman portraiture had long sunk, and the intractable nature of mosaic as a material do not allow us to judge from these representations what was her actual appearance.

Justinian has left behind him an almost unparalleled reputation as a conqueror, a builder, and a lawgiver, besides a less happy record of theological activity. It is mainly, however, with his foreign policy that we shall have to concern ourselves: the other spheres of his labour are better fitted for another work. But his dealings with Africa, Italy, and Spain form a great landmark and turning-point in the history of southern Europe, and their results were not entirely exhausted till the eleventh century. His long struggles with Persia are less interesting and less important, but they filled a great space in the view of contemporary observers, and were not without their moment.

Justinian's reign opened with a fierce war with the old Persian king Kobad. The struggle which this monarch had waged with Anastasius, twenty-five years before, had been so indecisive that the Sassanian longed for a new trial of arms. Almost immediately on Justinian's accession he issued his declaration of war, using as a pretext the erection of some fortifications near Nisibis, which were being constructed by Belisarius, governor of Daras, a young officer whose name was destined to be intimately associated with the whole history of Justinian's reign. The war opened with a defeat in the open field, suffered by the Roman army of Mesopotamia; but when reinforcements came up the Persians retreated beyond their frontier. After the winter of 528-29 was over neither side advanced in force, and all that occurred was a flying Roman raid into Assyria, and an equally hasty Persian incursion into Syria, both of which did some harm, but had no practical result on the fate of the war. Things went far otherwise in the next year, 530: the Persians crossed the frontier in full force, and marched on Daras, where they were met by Belisarius, who had lately been appointed commander-in-chief in the East. Under the walls of Daras the decisive battle of the war was fought, in which Belisarius, with 25,000 men, defeated 40,000 Persians by means of his tactical skill. The plan which he worked was to draw back his centre, containing all the Roman infantry, and when the Persians followed it, to launch against their exposed flanks all his cavalry, a miscellaneous gathering of Hunnish light horse, Teutonic Heruli from the Danube, and Roman Cataphracti or cuirassiers. This plan, much resembling Hannibal's manoeuvre at Cannae, and perhaps consciously copied from it, resulted in the complete rout of the Sassanian host.

After this defeat Kobad commenced abortive negotiations for peace, but the war was protracted into the next year, and Belisarius did not fare so well in 531. In stopping a Persian raiding force on the middle Euphrates, which aimed at Syria, and had turned the southern flank of the Mesopotamian fortresses, he suffered serious loss at the affair of Callinicum. Though he was defeated, his resistance had yet turned and frustrated the Persian expedition. Four months later king Kobad died, and his successor Chosroes I. made peace on the base of the status quo ante, fearing to continue the Roman war while his throne was insecure. (September, 531.)

The end of the Persian war left Justinian free to cast his eyes on the affairs of his neighbours to the West. Though so indecisive, it had not been without its uses, for it had permitted him to test the solidity of his army, and to discover several officers of merit, and one general of commanding ability — the young victor of Daras. Belisarius was now twenty-six years of age: he was, like his master, a native of the borderland between Thrace and Illyricum, bred at an unknown village named Germania, but not, as the name of his birthplace might seem to suggest, of Teutonic but of Thracian blood. He had entered the army at a very early age, and had fought his way up to the post of governor of the great fortress of Daras before he was twenty-four. His favour with Justinian had been confirmed by his marriage with Antonina, the friend and confidante of the empress Theodora. She was a clever, unscrupulous, domineering woman, several years older than her husband, and exercised over him a domestic tyranny which any man less easy tempered than the young general would have found unbearable. The position of Belisarius and Antonina at the Court of Justinian has been not unaptly compared to that of Marlborough and his imperious wife at the court of Queen Anne; but it is only fair to the East-Roman to say that he was in every way a better man than the Englishman, while his wife had all the faults of Duchess Sarah, without her one redeeming virtue of fidelity to her spouse.

Before he was able to turn his attention to the West, and just after the crisis of the Persian war had passed, Justinian was exposed to a sharp and sudden danger, the most perilous experience of his whole career. We have already spoken at some length of the rivalries of the Blue and Green factions, and explained how, in the early sixth century, the Greens were reckoned heterodox and supporters of the house of Anastasius, while the Blues were orthodox and favoured Justinus and his nephew. Accident conspired with the innate turbulence of the factions to stir them up into fierce disorder in the year 532, and brought about the celebrated 'Nika' sedition. To provide for the expenses of the Persian war, Justinian had not only drawn upon the hoarded wealth of Anastasius, but had imposed heavy additional taxation. This act made his instruments the Quaestor Tribonian and the Praetorian Prefect John of Cappadocia very unpopular. Both of them were suspected — and not incorrectly — of having used the opportunity to fill their pockets at the expense of the public, and John the Cappadocian had made himself particularly odious by his cruel treatment of defaulting debtors. In January 532 there were riotous scenes in the circus, caused by the protests of the Greens against the oppression they were suffering. There soon followed tumults in the streets, and the factions settled their grievances with bludgeon and knife. Justinian often allowed the Blues a free hand in dealing with their adversaries, but, on this occasion, his supporters had gone too far. The police seized many ring-leaders of both factions, and seven of the chiefs were condemned to the axe or the cord. While an angry crowd stood round, five of the rioters were put to death, but when the last two, a Blue and a Green, were being hung, the cord slipped twice, owing to the nervousness of the executioner, and the criminals fell to the ground. The populace then burst through the police and hurried off the men to sanctuary in a neighbouring monastery. This incident proved the beginning of a fearful uproar. Instead of dispersing, the mobs paraded the place shouting for the dismissal of the unpopular ministers John and Tribonian. Blues and Greens united in the cry, the whole city poured out into the streets, and the police were trampled down and driven away.

Frightened by the storm Justinian had the weakness to yield; instead of sending out the imperial guard to clear the streets, he announced that he had determined to remove the obnoxious Quaestor and Prefect. This only made matters worse; after burning the official residence of the prefect of the city, the mob mustered in a most threatening attitude outside the palace. This constrained the emperor to use force, but he happened to be very short of soldiery at the moment. All the garrison of Constantinople save 3500 of the scholarii, or imperial guard, had been sent off to the Persian war. Only two regiments had as yet returned, a corps of 500 cuirassiers under Belisarius, and a body of Heruli of about the same number. Five thousand men were hardly enough to cope with an angry populace of half-a-million souls in the narrow streets of the capital.

When attacked by the troops the rioters set fire to the city, and an awful conflagration ensued. The great church of St. Sophia perished among the flames, together with all the houses and public buildings to the north and east of it. Blood having once flowed, the mob were set upon something more than a riot — a revolution was in the air, and the Greens, who took the lead in the struggle, sought about for their favourite the patrician Hypatius, the nephew of their old patron Auastasius I. But Hypatius was a prudent and cautious person, with no ambition to risk his head; he had entered the palace and put himself in Justinian's hands to keep out of harm's way. It was not till the emperor, who feared traitors about him, ordered all senators to retire to their homes that Hypatius fell into the hands of his own partisans. The unhappy rebel in spite of himself was at once hurried off to the Hippodrome, placed on the imperial seat, and crowned with a diadem extemporised from his wife's gold necklace.

It was in vain that Justinian issued from the palace next day, and proclaimed an amnesty; he was chased back with insulting cries. Losing heart he summoned the chief of his courtiers and guards, and proposed to them to abandon Constantinople and take refuge in Asia, as Zeno had done in a similar time of trouble. John of Cappadocia and many of the ministers advised him to fly; but the intrepid Theodora stepped forward to save her husband from destruction. 'It has been said,' she cried, 'that the voice of a woman should not be heard among the councils of men. But those whose interests are most concerned have the best right to speak. To death the inevitable we must all submit, but to survive dignity and honour, to descend from empire to exile, to such shame there is no compulsion. Never shall the day come when I put off this purple robe and am no more hailed as sovereign lady. If you wish to protract your life, O Emperor, flight is easy; there are your ships and there is the sea. But consider whether, if you escape to exile, you will not wish every day that you were dead. As for me, I hold with the ancient saying that the imperial purple is a glorious shroud.'

Spurred on by the fiery words of his wife Justinian tried the fortune of war once more. A few reinforcements had arrived; with these, and the harassed troops who had already faced five days' street-fighting, Belisarius once more sallied forth from the palace. The rebels were off their guard, for a false rumour had got about that Justinian was already fled. At this moment the mob was crowding the Hippodrome and saluting their creature with shouts of Hypatie Auguste tu vincas. After a vain attempt to break in by the imperial staircase, Belisarius assaulted the main side gate of the circus, and burst in at a point where the conflagration had three days before made a breach in the wall. Penned into the great amphitheatre, and taken by surprise, the rebels made a weak resistance. Soon they turned to fly, but all the issues were choked, and the victims of the sword of Belisarius were numbered by the ten thousand. Hypatius and his brother were caught alive and brought to Justinian, who ordered them to be beheaded. The next day he heard of all the facts concerning the unwillingness of Hypatius, and gave his body honourable burial. It was many years before the Blues and Greens ever vexed him by another riot. The awful carnage in the circus kept the city quiet for a whole generation.

Justinian was now free from trouble at home and abroad, and turned to those ambitious schemes of foreign policy which were to occupy the rest of his reign. The dream of his heart was to reunite the Roman Empire, by bringing once more under his sceptre all those western provinces which were occupied by Teutonic kings, and paid only the shadow of homage to the imperial name. A few years before, the dream would have seemed fantastically overweening, but of late matters had been growing more and more promising. Justinian was, compared with his four predecessors, young and vigorous; he had an immense store of treasure, all the hoard of Anastasius, a large and efficient army, and at least one general of first-rate ability. His throne was firmly rooted; his eastern frontier secure; nothing now prevented him from undertaking wars of aggression.

Meanwhile, everything in the West favoured his projects. In Italy the great Theodoric was dead, and, since his death, the Ostrogothic kingdom had been faring ill. The old hero had left his realm to his grandson Athalaric, a boy of eight years old, under the guardianship of his mother Amalaswintha, the widow of Eutharic. The daughter of Theodoric was a clever and masterful woman, but she had a difficult task in teaching the turbulent Ostrogoths to obey a female regent. They murmured at all her doings, and most especially at her taste for Roman and Greek letters, and her frequent promotions of Roman officials. She strove to bring up her son, it was said, more as an Italian than a Goth, placing him under Roman tutors and keeping him tight to the desk, in spite of the saying of Theodoric that 'he who has trembled before the pedagogue's rod will not face the spear willingly.' It was as much as Amalaswintha could do to keep the Goths in their obedience while her son was young, but when he had attained the age of twelve or thirteen, and began to show some will of his own, the murmurs of the people grew louder. At last, when he had one day been chastised by his mother, he burst into the guard-room, and bade his subjects take note how a king of the Goths was treated worse than a slave. This scene produced a tumult, and the chiefs of the Goths took the education of the boy out of his mother's hands, though they left her the regency. Handed over to unsuitable companions Athalaric grew idle, drunken, and reckless; he was of a weakly habit of body, and, before he reached manhood, had developed the symptoms of consumption. Meanwhile, Amalaswintha was contending for power with the chiefs of the Goths, and had earned much unpopularity by putting to death, without form of trial, the three heads of the party which opposed her. So uncertain was her position that she sent secretly to Justinian in 533 to beg him to give her refuge at Dyrrhachium if she should be forced to fly. The emperor soon grasped the position — a divided people, an unpopular regent, a boy-king sinking into his grave invited him to active interference in Italy.

In Africa the condition of affairs was equally tempting. We have already mentioned how, on the death of king Thrasamund, the Vandal throne had fallen to his kinsman Hilderic, the son of king Hunneric and the Roman princess, Eudocia. Hilderic was elderly, unversed in affairs of state, and a conscientious Catholic, inheriting from his Roman mother that orthodoxy which his Arian subjects detested. He had but a short reign of seven years, but in it he succeeded in alienating the affections of the Vandals in every way. He incurred great odium for putting to death his predecessor's widow Amalafrida, the sister of the great Theodoric, because he found her conspiring against him. His wars were uniformly unsuccessful, the Moors of Atlas cut to pieces a whole army, and pushed their incursions close to the gates of Carthage. Probably his open confession of Catholicism, and promotion of Catholics to high office, were even greater sources of wrath. In 530 his cousin Geilamir organised a conspiracy against him, overthrew him with ease, and plunged him into a dungeon. Justinian professed great indignation at this dethroning of an orthodox and friendly sovereign, and resolved to make use of it as a grievance against the new king of the Vandals. Just before the 'Nika' sedition broke out he had sent an embassy to Carthage to bid Geilamir replace his cousin on the throne, and be contented with the place of regent. The usurper answered rudely enough: 'King Geilamir wishes to point out to king Justinian that it is a good thing for rulers to mind their own business.' He trusted to the remoteness of his situation and the domestic troubles of Justinian, and little thought that he was drawing down the storm on his head.

For Justinian had fully made up his mind to begin his attack on the West by subduing the Vandals. All things were in his favour, notably the facts that an Arian king was once more making life miserable to the African Catholics, and that Vandal and Ostrogoth had been completely estranged by the murder of Amalafrida nine years before. Amalaswintha favoured rather than discouraged the emperor's attack on her nearest Teutonic neighbours. There was yet one more piece of good fortune: king Geilamir had just sent off the flower of the Vandal troops to an expedition against Sardinia.

Encouraged by these considerations, Justinian prepared an army for the invasion of Africa in the summer of 533, though some of his ministers, and above all the financier, John of Cappadocia, warned him against 'attacking the ends of the earth, from which a message would hardly reach Byzantium in a year,' a ridiculous plea to any one who remembered the ancient organisation of the empire. The army was not very large: it consisted of 10,000 foot and 5000 horse, half regular troops from the Asiatic provinces, half Hunnish and Herulian auxiliaries. But its commander, Belisarius, was a invades host in himself, and confidence in him buoyed up many who would otherwise have despaired. The voyage was protracted by contrary winds to the unprecedented length of eighty days, but at last the armament cast anchor at Caput Vada, on the cape which faces Sicily, in the beginning of September. The Vandals were caught wholly unprepared: their king was absent in Numidia, their best troops were in Sardinia, their fleet had not been even launched. A blind confidence in their remoteness from Constantinople had led them to despise all Justinian's threats, and no preparation whatever had been made against an invasion. Geilamir hurried down to the coast, put his prisoner Hilderic to death, and summoned in his warriors from every side; but it was eleven days before he mustered in sufficient force to attack the Romans, and meanwhile Belisarius had advanced unopposed to within ten miles of the gates of Carthage. The provincials received him everywhere with joy; for he proclaimed that be came to deliver them from Arian oppression, and kept his soldiery in such good order that not a field or a cottage was plundered.

Belisarius had reached the posting-station of Ad Decimum, and was advancing cautiously with strong corps of observation securing his flank and front, when suddenly he was assailed by the whole force of the Vandals, who outnumbered him in at least the proportion of two to one. He was beset on three sides at once; one corps of Vandals under the king's brother Ammatas issued from Carthage to attack him in front; another body beset his left flank; the main army under Geilamir himself assailed the rear of his long column of march. But the Vandals mismanaged their tactics, and failed to combine the three attacks. First the troops from Carthage came out, and were beaten off with the loss of their leader; then the turning corps was driven back by the Hunnish cavalry, whom Belisarius had kept lying out on his flank. When the main Vandal army came up there was more serious fighting with the centre and rear of the Roman column. Geilamir furiously burst through the line of march, and cleft the Roman army in twain, but he did not know how to use his advantage. Instead of improving his first success, he halted his troops, and allowed Belisarius to rally and re-form his men. It is said that he was so transported with grief at finding the corpse of his brother, who had fallen in the earlier engagement, that he gave no more orders, and cast himself weeping on the ground. Presently, the Romans were in good array again; their victorious vanguard had returned to aid the centre, and they fell once more, as the evening closed in, on the stationary masses of the Vandals.

The conquerors of Africa must have forgotten their ancient valour, for, after a very paltry resistance, they turned and fled westward under cover of the night.

Carthage at once threw open its gates, and Belisarius dined next day in the royal palace on the meal that had been prepared for the Vandal king. Geilamir reaped now the reward for the hundred years of persecution to which his forefathers had subjected the Africans. Every town that was not garrisoned opened its gates to the Romans, and the provincials hastened to place everything they possessed at the disposal of Belisarius. His entry into Carthage was like the triumph of a home-coming king, and the order and discipline of his troops was so great that none even of the Vandal and Arian citizens suffered loss.

Geilamir meanwhile retired into the Numidian hills, with an army that had suffered more loss of morale than loss of numbers. He was soon joined by the troops whom he had sent to Sardinia; having subdued that island they returned, and raised his forces to nearly 50,000 men. Finding that Belisarius was repairing the walls of Carthage before marching out to finish the campaign, Geilamir resolved to take the offensive himself. Descending from the hills he marched on Carthage, and met the Roman army at Tricameron, twenty miles westward of the city.

Here Belisarius won a pitched battle after a struggle far more severe than that he had gone through at Ad Decimum. Thrice the Romans were beaten back, but their gallant leader rallied them, and at last his cuirassiers burst through the Vandal ranks and slew Tzazo, the king's brother. Geilamir turned to fly, though his men fought on until their retreat was cut off. Almost the whole Vandal race perished in this fight and the bloody pursuit which followed. Geilamir himself took refuge in the heights of Mount Atlas among the Moors, and dwelt among them miserably enough for a few months.

Discovering that he could not raise a third army, and that life was unendurable among the filthy barbarians, he determined to surrender, and yielded himself and his family to Belisarius, on the assurance that he should receive honourable treatment, in spite of the fact that he had murdered the emperor's friend Hilderic.

In the spring of 534 Belisarius was able to return in triumph to Constantinople, bringing with him the king and most of the surviving Vandals as captives. His ships were loaded with all the plunder of the palace of Carthage, the trophies of a century of successful pirate raids, including the plate and ornaments which Gaiseric had carried off from Rome in 455. It is said that the emperor recognised among this store the seven-branched candlestick and golden vessels of the temple of Jerusalem, which Titus Caesar had taken to Rome when he conquered Judea four hundred years back. He sent them to be placed in the Church of the Holy Sepulchre, in the Holy City where they had been first consecrated. Belisarius was allowed the honours of an ancient Roman triumph, a privilege denied to a subject for four centuries; he entered the Hippodrome in state, and laid his prisoners and his booty at Justinian's feet, while senate and people saluted him as the new Scipio Africanus, a title which he had fairly earned. Next year he was promoted to the consulship, and given every honour that the emperor could devise. His captive, king Geilamir, was kindly treated, and presented with a great estate in Phrygia, where he and his family long dwelt in ease.

The year of the triumph of Belisarius saw new opportunities arising for him and for his master. In the autumn of 534 died the sickly and debauched youth who held the title of king of the Ostrogoths; he had not yet attained his eighteenth birthday. His mother, Amalaswintha, was now left face to face with the wild Goths, stripped of the protection of the royal name, and exposed to the enmity of the families of the chiefs whom she had executed. In despair of inducing the Goths to endure the rule of a queen-regnant, she determined to choose a colleague, and confer on him the title of king. Theodoric's next male heir after Athalaric was a certain Theodahat, the son of his sister Amalaberga. This prince had been excluded by his uncle from all affairs of state for his notorious cowardice, covetousness, and duplicity. He was a Romanised Teuton of the worst type, and, as was truly said, Vilis Gothus imitatur Romanum; he had pronounced literary tastes, called himself a Platonic philosopher, and showed some care for the arts, but was wholly mean and corrupt. Amalaswintha thought to presume on the cowardice of her cousin, and to force him to become her tool; she forgot that even a coward may be ambitious. At the queen's behest the assembly of the warriors of Italy hailed Theodahat and Amalaswintha joint rulers of the Ostrogoths, But in less than six months the intriguing king had suborned his partisans to seize and imprison his unfortunate cousin. She was cast into a castle on the lake of Bolsena, and shortly afterwards murdered, with Theodahat's connivance, by some of the kinsfolk of the nobles whom she executed five years before. (May, 535.)

Justinian had now an even better casus belli in Italy than he had possessed in Africa. His ally had been dethroned and murdered, and her crown was possessed by a creature far inferior to Geilamir, who was at least a warrior if an unfortunate one. The miserable Theodahat grovelled with fear when he received the angry ultimatum of Justinian. He even made secret proposals to the emperor's ambassadors to the effect that he would abandon his crown and betray his people, if only he were granted his life and a suitable maintenance. When even this did not avail, he took to consulting soothsayers and magicians. We are told that a Jewish seer bade him pen up thirty pigs — to represent unclean Gentiles, we must suppose — in three sties, calling ten 'Goths,' ten 'Italians,' and ten 'Imperialists.' He was to leave them ten days without food or water, and then take augury from their condition. When Theodahat looked in at the appointed hour, he found all the 'Goth' pigs dead save two, and half of the 'Italians,' but the 'Imperialists,' though gaunt and wasted, were all, or almost all, alive. This the Jew told the downcast king would portend a war in which the Gothic race was to be well-nigh exterminated, and the Italians to be terribly cut down, while the Imperial armies would conquer after much toil and privation!

While Theodahat was vainly busy with his soothsayers, the Roman armies had already attacked the Gothic province in Dalmatia. The wretched usurper had to face war, whether he willed it or no. Justinian had determined, as was but natural, to intrust the Ostrogothic war to the conqueror of Africa, and, in the autumn of the year of his consulship, Belisarius sailed for the West with a small army of 7500 men, of whom 3000 were Isaurians, and the rest equally divided between Roman regulars and Hunnish and Herule auxiliaries. It was a small force with which to attack a king who commanded the swords of a hundred thousand gallant Germans, but reinforcements were to follow, and Theodahat's cowardice and incapacity were well known.

In September 535 Belisarius fell on Sicily; here as in Africa the provincials hastened to throw open the gates of their cities to the invader. There were few Goths in Sicily; they garrisoned Palermo, but Belisarius took the place by a sudden assault, after lying only a few days before its walls. By the approach of winter the whole island was in his hands. He would have hastened on to attack Italy, but for a mutiny which broke out in Africa and compelled him to cross the sea and spend some time in the neighbourhood of Carthage.

Meanwhile the poor craven Theodahat did nothing but besiege the ears of Justinian with more fruitless proposals for peace. He was as unprepared as ever for resistance when Belisarius crossed over the straits of Messina, in April 536, and overran Bruttium and Lucania. So greatly were the Goths of the south discouraged by his helplessness, that Ebermund, the Count of Lucania, surrendered to Belisarius, and entered the imperial service with all his followers. It was not till he had pushed on to Naples that Belisarius met with any opposition; all through southern Italy the city gates swung open the moment that he touched them with his spear. The old Greek city of Naples, however, held by a strong Gothic garrison, made a very obstinate defence, and held out for many weeks, awaiting the arrival of a relieving army. King Theodahat had gathered a great army at Rome, but the coward dared not close, and kept 50,000 men idle, while 7000 Romans were beleaguering Naples. At last the city fell, a party of Isaurian soldiers having found their way up a disused aqueduct, and stormed one of the gates from within. The news of the fall of Naples raised the wrath of the Goths against their wretched king to boiling point. At a great folkmoot at Regeta in the Pomptine Marshes the army solemnly deposed Theodahat, and, as no male Amal was left, raised on the shield Witiges, an elderly warrior of respectable character, who had won credit in the old wars of Theodoric. The dethroned king fled away to seek refuge at Ravenna, but a private enemy pursued him and cut his throat 'like a sheep' long ere he had reached the City of the Marshes.

The choice of Witiges was a fearful error on the part of the Goths; they had mistaken respectability for talent, and paid the penalty in seeing the stupid veteran wreck all their hopes. The first blunder on the part of the new king was to draw his army northward on the news that the Franks were crossing the Alps to ravage the valley of Po. He left only 4000 men in Rome, and marched on Ravenna with all the rest. The moment that he was departed Belisarius moved northward to attack the imperial city. It fell into his hands without a blow; the Gothic garrison felt that they were left deserted among a populace ready to betray them to the enemy; indeed Pope Silverius and the Senate had already written to pray Belisarius to deliver them. When the Imperialists appeared before the southern gate, the Goths fled out of the northern, in a panic that was inexcusable, for they were well-nigh as numerous as the 5000 men that Belisarius brought with him. (December 9, 536.)

Belisarius was now master of Rome, but he knew that his hold on it was precarious. Witiges had settled matters with the Franks by paying them 130,000 gold solidi and ceding his Transalpine dominions in Provence. After marrying Mataswintha, the sister of the late king Athalaric, and the last scion of the house of the Amals, he resolved to return and deliver Rome, All north Italy had sent him its Gothic warriors, and 100,000 men marched under his banner to besiege Rome in the spring of 537.

The defence of Rome is the greatest of all the titles to glory that Belisarius won. The walls of Aurelian were strong, but there were only 5000 men to defend their vast circuit, and within was an unruly mass of cowardly citizens, liable to all sorts of panic fears — mouths to be fed without hands to strike, for hardly a Roman took arms to aid the imperial troops. In the middle of March the Goths appeared before the walls, and pitched seven camps opposite the northern and eastern gates of the city. They then cut all the aqueducts which supplied Rome with water, and commenced the construction of siege-engines for a great assault. With the want of thoroughness that he always displayed, king Witiges made no adequate preparation for blockading the southern side of the city, or for stopping its communications with Ostia and Naples. All through the siege convoys of provisions and reinforcements were frequently able to creep into Rome by night, eluding the outposts which were all that Witiges placed on the side of the Tiber and the Campagna.

A fortnight after arriving in front of the walls Witiges had his engines ready, and delivered his great assault on the northern and north-eastern fronts of the city. Everywhere the attack failed; the towers and rams which the Goths had drawn forward never reached the walls; the oxen which drew them were shot down before they neared the ditch. But thousands of wild warriors with scaling-ladders delivered assaults against innumerable portions of the enceinte. In most cases they failed entirely; the walls of Aurelian were too strong; but at two points, at opposite ends of the city, they nearly won success. At the Praenestine gate a battering-ram broke in the outer bulwarks, and a swarm of Goths was only held back by an inner entrenchment till the reinforcements of Belisarius arrived. But greater danger still was encountered at the Mausoleum of Hadrian (castle of St. Angelo), just beyond the Aelian Bridge. There the Goths filled the ditch, overwhelmed the defenders with arrows, and were fitting their ladders to the embrasures, when they were at last checked by a strange expedient. The walls of the mausoleum were lined with dozens of splendid statues, some of them figures of emperors, others the ancient spoils of Greece. At the supreme moment the desperate garrison flung these colossal figures on the besiegers below, and drove them off by the hail of marble fragments.

At the end of the day Belisarius was everywhere successful; 20,000 Goths had fallen, and the self-confidence of Witiges was so broken that he never again tried a general assault. He relied instead on a blockade, but, though he inflicted great misery on the garrison, and still more on the populace, he never closed the roads or the river sufficiently to exclude occasional convoys of provisions. He did not prevent Belisarius from transferring to Campania the greater part of the women, aged men, and slaves in the city. Meanwhile the summer drew on, and the Gothic hosts began to suffer from malaria, and from the filthy state of the crowded camps. On the other hand, Belisarius at last began to receive reinforcements from Constantinople, and was able to make sallies, in which his horsemen handled the Gothic outposts very roughly.

When both assault and blockade had been proved ineffectual, and when an attempt to creep into the city through the empty aqueducts had been foiled, Witiges would probably have done well to raise the siege, and throw on Belisarius, whose army was still very small, the burden of taking the offensive. Instead of doing this he lay obstinately in his camp for a year and nine days, watching his army melt away under the scourge of pestilence, and allowing the numbers and boldness of the Imperialists to increase. At last Belisarius had been so strongly reinforced that he was able, while still holding Rome, to put a second force in the field. This he sent, under an officer named John the Bloody, through the Sabine hills to make a dash into Picenum and menace Ravenna. John, a very able officer, seized the important town of Rimini, only thirty-three miles from Ravenna, in February 538. The news that his capital was being threatened, and that the enemy was in his rear, at last forced the sluggish king of the Goths to move. He set his seven camps on fire, and retired up the Flaminian Way into Picenum. Thus the prudence and valour of Belisarius were at last vindicated, and the Romans, after a siege of 374 days, could once more breathe freely.

Middle Italy was now lost to the Goths, and the scene of operations shifted into Picenum, north Etruria, and the valley of the Po, where the war was to endure for two years more (538-40). It resolved itself into a struggle for the coast towns between Ravenna and Ancona, and for the command of the passes of the Apennines. One half of the Roman army was concentrated at Rimini and Ancona, while Belisarius himself with the. other was occupied in clearing the Gothic garrisons out of northern Etruria. Two Gothic armies at Ravenna and Auximum penned the northern Roman force into the narrow sea-coast plain, and at last laid siege to both Rimini and Ancona. Here Witiges seemed for once likely to succeed, but, when the garrisons had been brought to the last extremity, they were relieved by new forces from Constantinople commanded by the eunuch Narses the praepositus sacri cubiculi.

Thrown on the defensive Witiges drew back to Ravenna, and allowed the Romans to overrun the province of Aemilia, and even to cross the Po, and raise an insurrection in the great city of Milan. There now followed a long pause: Belisarius found that Narses was set on asserting an independent authority over the newly-arrived army, and had to send to the emperor to beg him to recall the eunuch. Meanwhile he laid siege to the last two Gothic fortresses south of Ravenna, the towns of Fiesole in Etruria and Auximum (Osimo) in Picenum. Both cities made a gallant resistance, and while Belisarius was at a standstill Uraias, the warlike nephew of Witiges, stormed and sacked Milan, and restored the Gothic dominion north of the Po (539). Meanwhile the king took the only wise step which occurred to him during the whole war: he sent ambassadors to the East to inform Chosroes, king of Persia, that well-nigh the whole Roman army was occupied in Italy, and that he might overrun Syria and Mesopotamia with ease. Taken two years earlier, this step might have saved the Goths, but now it was too late: Chosroes moved, but moved only in time to hear that Witiges was dethroned and a captive.

After holding out seven months, Auximum surrendered to Belisarius at mid-winter, 539-40. Witiges had done nothing to save the gallant garrison, alleging that a Frankish raid into the valley of the Po prevented him from moving. The excuse was true but insufficient, for when the Franks of Theudebert, thinned by disease, turned home again, the Gothic king did not stir any the more.

At last, in the spring of 540, Narses had been recalled, and Belisarius had full possession of all Picenum and Etruria, and could safely advance on Ravenna. After posting a covering force to ward off any attempt to relieve the town by the Goths of northern Italy, he drew his main army round the great fortress in the marshland, the chosen home of Theodoric, the storehouse of the hoarded wealth of the Amals. The defence was weak, far weaker than that of the smaller stronghold of Auximum. Witiges seemed to have the power of communicating his sloth and hesitation to all who came near him. He listened first to offers from Theudebert the Frank, then to proposals for surrender sent in by Belisarius. At last he determined to close with the terms offered by Justinian, that he should resign all Italy south of the Po, give up half the royal hoard, and reign in the Transpadane as the emperor's vassal. The terms were not hard, for Justinian had just been attacked by Persia, and wished to end his Italian war at once. It would have been well for all parties if they had been carried out; but two wills intervened: the Gothic nobles were wildly indignant at their master's cowardice: Belisarius, looking at his military advantages, thought the terms too liberal. From this discontent came an extraordinary result: the Teutonic chiefs boldly proposed to the imperial general that he should reign over them, — whether as king of the Goths or Roman Caesar they cared not, — but their swords should be his, and the craven Witiges should be cast away, if he would take them as his vassals and administer Italy. Belisarius temporised, and the simple Goths, believing that no man could resist such an offer, threw open the gates. But the great general was loyal to the core: instead of proclaiming himself emperor, he took over the town in Justinian's name, bade the Gothic warriors disperse each to his own home, and shipped all the golden stores of Ravenna off to Constantinople. It seemed as if the monarchy of the Goths was ended: nothing remained to them save Pavia, Verona, and a few more north Italian cities. Justinian resolved to recall Belisarius before these places should fall; meaner generals would suffice to take them. Two motives stirred the emperor: his great captain was wanted on the eastern frontier to keep back the advancing Persian; but suspicion also played its part: Justinian was not too well pleased that Belisarius had overruled his project of making peace with Witiges, and he had been somewhat frightened by the Gothic proposal to make Belisarius emperor. It had been declined, it is true, but might not the seeds of disloyalty have sunk into the heart of the general? It would be safer to bring him away from the temptation.

So, by the imperial mandate, Belisarius sailed for the Bosphorus, taking with him the captive Witiges, and all the gold and gems of the great hoard of the Amals. He was denied a formal triumph such as he had won by his Vandal victory, but none the less his reception was magnificent. His personal body-guard of 7000 chosen men had followed him to the capital, and, as they passed through the streets, the populace exclaimed 'the household of one man has destroyed the kingdom of the Goths.' Happy would it have been for the great general if he had died at the moment of this his grandest success. He was reserved for lesser wars and years of chequered fortune (540).

CHAPTER VI: JUSTINIAN — (continued) — 540-565 A.D.

Justinian as builder — His ruinous financial policy — His second Persian war — Chosroes takes Antioch, 540 — Campaigns of Belisarius and Chosroes — The Great Plague of 542 — Peace with Persia — Baduila restores the Ostrogothic kingdom in Italy — His campaign against Belisarius — Two sieges of Rome — Success and greatness of Baduila — Narses invades Italy — Baduila slain at Taginae, 552 — End of the Ostrogothic kingdom — Narses defeats the Franks — Justinian attacks Southern Spain — Third Persian War, 549-55 — Justinian as Theologian — Belisarius defeats the Huns — Later years of Justinian — His legal reforms.

The year 540 was the last of Justinian's years of unbroken good fortune. For the rest of his long life he was to experience many vicissitudes, and see some of his dearest schemes frustrated, though, on the whole, the dogged perseverance which was his most notable characteristic brought him safely through to the end. The first difficulty which was destined to trouble him, in the latter half of his reign, was a financial one. He had now come to the end of the hoarded wealth of Anastasius; the military budget of his increased empire required more money, for Africa and Italy did not pay their way, and now a new Persian war was upon his hands. In addition, his magnificent court and his insatiable thirst for building called for huge sums year after year. It is impossible to exaggerate Justinian's expenditure on bricks and mortar: not only did he rebuild in his capital, on a more magnificent scale, all the public edifices that had been burnt in the 'Nika' riot, but he filled every corner of his empire, from newly-conquered Ravenna to the Armenian frontier, with splendid forts, churches, monasteries, hospitals, and aqueducts. Whenever a Byzantine ruin is found in the wilds of Syria or Asia Minor it turns out, in one case out of every two, to be of Justinian's date. In the Balkan peninsula alone we learn to our surprise that he erected more than 300 forts and castles to defend the line of the Danube and the Haemus, the side of the empire which had been found most open to attacks of the barbarian during the last century. The building of his enormous cathedral of St. Sophia alone cost several millions, an expenditure whose magnificent result quite justifies itself, but one which must have seemed heartrending to the financiers who had to find the money at a moment when the emperor was involved in two desperate wars.

Justinian poured forth his treasures with unstinting hand in the arts both of war and of peace. But to replenish his treasury — that jar of the Danaides — he had to impose a crushing taxation on the empire. His finance minister, John of Cappadocia, was the most unscrupulous of men, one who never shrank from plying extortion of every kind upon the wretched tax-payers: as long as he kept the exchequer full Justinian winked at his iniquitous and often illegal proceedings. It was only when he chanced to quarrel with the empress Theodora that John was finally disgraced. His successors were less capable, but no less extortionate: ere ten years had passed the Africans and Italians, groaning under the yoke of the Greek Logothetes, were cursing their stars that ever they had aided Belisarius to drive out the Arian Goth and Vandal. As Justinian's reign went on the state of matters grew worse and worse; for a crushing taxation tends to drain the resources of the land, and at last renders it unable to bear even a burden that would have once been light. Historians recapitulate twenty new taxes that Justinian laid upon the empire, yet at the end of his reign they were bringing in far less than the old and simpler imposts of Anastasius and Justin had produced.

This ruinous draining of the vital power of the empire only began to be seriously felt after 540, when, for the first time, Justinian was compelled to wage war at once in East and West, and yet refused to slacken from his building. The Gothic war — contrary to all probability and expectation — was still destined to run on for thirteen years more; the Persian lasted for sixteen, and, when they were over, the emperor and the empire alike were but the shadow of their former selves: they were unconquered, but drained of all their strength and marrow.

We have already mentioned that the young king Chosroes of Persia, stirred up by the embassy of Witiges, and dreading lest the power which had subdued Carthage and Rome should ere long stretch out its hand to Ctesiphon, had found a casus belli, and crossed the Mesopotamian frontier. Some blood-feuds between Arab hordes respectively subject to Persia and Constantinople, and a dispute about the suzerainty of some tribes in the Armenian highlands formed a good enough excuse for renewing the war at a moment when Justinian's best general and 50,000 of the flower of his troops were absent in Italy and Africa.

In the spring of 540, at the very moment when Belisarius reducing Ravenna, Chosroes marched up the Euphrates, leaving the frontier fortresses of Daras and Edessa on his flank, and launched a sudden attack on north Syria. He had been expected not there but in Mesopotamia, and all preparations for defence were out of gear. Before any resistance was organised Chosroes had crossed the Euphrates, sacked Beroea, and ransomed Hierapohs for 2000. lbs. of gold. But it was at Antioch, the third city of the Roman Empire, and the seat of the Praetorian Prefect of the East that the Persian monarch was aiming. It was more than two centuries and a half since the city of the Orontes had seen a foreign foe, and its walls were old and dilapidated. A garrison of 6000 men was thrown in, and the Blues and Greens of the city armed themselves to guard the ramparts. But there was no Roman army in the field to protect the city from the approach of the Persian: Buzes, the general of the East, refused to risk his small army in a general engagement, and had retired no one knew whither. The siege of Antioch was short, for the defence was ill-managed: the garrison cut its way out when the walls were forced, but the town, with all its wealth, and a great number of its inhabitants who had not found time to fly, became the prize of Chosroes. The Persian plundered the churches, burnt the private houses, and drove away a herd of captives, whom he took to his home, and established in a new city near Ctesiphon, which he called Chosroantiocheia.

The great king then ransomed the neighbouring cities of Chalcis and Apamea, and recrossed the Euphrates into Mesopotamia. Here, where strong and well-armed fortresses blocked his way, Chosroes found that he could effect nothing; after looking at Edessa he found it too strong, and made his way to Daras. To this town he laid siege, but was beaten off without much difficulty, and then returned home for the winter (540).

The Persians were never destined to win again such successes as had fallen to them in this the first year of the war. By the next spring Justinian had reinforced the eastern frontier with all his disposable troops, and the mighty Belisarius himself had arrived to take command of the army of Mesopotamia. But it was not fated that the great king and the great captain should ever measure themselves against each other. Hearing that the frontier to the south was now well guarded, the Persian had resolved to make a dash at a new point of the Roman line of defence. While expected on the Euphrates he quietly marched north through the Median and Iberian mountains, crossed many obscure passes, and appeared on the Black Sea coast by the river Phasis. The Romans here held the shore by their great castle of Petra, while the Lazi, the tribes of inland Colchis, were Roman vassals. Chosroes overran the land, constrained the Lazi to do him homage, and, after a short siege, took Petra.

Meanwhile Belisarius, on finding the Persian invasion of Mesopotamia delayed, had crossed the frontier in the far south, beaten a small Persian force in the field, and ravaged Assyria from end to end, though he could not take the great fortress of Nisibis. On hearing of this raid Chosroes returned from Colchis with his main army, whereupon Belisarius retired behind the ramparts of Daras. The campaign had not been eventful, but the balance of gain lay on the side of the Persians, whose frontier now touched the Black Sea.

Nor was the next year (542) destined to see any decisive fighting. Belisarius had concentrated his army at Europus on the Euphrates and waited to be attacked, but save one raid no attack came, though Chosroes had brought the full force of his empire up to Nisibis. The Roman chronicles ascribe his sluggishness to a fear of the reputation of Belisarius, but another cause seems to have been more operative. The great plague of 542 had just broken out in Persia, and its ravages were probably the real cause of the retreat and disbanding of the army of Chosroes, much as in 1348 the 'black death' caused English and French to drop for a time their mutual hostilities.

This awful scourge merits a word of notice. It broke out in Egypt early in the year, and spread like wildfire over Syria, the lands of the Euphrates valley, and Asia Minor, thence making its way to Constantinople and the West. It is impossible to make out its exact nature, but we know that it was accompanied by ulcers, and by a horrible swelling of the groin. Few whom it struck down ever recovered, but of these few was Justinian himself, who rose from his bed when the rumour of his death was already abroad and a fight for the succession imminent. At Constantinople the plague raged with such violence that 5000, and even 10,000 persons are said to have died in a single day. The historian Procopius marvelled at its universal spread. 'A man might climb to the top of a hill, and it was there, or retire to the depths of a cavern, but it was there also. It took no note of north or south, Greek or Persian, washed or unwashed, winter or summer: in all alike it was deadly.' This awful scourge, which is thought to have carried off a third of the population of the empire, was not the least of the causes of that general decay which is found in the later years of Justinian's reign. It swept away tax-payers, brought commerce to a standstill, and seems to have left the emperor himself an old man before his time.

The plague then sufficiently accounts for the stagnation of the war in 542. Perhaps we may also allow something for the personal troubles of Belisarius, who, in the previous winter, had fallen on evil times. He had detected his intriguing wife Antonina in unfaithfulness, and, for throwing her into a dungeon, and kidnapping her paramour, had incurred the wrath of Theodora, which seriously handicapped him in the rest of his career, so great was her influence with her imperial spouse. He was no longer supported from Constantinople as he had once been, and was at last compelled to disarm Theodora's displeasure by liberating his wife. The imperial ill-humour may, perhaps, have stinted his resources during the summer that followed his domestic misfortune.

In 543, the plague having somewhat abated, Chosroes once more assumed the offensive, and moved towards Roman Armenia, following the valley of the upper Euphrates; but a fresh outbreak of pestilence forced him to turn back, and the Romans were consequently enabled to invade Persarmenia. Belisarius was not with them, and they suffered a serious defeat from an inferior force, and returned with discredit to their old cantonments. The great general had been recalled with ignominy to Constantinople. Justinian had heard that, when the news of his supposed death had reached the army of the Euphrates, Belisarius had shown some signs of arranging for a military pronunciamento. He did not make this his pretext for recall, but dwelt on some unsettled charges of money lost from the Vandal and Gothic treasures, for which there was some foundation, for Belisarius, like Marlborough, had an unhappy taste for hoarding. For some months the general was in disgrace: his body-guard was dispersed — 7000 men was too large a comitatus for even the most loyal of men — and much of his wealth confiscated, but, on his consenting to be reconciled to his wife, and to depart for Italy, the empress Theodora consented to forget her displeasure and allow Justinian to give Belisarius the charge of a new war (543).

But, before relating the doings of the humbled and heartbroken Belisarius in the West, we must finish the Persian war. In 544 Chosroes, freed alike from the plague and from the fear of Belisarius, invaded Mesopotamia and laid siege to its capital Edessa. After a siege of many months, in which the gallant garrison beat off every effort both of open force and of military engineerings, — mounds, mines, rams, and towers availed nothing against them, — Chosroes withdrew humbled to Nisibis, and began to negotiate for a truce; it was successfully made on the terms that the Persians should retain the homage of their conquests in Colchis, and receive 2000 lbs. of gold on evacuating their other conquests — which were of small value. On the all-important Mesopotamian frontier the great fortresses had held good, and there was nothing of importance for the king to restore. This truce was concluded for five years, at the end of which the war was renewed (545-550).

Meanwhile all Italy was once more aflame with war. After Ravenna surrendered, and Witiges was led captive to Byzantium, all the Gothic fortresses surrendered save two, Verona and Pavia, the only towns of northern Italy in which the Teutonic element seems to have outnumbered the Roman. The remnant of the Ostrogoths in Pavia, though they did not number 2000 men, took the bold step of proclaiming a new king, a warrior named Hildibad, who was the nephew of Theudis, king of Spain, and who promised his uncle's help to his followers. Hildibad's resistance might have been crushed if he had been promptly attacked, but the Roman commanders were occupied in taking over the towns that made no resistance, and in quelling some disorders among their own men. After Belisarius left, there were five generals in the peninsula of whom none was trusted with supreme authority over the rest. Each left to another the task of treading out the last sparks of Gothic resistance, and gradually Hildibad grew stronger as the scattered remnants of the army of Witiges made their way to his camp. When he recovered most of Venetia, the Romans thought him worthy of notice, but he won a battle near Treviso over the army that came against him. The Italians were now far from showing the devotion to the imperial cause that they had once displayed. The Logothetes from Constantinople were harassing them with new imposts, and most especially with the preposterous attempt to gather the arrears of taxation for the years during which the war had raged, a time at which the emperor had, as a matter of fact, no firm hold on the country.

In 541 Hildibad was murdered by a private enemy ere yet he had succeeded in freeing all the land north of the Po. But this hero of the darkest hour, who had saved the Goths from extinction when salvation seemed impossible, found a still worthier successor. After a few months, during which a certain Rugian, named Eraric, ruled at Pavia, Hildibad's nephew, Baduila, was raised on the shield and saluted as king. Baduila was, after Theodoric, the greatest of all the Goths of East or West: he showed a moral elevation, a single-hearted purity of purpose, a chivalrous courtesy, a justice and piety worthy of the best of the knights of the Middle Ages. As a warrior his feats were astonishing: he out-generalled even the great Belisarius himself. The only stain on his character, during eleven years of rule, are one or two unjustifiable executions of prisoners of war who had roused his wrath, and caused the old Gothic fury to blaze forth.

From the first moment of his accession Baduila went forth conquering and to conquer. The Roman generals frightened by his first successes were at last induced to combine: he foiled them at Verona, followed them across the Po, and inflicted on them at Faenza in Aemilia a decisive defeat in the open field, though they had 12,000 men to his 5000. Then crossing the Apennines he won all Tuscany by a second battle on the Mugello near Florence. By these two victories all Italy north of Rome, save the great fortresses, fell into his hands: Rome and Ravenna, with Piacenza in the valley of the Po, and Ancona and Perugia in the centre, were left as isolated garrisons, rising above the returning tide of Gothic conquest. All the surviving Goths had rallied under Baduila's banner, and many of the imperial mercenaries of Teutonic blood took service with him when the cities which they garrisoned were subdued. After conquering Tuscany and Picenum, Baduila left Rome to itself for a space — the memories of its last siege were too discouraging — and spent the year 542 in overrunning Campania and Apulia. The Italians kept apathetically quiet, while the imperial garrisons were few and scattered. In six months south Italy was once more Gothic up to the gates of Otranto, Reggio, and Naples. The siege of the last-named town was Baduila's first exercise in poliorcetics: the place was very gallantly defended, and only surrendered when famine had done its work, and after an armament sent from Constantinople to its relief had been shattered by a storm almost in sight of the walls, along the rocks of Capri and Sorrento. In spite of this desperate resistance, it was noted with surprise that Baduila treated both garrison and people with kindness, sending the one away unharmed, and preserving the other from plunder. It was at the time of the fall of Naples that an event occurred which was long remembered as a token of the justice of Baduila. A Gothic warrior had violated the daughter of a Calabrian: the king cast the man into bonds and ordered his death. But many of the Goths besought him not to slay a brave warrior for such an offence. Baduila heard them out, and replied that they must choose that day whether they preferred to save one man's life, or to save the whole Gothic nation. At the beginning of the war they would remember how they had great hosts, famous generals, vast treasure, splendid arms, and all the castles of Italy. But under king Theodahat, a man who loved gold better than justice, they had so moved God's anger by their unrighteous lives that everything had been taken from them. But the divine grace had given the Goths one more chance of working out their salvation: God had opened a new account with them, and so must they do with him, by following justice and righteousness. The ravisher must die, and as to being a brave warrior, they should remember that the cruel and unjust were never finally successful in war, for as was a man's life, such was his fortune in battle. The officers caught their sovereign's meaning and withdrew, and the criminal was duly executed.

In 542, the year of the plague, Justinian had been able to do little for Italy, but in that which followed, when he heard that Naples had fallen, he determined to send the newly-pardoned Belisarius back to the scene of his former glories. Denied the services of his own body-guard the great general recruited 4000 raw troops in Thrace, and made ready to return. Baduila meanwhile was besieging Otranto, and clearing Apulia of the Imperialists.

In the next year the Gothic king and the Roman general came for the first time into contact; contrary to expectation it was not Belisarius who had the better of the struggle: broken in spirit, badly served by his raw recruits, and by the demoralised army of Italy, and unaided by Justinian, who was straining every nerve to keep up the Persian War, he accomplished little or nothing. Based on the impregnable fortress of Ravenna he was able to seize Pesaro, and to relieve the garrisons of Osimo and of Otranto, but that was all. Baduila ravaged Italy unmolested, and began to make preparations for the siege of Rome: if he was to be checked — as Belisarius wrote to his master — more men and money to pay them were urgently needed.

Justinian could not, or would not, send either men or money in adequate quantity, and Baduila was able to invest Rome. Unlike Witiges, he succeeded in barring all the roads, and in blocking the Tiber by a boom of spars. Famine was soon within the walls, but the Goths made no attempt at a storm, leaving hunger to do its work. Bessas, the governor of Rome, sought for aid from all sides, and corn ships were sent him from Sicily, but Baduila seized them all as they were tacking up the Tiber channel. Then Belisarius came round to Portus, at the mouth of the river, with all the men he could muster, a very few thousands, and endeavoured to force his way to Rome by breaking Baduila's boom, and bringing his lighter war-vessels up the Tiber. He left his wife, his stores, and his reserves at Portus, sailed up the river, and succeeded, after a hot engagement, in burning the towers which guarded the boom. But, in the moment of success, news came to him that the Goths were attacking Portus in his rear, and that his wife and camp were in danger. He turned back, found that the fighting at Portus was only an insignificant skirmish brought on by the rashness of the officer in command there, and so missed his chance of forcing the boom. Disappointment, or the malarial fever of the marshy Tiber-mouth, laid him on a bed of sickness next day, and, before he was recovered, Rome had fallen. Some of the famished garrison threw open the Asinarian Gate at midnight, and admitted the Goths, after the siege had lasted thirteen months (545-546). The blame of the fall of the city rested mainly on the governor Bessas, who doled out his stores with a sparing hand to soldiery and people alike, while he was secretly selling the corn at exorbitant prices to the richer citizens. The troops were starving, yet vast quantities of provisions were found concealed in the general's praetorium.

Baduila gave up the plunder of the city to his long-tried troops, but sternly prohibited murder, rape, or violence. By the confession of his enemies themselves only twenty-six Romans lost their lives, though 20,000 war-worn troops had poured into the city at midnight, wild for plunder and revenge. The king made the churches into sanctuaries, and the multitudes that gathered in them suffered no harm.

Baduila looked upon Rome as the chief lair of his enemies, the home of a faithless people, and the snare of the Goths. He resolved neither to make it his capital nor to garrison it, but to make a desert of it. The people were driven out, the gates burnt, and great breaches were made all round the walls of Aurelian. Then he harangued his army, bidding them remember how, in the days of Witiges, 7000 Imperialists had robbed of power and wealth and liberty 100,000 rich and well-armed Goths. But now that the Goths were become poor, and few, and war-worn, they had discomfited more than 20,000 Greeks. The reason was that in the old days they had angered God by their pride and evil living; now they were humbled and chastened in spirit, and therefore they were victorious. For the future they must remember that if just they would have God with them; but, if they fell back into their former ways, the hand of Heaven would work their downfall.

This done, he drew off with his army, leaving Rome desolate, and without a living soul within its walls. For forty days the imperial city was given up to the wolf and the owl, but at last Belisarius, who still lay at Portus with his small army, marched within the walls, hurriedly barricaded the breaches and the gateless portals, and prepared to hold Rome for a third siege. The Goths had been too slack in casting down the walls, and the hasty repairs of Belisarius made the city once more tenable against any coup-de-main. In great disgust Baduila rushed back from Campania, and tried to force the barricades. After three assaults he recognised that they were too strong, and retired to central Italy, leaving, however, a strong corps of observation at Tivoli, to keep Belisarius from issuing out of the city for further operations.

For two years more Belisarius and Baduila fought up and down the peninsula, but the Goth kept the superiority; though sometimes foiled, he had, on the whole, the advantage. Belisarius, like Hannibal during the later years of his sojourn in Italy, flitted from point to point with his small army, looking for opportunities to strike a blow, but seldom finding them. Justinian, though now freed from the Persian War, sent no adequate supplies or reinforcements, and seemed content that his general should hold no more than Rome and Ravenna. In 548 Belisarius was recalled on his own or his wife's request. He felt that he could do no more with his inadequate resources, he had outlived the desire of glory, and his old age was at hand. Justinian received him with kindness, made him magister militum and chief of the Imperial Guard, and bade him live in peace in Constantinople.

The sole check on Baduila was now removed, and, in the four years that followed, the gallant Goth cleared the whole country, save Ravenna, of the presence of the imperialist soldiery. He retook Rome in 549, and captured or slew the whole garrison. This time, instead of dismantling the city, he determined to make it his capital. He reorganised the Senate, bade the palace be repaired, and celebrated games in the circus as his great predecessor, Theodoric, had done. It would seem that he now felt himself so strong that he feared no return of the imperialist armies, and lost his old dread of walled towns. He sent embassies to Justinian, bidding the emperor recognise accomplished facts, and return to the old relations that had subsisted between the Goths and the emperor in the happy days of Anastasius and Theodoric. But the stern ruler of the East was immovable. He quietly persisted in the war, and merely began to collect once more an army for the invasion of Italy. The first expedition he placed under count Germanus, his own nephew, who was looked upon as the destined heir to the empire. But a sudden invasion of Macedonia by the Slavs drew aside Germanus to Thessalonica. He achieved a success over the invaders, but died soon after, and his army never crossed the Adriatic. Baduila meanwhile was in full possession of Italy. When he found that the armament of Germanus had dispersed, he built a fleet, conquered Sardinia, and then crossed into Sicily, and ravaged that island, against whose people the Goths bore an especial grudge for their rebellion and eager reception of Belisarius fifteen years before.

It was not till 552 that Baduila was forced to fight on the defensive once more, and protect Italy from the last of the armies of Justinian. This time the emperor had chosen a strange commander-in-chief, the eunuch Narses, his chamberlain, or praepositus sacri cubiculi, who had once before been seen in Italy, in 538, when he had intrigued against Belisarius. Narses was known as clever, pushing, and persistent, but his choice as a general-in-chief was one of those strange appointments of Justinian's which looked like freaks of folly, but turned out to have been guided by the deepest knowledge of character. Being better trusted than Belisarius, he was better equipped for war. Besides a large detachment of the regular troops of the East, he was allowed to hire no less than 10,000 German auxiliaries from the Danube — Herules, Lombards, and Gepidae. His whole force must have been more than 20,000 strong, thrice the size of the army that had followed Belisarius. Narses had resolved to turn the head of the Adriatic and advance through Venetia, but, while he was executing this long march, he sent a fleet to threaten the east coast of Italy. Off Ancona his armada met and defeated the Gothic ships, which Baduila had brought round to watch the Adriatic. This engagement seems to have induced the Goths to expect a Roman landing in Picenum, and only a small portion of Baduila's army was sent into Venetia, under count Tela, to watch the passes of the Carnic Alps. Narses succeeded in eluding this force by hugging the sea-coast, and using his ships to ferry him over the Po-mouth. He reached Ravenna without striking a blow, and there was joined by such Roman troops as were already in Italy.

Then, neglecting all the Gothic fortresses, he marched straight on Rome: not by the Flaminian Way, the great road between north and south — for that was held by the Goths — but by following a minor pass up the valley of the river Sena. He had just crossed the Apennines when Baduila met him at Taginae, in Umbria, under the very shadow of the mountains. The Gothic king had called up all his forces from central Italy, and was joined by Teia and the northern army on the eve of the fight, but he was still inferior in numbers to the Imperialists. Narses showed himself an able general. Knowing that the Goths mainly trusted to the wild rush of their heavy cavalry, he dismounted all his barbarian auxiliaries, and formed them in a serried mass in his centre; 8000 Roman archers flanked them, and 1500 chosen Roman cavalry were held in reserve on his left wing. Baduila bade his men use the lance alone, and himself led the horsemen of his comitatus in a gallant charge on the enemy's centre. From noon till dusk the Gothic knights dashed again and again at the phalanx in the middle of the Roman line: they could not break it, and meanwhile they were shot down in hundreds by the archers on the wings. The battle, in fact, was much like the English fight at Cressy; at both the archery and dismounted horsemen beat back the unsupported cavalry of the assailant. At last, towards dusk, the wrecks of the Gothic cavalry reeled back in disorder upon their infantry, and Narses bade the 1500 cuirassiers of his reserve to strike at the hostile flank.

All was over with the Goths. Their line broke and fled, their gallant king was mortally wounded in the pursuit, and darkness alone saved the army from annihilation. So perished Baduila, last Ostrogothic king of Italy, and 'first of the Knights of the Middle Ages,' as he has been not inaptly styled. There was still, however, fighting to be done. The warriors who had escaped from Taginae proclaimed count Teia king, and though most of the Italian towns accepted the death of Baduila as ending the war, a few still held out. Rome, manned by an inadequate garrison, was stormed with ease, and its keys sent, now for the third time, to Justinian. King Teia, after ranging up and down the land in a vain attempt to keep up the war, was brought to bay in Campania. His little army, penned up in the hills above Sorrento, made a sudden dash to catch the eunuch-general unprepared. But Narses was ready for them, and on the banks of the Sarno the last of the Goths were Overwhelmed with numbers, and saw their king slain in the forefront of the battle. Then the poor remnants of the rulers of Italy sent to offer submission. They would leave the peninsula, with bag and baggage, wife and child, and betake themselves beyond the Alps, if only a free passage were granted to them. So, in the autumn of 553, the few remaining Gothic garrisons laid down their arms, gathered together, and disappeared over the passes of the Alps into the northern darkness. We have no tidings of the fate of these last survivors of the great Ostrogothic race. Whether they became the vassals of the Frank, or mingled with the Bavarians, or sought their kinsmen, the Visigoths of Spain, no man can tell.

So perished the Gothic kingdom, which had been erected by the genius of Theodoric, by the same fate which had smitten the pirate-realm of the Vandals seventeen years before. Both fell because the ruling race was too small to hold down the vast territory that it had overrun, unless it could combine frankly and freely with the conquered Roman population. But the fatal bar of Arianism lay m each case between masters and servants, and when the orthodox armies of Constantinople appeared, nothing could restrain the Africans and Italians from opening their gates to the invader. The Ostrogoths had been wise and tolerant, the Vandals cruel and persecuting, but the end was the same in each kingdom. It was only in the measure of the resistance that the difference between Goth and Vandal appeared. Sunk in coarse luxury, and enervated by the African sun, the Vandals fell in one year before a single army. The Ostrogoths, the noblest of the Teutons, made a splendid fight for seventeen years, beat off the great Belisarius himself, and only succumbed because the incessant fighting had drained off the whole manhood of the tribe. If Baduila could have mustered at Taginae the 100,000 men that Witiges had once led against Rome, he would never have been beaten. It is one of the saddest scenes in history when we see the well-ordered realm of Theodoric vanish away, and Italy is left an unpeopled desert, to be disputed between the savage Lombard, the faithless Frank, and the exarchs of distant Byzantium.

The conquest of Italy by Narses was destined to have one further episode ere it was yet complete. When Teia's fate was known, the ministers of the young Frankish king Theudebald of Metz launched a great army into the peninsula, under two Suabian dukes Chlothar and Buccelin. Their hosts pressed down the peninsula, following the one the western coast, the other the eastern. But Chlothar's army was destroyed by famine and pestilence, and Buccelin's was annihilated at Casilinum, in Campania, by Narses, Against the mass of Frankish foot-soldiers, with spear and battle-axe, Narses employed the same tactics as against the Gothic horse. A solid centre of dismounted Teutons, Lombards, and Heruli, kept the Frankish column in check, while wings of Roman archers and cuirassiers swung round the flanks of the invader, enveloped him, and destroyed him. Of 40,000 of Buccelin's men it is said that not a hundred escaped, so far worse did they fare than the Goths had fared at Taginae in the previous year. The

Frankish ravages put the last finishing touch to the misery of Italy. Alike in the northern plain, in Picenum and Aemilia, and in the neighbourhood of Rome, the whole population had disappeared. Justinian and Narses had restored peace, but it was the best example ever seen of the adage, solitudinem faciunt pacem appellant.

To these same years belongs the story of Justinian's invasion of southern Spain, an episode which will be found narrated at full length in the chapter dealing with the Visigoths.

We must now turn back to Justinian's fortunes in the East. It will be remembered that his Second Persian War had been ended by a five years' truce in 545, after the great plague and gallant defence of Edessa. The five years of peace that followed were not very notable in the history of the empire save for one important event. Theodora, the colleague and other self of Justinian, died of cancer in 548, and with her death much of her husband's vigour, if not of his persistence, seems to have vanished. Deprived of his councillor and helpmate the emperor became gloomy and morbid. His midnight studies took the direction of theology alone, and he launched out into a futile ecclesiastical controversy on 'The Three Chapters.' This was a wholly unnecessary dispute as to whether three documents of three patristic writers, Theodore, Ibas, and Theodoret — all long dead — contained heretical matter or not. But it succeeded in convulsing the whole Eastern Church, and led Justinian into a quarrel with the Roman see, which refused to condemn the 'Three Chapters.' He seized Pope Vigilius, and brought him to Constantinople, to compel him to fall in with his own views. After detaining the unfortunate pontiff in the East for six years, and even dragging him from sanctuary and imprisoning him in an island, the emperor succeeded in inducing him to declare that Theodore and the two other theologians had indeed fallen into grievous heresy (A.D. 553). Justinian was triumphant, but Vigilius found that he had thereby introduced schism into Italy and Africa, where many bishops stood by the 'Three Chapters.' An African council went so far as to excommunicate Vigilius, and for a century some of the north Italian churches were out of communion with the Roman see.

But long ere Vigilius had yielded Justinian was once more at war with Persia. When the five years' truce ran out at the end of 549, the imperial troops advanced to recover the suzerainty of Colchis, the one point that had been yielded to Chosroes in the treaty of 545. But strangely enough, while the war was renewed on the Black Sea, it did not recommence on the

Mesopotamian frontier. Both parties concurred to renew the truce for everything except Colchis, and on that limited arena alone the hostilities proceeded. The struggle recalls, in this curious feature, the way in which the French and English fought in India in the eighteenth century, while in Europe they were at peace. The conditions of the war were favourable to Justinian, whose armies had free access by sea to the Colchian coast, while the Persians had to reach it by the wild passes over the Armenian and Iberian mountains. The dreary but very bloody Colchic or Lazic war went on for six years, draining alike the Persian and the imperial treasuries; but at last the Romans had the better in the struggle, secured the homage of the Lazic king, and drove the Persians far back into the interior (555). Finally, after interminable negotiations Chosroes made peace, surrendering his claim on Colchis in consideration of an indemnity of 30,000 solidi (£18,000) per annum.

This was the last of Justinian's great wars; but the end of his reign was far from being peaceful or prosperous. It was especially noteworthy for the repeated inroads of the Huns and Slavs into the Balkan peninsula. The greatest raid was in 558, when the Cotrigur Huns under their khan Zabergan eluded the garrisons on the Danube, crossed the Balkans, and rode at large over the whole of Thrace. One body of 4000 horse pushed their incursions up to the very gates of Constantinople, and so alarmed Justinian that he bade the aged Belisarius to buckle on his arms once more, and save the capital. The military resources of the empire were so scattered that Belisarius could only count on 300 of his own veterans, on the 'Scholarian Guards' and a levy of half-armed Thracian rustics. By skilfully posting this small force, and inducing the Huns to attack his line exactly where it was strongest, he routed the barbarians, and returned in triumph from this his last campaign.

After this final feat of the old general it is sad to learn that his master had not even yet learned to trust him. Four years later there was a futile conspiracy against Justinian, and Belisarius was accused of having known of it. He was disgraced, and put under ward for eight months, before the emperor convinced himself that the charge was false. Restored at last to favour, he lived two years more in possession of his riches and honours, and died in March 565. His thankless master followed him to the grave before the end of the same year. On the 11th of December 565, Justinian, after living more than seventy years, and reigning for thirty-eight, descended to the tomb.

We have spoken of Justinian's wars, of his buildings, of his financial policy, of his ecclesiastical controversies. But for none of these is he so well remembered as for his activity in yet another sphere. It is by his great work of codifying the Roman law, and leaving it in a complete and Legal reforms orderly form as a heritage to the jurists of the of Justinian, modern world that he earned his greatest title to immortality. This was an achievement of the first half of his reign, carried out with the aid of the best lawyers of Constantinople, headed by Tribonian, the able but greedy quaestor against whom the rioters in the 'Nika' sedition had raged so furiously.

Roman law had hitherto consisted of two elements — the constitutions and edicts of the emperors, and the decisions of the great lawyers of the past. Both these elements were somewhat chaotic. Five centuries of imperial edicts overruled and contradicted each other in the most hopeless confusion; Pagan and Christian ideas were intermixed in them, many had gone completely out of date, and new conditions of society had made others impossible to work. Nor were the responsa prudentum or decisions of the ancient jurisconsults any less chaotic; in modern England the difficulties of 'case made law,' as it has been happily called, are perplexing enough to enable us to understand the troubles of a Constantinopolitan judge, confronted with a dozen precedents of contradictory import.

Justinian removed all this confusion by producing three great works. His Code collected the imperial constitutions into a manageable shape, striking out all the obsolete edicts, and bringing the rest up to the requirements of a Christian state of the sixth century. His Digest or Pandects did the same for the decisions of the ancient lawyers, laying down the balance of authority, and specifying the precedents which were to be accepted. Lastly, the Institutes gave a general sketch of Roman law in the form of a commentary on its principles for the use of students. These volumes were destined to be the foundation of all systematic jurisprudence in modern Europe; their compilation was the last, and not the least, of the works of the ancient Roman spirit of law and order, incarnate in the last great emperor of Roman speech, for none of Justinian's successors could say, as could he himself, that Latin was his native tongue. After-ages remembered him, above all things, as the compiler of the Code, and it was as its framer that he is set by Dante in one of the starry thrones of the Christian paradise.

In spite of all his great achievements it cannot be disputed that Justinian left the empire weaker than he found it. Its territorial expansion in Italy,

Africa, and Spain did not compensate for the exhaustion of the Eastern provinces. By his ruthless taxation Justinian had drained off their vital energies, and left them poorer and weaker than they had ever been before. Even his armies felt the reaction; at the end of his reign we read that they were sinking both in numbers and efficiency; the new and extended frontiers were more than they could guard, and the old race of generals who had followed Belisarius was dead. Justinian himself is said to have neglected their pay and maintenance, while he set his aged brains to wrestle with the problem of the 'Three Chapters' or the heresy of Aphthartodocetism. Like Louis XIV. of France, whom he resembles in many other respects, Justinian closed a reign of unparalleled magnificence as a gloomy pietist, whose despotism drained and crushed a people who had grown to abhor his very name.

CHAPTER VII: THE EARLIER FRANKISH KINGS AND THEIR ORGANISATION OF GAUL — 511-561.

The Sons of Chlodovech — Theuderich conquers Thuringia, 531 — Childebeit and Chlothar conquer Burgundy, 532 — Their war with the Visigoths — Theudebert invades Italy — Chlothar reunites the Frankish kingdoms, 558 — Organisation of the Frankish realm — The great officials — Mayors of the Palace — Counts and Dukes — Local government, the Mallus — Legal and financial arrangement.

Chlodovech left four sons: one, Theuderich, borne to him by a Frankish wife in early youth; three, Chlodomer, Childebert, and Chlothar, the offspring of his Burgundian spouse, Chrotechildis. In accordance with the old Teutonic custom of heritage-partition, the four young men divided among themselves their father's newly-won realms, though the division threatened to wreck the Frankish power in its earliest youth. Theuderich, the eldest son, took the most compact and most Teutonic of the parts of Chlodovech's realm, the old kingdom of the Ripuarian Franks along the Rhine bank from Koln as far south as Basle, with the new Frankish settlements east of the Rhine in the valley of the Main, He fixed his residence, however, not at Koln, the old Ripuarian capital, but in the more southerly town of Metz on the Moselle, an ancient Roman city, though one less hitherto famous than its greater neighbour Trier. In addition to Ripuaria Theuderich took a half share of the newly-conquered Aquitaine, its eastern half from Clermont and Limoges to Albi.

While Ripuaria was given to Theuderich, his brother Chlothar obtained the other old Frankish realm, the ancient territory of the Salian Franks from the Scheldt-mouth to the Somme, together with his father's first conquests from the Gallo-Romans in the valley of the Aisne. His capital was Soissons, the old stronghold of Syagrius, in the extreme southern angle of his realm. The remaining two brothers, Chlodomer and Childebert, reigned respectively at Orleans and Paris, and ruled the lands on the Seine, Loire, and Garonne which Chlodovech had won from Syagrius and Alaric. Their kingdoms must have been far less strong, because far less thickly settled by the Franks, than those of Theuderich and Chlothar. Chlodomer's dominion comprised the whole valley of the middle and lower Loire, and Western Aquitaine, including Bordeaux and Toulouse. Childebert had a smaller share — the Seine valley and the coasts of the Channel from the mouth of the Somme westward.

The four brother kings were all worthy sons of their wicked father — daring unscrupulous men of war, destitute of natural affection, cruel, lustful, and treacherous. But they were eminently suited to extend, by the same means that Chlodovech had used, the realms that he had left them. The times, too, were propitious, for during their lives was removed the single bar that hindered the progress of the Franks, the power of the strong Gothic realm that obeyed Theodoric the Great.

Although the sons of Chlodovech not unfrequently plotted each other's deposition or murder, yet they generally turned their arms against external enemies, and even on occasion joined to aid each other. The object which each set before himself was the subjection of the nearest independent state. Theuderich therefore looked towards inner Germany and the kingdom of the Thuringians, on the Saal and upper Weser; Childebert and Chlodomer turned their attention towards their southern neighbours the Burgundians.

Both these states were destined to fall before the sons of Chlodovech, but neither of them without a hardly fought struggle. Theuderich was distracted from his first attempts against Thuringia by a great piratical invasion of the Lower Rhineland by predatory bands from Scandinavia, led by the Danish king Hygelac (Chrocholaicus), who is mainly remembered as the brother of that Beowulf whom the earliest Anglo-Saxon epic celebrates (515). The son of the king of the Ripuarians slew the pirate, and next year the Thuringian war began. It did not terminate till 531, when Theuderich, calling in the aid of his brother Chlothar, utterly destroyed the Thuringian realm, and made it tributary to himself. The Frank celebrated his victory first by an unsuccessful attempt to murder his brother and helper Chlothar, who was fain to fly home in haste, and next by the treacherous murder of Hermanfrid, the vanquished Thuringian king, who had surrendered on promise of life. Theuderich led him in conversation around the walls of the city of Zulpich, and suddenly bade his servants push him over the rampart, so that his neck was broken. Southern Thuringia, the region on the Werra and Unstrut, was for the future a tributary province of the Franks. Northern Thuringia, between Elbe and Werra, was overrun by the Saxons, and never came under Theuderich's power.

While the king of Ripuaria was warring in Germany, his younger brothers had assaulted Burgundy. In 523 Childebert and Chlodomer attacked the unpopular king Sigismund, the slayer of his own son, as we have elsewhere related. They beat him in battle, took him prisoner, and threw him with his wife and son down a well. But Gondomar, brother of Sigismund, restored the fortune of war in the next year, and routed the Franks at Veseronce, in a battle where Chlodomer was slain (524). Before pursuing the Burgundian war the brothers of the dead man resolved to plunder his realm. The king of Orleans had only left infant children, so Childebert and Chlothar found no difficulty in overrunning his lands on the Loire. The three young boys, to whom the realm should have fallen, were captured and brought before their uncles. Childebert, the ruffian who was of a milder mood, proposed to spare their lives, but Chlothar actually dragged them away while they clung to his brother's knees, and cut the throats of the two eldest with his own hands. The youngest was snatched up arid hidden by a faithful servant, and lived to become a monk, and leave his name to the ;monastery of Chlodovald' (St. Cloud).

Of Chlodomer's realm Childebert took the lands on the upper Loire and the capital city Orleans, Chlothar the Loire-mouth and the part of Aquitaine south of it. Hearing a false report that his eldest brother, Theuderich had fallen in battle with the Thuringians, Childebert now invaded East Aquitaine, a part of his brother's heritage. But Theuderich returned in wrath, and the king of Paris and Orleans resolved to go instead against the Visigoths, and to drive them from the land between the Cevennes and the Pyrenees. The great Theodoric was just dead, so no help from Italy could be expected by the Visigothic king Amalric, the grandson of the departed hero. Childebert found his pretext in the complaint that his sister Chrotechildis, the wife of Amalric, had been debarred from the exercise of the Catholic religion and cruelly ill treated by her Arian husband. With this holy plea as his casus belli he marched against Narbonne, defeated Amalric in battle, and drove him over the Pyrenees to the gates of Barcelona. There he was slain, either by the sword of the pursuing Franks, or by the Visigothic army, enraged at the cowardice which he had displayed in the struggle. On his death the Goths raised on the shield and saluted as king the aged count Theudis, the regent who had ruled Spain for Theodoric the Great during the minority of Amalric. Thus ended the race of the Baitings as rulers of the Visigoths; their succeeding kings were not of the old royal house. Theudis, who was suspected of having had some hand in his late pupil's murder, soon justified the choice of the Goths, by recovering Narbonne and the other cities of Septimania from the Franks. Childebert had turned off to another quest, and the old Visigothic possessions north of the Pyrenees were retaken without much trouble (531).

The enterprise which had called away Childebert was a new attempt to conquer Burgundy, in which his brother Chlothar had promised to join him. In the spring of 532 the kings of Paris and Soissons united their forces, and marched up the valley of the Yonne. They laid siege to Autun, and when Gondomar the Burgundian monarch came to its relief, beat him with such decisive results that he fled into Italy and abandoned his kingdom. A few sieges put the victorious Frankish brethren in possession of the whole Burgundian realm as far as the borders of the Ostrogoths on the Alps and the Drome.

When Burgundy had been conquered, the Franks began to prepare for a new campaign against the Visigoths, in which Theuderich intended to share no less than his brothers. But this scheme was frustrated by the death of the king of Ripuaria early in the year 533. He left a son, Theudebert, already a grown man and a good warrior, but in true Merovingian fashion the uncles of the heir made a vigorous attempt to seize and divide his realm. It was only the prompt and enthusiastic way in which the Ripuarians rallied around their young king that saved him from the fate of his cousins, the princes of Orleans. Not merely, however, did Theudebert hold his own, but he compelled his uncles to give him a share of the newly-conquered Burgundy, when the partition of that country was finally made.

Theudebert was, in fact, well able to take care of himself, and soon showed that he was as unscrupulous and enterprising, if not quite so bloodthirsty, as his father and uncles. Yet he was, for a Meroving, not an unfavourable specimen of a monarch, and the chroniclers tell us that he ruled his kingdom with justice, venerated the clergy, built churches, and gave much alms to the poor. That as a politician he was shifty and treacherous was soon to be shown by his dealings with Italy. In 535 the emperor Justinian, on the eve of his invasion of the Ostrogothic kingdom, bribed the three Frankish monarchs, by a gift of 50,000 solidi, to attack Italy from the rear. Uncles and nephew alike were ready to take the money and join in the plunder of the peninsula. But in the next year the Gothic king Witiges, eager to free himself from a second war, offered to cede Provence and Rhaetia to the Franks if they would make peace with him, and grant him the aid of their arms. The three kings gladly agreed, and lent him an auxiliary force of 10,000 men, who joined the Goths in recovering Milan. Theudebert and Childebert are said to have cheated Chlothar of his third of the gains, the former having got the money and the latter the land which Witiges made over.

In 539 Witiges and Belisarius were locked in such deadly conflict that the Franks thought it a good opportunity to endeavour to invade Italy on their own behalf. Theudebert came over the Alps in person, with an army of 100,000 men, all footmen armed with lance and axe, save 300 nobles who rode around the king with shield and spear. First falling on his friends the Goths, then attacking the East-Romans in turn, Theudebert drove across the north of Italy, sacking Genoa, and wasting all the valley of the Po as far as Venetia. All the open country was in his hands, and the Goths and Romans had to shut themselves up in their fortresses. But a disease brought on by foul living fell upon the Franks, and so thinned their ranks that Theudebert had to retire homeward, relinquishing all he had gained save the possession of the passes of the Cottian Alps. It was, however, with his Italian plunder that he struck the first gold money which any barbarian king coined in his own name. Instead of placing the head of the emperor on his solidi, as had hitherto been the practice of Goth, Frank, and Burgundian, he represented his own image with shield and buckler, and the inscription Domimis Noster Theudebertus Victor, without any reference to Justinian as emperor or overlord. Some of the pieces make him assume the more startling title of Doniinus Theudebertus Augustus, as if he had aimed at uniting Gaul and Italy, and taking the style of Western Emperor; and, strange as this design may appear, it receives some countenance from a chronicler who declares that, after his Italian conquests, Theudebert was so uplifted in spirit that he designed to march against Constantinople, and make himself lord of the world (539).

When in the next year the faithless Theudebert planned another expedition to reconquer north Italy, and had the effrontery to offer his alliance once more to king Witiges, we need not marvel that the Ostrogoth refused to listen for a moment to the overture, and chose rather to open negotiation with his East-Roman foes. The surrender of Ravenna and the triumph of Belisarius followed, and Theudebert found that, in invading the peninsula, he would have the emperor as his foe rather than the king of the Goths. He refrained for the time from following up his first successes, but it is strange to find that when the Gothic cause had again triumphed in the hands of king Baduila, and north Italy was once more torn asunder between Roman and Teuton, the Frank did not take advantage of the renewed troubles to make a second expedition. It is probable that in these years, 541-45, he was occupied in another conquest, that of the land between the Danube and the Noric Alps, which now bore the name of Bavaria. The German tribes in the ancient Noricum, who had been subject to Theodoric in the great days of the Gothic Empire, the remnant of the Rugians, Scyrri, Turcilingi, and Herules, had lately formed themselves into a federation under the name of Bavarians, and had chosen a duke Garibald as their prince. We have no details of Theudebert's wars against them, but merely know that by the end of his reign he had made the Bavarians tributary to the Franks. Their conquest in all probability fills the unrecorded time between Theudebert's expedition to Italy and his death in 548. For some years at the end of this period we know that he was sick and bedridden, so that it is fair to put the subjection of Bavaria somewhere about 543, five years before the death-date of the Ripuarian king. Theudebert left his kingdom to his young son, Theudebald, a weak and sickly boy, whose accession, knowing the character of his great-uncles, we are surprised to hear was not troubled by any opposition.

While Theudebert had been busied in Italy, the other two Frankish kings, Childebert and Chlothar, though now they were both advanced in years, had made a second expedition against the Visigoths, and in 542 overran the Gothic province north of the Pyrenees, and then crossed into the valley of the Ebro. They took Pampeluna, and advanced as far as Saragossa, to which they laid siege, but in front of that city they received a crushing defeat from Theudigisel, the general of the old Gothic king, Theudis, and were driven back into Gaul without retaining one foot of their conquests. Narbonne and the Mediterranean shore still remained an appendage of the kingdom of Spain.

A similar fate to that which attended the armies of his great-uncles in Spain was destined to befall the first expedition which Theudebald of Ripuaria despatched to Italy. The boy-king was too young to head the army, but the Eastern Frankish magnates who governed in his name had resolved to renew the enterprise of king Theudebert. Two dukes of Alamannian race, Buccelin and Chlothar, who seemed to have possessed the chief influence at the court of Metz, set out in 551, while King Baduila was engaged in his last desperate struggle with the East-Romans, and overran part of Venetia. Holding to the alliance of neither Roman nor

Goth, they threatened to attack both; but Narses, when he marched into Italy from Illyria, left them alone, and proceeded to assault king Baduila, without paying attention to the northern invaders. It was only in the next year, when Baduila and his successor Teia had both been slain, that the armies of the Franks broke up from their encampments in northern Italy, and marched down to challenge the supremacy of the victorious Narses in the desolated peninsula. How they fared we have had to relate in the preceding chapter. Chlothar and his division perished of want, or plague, in Apulia. Buccelin and the main body were defeated and exterminated by Narses at the battle of Casilinum. By the end of 553 all the gains of the Franks in Italy were gone, and 75,000 Frankish corpses had been buried in Italian soil or left to the Italian vultures.

Less than two years after the armies of his generals had been exterminated by Narses the weakly Theudebald died, and, as he left no brother or uncle, the East-Frankish realm was heirless. It fell by the choice of the Ripuarian folk-moot to Theudebald's great-uncle, the aged Chlothar, king of Soissons, who thus became possessed of three-fourths of the Frankish Empire. As his brother, the still older Childebert, king of Paris, was childless, it was now certain that after fifty years of division the empire of Chlodovech was about to be once more reunited (555).

Though verging on his seventieth year, Chlothar was still energetic enough to go forth to war. When the dominions of Theudebald passed into his hands, he took up the scheme which his brother Theuderich, now twenty years dead, had once entertained, of subduing all the nations of inner Germany. Beyond the vassal Thuringians lay the independent Saxons, and against them Chlothar led out, in 555, the full force of both the Ripuarian and the Salian Franks. The Saxons, on the other hand, induced many of the Thuringians to rise in rebellion, and endeavour to shake off the Frankish yoke. The fortune of war was at first favourable to Chlothar, who put down the Thuringian insurrection without much difficulty, but when, in the next year, he led his host into the unexplored woods and moors of Saxony, he suffered such a terrible defeat that he was fain to flee behind the Rhine, and cover himself by the walls of Koln. The pursuing Saxons devastated the Trans-Rhenane possessions of the Franks up to the gates of Deutz. They were not destined to become the vassals of their western neighbours for another two hundred years.

The news of Chlothar's disaster in Germany, and the false report of his death, which rumour added to the news, brought on trouble in Gaul.

Chramn, the eldest son of Chlothar, and Childebert of Paris, his aged brother, at once took arms to divide his kingdom. Nor when the news came that he still lived did they desist from their attempt. They sent to stir up the Saxons, and persisted in the war. But, before they had actually crossed swords with Chlothar, the old king of Paris died, and Chramn, reduced to his own resources, was fain to throw himself on his father's mercy (558).

Thus Chlothar, by Childebert's death, gathered in the last independent fragment of his father's vast heritage, and reigned for three years (558-561) over the realm of Chlodovech, swelled by the conquests of Burgundy, Thuringia, Provence, and Bavaria, made since the division of the Frankish Empire.

Chlothar was the worst of his house. It will be remembered how his career had begun by the brutal murder of his nephews. It was destined to end by an even greater atrocity. His undutiful son, Chramn, though pardoned in 558, rebelled again in 560, with the aid of the Bretons of Armorica. Chlothar pursued, defeated, and caught the rebellious prince. Then he bound him, with his wife and his young sons, to pillars of a wooden house, and burnt them alive by firing the building. This shocking deed roused even the brutal Franks to horror, and it was noted as the judgment of heaven that the king died exactly a year after he had given his heir to the flames. The wicked old man's body, however, was buried in great state in the church of St. Medard, as though he had been the best of sovereigns (561). His kingdom fell to his four sons, destined to a new division just fifty years after its first partition among the sons of Chlodovech.

The realm of the Merovings having now attained to its full growth, and assumed the shape which it was to keep till the fall of the dynasty, we may proceed to give the chief facts concerning its social and political organisation.

Like all the other Teutonic states which were erected on the ruins of the western provinces of the Roman Empire, it possessed a political constitution which had advanced very far beyond the simple state of things described in the Germania of Tacitus. The conquests of the Franks had resulted in the increase of the kingly power to a height which it had never reached in earlier days. As the permanent war-chief, in a time when war was incessant, the king had gradually extended his power from supreme command in the field into supreme command in all things. He and his war-band of sworn followers had borne the brunt of the fighting, and naturally reaped the greater part of the profit. The check exercised by popular assemblies on the royal power seems almost to have disappeared after the first days of the conquest. In the time of Chlodovech himself we find some traces of them still remaining. Once or twice the army, in the capacity of public assembly of the manhood of all the Franks, seems to assert itself against the king, but even this check gradually disappeared. The Frankish Empire grew too broad for any public folk-moot of the nation to be able to meet, and the king only took counsel of such magnates — high officers of the household, bishops, and provincial governors — as he chose to summon to his presence. Two additional factors gave increased strength to the monarch. The first was the high respect paid to the supreme power by the conquered Gallic provincials, men long habituated to the despotic government of Rome — a respect far greater than any that the Franks had been accustomed to give their kings. The habit of obedience of the Gallo-Roman was soon copied by the Frank. The second factor was the enriching of the king by the vast extent of the old imperial domain land in Gaul, which was transferred at the conquest to the Frankish king, and became his private property, placing a vast store both of land and money at his disposal.

The Merovings, then, were despotic rulers, little controlled by any constitutional checks, and only liable to be deposed by their subjects if their conduct became absolutely unbearable. Their worst danger was always from their ambitious relatives, not from their people.

The Frankish king was distinguished from his followers by the regal privilege of wearing long hair, — to shear a king's head was the best token of deposing him, — by his royal diadem, and kingly spear. Occasionally he borrowed trappings from the Romans, as when, for example, Chlodovech was invested with the robes of Patrician after his Gothic War. But the national dress was generally adhered to.

The government of the realm was managed by two groups of ministers — the royal household, or palatium, and the provincial governors. The household followed the person of the king in all his movements. It was mainly composed of personal companions, bound by the oath of fidelity, the comites of earlier days, who had once formed the king's war-band, but now constituted his ministers and officials. These personal adherents were called by the Franks antrustions. We have already seen that the Goths called the same class saiones, and the English gesiths.

The chief of the royal household, or palatium, was the official whom later generations usually called the Major Palatii, or 'Mayor of the Palace.' He was the king's first servant, charged with the overseeing of the rest of the household officials, and ready to act at need as the king's other self in matters of war, justice, or administration. In the days of the first warlike Frankish kings the Mayor of the Palace was kept in his place by the activity of his master, and was no more than an important official. But, as the Merovings decayed in personal vigour, their mayors grew more and more important, till at last we shall see them taking the place of regent and practical substitute for the king. The old English monarchies had no officials who can be compared in importance to them, but, under the Anglo-Normans, the position of the Justiciar was much like that occupied by the Frankish Major Palatii.

After the Mayor of the Palace, the chief ministers of the royal household were the Marshall (comes stabuli), charged with the oversight of the royal stables; the Comes Palatii, who acted as legal adviser and assessor to the king; the Treasurer; and the Referendarius, or royal secretary. Though primarily household officials, all these are occasionally found detached from the court on external business, commanding armies, or sent on embassies.

At first all the posts were given to Franks, save that of the Referendarius, to fill which it would have been hard to find an educated man of Teutonic blood. But, by the end of the sixth century, men of Gallo-Roman origin were occasionally found in occupation of them, and in the seventh century this became quite common. In 605 we find even the office of Major Falatii, the most important of them all, in the hands of the Gallo-Roman Protadius.

The provincial, as distinguished from the central, government of the Frankish realm was exercised by officers who bore the names of Count and Duke (comes, dux, Graf, Herzog), The whole realm was divided into countships. In the purely Teutonic half the unit was the old tribal district, which the Roman called Pagus and the Frank Gau. A count was appointed to each of these tribal units. In the Romano-Gallic half of the kingdom the countship was composed of the civitas, or city with its dependent district, which had survived from the times of the Western Empire, and often represented the original Celtic tribe. The count was both a military and civil official. He administered justice, led the armed levy of his district, and saw to the raising of taxes.

Several countships were often united and placed under a single official of higher rank, the dux, when the counts had to follow and obey. These unions of countships were most common on the frontier, where a strong and united defence against foreign enemies would be needed, and where it would have been unsafe to leave the charge of the border to half a dozen counts, who might or might not co-operate willingly with each other. In Provence and Burgundy the dux was also known by the Roman title of Patrician.

The provincial no less than the household officials of the Frankish kings were originally all of Teutonic birth. But, in the sixth century Gallo-Romans are found intrusted with both the lesser and the greater charges. We shall have to make mention of one of these native dukes, the Burgundian Eunius Mummolus, more than once, when recounting the history of the last years of the sixth century.

The provincial governor, count or duke, was assisted by a deputy, or vicarius, whom he nominated to fill his place during his absence at the court or the wars, or while he was engaged in some specially absorbing task at home. The minor administration of the countship was carried out by centenarii, or hundred-men, called also on occasion tribuni. The countship was divided into hundreds, and over each of these there presided a hundred-man, who was appointed by the count to act as a police magistrate in time of peace, and to head the men of his district in time of war. Petty law cases came before him, but at stated periods the count went round all the hundreds in his countship, and administered justice at a public assembly of the inhabitants.

The count's tribunal was called the Mallus. He sat in company with a few assessors, chosen from the chief men of the district. These magnates were called Rachimburgi, or Boni Homines. They were summoned by the count, and had no authority independent of his, but by ancient custom — both Roman and Teutonic — assessors had always been called in to aid the chief judge. The system is found alike at the tribunal of the Roman provincial magistrate presiding in his conventus, and in the primitive German law courts described by Tacitus. The count, sitting in his Mallus, had full power of life and death, and authority in all cases, save where the persons concerned were so great that the case might be called before the King's High Court, and tried by the king himself and the Comes Palatinus.

The Franks not unfrequently enforced the death penalty for murder, arson, brigandage, and other great crimes. But they used also the system of weregeld, like our own Anglo-Saxon forefathers. With the consent of the family of the victim, almost every murder could be condoned on the payment of sums varying from 30 gold solidi for a slave to 1800 for a freeman of high rank. In cases when the proof of a crime was difficult on the evidence produced, the Franks often made use of oaths and compurgations. The accused for himself, or a body of his supporters in his behalf, made a solemn oath that he was innocent, and this sufficed to acquit him if no further evidence was produced. Judicial combats were also not unfrequent. They appear among the Burgundians, however, before they were taken up by the Franks. Nor was the custom unknown of submitting criminals whose conviction was difficult to the ordeal: that by boiling water, where the accused plunged his hand into a caldron, was the one most frequently used.

It will be noticed that there was no trace of popular government in this Frankish administration. The king chose the count and the count the hundred-man. The king was not controlled or checked by any popular assembly of the nation, nor the count or hundred-man by any meeting of the people of his district. The king promulgated edicts and laws on his own responsibility, and similarly the count administered his countship without any thought of rendering account to any one save the king. Such assemblies as took place were summoned to hear the decisions of king or count, not to debate upon them, or recommend their modification. The ancient German freedom had disappeared, to give place to an autocracy as well defined as that of the vanished Roman empire.

Besides dukes and counts, the king kept other officials in the provinces. These were the domestici, who were charged with the control of the royal domain-land throughout the kingdom. They were the king's private bailiffs for his own possessions, acting much as the 'Procurators of the Fiscus' had once acted for the Roman emperors in the ancient provinces. There were other domestici in the palace, whose offices were also financial, and who must apparently have served as underlings to the high treasurer.

The revenue of the Merovings seems chiefly to have fallen under four heads. The first was the profits of the royal domain, worked by the domestici. The second was the produce of custom dues, levied both on the land and the sea-frontier of the empire. The third was the produce of fines and compositions in the law courts, of which one-third always went to the king. But the fourth, and most important, was the regular annual tribute of the countships. Each district was assessed in the king's books for a defined sum, and this the count had to raise and send in, on his own responsibility. It seems that at first only the Gallo-Roman districts were charged with tribute. Theudebert, the grandson of Chlodovech, we are told, first subjected the native Frankish districts to the impost, a grievance so deeply felt that, when he died, the Austrasians rose, and slew Parthenius, the minister who had suggested to the king this method of increasing his revenue.

From this short sketch of the constitution of the Frankish realm it will be seen that its organisation lay half-way between the almost purely Teutonic forms of the government of early England and the almost purely Roman methods employed by Theodoric the Great in Italy. This is what might have been expected. The Frankish kingdom was by no means a primitive Teutonic state, but it was far more so than the Ostrogothic realm in Italy.

CHAPTER VIII: THE VISIGOTHS IN SPAIN — 531-603

Weakness of the Visigothic kingdom — Civil wars and murders of Kings — The Romans invade Andalusia, 554 — Reign of Leovigild — He restores the power of the Visigoths — His conquests — Rebellion and death of his son Hermenegild — Reign of Reccared — He converts the Goths to Catholicism — Consequences of this conversion.

We have already, while dealing with the fortunes of Chlodovech the Frank and Theodoric the Great, related the story of the expulsion of the Visigoths from Aquitaine, and of the extinction of their royal house — the heaven-born Balts — by the deaths of Alaric II. and Amalric, both slain by the sword of the Franks.

In 531 the Visigoths, deprived of all their dominions north of the Pyrenees, and followed into the Iberian peninsula by the victorious Franks, found themselves without any prince of the old royal line who could be raised to the throne, and deliver them from their enemies. The host proceeded, according to Teutonic custom, to elect a king, and chose the old count Theudis, the Ostrogothic noble who had acted as regent for Amalric during the long years of his minority. The veteran justified their choice by recovering part of the lost lands beyond the Pyrenees — the rich province of Septimania, with its cities of Narbonne, Nismes, and Carcassonne. Ten years later Theudis had to face another Frankish invasion, and again succeeded in repelling his adversaries, after a bloody battle in front of Saragossa (542).

Preserved from the danger of Frankish conquest, the Visigothic nation had to face the problem of reorganising its constitution under the new conditions of its existence. It had previously looked on Gaul rather than on Spain as its home. Toulouse had been the favourite abode of its kings, not Barcelona or Toledo. Gaul was now lost, save one province, and it was in Spain alone that the Visigothic name was to survive. But even worse than the loss of its ancient home was the loss of its ancient royal house. Nothing could be more ruinous to a Teutonic tribe in those days than the extinction of the line of its old heaven-descended kings. When it had become necessary to choose a ruler from among the ranks of the nobility, every ambitious count and duke could aspire to the throne. Each election was bitterly contested, and the candidates who had failed to win the favour of the host retired to plot and intrigue against their more fortunate rival. When no one had any prescriptive hereditary right to the succession on the reigning king's death, the temptation to make away with him by violence, and endeavour to seize his heritage, was irresistible. Hence it came to pass that of the twenty-three Visigothic kings of Spain — from Theudis to Roderic — no less than nine were deposed, and of these seven were murdered by their successors. The average length of their reigns was less than eight years, and only in eight instances did a son succeed a father on the throne. There was but one single case of grandfather, father, and son following each other in undisputed succession.

In relating the history of the Franks in Gaul, we have had occasion to point out the comparative ease with which the Frank and the Roman provincial coalesced to form a new nation. We have seen how from the first the Gaulish bishops were employed as ministers and confidants by the Merovings, and how, in a short time, Gallo-Roman counts and dukes were preferred to high places in the Frankish palace and army. In Spain no such easy union between the Teutonic conquerors and the provincials was possible, because the great bar of religion lay between them. Unlike the Franks, the Visigoths were Arians, having preserved the heretical form of Christianity which their forefathers had learnt beyond the Danube in the fourth century. The Spanish provincials, on the other hand, were almost to a man fanatically orthodox. The Goths formed a religious community of their own, quite apart from the Spaniards, with Arian bishops and priests to minister to them: and their kings could not acknowledge or utilise the native bishops as the Merovings had done in Gaul. The provincials hated their rulers as heretics as well as barbarians, and never acquiesced willingly in their domination. They were not indisposed to favour the advance of the orthodox Frank, and welcomed the coming of the troops of the East-Roman emperors to their shores in the sixth century. While the Visigoths remained Arian they raised no Spaniard to power or office; it was not till they became Catholic, in the very end of the sixth century, that the first Roman names are found among the servants of the king. For the first seventy years of their rule in Spain the Visigoths were completely estranged from their subjects (511-587).

The masters of Spain, then, were a not very numerous tribe, scattered thinly among masses of an oppressed subject population. They were masters by the power of the sword alone, but their military force was crippled by the weakness of their elective kings, who were too much occupied in maintaining their precarious authority over the discontented chiefs to allow of their making their arms felt abroad. Nearly all the wars of the Visigoths were either civil broils between rival kings, or defensive campaigns against the intrusive Frank from beyond the Pyrenees.

There is yet one more point to add to this picture of the distracted realm of the Visigoths; they were not even masters of the whole of the Iberian peninsula, but had to contend with fierce and watchful enemies within its limits. In the western Pyrenees, and on the shores of the Gulf of Biscay, the Basques preserved a precarious independence, and descended from their fastnesses to plunder the valley of the Ebro, whenever the Goths were engaged in civil discords. Farther to the west there still subsisted in the ancient Galicia and Lusitania the kingdom of the Suevi — the original Teutonic conquerors of Spain. The early Visigothic kings had driven them into the mountains of the West, but had never followed them into their last retreats, to compel them to make complete submission. Suevic kings reigned at Braga over the country north of the Tagus and west of the Esla and Tormes till the last years of the sixth century. Whenever a favourable opportunity occurred, they took part in the civil wars of the Visigoths, and harried the valley of the upper Douro and the lower Tagus.

The inner organisation of the Visigothic realm presents a very different picture from the centralised despotism, with everything depending on the king, which we have described as existing among the early Franks in Gaul. Like the Franks the Visigoths had divided their conquest into districts, governed by counts or dukes, generally using as the unit of division the old Roman boundaries of provinces and civitates. But the Visigothic governors were far less under the control of their elective kings than were the Frankish counts under the hand of the despotic Merovingians. Each of them kept a bodyguard of personal dependants called — as among the Ostrogoths — saiones, or sometimes bucellarii, whom he could trust to follow him even against the king. It was the possession of this armed following among a helpless, weaponless mass of provincials which enabled any count or duke who was popular and ambitious to dare an attempt at rebellion, whenever his master was weak or unfortunate. There seems to have been a comparatively small body of lesser freeholders — ceorls as they would have been called in England — among the Visigoths. There is little trace of any intermediate class between the nobles — whether official nobles, palatini, or nobles of birth — and their sworn followers the saiones. In fact, the kingdom might fairly be called feudal in its organisation, consisting as it did of a servile population of Hispano-Roman blood, held down by a sprinkling of Gothic men-at-arms, each bound by oath to follow some great noble, who considered himself the equal of his king, and vouchsafed him only the barest homage. As yet the king had no opportunity of supporting himself by calling in to his aid either the Church or the subject Roman population; his Arianism prevented him from having recourse to any such expedient.

The difference between Roman and Goth was indeed accentuated in every way. There were different codes of law for subject and master, the former using a local adaptation of the Theodosian code known as the Breviarium Alarici, while the latter was judged by old Gothic customary law not yet reduced into written form. Even marriage between the two races was illegal, till about 570 king Leovigild broke the prohibition by taking to wife Theodosia, the daughter of Severianus. Spain sadly needed some ruler like Theodoric the Great, to act as a mediator and redresser of wrongs between the two nations who dwelt within its borders.

An evil end fell upon all the first three Visigothic kings who ruled in Spain. The aged Theudis enjoyed seventeen years of power, and, as we have already related, was successful in beating off three successive attacks of the Franks on the peninsula. But the end of his reign was clouded by disaster; frightened by the rapidity with which the armies of Justinian had crushed Vandal and Goth, he resolved to create a diversion in favour of his own Italian kinsmen, by attacking the newly-created imperial province of Africa. But his army was almost annihilated in front of the fortress of Septa (Ceuta), the westernmost bulwark of the African province, and he himself returned to Spain with his military reputation wrecked in his extreme old age. Four years later he was murdered at Seville by an unknown assassin, who either was, or feigned to be, insane (548).

The Visigothic chiefs then elected as their king, Theudigisel, the general who had beaten the Franks at Saragossa in 542, and had ever since been reckoned the best warrior of their race. But the new king was brutal and debauched; his excesses provoked the anger of the nobles, and only seventeen months after his accession he was murdered. 'While he sat at supper with his friends, and waxed merry over the wine, the lamps were extinguished, and he was slain on his couch by the sword of his enemies.'

The majority of the Visigoths then chose Agila as their ruler, but, though he was acknowledged as king at Toledo and Barcelona, the counts of the South refused to recognise him. When he invaded Andalusia he suffered a fearful defeat in front of Cordova, and saw his son and heir slain before his eyes. But he still held all Spain north of the Sierra Morena, and seemed so strong that the chief of the rebels, count Athanagild, resolved to call in to his aid the arms of the East-Romans. Justinian embraced with joy this opportunity of getting a footing in Spain, and by his orders Liberius, governor of Africa, crossed the Straits, and landed at Cadiz. Many towns at once opened their gates to the Roman troops, for the oppressed provincials thought that Liberius would deliver them for ever from the Goths, and restore the imperial authority in the whole peninsula. Roused to desperation, Agila summoned up all his forces, crossed the Sierra Morena for a second time, and engaged the armies of Athanagild and Liberius in front of Seville. Again he suffered a disastrous defeat, and was constrained to fly to Merida. Then his soldiery, seeing that the Gothic race was ruining itself by fratricidal strife, while the Romans were occupying town after town, suddenly ended the civil war by murdering their chief, and saluting the rebel Athanagild as king of the Visigoths. For, as a Frankish chronicler observed, 'the Goths have long had the evil custom of slaying with the sword any king who does not please them, and of choosing in his stead some one who better suits their inclination.' The Franks, on the other hand, boasted of their unshaken fidelity to the house of Chlodovech, outside whose limits they never looked when a king had to be chosen.

Athanagild was now king of Spain, but he soon found that by calling in the Romans he had raised up a demon whom he was not strong enough to control. The generals of Justinian utterly refused to evacuate the towns they had seized during the civil war. They were in possession of the majority of the harbours of the south coast of the peninsula, on both sides of the Strait of Gibraltar, from the promontory of St. Vincent on the Atlantic to the mouth of the Sucre on the Mediterranean. And not only were Cadiz, Malaga, and Carthagena in their hands, but also many of the inland towns of Andalusia, including the great city of Cordova. Athanagild never succeeded in evicting them from these conquests; for thirty years the Constantinopolitan Caesars were acknowledged as rulers at Cordova and Granada, and it was fully sixty years before the sea-coast towns were all won back by the Goths. Although defeated in the open field by Athanagild, the generals of Justinian clung successfully to their walled towns, till at last the Gothic king was forced to make a truce with them, and leave them unsubdued.

Although Athanagild maintained himself on the throne for thirteen years, and died a natural death — unlike his five predecessors on the Visigothic throne — he does not seem to have been a very powerful or successful monarch. The scanty annals of the century preserve few facts about him, and he is best remembered as the father of the two unhappy sisters, Brunhildis and Galswintha, 'the pearls of Spain,' whom he gave in marriage to the Frankish kings, Sigibert and Chilperich. These alliances were founded on political needs; the marriage of Brunhildis — the first wed of the two princesses — was destined to secure the aid of the king of Austrasia against any attempts of his brothers of Paris, Soissons, and Burgundy against Spain. The fame of the beauty and wealth of Brunhildis then led the wicked Chilperich of Soissons to ask and obtain her sister's hand, which Athanagild granted in order to secure another ally. Luckily for himself the old Gothic king died soon after, before he had time to hear of Galswintha's troubled wedlock and miserable end (568).

The death of Athanagild was followed by five months of anarchy; the Visigothic nobles could not agree to choose any king; each took arms, assaulted his neighbours, and did all that was right in his own eyes, for the 'king's peace' died with the king. At last the governors of Septimania agreed to elect Leova, duke of Narbonne, as their ruler; but the counts who dwelt south of the Pyrenees refused to accept the nominee of the Gallic province. After some fighting, however, Leova proposed to them to take as his colleague his brother Leovigild, who was well known and popular in the south, and the majority of the nobles of Spain agreed to accept him. Leova retained his kingly title and his own Septimanian realm, while Leovigild reigned in the peninsula as king of Spain. The division of the kingdom, however, only lasted four years, as Leova died without issue in 572, and his brother then united Septimania to Spain.

Leovigild was the first man of mark who had reigned over the Visigoths for a hundred years; he may be styled the second founder of the Visigothic kingdom, for he dragged it out of the depths of anarchy and weakness, gave it a new organisation, and smote down its enemies to east and west. Without his strong hand it seems possible that the realm would have gone to pieces, and become the prey of the Franks and the East-Romans.

For the first eight years of his reign Leovigild was forced to fight hard with enemies on all sides, before he could win a moment for repose. His first blows were struck against the Imperialists, who had gone forth from Cordova and Cadiz and conquered the whole of Andalusia. After winning several battles in the open field, and storming Baza and Assidonia, he drove the

Romans within the walls of Cordova. This great city, defended by a strong garrison and a fanatically Catholic population, kept the king at bay for a whole year; but in 571 it was betrayed to him by its Gothic inhabitants and fell, after having been more than twenty years in the hands of the Imperialists. The East-Roman power now shrank back behind the Sierra Nevada, and comprised nothing more than the coast-strip from Lagos to Carthagena.

Leovigild then turned against the Suevi, who had seized the valley of the middle Douro, and were pushing into the very heart of the peninsula. They had lately been converted to Catholicism, and were welcomed by the provincials of central Spain, who hoped to gain an orthodox instead of an Arian master. But Leovigild beat the Suevic king Theodemir in the field, stormed his fortress of Senabria, and compelled him to do homage.

For two years more Leovigild was occupied in putting down sporadic rebellions of the Roman provincials in all the more remote and mountainous corners of Spain — especially in Cantabria, on the shores of the Gulf of Biscay, and among the Murcian mountains in the South. He captured and put to death Aspidius and Abundantius, the chief leaders of these revolts, and punished their followers by wholesale executions. At last, after eight years of war, the whole of the ancient Visigothic dominions, save the towns on the Andalusian coast, were once more subdued and under control (576).

The hand of Leovigild was no less hard upon the factious nobility of his own nation than upon the foreign enemies of Spain. He sought out and executed, one after another, all the more unruly of the Visigothic chiefs — 'all the race of men who had been wont to slay their kings,' as a Frankish chronicler styled them. In their stead he appointed counts and dukes from among his own comitatus, whom he thought that he could trust. At last the king's mandate was obeyed through all the realm, from Nismes to Seville, as it had never been obeyed before, and it seemed likely that a strong autocratic royalty would prevail among the Visigoths as it did among the Franks. Leovigild now fixed his court permanently at Toledo, and assumed all the splendour and state of the ancient Roman Caesars — the diadem, the sceptre, the purple robe, and golden throne. Before him the kings of the

Visigoths had been indistinguishable in manners and apparel from their own nobles; they only differed from them by bearing the royal name, and keeping up a larger body of oath-bound saiones. At the same tim'e that he fixed his seat at Toledo, Leovigild took another opportunity of asserting his power and independence. The coinage of the Visigoths had hitherto been a mere barbarous imitation of the imperial currency of Rome and Constantinople, but from henceforth the name of the Gothic king was placed upon all the gold tremisses of Spain. For a few years Leovigild added the name of Justin II. to his own, but he soon cast away the last sign of the old dependence on the empire, and the inscription, LIVIGILDVS INCLITVS REX, was the sign of the disavowal of the last nominal connection of Spain with the heirs of Constantine.

The troubles of Leovigild, however, had not yet come to an end. His worst enemies were to be those of his own house. Before his accession to the throne he had married, contrary to Gothic custom, a noble Roman lady named Theodosia, daughter of Severianus, sometime governor of Carthagena. By her he had two sons, Hermenegild and Reccared. When she died he endeavoured to strengthen his position by marrying Godiswintha, the widow of his predecessor Athanagild; and some years later, when his son Hermenegild reached manhood, he determined to seek for him another bride from the family of Athanagild. Accordingly he asked for, and obtained the hand of his wife's granddaughter, Ingunthis, the daughter of Sigibert of Austrasia and Brunhildis. At the age of thirteen she was wedded to Hermenegild. This marriage was destined to have the most unhappy results. The daughter of Brunhildis was fated to be as much the cause of woe to Spain as her mother had been to Gaul. She had been reared in Austrasia as a Catholic, and, in spite of her tender age, refused to conform to the Arian creed of the Visigoths. If the Frankish chronicles are to be believed, she was subjected to the most violent treatment by her grandmother Godiswintha, to force her to abandon the orthodox faith. But though beaten, starved, and flung into a fish-pond, she still refused to renounce the faith of her childhood. At last Leovigild, tired of the perpetual disputes between his wife and his daughter-in-law, which made his palace unbearable, sent off Hermenegild to Seville to govern part of Andalusia.

This step proved most unfortunate. The young prince fell entirely under the influence of his wife and of his mother's brother, Leander bishop of Seville. Won over by their pleadings, he declared himself a Catholic, and was rebaptized, and received into the orthodox church. He knew that his conversion would bring on him his father's wrath, and the loss of his prospect of succeeding to the Visigothic crown. But he was unwilling to suffer degradation meekly, and promptly proclaimed himself king, allied himself with the Suevi and the East-Romans, and called the orthodox to arms all over Spain.

Leovigild had never had to face a more dangerous crisis. The rebellion of his son had called out against him all the elements of disorder in the peninsula. The Suevi swarmed down the Douro; the Imperialists reoccupied Cordova; Merida, Seville, and Evora hailed Hermenegild as king; and the discontented provincials, headed by their bishops, began to stir all over the country. It is the greatest testimonial to Leovigild's abilities that he knew how to deal with all these dangers. First, he turned against the incipient rebellion in the north, and put it down by banishing or imprisoning some dozen bishops, and by defeating in battle the Basques, who had come down from their hills to join in the struggle. After beating them, he founded on their border the town of Vittoria as a memorial of his success — a town destined to be better remembered for the great English victory of 181 3 than for this ancient triumph.

Hermenegild was nearly two years in possession of the valley of the Guadalquivir, but in 582 his father suddenly descended upon him, and drove him within the walls of Seville. The Suevi came up to raise the siege, but Leovigild routed their king Miro, and returned to resume his leaguer. After many months of blockade he stormed the town, but Hermenegild and his wife escaped to the Romans. The rebel prince took refuge in the castle of Osset, whither the king followed him, and, by the huge bribe of 30,000 solidi, induced the Imperialist Government to sell the town. Hermenegild was dragged from sanctuary, and brought before his father, who pardoned his rebellion, but stripped him of his princely insignia, and sent him to live in honourable confinement at Valencia as a private person.

Leovigild then turned against the Suevi, overran their whole country, and captured their last king, Andica, whom he interned in a monastery. Thus the rebellion of Hermenegild had not only failed to ruin the Gothic state, but had actually led to the subjection of the troublesome neighbour-kingdom in the north-west, which had hitherto escaped the Visigothic sword.

Hermenegild's fate was destined to be a sad one. His father promised to restore him to his former place if he would abandon the orthodox faith, but he steadfastly refused, and was presently cast into prison. But chains had no more effect on his constancy than prayers and promises. His father grew angry, and bade him expect the worst if he persisted in his obstinacy. On Easter Day 585, he sent an Arian bishop to administer the sacrament to the prisoner. Hermenegild drove the heretical prelate from his cell with cries and imprecations. The news was brought to his father, who, in a moment of ungovernable rage, like that which induced our own Henry II. to order the death of Becket, bade his guards seize and behead his inflexible son. So perished Hermenegild, whom after-generations, forgetting his undutiful rebellion, and remembering only his constancy in the orthodox faith, saluted as a saint. His wife and infant son were sent to Constantinople by the Roman governor of Malaga. Ingunthis died on the voyage, but the boy, Athanagild, lived and died obscurely at the court of the emperor Maurice.

Leovigild had now to face the wrath of the Franks. Guntram, the uncle, and Theudebert, the brother of Ingunthis, took arms to avenge her husband's execution. They sent a fleet to land a force in Galicia, and raise the newly-conquered Suevi, while a Burgundian army entered Septimania, and attacked Nismes and Carcassonne. But Leovigild's military skill and constant good fortune in war did not fail him. While he himself cut to pieces the army which had landed in Galicia, his son, Reccared, drove the Burgundians out of Septimania, with the loss of their general and half their army. Father and son met in triumph at Toledo, but the hardships of a winter campaign had been too much for Leovigild, who died soon after his return to his capital, on the 13th of April 586, a year to the very day from the date of his eldest son's execution, a coincidence which the orthodox did not fail to point out as marking the wrath of heaven.

Leovigild, some time before his death, had induced the Visigoths to elect his second son, Reccared, as his colleague, and to salute him as king. There was, therefore, no tumultuous election or civil war when the old king died, and his heir quietly took his place. Reccared was destined to set his mark on the history of the Visigothic kingdom no less firmly than his father had done. If Leovigild saved the state from anarchy by his strong arm, Reccared set it on a new and altered course of existence, and introduced a new element into its political and religious life by the great change which is connected with his name — the conversion of the Visigoths to the orthodox faith. Reccared was the son of a Roman mother, but, unlike his brother Hermenegild, he never showed any discontent with Arianism in his father's lifetime. No sooner, however, was the old man dead than his successor began to take steps which threw the Arians into a state of excitement and apprehension. He summoned Catholic and Arian bishops before him, and many times bade them dispute in his presence on the mysteries of the Trinity. This he did more to prepare the people for the coming change than because he was himself in any doubt as to his future conduct.

Reccared thoroughly grasped the fact that the Visigothic state would never be established on a really firm basis as long as the governing caste were separated from the bulk of their subjects by the fatal barrier of religion. The Goths were too few to amalgamate the provincials with themselves, and had shown no signs of wishing to do so. But if no such amalgamation took place, the Gothic monarchy was doomed to disappear some day in a political convulsion, when the moment should come that found no strong and capable ruler on the throne. Leovigild had only staved off such a crisis by prodigies of activity and courage. Now Reccared had made up his mind that the Arianism of the Goths was more a matter of conservative adherence to ancestral prejudices and of race-pride, than of real conviction or fanatical faith. He thought that if the king led the way, and if mild and cautious changes were made, without any sudden blow or attempt at enforced conformity, his countrymen might insensibly be led within the pale of the Catholic church. The course of events proved that he was entirely right; and the conversion of the nation was managed all the more surely because it was carried out by a cautious and unemotional statesman, and not by an enthusiastic saint.

The completion of Reccared's scheme occupied the years 586-88. When he declared himself a Catholic, and accepted the solemn blessing of his uncle, the Metropolitan of Seville, the greater part of his comitatus followed his example. In quick succession many Gothic counts, and a large portion of the Arian episcopate conformed to orthodoxy. The Church on its side made the change easy, by not insisting on any new baptism of the converts. It was enough if they attended a Catholic place of worship, and received the blessing of an orthodox priest.

It was not to be expected, however, that so momentous a change would pass over the country without provoking trouble. There were many Goths, both clergy and laymen, who viewed Arianism as the sacred religion of their ancestors, and the badge of their conquering race. Three rebellions broke out in quick succession, in regions as far apart as Septimania and Lusitania, while the king's step-mother Godiswintha and bishop Athaloc, the chief of the Arian clergy, placed themselves at the head of the rising.

But the greater part of the Visigoths looked on in apathy, and allowed a small body of fanatics to fight out the question of religion with the king. The Arians were put down, and gave no further trouble. The whole sect seems to have melted away in a few years, and ere long the Visigoths were as proud of their Catholicism as they had once been of their heterodoxy.

While Reccared was busy with the suppression of the Arian rebels, the Frankish king Guntram of Burgundy thought that a good opportunity had arisen for conquering Septimania. He sent a great army down the Rhone, but near Narbonne it was completely defeated by Reccared's general, duke Claudius, the first man of Roman blood who had ever been promoted to high rank by a Visigothic king. This was the last time that a Frankish conquest of Septimania was ever seriously attempted (589).

Reccared reigned for twelve years more, with great good fortune both at home and abroad. He subdued the Basques, kept the Imperialists penned in to their line of harbours along the south coast, and repressed several minor tumults raised by discontented Gothic nobles. In every crisis he found the Catholic bishops his best support, and must have constantly congratulated himself on having turned his most dangerous enemies into the strongest bulwark of his throne. But by placing himself in their hands he had begun to expose Gothic royalty to a new danger, that of too great dependence on the Church. The National Council — the Witan as it would have been called in England — was completely swamped by the churchmen. There were more than sixty bishops in Spain, while the number of dukes and counts who were usually summoned to the Assembly was considerably less. The bishops — men more clever, more wise, and better organised than their lay colleagues — soon came to exercise a dominating influence in the council. The spiritual pressure which they could bring to bear on the king was too great to be disregarded. Hence it came to pass that ere the end of his reign Reccared, though peaceful and tolerant himself, was urged into acts of persecution, not only against his old co-religionists, the Arians, but against the Jews — a race who had hitherto prospered in Spain, and who had gathered in a very considerable portion of its wealth and commerce. Formerly the Visigothic kings, like the great Theodoric in Italy, had been very tolerant, and had not seldom employed Jews as collectors of revenue and in minor official posts. All this came to an end with the conversion of Reccared, though in his day the discouragement alike of Arian and Jew went no further than making them incapable of holding any office, and prohibiting the public exercise of their worship.

After a reign of fifteen years, king Reccared died in 601, leaving the throne to his son, Leova II., the only instance in Gothic Spain of a succession of three generations of the same house on the throne. The new monarch was just twenty. He was a devoted admirer and follower of the Catholic bishops, and, by all accounts, showed more piety than capacity. The accession of a weak and inexperienced youth was the opportunity for which the unruly Visigothic nobles, crushed for thirty years under the strong hands of Leovigild and Reccared, had been long waiting. In the second year of his reign Leova was surprised and murdered by conspirators under the guidance of a certain count Witterich, who had headed an Arian rising in 588, but had been spared on conforming to Catholicism. He now repaid Reccared's clemency by murdering his son (603).

After thirty-three years of strong government, Spain once more fell back into the state of civil strife from which it had been rescued by Leovigild. But the character of the struggle was now changed; for the future it was a contest between the Catholic hierarchy and the Visigothic nobles, as to which should appoint and control the king.

BOOK II

CHAPTER IX: THE SUCCESSORS OF JUSTINIAN — 565-610

Justin II. and his unhappy financial policy — His troubles with the Persians and Avars — Reign of Tiberius Constantinus — Accession of Maurice — His victory over Persia — His failure against the Slavs and Avars — Disasters in the Balkan Peninsula — Fall of Maurice — Tyranny of Phocas — His unfortunate war with Persia — He is dethroned and slain by Heraclius, 610,

The forty years which followed the death of Justinian were a period of rapid decline and decay for the East-Roman world. The empire was paying, by exhaustion within and the loss of provinces without, for the spasmodic outburst of energy into which it had been galvanised by the great emperor. He left to his heirs broad and dangerous frontiers in his newly-acquired provinces, with an army which had got somewhat out of hand, and a civil population shorn to the skin by the excessive taxation of the last twenty years.

Justinian's heirs were, unhappily for the empire, princes who tried to maintain their great predecessor's ambitious policy, at a moment when the less brilliant, but more cautious and economical, rule of a second Anastasius would have been the best thing for the East-Roman world. The Emperor's nephew, Justinus, son of his sister Vigilantia, mounted the throne on his decease without meeting with any opposition. He had served his uncle as Curopalata, or Master of the Palace, for the last ten years, and had been able to make things ready for his own peaceful succession, though Justinian had never consented to allow him to be crowned as his colleague as long as he lived. Justin was married to Sophia, the niece of the empress Theodora, a lady who resembled her aunt in her masterful spirit, but was far from rivalling her abilities. Justin and his wife had led a somewhat repressed and constrained existence during the old emperor's life, and were set upon asserting their individuality the moment that Justinian was buried. Justin had high ideas of the dignity of the imperial name and the majesty of the empire, and had determined to inaugurate a spirited foreign policy when he seized the helm of affairs. His first measure was to refuse to continue any of the comparatively trifling subsidies to barbarian princes on the frontier, which Justinian had been content to pay in order to keep them from petty raids — much as the Indian Government to-day subsidises the chiefs of the Khyber Pass. This involved him in a long and ultimately dangerous war with the Chagan of the Avars, a Tartar tribe newly established on the north bank of the lower Danube, whom Justinian had paid to keep off the Huns and other troublesome neighbours. The Avars, originally a race of no great importance, obtained at this moment a great extension of power and territory by allying themselves with the Lombards, in order to destroy the Gepidae, the Gothic tribe who dwelt north of Sirmium on the middle Danube. After exterminating their Teutonic neighbours, the Lombards passed on to invade Italy, and left the Avars in possession of the whole line of the Danube, from Vienna to its mouth. Thenceforth the Avars were a scourge to the already half-desolate provinces of Moesia and Illyricum. They ranged over the whole territory up to the Balkans, in spite of the innumerable fortresses which Justinian had built and garrisoned to defend the Danube bank. This trouble was continually growing worse all through the reign of Justin II., and became an actual source of danger, as well as of mere annoyance, in the time of his successors.

Another refusal of Justin to make a payment of money, which he considered degrading to his majesty, was destined to bring on a struggle even more ruinous than that with the Avars. It will be remembered that the peace between Justinian and Chosroes of Persia, concluded in 562, had stipulated for some payments from the East-Romans to the king. In 571 Justin refused to fulfil his obligations, and plunged the empire into a wholly unnecessary war with his great Oriental neighbour. Several causes conspired to induce Justin to undertake this struggle. He was implored by the Christian population of Persian Armenia to deliver them from the fire-worshipping Sassanians, and the Turks of the Oxus had sent an embassy to promise him help from the East if he would assault Chosroes. Dizabul, their great Khan, engaged to distract the forces of the enemy by crossing the Oxus and invading northern Persia, while Justin's generals were to cross the Tigris and attack Media.

This war, which the emperor undertook with such a light heart, was destined to last no less than nineteen years (572-591), and to drag on into the reigns of two of his successors. It was quite as inconclusive, and quite as costly in men and money, as had been the previous struggle in the reign of Justinian. On the whole, the Romans lost no territory during its course. Their farthest frontier stronghold of Daras was the only place of importance that fell into Persian hands in the earlier years of the war, and the secondary fortress of Martyropolis, in the Armenian Highlands, the only loss of its later years. Both were destined to be recovered, and the second Roman line of defence, based on Edessa and Amida, held good. If the armies of Chosroes once succeeded in penetrating into Syria, it is only fair to add that the imperial troops made several incursions into the Persian border-lands of Arzanene and Corduene. It was not so much by the loss of fortresses or the ravaging of territory that the war was harmful to the empire, as by the long, fruitless drain of taxation that it brought about. Where the tax-gatherer of Justinian's time had shorn the population close, the tax-gatherer of Justin's was obliged to flay them, in order to wring out the necessary solidi. Having begun the war at his own pleasure, Justin found that he could not conclude it in a similar way. The Persians hoped to win by exhausting the empire's resources, and were set on protracting the weary game.

In the ninth year after his succession to the throne, Justin was seized with suicidal mania, and had to be placed in close restraint for all the rest of his life. On his first lucid interval he nominated as his colleague, and crowned as Caesar, a respectable military officer, named Tiberius Constantinus, who, in conjunction with the empress Sophia, acted as regent for the demented emperor till 578. Sophia, a proud and restless woman, kept most of the power in her own hands, for Tiberius was not of a pushing or ambitious disposition. His accession to power made little or no difference in the policy of the court, which was still guided by the empress.

While Justin saw the Balkan peninsula ravaged by the Avars, and the Mesopotamian frontier beset by the Persians, he was destined to suffer a still more grievous loss in another region of his empire. The Lombards, emigrating from the middle Danube, followed the track that the Ostrogoths had taken eighty years before, and threw themselves on the newly-recovered province of Italy, only fifteen years after it had been finally secured to the empire by the victories of Narses at Taginae and Casilinum. Their fortunes will be described in another chapter. Here it must suffice to say that ere the end of the reign of Justin II. they had torn two-thirds of the peninsula from the grasp of the East-Roman governors.

In 578, four years after he had fallen into a state of lunacy, Justin II. died, and his colleague, Tiberius Constantinus, became sole ruler of the empire.

Tiberius II. was a thoroughly upright and well-intentioned man, who had been chosen as heir by his predecessor solely on the ground of his merits, and in spite of the fact that Justin had a son-in-law and several cousins to whom he might have left the legacy of power. Like Titus in an earlier age, Tiberius II. was the darling and hope of the whole population of the empire, and, like Titus, he was cut off in the flower of his years after a very short reign. He had time, however, to give some earnest of his good intentions by cutting down the grinding taxation of Justin II. by a fourth, and remitting all arrears owed to the state. But he was unable to do away with the cause which made taxation so heavy, the wretched lingering Persian war, and, till the empire could obtain peace within and without, the remission of taxation only meant the inadequate performance of the duties of the state, and the rapid accumulation of public debt. Tiberius succeeded, however, in making a truce with the Avars, though to obtain it he had to give up the great border-fortress of Sirmium, the central point for the defence of the line of the Danube and Save, and also to promise to make one of those payments of money which his predecessor had regarded as degrading the majesty of the empire. Being free from war in the Balkans, Tiberius concentrated no less than 200,000 men on the Persian frontier, and his troops, under the general Maurice, won many successes, and invaded Media. But the obstinate king Hormisdas, who had now succeeded Chosroes on the throne, refused to listen to any proposals for peace, and the war dragged on.

In the fourth year of his reign Tiberius was suddenly stricken down by disease, and died while only on the threshold of middle age. Like his predecessor, he chose as his heir not any relative, but the best man that he knew. Eight days before his death he invested with the royal diadem his general Maurice, who had lately distinguished himself by a great victory in Mesopotamia, and was universally respected for his sterling merit and modesty. Maurice immediately married his benefactor's daughter, Constantina, and ascended the vacant throne in peace.

Like Tiberius Constantinus, Maurice was an eminently well-meaning ruler, and a man not destitute of ability, but the times were too hard for him, and his very virtues often conspired to lead him into unfortunate actions. His reign of twenty years (582-602), though not wanting in successes, was still a continuation of the unhappy period of decline and decay which had set in since the year of the great plague of 542. The worst of the troubles of Maurice was the complete exhaustion of the imperial finances. The liberality of Tiberius II. had drained out the last solidus from the already depleted treasury, and the new emperor started with a deficit, which remained as a perpetual nightmare to him all through his reign. Maurice was of a prudent and economical disposition; the adverse balance cut him to the heart, and he adopted all sorts of schemes — wise and unwise — to make receipts and expenditure balance. The war expenses were, of course, the main disturbing element, and Maurice went so far in his zeal for retrenchment that while hostilities were still in progress he endeavoured, on more than one occasion, to cut down the soldiers' pay, and economise the expenditure of provisions and military stores. This policy had the most disastrous results. Several times it led to mutiny, and at last it cost Maurice his throne and life.

The Persian war continued through the first nine years of Maurice's reign, as long as the reckless and obstinate king Hormisdas remained in power. On the whole it was fortunately conducted. Two able officers, named Heraclius and Philippicus, obtained the mastery over the Persians, and won several battles. They would have done even more if Maurice's policy of 'economy at any price' had not led to mutinies among the soldiery, who struck work, and retired behind the border when they heard that their pay was to be reduced. It is hard to conceive how Maurice could be so unwise; for he had considerable military experience, and wrote an excellent book on tactics. The Strategicon, which served for three hundred years as the manual of all Byzantine officers. Apparently the economist prevailed over the soldier in his composition.

Luckily the mutiny of 588 did not ruin the empire; the troops returned to duty when their grievance was removed, and won more victories over the Persians. Hormisdas grew unpopular with his subjects, and was deposed and slain by a usurper named Varahnes. His young son, Chosroes, fled to the Roman camp, and threw himself on the mercy of his hereditary foe. This led to the end of the war; Maurice lent the young prince supplies and auxiliaries to start a rebellion against Varahnes. The rising succeeded, and the grateful Chosroes made peace with the empire the moment that he was restored to his father's throne (591). The terms, like those of the peaces of 532 and 562, amounted to little more than the restoration of the state of things which had preceded hostilities. Maurice recovered the lost fortresses of Daras and Martyropolis, and gained the Christian districts of Persarmenia, a new acquisition to the empire, but not one of much importance.

But the troubles of Maurice, military and financial alike, did not cease with the end of the Persian war. The faithless Avars, disregarding the terms of peace which they had sworn to Tiberius II. in 581, were once more ravaging the Balkan peninsula. In the second year of Maurice's reign they burst over the Danube, and seized the fortresses of Singidunum and Viminacium, whose garrisons had been reduced by the needs of the Persian war. Unable to raise a new army, Maurice sent them a subsidy which kept them quiet for two years, but in 585 the Tartar horde took arms once more, and threw themselves upon Thrace. Nor was it only with the wild Avars that Maurice had to deal. We now hear of the Slavs as becoming for the first time a serious danger to the empire. Their tribes had for some time dwelt in obscurity along the lower Danube and in the South-Russian plains, having flooded in to occupy the void space left by the migration of the Goths in the fourth century. At the accession of Maurice some of them were subject to the Avars, others were still independent, but all showed a tendency to move southward over the Danube. The Slavs were individually not very dangerous enemies to the empire; they were in the very lowest stage of civilisation, hardly yet accustomed to till the soil, and living the precarious life of fishers and hunters. They did not fight in the open field, but lurked in forests and morasses, issuing forth to plunder by night, and only attacking their foes when they could take them by surprise. It is said that they practised the curious stratagem of lying hid in shallow pools, showing nothing above the surface of the water save the point of a hollow reed, through which they breathed. The story sounds improbable, but Byzantine authors quote several occasions on which it was actually used.

Many Slav tribes, seeking refuge from the domination of the Avars, crossed the Danube in their light canoes, and established themselves in the wooded slopes of the Balkans, or the marshes of the Dobrudscha, where they found the cover that they loved. The Moesian provincials had been so thinned by two hundred years of raiding suffered at the hands of Goth, Hun, and Avar, that the Slavs found the land almost wholly uninhabited. Outside the great Danube fortresses, and the large towns like Naissus or Sardica, the population had almost entirely disappeared. Avoiding battles with the garrisons of the towns, the Slavs slipped between them, and spread over the face of the deserted land, pitching their rude huts in the most secluded spots that they could find. They were not only intruders, but enemies, for they were keenly set on plunder, waylaid every party of travellers that strove to pass from town to town, and laid ambuscades for every body of soldiers that was not too numerous for them to cope with.

From 585 to the very end of his reign Maurice was engaged in a desperate struggle against Slav and Avar, which raged over the whole of the Balkan peninsula. The invaders gradually pressed southwards, though they suffered many defeats, and though whole tribes of Slavs were sometimes exterminated. The enemy, though individually contemptible, seemed to draw on endless reserves of strength, as horde after horde slipped across the Danube, and threw itself into the glens of the Balkans. The effect of these invasions is well described by a contemporary chronicler, John of Ephesus: 'The first years of Maurice were famous for the invasion of the accursed people called Slavonians, who overran Greece and all the lands about Thessalonica and Thrace, plundering many towns, and devastating and burning, and reducing the people to slavery. They have made themselves masters of the whole country, and settled in it by main force, and dwell in it as though it were their own. Four years have now passed, and still they live at their ease in the land, and spread themselves abroad, as far as God permits them, and ravage and burn and take captive, and still they encamp and dwell there.'

Ever since the Persian war ended, the reign of Maurice had been one unbroken series of misfortunes; the only remedy that the emperor could find for the evil times was an economy that verged on avarice. This foible at last caused his ruin. In 599 the Chagan of the Avars demanded of him ransom-money for 12,000 Roman prisoners who had fallen into his hands; the emperor refused to pay it, though he had the required sum of solidi ready at hand. The Chagan thereupon massacred the whole body of prisoners. The Roman world raised a cry of horror, and threw the blame upon the avarice of Maurice, not the savagery of the Avars. Henceforth his throne was unsafe; but the crowning blow to his power was given by another piece of unwise economy. After a successful campaign against the Slavs in 601, the army of the Balkans had pursued them across the Danube. Maurice sent orders that the victorious troops should winter in the open field, upon the bleak townless plains of Wallachia, in order to save supplies.

Instead of obeying, the soldiery drove away their generals, placed a Thracian centurion named Phocas at their head, and marched on Constantinople, loudly proclaiming that they were coming to depose the emperor. So unpopular had Maurice made himself with the army, that he found that he could not trust even his household troops, and in despair armed the Blue and Green factions, and set them to guard the city walls. But the factions were a broken reed when disciplined troops had to be faced, and Maurice soon found himself deserted by every one. He fled to Chalcedon, hoping to raise aid in the Asiatic provinces, where he was less unpopular than in Europe. Meanwhile, the army entered the capital, and proclaimed Phocas as emperor, though he was but a rough uncultured boor, who had headed the mutineers simply in virtue of having louder lungs and a heavier hand than his comrades. The usurper sent officers to seize his unfortunate predecessor, and caused him to be beheaded, along with his four sons, the youngest of whom was a mere infant in arms. Maurice met his death with a courage and dignity that moved the hearts of those who had so lately reviled him. 'Just art Thou, O Lord God, and just are Thy judgments,' he exclaimed as the executioner raised his sword, and died with a prayer on his lips.

From the foundation of Constantinople down to the death of Maurice the Eastern crown had never before been the prize of successful rebellion, nor had any legitimate emperor fallen by the hands of his subjects. Revolts there had been, but they had never gained permanent success. It was an evil day for the empire when the army found that they could make an emperor, and the orderly succession of elective Caesars, chosen by their predecessors or by the Senate, came to an end.

The new ruler of Constantinople proved to be a brutal ruffian, beside whose vices the faults of Maurice seemed shining virtues. Ignorant, cruel, licentious, and thriftless, he made his lusts his masters, and soon became the detestation of all his subjects. Phocas showed ability in one thing only, he was most successful in tracking out and frustrating the numerous conspiracies which were ere long framed against his life. All whom he rightly or wrongly suspected were visited with cruel deaths; among others he slew his predecessor's widow, Constantina, and her three little daughters, because he found that their names were often used as a rallying cry by plotters. On mere suspicion he seized and burnt alive Narses, the general of the East, the most distinguished officer in the army. Other objects of his dread were flogged to death, strangled, or cruelly mutilated.

Meanwhile, the reign of terror at home was accompanied by disaster without. The decaying military and financial strength of the empire suddenly collapsed into utter ruin under the rule of the vicious boor who had replaced the economic Maurice. The Slavs and Avars wrought their wicked will unhindered on the European provinces, and pushed their ravages up to the wall of Anastasius. In the East matters fared even worse. The young and able king of Persia made the murder of his benefactor Maurice a casus belli, and took arms to avenge his 'friend and father.' From the first opening of the war the Romans fared badly; never had such an unbroken series of disasters met their arms. Early in the struggle Phocas had provoked the Eastern army by recalling and burning alive their commander Narses. They fought feebly, were ill-supplied by the incapable tyrant, and badly led by his creatures who were placed at their head. In 606 there came a sudden collapse; the great frontier fortress of Daras fell, and from that moment the Persians pushed on without meeting a check. They overran all Mesopotamia, ravaged northern Syria, and pushed their incursions into Asia Minor, where no enemy had been seen for a century. The armies of Phocas seem to have dispersed, or shut themselves up within city walls, for we hear of no resistance to the invader. In 608 matters grew worse still; from their base in Mesopotamia and north Syria the Persians struck out boldly towards Constantinople. Overrunning Cappadocia, Galatia, and Bithynia their raiding bands crossed the whole peninsula, and even penetrated to Chalcedon and eyed the imperial city across the Bosphorus. Phocas, instead of hastening to organise new troops, contented himself with ordering a persecution of the Jews, whom he accused of having betrayed to the Persians some of the towns of Syria.

In 609 the enemy once more overran Asia Minor, capturing among other places the great city of Caesarea in Cappadocia. Again they met with little or no opposition; the emperor's attention was entirely taken up with real or imaginary plots in the capital. It seemed that he would allow the empire to be torn from him piecemeal, without striking a blow.

But relief was at last about to come to the suffering people of New Rome. In Africa there ruled as exarch Heraclius, the veteran officer whose victories had closed the old Persian wars of the time of Maurice. He was capable and much beloved both by the provincials and by his army; under his able rule Africa, alone among the provinces of the empire, enjoyed peace and prosperity. In 609 Heraclius received emissaries from Priscus, the commander of the imperial guard, one of the innumerable persons who had fallen under the suspicion of Phocas. The messengers bade Heraclius strike boldly at Constantinople, for Phocas was universally detested, and no one would raise an arm in his defence. At the same moment the exarch learnt that his tyrannical master had already conceived doubts of his loyalty, and had thrown his wife and daughter into prison.

Seeing that he must strike hard or be crushed, Heraclius determined to rebel. He spent the winter of 609-10 in fitting out a fleet, and launched it against Constantinople before Phocas had learnt of his revolt. The command was given to his eldest son, who also bore the name of Heraclius, for the exarch himself was old and ailing. At the same time, to make a diversion, he sent a body of cavalry under his nephew, Nicetas, to invade Egypt by land; they were to follow the line of the long coast-road through Tripoli and Cyrene.

When the fleet of the younger Heraclius reached the Dardanelles it met with no resistance; on the news of its arrival, Priscus brought the imperial guard to join the rebels, and the emperor found himself deserted by all his soldiery. He strove, like his predecessor Maurice, to arm the factions of the Blues and Greens; but no one would strike a blow in behalf of such a worthless tyrant. Heraclius sailed unopposed to the Bosphorus, and as he arrived off the palace he met a boat containing the wretched Phocas, whom a private enemy had seized and cast into chains. The prisoner was brought on deck and cast at the feet of his conqueror. 'Is it thus,' cried Heraclius, 'that you have governed the empire?' 'Will you,' the fallen tyrant replied, 'govern it any better?' Heraclius spurned him with his foot, and promptly consigned him to the headsman.

Thus perished the first, but by no means the last, military usurper who sat on the Constantinopolitan throne, overthrown, as he had been elevated, by an armed rebellion. All the world with singular unanimity testified to the worthlessness of Phocas, save one single adherent; but this was no less a person than Pope Gregory the Great. Much to his discredit the great pontiff had been a supporter, nay, even a flatterer, of the Thracian boor who wore the eastern diadem with such ill grace. But Gregory had been an enemy of the unfortunate Maurice, because that prince — though orthodox in matters of doctrine — had shown scant respect to the See of Rome. He had called some of Gregory's epistles 'fatuous,' and had allowed John 'the Faster,' patriarch of Constantinople, to assume the title of 'oecumenical bishop,' a style which filled Gregory with horror, and caused him to exclaim that the times of Antichrist were at hand. Gregory therefore looked on Maurice's murderer as the avenger of the outraged dignity of the See of Rome, and did not shrink from heaping upon him epithets of unseemly adulation; the choirs of angels, he said, sang with joy in heaven at the accession of such a worthy Caesar! Truly this was a painful episode in the life of a man who, in spite of all his faults, has been justly hailed as a saint.

CHAPTER X: DECLINE AND DECAY OF THE MEROVINGIANS — 561-656.

The sons of Chlothar divide the Frankish realm — Wars of Sigibert and Chilperich — The fortunes of Brunhildis — Continued wars of Neustria and Austrasia — Tyranny of Chilperich and Fredegundis — Decay of the Royal Power among the Franks — The House of St. Arnulf and Pippin — Brunhildis regent in Austrasia — Wars of her grandsons — Pier death — Chlothar II. sole king — His weakness — His successor Dagobert I. last free king of the Merovingian line — Rise of the Mayors of the Palace.

After the first eighty years of its existence, the Frankish kingdom, which under three generations of warlike monarchs had continued to extend its borders so fast and so far, ceased suddenly to grow, and was given up for a century and a half to ruinous civil wars, as objectless as they were tedious and confused. In surrendering their primitive Teutonic freedom to their royal house, in return for the glory and aggrandisement which union under a single despotic hand gave to their hitherto weak and scattered tribes, the Franks had bartered away their future. As long as the house of Chlodovech were able and active, their subjects could console themselves for submitting to an autocrat by sharing in the power and plunder which a century of successful war brought in to them. But when the Merovings, though still retaining their despotic authority, grew weak and incapable, showing no trace of their ancestor's qualities, save an inveterate tendency to treachery and fratricide, an evil time came upon the Frankish race. They paid for their early aggrandisement by being condemned to five generations of useless civil wars at home, and powerlessness abroad, while their hereditary monarchs sacrificed everything to their unending family feuds. Nothing more could be hoped for the Franks till they had rid themselves of the nightmare-incubus of this wicked house, whose repulsive annals are, on the whole, the most hopeless and depressing page in the history of Europe. From generation to generation their story reeks with blood; there is nothing that can be compared to it for horror in the records of any nation on this side of the Mediterranean. We have to search the histories of the courts of Mohammedan Asia to discover a parallel. The

Franks only found salvation in the growth of checks on the royal power by the development of the great provincial governors, and by the final deposition of the Merovings in favour of the great house of the descendants of St. Arnulf, the Mayors of the Palace, whose strong hand at last stayed the fratricidal wars of the seventh century. And even when the new dynasty had mounted the throne, the Frankish realm showed fatal signs of the demoralisation it had suffered under the old royal house. The tendency of the race to acquiesce in the unwise habit of heritage-partition, and the unhappy grudge between the eastern and the western Franks, were direct legacies of the Merovings.

We left the whole Frankish realm concentrated in the hands of the aged Chlothar, last surviving son of Chlodovech. When, however, this hoary ruffian, fresh from the murder of his eldest son, sank into his grave, in the year 561, his four surviving children parted the kingdom once more among themselves, not without a preliminary fight, in which Chilperich, the youngest of the four, having laid hands on his father's treasures, and raised an army with their aid, tried to put down his kinsmen, but failed. When he had been defeated and brought to submission, the realm was made into four shares. Charibert, the eldest son, took Paris and Aquitaine; Guntram the Burgundian kingdom; Sigibert the Ripuarian land on the Rhine, and the tributary Thuringian and Bavarian lands beyond it; lastly, the restless Chilperich was given his father's original share, the old Salian land between Meuse and Somme, with certain districts farther south added to it, so that it extended nearly as far as the gates of Rouen and Rheims.

Of these four brothers, Charibert died young, in 567. He is only remembered because his daughter Bertha married Ethelbert, the king of Kent, and was, twenty years later, the protector of the mission of St. Augustine. Charibert's lands on the Seine and Loire were parted among his three brothers, Guntram and Chilperich each taking the part that lay nearest to his own frontier, while their distant Ripuarian brother, Sigibert, had Tours, Poictiers, and Bordeaux, separated from his other dominions by the whole breadth of Burgundy.

The tale of the wars and tumults which the three surviving sons of Chlothar I. raised against each other is a long recital of objectless strife and treachery. The uneasiest spirit of the three was the wicked Chilperich, 'the Nero and Herod of his time,' as Gregory of Tours very rightly styles him. The usual fraternal hatred of the Merovings was embittered between him and Sigibert by an additional grievance. While Sigibert was away beyond the Rhine striving with the wild Avars, who had pushed their incursions along the Danube into Bavaria and Suabia, his brother, the king of Soissons, invaded Ripuaria, and tried to seize it for himself. Sigibert returned in haste, and succeeded in driving Chilperich back beyond the Meuse, and preserving his eastern border.

This would have been cause enough for revenge, but a worse was to follow. Chilperich and Sigibert had married two sisters, the daughters of the Visigothic king, Athanagild. Galswintha was the spouse of Chilperich, Brunhildis of Sigibert. They were princesses famed all over the Western world for their beauty and abilities no less than for the enormous dowries which their father had bestowed upon them. Before his marriage Chilperich had kept a perfect harem of concubines, though on the arrival of Galswintha he had for the moment banished them. But Fredegundis, the chief among his former favourites, retained such an empire over him that after a few months he openly brought her back to the palace, and insulted the queen by her presence. When Galswintha indignantly declared that she should return to her father, the wicked king had her murdered, and publicly married Fredegundis within a few days (567).

Brunhildis, the sister of the murdered queen, and the spouse of Chilperich's elder brother the king of Ripuaria, devoted the rest of her life to the task of avenging Galswintha's death on the king of Soissons and his paramour. She was a strong-willed, fearless, able woman, and her influence over her husband was unbounded. For forty years the houses of Sigibert and Chilperich and their unhappy subjects were destined to shed their blood on the battle-field that the slaughter of Galswintha might be atoned for.

It is in these wars that the final partition of the Frankish realm into its two permanent divisions took shape, and that new names for these divisions came into use. The Ripuarian realm of king Sigibert, from the borders of Bavaria and Thuringia as far as the Meuse and Scheldt, is for the future known as Austrasia — the Eastern kingdom; Chilperich's less purely Teutonic realm, from the Meuse and Scheldt as far as the Loire, gets the name of Neustria, the New kingdom, or the New West kingdom, as others interpret it.

The beginning of the wars of Neustria and Austrasia follows immediately on the death of Galswintha. As the avenger of blood, king Sigibert entered his brother's kingdom, and drove him westward. But the hostilities were suspended by a great Lombard invasion of Gaul. The new conquerors of

Italy had passed the Alps, and thrown themselves upon the Frankish realm. Guntram of Burgundy, whose kingdom bore the brunt of the assault, prevailed upon his brothers to cease their struggles and unite to cast out the Lombards from Provence and the Rhone valley. By his decision Chilperich gave up as weregeld for his wife's murder, her dowry and five Aquitanian cities, which had been bestowed upon her at the marriage. These were made over to Brunhildis, who took them, but nevertheless bided her time for a fuller revenge (568).

Four years of Lombard wars kept the Frankish kings engaged on their southern borders, and they were at last successful in forcing the invaders beyond the Alps, in a series of campaigns in which the chief glory was gained by the Romano-Gallic duke, Eunius Mummolus, who led the armies of Guntram of Burgundy. But in 573 the civil war between Sigibert and Chilperich burst forth again. It spread at once over the whole of the Frankish realm; for Chilperich attacked his brother's dominions in Aquitaine, while Sigibert pressed on beyond Meuse and Scheldt. There followed two years of fierce fighting, attended by the most barbarous wasting of the land. Chilperich's sons burnt every open town between Tours and Limoges; Sigibert's troops from beyond the Rhine devastated the valley of the Meuse. The Austrasians had the better in the struggle, and Chilperich sued for peace, offering large territorial concessions. But it was his life and not his lands that Brunhildis wanted. Her husband was induced to decline his brother's proposals, and pushed his victorious arms into the heart of Neustria, after a battle in which Chilperich's son and heir, Theudebert, was slain. The king of the West abandoned his capital, and fled north to hide himself and his wife behind the walls of Tournay. Most of the Neustrian counts came to do homage to Sigibert at Paris, and when he had chased his brother behind the Scheldt, the Austrasian had himself lifted on the shield, according to old Frankish custom, and saluted as King of all the Franks at Vitry, near Arras. He sent for his wife and children to Paris to share in his triumph, and determined to end the war by the siege of Tournay. But, when all Gaul seemed at his command, two murderers, hired by queen Fredegundis, came before him with a pretended message, and stabbed him while he listened to their words (575).

The death of Sigibert changed the whole aspect of affairs in Gaul, and raised his assassin from the depth of despair to the height of fortune. The Austrasian army dispersed when its commander was slain, and the Neustrian counts flocked to Tournay to do homage again to Chilperich.

Queen Brunhildis, who lay at Paris with Sigibert's infant son and heir Childebert, was seized and imprisoned by the partisans of the Neustrian king. Her little four-year-old son only escaped from his uncle's clutches by being let down in a basket from his mother's prison window, and received by a faithful adherent, who rode away with him to Metz. If Chilperich had laid hands on the boy, the Austrasian royal house would have been ended in the promptest way.

The East-Frankish counts and dukes, when the news of Sigibert's death reached them, resolved not to submit to his murderer, but to take a step unheard of heretofore in the annals of the Merovings. When they found that the boy Childebert had escaped, they bound his father's diadem about his brows, and saluted him as king. Hitherto the Franks had always lived under the strong hands of a grown man, and the provincial governors had been as powerless as the meaner people under the autocratic sway of the ruler; but in the long minority that would follow the accession of a four-year-old child, they found their opportunity for lowering the royal power, and dividing many of its privileges among themselves. From this point begins the degradation of the kingly office, which was to be the rule henceforth among them; and the counts and dukes, as well as the great officers of the palace, were destined to acquire, in the early years of Childebert, a control over the central power which they had never hitherto possessed.

Meanwhile the fate of the little king's mother, Brunhildis, had been a strange one. Chilperich had seized her treasures, and thrown her into prison at Rouen. There she caught the eye of Merovech, her captor's eldest surviving son, who was charged by his father with the command of an army destined to attack the Austrasian king's dominions beyond the Loire. Merovech was so infatuated by the beauty of the captive queen that, braving his father's displeasure, he delivered her from her dungeon, and induced Praetextatus, bishop of Rouen, to marry them in his cathedral. King Chilperich immediately flew to Rouen in great wrath, and at his approach the newly-married pair took sanctuary under the bishop's protection. After some hesitation the king of Neustria promised to spare their lives, but, when his son surrendered himself, he took him away to Soissons, and shortly afterwards tonsured him, and compelled him to become a monk. Brunhildis escaped to Austrasia, whither her husband strove to follow her. He fled from his monastery, and had almost reached the frontier, when the emissaries of his stepmother, Fredegundis, caught him, and murdered him (577).

In Austrasia there now commenced a struggle between the liberated queen-mother and the great officers of state, for the guardianship of the little six-year-old king. The struggle was an obstinate one; for if the Frankish nobles were hampered by the autocratic traditions of the kingship, Brunhildis, on the other hand, was a foreigner, and met with little support save among the Gallo-Roman clergy and officials, who found some protection, under the shield of the king, from the arrogance and violence of their Frankish fellow-subjects. In Neustria or Aquitaine, where the Roman elements were stronger, Brunhildis might have done more, but her lot was cast in Austrasia, where the Germans were entirely preponderant.

To protect the young Childebert against the attacks of Chilperich, his mother allied herself with the boy's uncle, Guntram, king of Burgundy. Guntram, who had no children of his own, designated Childebert heir to all his dominions, and took up his cause with vigour. But he was not a very warlike prince, and it was as much as he could do to protect his own realm against the active and ruthless king of Neustria. Though Burgundy and Austrasia were allied, Chilperich succeeded in conquering their united armies, under the Burgundian general, Mummolus, and seizing Tours, Poictiers, and all the north of Aquitaine. He would probably have carried his arms further if internal troubles had not arisen to check him. The Bretons of Armorica burst into rebellion, and had to be put down, and other risings were excited by his ruthless and excessive taxation. But his worst vexations were those of his own household, caused by the strife of his elder sons with their Stepmother, Fredegundis. All through these years the wicked queen had been fearfully active. Theudebert and Merovech, the eldest of her husband's family, were dead, but their brother, Chlodovech, still stood between Fredegundis' children and the throne. In 580 the plague swept all over Gaul,, and two sons of Fredegundis' were carried off by it. She accused their step-brother of having caused their death by witchcraft, and got her husband to permit her to execute him. But when her last child died, two years later, the wretched woman's rage and grief led her into the wildest outbursts of cruelty. She accused numbers of persons about the court of magic arts practised against her boy, and burnt them alive, or broke them on the wheel. Many other acts of murder and treachery are attributed to her, notably the death of Praetextatus, bishop of Rouen, whom she detested for the part he had taken in the marriage of Merovech and

Brunhildis, and her crimes fill many a page in the gloomy annals of Gregory of Tours. A legend tells how two holy bishops once stood before the gate of the palace at Soissons. 'What seest thou over this house?' said one. 'I see nothing but the red standard which Chilperich the king has ordered to be set up on its topmost gable.' 'But I see,' said the first, 'the sword of God raised above that wicked house to destroy it altogether.'

Meanwhile, Chilperich's wars with his brother of Burgundy and his nephew of Austrasia continued to fill central Gaul with blood and ashes. They ceased for a moment when the Austrasian nobles, against the will of Brunhildis, forced their little king to make peace and alliance with his father's murderer. But no one could long trust Chilperich, and after less than a year the old league between Austrasia and Burgundy was renewed.

In 584 Chilperich, to the great joy of all Gaul, was murdered by an unknown hand: — 'As he was returning from the hunt to his royal manor of Chelles, a certain man struck him with a knife beneath the shoulder, and pierced his belly with a second stroke, whereupon he fell down and breathed out his foul soul,' says the chronicler. He was perhaps the worst of the wicked Merovings — cruel, unjust, gluttonous, and drunken, vain, boastful, and irreligious, the worthy son of the ruffian Chlothar, and grandson of the murderer Chlodovech. But his untiring energy and reckless courage bore him safely through many an evil day, and he died leaving the kingdom he had inherited in 561 increased to three times its original bulk.

Queen Fredegundis had borne one more son, named Chlothar, to her husband just four months before his murder, so that Neustria was not left altogether without an heir. But Fredegundis feared that Guntram and his nephew would now seize the whole realm, and slay her with her infant. She took sanctuary at Paris; but when the king of Burgundy arrived he showed his superiority to the morals of his family by sparing the life of the wicked queen, and recognising her son as king of Neustria. Brunhildis sought in vain to induce Guntram to give over to her the murderess of her husband; he refused, and Fredegundis took advantage of his kindness to hire assassins to make attempts on the lives both of Brunhildis and her son the young king of Austrasia. Luckily the project failed in both cases.

The civil wars of the Franks now ceased for a moment. Guntram, a mild and not unamiable character, controlled both his nephews, the fifteen-year-old Childebert of Austrasia, and the one-year-old Chlothar II.; and for nine years the three kingdoms had a certain measure of peace, broken only by wars with the Lombards and Visigoths. Guntram seems to have hoped that the fratricidal wars of his family might be staved off for a space by turning the energy of the Franks against their southern neighbours, and engaged himself in a war with Reccared, king of Spain, while the Austrasian nobles were induced by the gifts of the emperor Maurice to assist the Byzantines in their struggle against the Lombards. Both wars were long and fruitless. In the West, the repeated attacks of the Burgundian armies on Septimania were all beaten back. In the East, the Austrasians twice crossed the Alps, and wasted the valley of the Po, but in 588 they received such a defeat at the hands of king Authari that they made peace with him and withdrew across the Alps. In 590 Childebert, who had now attained his twentieth year, and was governing for himself, renewed the struggle; but his army was thinned by famine and pestilence before the walls of Verona, and he was finally fain to renew the peace with Agilulf, the successor of Authari.

Unfortunate foreign wars, however, were better than strife in the heart of Gaul, and the last years of Guntram were fairly free from this pest. He was only troubled by one rebellion: a conspiracy between his illegitimate brother, Gundovald, and two great Romano-Gallic dukes, Mummolus and Desiderius, who were apparently wishing to become king-makers, and rule under the name of an obscure and incapable pretender. But the day of the complete triumph of the great State officials over the kingship had not yet come, and though he was for a moment master of all Aquitaine, Gundovald was easily put down, and executed in company with his chief supporter Mummolus (585).

Guntram died in 593, and his nephew Childebert received his dominions in Burgundy and Aquitaine, thus becoming ruler of four-fifths of the whole Frankish kingdom in his twenty-third year. Under his nominal sway Austrasia had been the theatre of a long struggle between his mother Brunhildis and the great counts and dukes, whose plots and riots were secretly abetted by Fredegundis. From her home in Neustria the ruthless widow of Chilperich did her best to set her nephew's kingdom in disorder, and promised lands and titles to the Austrasian chiefs if they would murder Brunhildis and Childebert, and proclaim her own son, Chlothar, king of Austrasia. But the stern and able Brunhildis unravelled and crushed all these conspiracies, and had the triumph of seeing her son attain his majority, and assume the rule in his own name.

The moment that the pacific Guntram was dead, Brunhildis and her son, freed from all restraint, set out to punish the intrigues of Fredegundis, and by invading Neustria to make an end of her and her boy Chlothar. But the fortune of war declared in favour of the Western Franks. At Droisy, near Soissons, the army of Childebert was defeated with the loss of no less than 30,000 men, and Neustria was saved from conquest. The war continued without definite result, for Childebert was prevented from using his full strength by a rebellion beyond the Rhine, among the Warni in Suabia. Probably his superior force must in the end have carried the day, but the entire aspect of affairs was suddenly changed by his unexpected death in 596, at the early age of twenty-six. He left two infant sons, Theudebert and Theuderich, to the care of their grandmother, who found herself, though she was now verging on old age, once more called upon to assume the regency.

The death of Childebert was to the kingly authority a fatal blow, from which it never recovered. His own long minority had raised the counts and dukes to a pitch of power which they had never gained before, and all the efforts of Brunhildis had not succeeded in fully holding them down. The equally long minority of his sons was the last blow to the kingship. Their grandmother struggled with all her might to retain the power for the kingly race, and to curb her unruly subjects. But though she worked with untiring energy and zeal, and kept the reins of government in her own grasp for some time, the treacherous nobles, bent on their own aggrandisement at the expense of the royal authority, were at last too much for her.

Of the two sons of Childebert II. Theudebert, the elder, became king of Austrasia, Theuderich, the younger, king of Burgundy, the legacy of his uncle Guntram. It was an uneasy inheritance to which they succceded, for Fredegundis saw her opportunity, and urged the Neustrians forward against her great-nephews. At Lafaux near Laon the Austrasians suffered a great defeat, and all the lands as far as the Meuse fell into the hands of the queen of Neustria. But in the moment of triumph, her son's throne being now firmly established, and her rival's power on the decline, the wicked Fredegundis died at Rouen. Her countless murders and cruelties met no chastisement on earth, and the son for whom she had risked so much was destined to carry out to a successful end the schemes in pursuit of which she had so long striven, and to unite all the Frankish realms under his sceptre (597).

The death of Fredegundis brought no relief to Brunhildis. For two years more she struggled on against the intrigues of the Austrasian nobility; duke Wintrio, who led the opposition against her, was seized and executed in 598. But in 599 a final rising took her by surprise, and she was forced to fly alone and unaccompanied from Metz to save her life. She escaped to Burgundy, where she took refuge with her younger grandson Theuderich, and was there received with all honour. Two successive Mayors of the Palace, Protadius and Claudius, both of Romano-Gallic blood, lent themselves to her schemes, and the royal power in Burgundy was still upheld by her strong hand.

The curse of fratricidal wars was never to depart from the house of the Merovings. When Theudebert II. and Theuderich II. grew up and reached early manhood, they united for a moment to attack their cousin Chlothar, and to recover from him the lands between the Meuse, the Seine, and the Loire, with Paris, Rouen, and Tours. But soon after they fell to strife, and it would seem that the old Brunhildis was greatly to blame for its outbreak. She was burning to revenge herself on the Austrasian nobles for the banishment she had endured at their hands, and stirred up the Burgundians to war. She and the Mayor Protadius were far more eager than the counts and dukes of Burgundy to begin the strife, and when the two armies came in sight of each other, the soldiers of Theuderich lowered their weapons, slew Protadius when he strove to force them on, and compelled their young king to make peace with his brother. But the curse that rested on the Merovings was not so easily to be exorcised; Brunhildis and Theuderich were determined to have their way, and ere very long the war was renewed. The Austrasians were beaten at Toul, their lands wasted, and the victorious Theuderich forced his way as far as Zulpich, in the very heart of his brother's realm. Here Theudebert withstood him for a second time, was again beaten, and fell into the hands of the Burgundians. He was led before his grandmother, who assailed him with bitter reproaches, and bade him be tonsured and become a monk. But this did not content the king of Burgundy; a few days later he had his brother dragged out of his monastery and put to death (612).

The revenge of heaven seemed to be called down by the wicked deed of the young king of Burgundy. Only five months after his brother's murder he was smitten down by an attack of dysentery, and died at Metz in the very prime of his early manhood (613).

Now for the third time the unhappy Brunhildis was left alone, with a helpless child as her only stay. Once more she steeled her heart and faced the situation; she led her great-grandson Sigibert, the eldest son of Theuderich, before the assembly of the East Franks, and bade them do homage to him as king of Austrasia and Burgundy. For a moment they bent before her, and Sigibert II. was acknowledged as ruler of the East Franks. But the Austrasians were determined to have no more of Brunhildis' rule; they sent secretly to Chlothar, king of Neustria, and bade him arm and invade his cousin's realm, for no hand should be raised against him. When the Neustrian king marched into Austrasia, Warnachar, the mayor of the palace, and most of the nobles of the land took arms and joined him. Brunhildis with her great-grandson fled to Burgundy, and raised an army there, with which she faced the Neustrians near the headwaters of the Aisne. But when Chlothar's army came in sight, the Burgundian patrician Aletheus and the dukes Rocco and Sigvald led off their troops, and joined the invader. In a moment the whole of Sigibert's army had deserted or dispersed. Brunhildis and the little king fled away as far as Orbe, hard by the lake of Neuchatel, where the emissaries of Chlothar overtook and captured them. They were led before the king of Neustria, the worthy son of Fredegundis. 'Here is the woman,' he cried, 'by whose intrigues and wars ten princes of the Franks have come to their deaths,' and he bade his soldiers scourge the old queen, and then bind her by hands and feet to the heels of a wild horse, who dragged her among stones and rocks till her body was torn limb from limb. The boy Sigibert and his younger brother Corbo were strangled.

Thus perished Brunhildis, and with her the greatness of the house of the Merovings. For the future it was the counts and the mayors of the palace who were to exercise real power among the Franks, and not the kings. Chlothar, who had conquered only by the treachery of the nobles, was, with all his descendants, to be their servant, not their master. Considering that she was a woman and a foreigner, it is wonderful that Brunhildis continued for so long to sway the councils of Austrasia. Save her abilities and her force of character, she had no advantage, yet she not only dominated in succession her husband, her son, and her grandson, but held down the unruly counts and dukes, who were neither allied to her by blood nor constantly under her eye and influence. The tale of her life has sufficiently shown her qualities and defects. That she was something more than a fury stirring up war and strife from personal revenge for the blood of her sister and her husband is clear enough. She was an administrator of marked ability. Almost alone among the rulers of the Franks, she is noted as a builder and a founder. Churches, hospitals, and monasteries she erected in great numbers. The old Roman fortresses and military roads were also her care. To this day some of the high roads of Belgium still bear her name, and as the 'Chaussees de Brunehaute' preserve her memory as the first potentate who cared for them after the Franks came into the land. That she was a sincerely religious woman would seem to be vouched for by the series of her letters to Gregory the Great, which moved the good pontiff's admiration. But sincere piety was not in those days, any more than in our own, inconsistent with a headstrong impatience of opposition, and an unscrupulous readiness to sweep obstacles out of the way. There is no doubt that Brunhildis struck down the Austrasian counts by the dagger, as well as by the sword, when they intrigued against her. She never forgave her own grandson Theudebert II. for allowing her to be driven out of his realm, and was not satisfied till, ten years after his offence, she caught him, and forced him to become a monk. Her enmity pursued not only Fredegundis and Chilperich, the murderers of her sister and husband, but their young son and their subjects long years after they themselves were dead. Yet, if she was relentless and unforgiving, we must remember that few rulers in history have suffered such wrongs and faced such odds. Compared with her contemporaries, Brunhildis might almost pass for a heroine and a saint.

Chlothar II., though he became king of all the Frankish realms by the murder of Brunhildis and her great-grandchildren, acquired little real power thereby. The Austrasians and Burgundians, who had combined with him to destroy the old queen, wrung terms from him which deprived him of many undoubted regal rights. The dukes Warnachar and Ratho, who were made mayors of the palace of the two realms. Stipulated that they were to hold their offices for life, not at the king's pleasure. For the future the mayorship became an office of far greater importance than it had yet been. Another step in the weakening of the kingship is shown by the fact that the legislation of the Franks from this time forward is always noted as being done by the king, with the counsel and consent of his bishops, counts, and dukes. A code of laws which Chlothar II. put forth for the Suabians, somewhere about the year 620, is indorsed not merely with his own authority, but with that of thirty-three bishops, thirty-four dukes, and sixty-five counts. The fact that the reign of Chlothar was exceptionally fertile in legislation is probably to be accounted for by the fact that he was compelled to listen to the demands of his nobles, and grant redress to their grievances, rather than by any particular taste of his own for the enacting of laws. When, for example, we hear that he 'met the mayor Warnachar, and all the bishops, and great men of Burgundy at Bonneuil, and there assented to all their just petitions,' we must remember that he was facing an irremovable mayor of the palace, and a nation who had freely given themselves into his hands on stated terms, and had no longer over them the unlimited authority that a Chlodovech or a Theuderich had owned a hundred years before. Nothing can show more clearly the growing weakness of the king than an incident which occurred at a great national gathering of Neustrians and Burgundians, at Clichy, towards the end of his reign. In the midst of the council a brawl arose, and the followers of a duke named Aegyna, slew Ermenhar, the steward of the palace of the king's son. At once all the Neustrians seized their arms, and drew apart into two bands. While Aegyna and his friends seized the hill of Montmartre, and formed their array on its brow, the larger party, headed by Brodulf, a kinsman of the slain man, started off to storm the position. The king was only able to keep the peace by inducing the Burgundians, who were not interested in the quarrel, to follow him, and to promise to attack whichever of the two sides should strike the first blow. He dismissed the assembly, and was unable to punish any one, either for the murder or for the riot which had ensued.

Chlothar, with his diminished royal prerogative, seems to have had neither the opportunity nor the power to engage in wars of conquest beyond the bounds of his realm. He had to look on, without stirring, while a great, if ephemeral, kingdom was built up beyond his eastern frontier. Behind the Thuringians and Bavarians, on the Elbe and Oder, there had dwelt for the last two hundred years, since the German races had migrated westward, a group of small and disunited Slavonic tribes, calling themselves Wiltzes, Sorbes, Abotrites, and Czechs. Their dissensions had kept them from being dangerous neighbours till the time of Chlothar. But about 620 a Frankish adventurer, named Samo, who had gone eastward, half as trader half as buccaneer, united many of the Slavonic tribes, and became their king. He gradually extended his power all down the valley of the Elbe, on both sides of the Bohemian mountains, and was soon to prove himself a serious trouble to the realm of the Merovings.

Towards the end of his reign, Chlothar II. made his son Dagobert king of Austrasia, while he was still a very young man. The chief councillors by whose aid Dagobert administered his realm were two men whose names form a landmark in Frankish history — Arnulf, bishop of Metz, and count Pippin the elder, the ancestors of the great house of the Karlings. Bishop Arnulf was the wisest and best of the prelates of Austrasia, and, after a long life of usefulness in church and state, won the name of saint by laying down his crozier and ring and retiring to a hermitage, to spend his last fifteen years in the solitudes of the Vosges. Count Pippin, a noble from the land between Meuse and Mosel, whose ancestral abodes are said to have been the manors of Hersthal and Landen, was appointed mayor of the palace, and lived in the closest concord and amity with Arnulf. They cemented their alliance by a marriage, Begga, the daughter of Pippin, being wedded to Ansigisel, the son of the bishop; for Arnulf, like many of the Frankish clergy, lived in lawful wedlock. From these parents sprang the whole of the line of mayors, kings, and emperors whose mighty deeds were to make their comparatively unimportant ancestors famous in history.

King Chlothar II. died in 628, and his son, Dagobert I., became ruler of all the Frankish realms. He was, for a Meroving, a very creditable ruler, though he lived with three wives at once, and indulged in occasional outbursts of wrong-headedness. For the two first years of his reign he chose to share the sovereign power with his brother Charibert, whom he made king of Aquitaine out of pure fraternal affection. But when Charibert died, in 630, he resumed his southern dominions, disregarding Charibert's three sons. Dagobert was the last of the Merovings whose will was of much importance in the ordering of the Frankish realms; his successors were to be mere shadows. Even in his own time the royal power was already of little force in Austrasia, where the king leant entirely upon the support of Pippin, who, with his son-in-law, Ansigisel, held the post of mayor of the palace for the whole sixteen years of Dagobert's reign. His loyalty to the king concealed the fact that he was far more powerful in the eastern kingdom than Dagobert himself. The king had several sharp quarrels with him, but never dared to depose him from his post lest trouble should ensue. In Neustria no great mayor of the palace had yet arisen, and there Dagobert was ruler in fact as well as name. Hence it is not surprising that he always dwelt west of the Meuse, and made Paris his favourite residence.

Dagobert was the last Meroving who took arms to extend the limits of the Frankish power. He supported the pretender Sisinand in Spain, by the aid of a Burgundian army, made an alliance with the emperor Heraclius against the Lombards, and entered into a protracted war with the Slavonic tribes of the East. On the Elbe, the kingdom of Samo the Frank was now at the height of its power. Dagobert took alarm at its rapid growth, and when the Wends plundered part of Thuringia, in 630, sent against them three great armies, comprising the whole military force of Austrasia. Two of these expeditions fared well, but the third suffered complete annihilation at Wogastisburg, in Bohemia, and the victorious Slavs ravaged Thuringia and Bavaria, from Saal to Danube, with fire and sword, till Radulf, duke of Thuringia, at last checked them, in 633.

Dagobert I. died in 638, He left two sons, Sigibert III., aged nine, and Chlodovech II., aged six. It was the long minority of these two boys which finally achieved the ruin of the Merovingian house. While Sigibert and Chlodovech were growing up to manhood, the future of the Frankish realms was being settled by the sword, the all-important issue at stake being the question whether the house of Pippin and Arnulf should retain permanent possession of the Austrasian mayorship of the palace or should sink out of sight. Pippin the Old died in 639, the second year of Sigibert's reign. His son Grimoald at once proclaimed himself heir to his father's office. But a great part of the Austrasian nobles, headed by Otto, the foster-father of the young king, refused to acknowledge his right to the mayorship, and a fierce war of three years was required to settle the dispute. At last the son of Pippin conquered, and for fourteen years (642-56) was undisputed master of Austrasia. King Sigibert, indeed, grew up to man's estate, but he was completely dominated by his servant, and never made any endeavour to take the power out of his hands. Hence he is known as the first of the Rois Faineants, or do-nothing kings, who were from henceforth to be the rule among the house of the Merovings.

In Neustria, meanwhile, the royal power was saved for a time by the cleverness of queen Nanthildis, a lady of great piety, the widow of Dagobert, who acted as guardian for her younger son Chlodovech. She enlisted in her cause the Neustrian mayor of the palace, Erchinoald, who was akin to the royal house himself, and therefore not unfavourable to its dominance. Not till these two passed away was the Western realm to sink into the same state as the Eastern. But the fall of royalty here, too, was now imminent.

CHAPTER XI: THE LOMBARDS IN ITALY, AND THE RISE OF THE PAPACY — 568-653

The Wanderings of the Lombards — Alboin conquers Northern Italy — His tragic end — Anarchy among the Lombard dukes — Reign of Authari, and Prankish wars — Conquest and conversion of Agihilf — Rothari the Law-giver — State of Rome and Italy — Career of St. Gregory — He founds the temporal power of the Papacy.

In the third year of Justin II., and only fifteen years after Narses had swept the Goth and Frank out of Italy, a new horde of barbarians came pouring down on that unhappy land. The ravages of eighteen years of war, and a terrible pestilence which supervened, had left all the northern parts of the peninsula desolate, and well-nigh uninhabited, — 'the land seemed to have sunk back into primeval silence and solitude.' The imperial troops held a few strong places beyond the Po, such as Verona and Pavia, but had made no effort to restore the military frontier along the Alps, and the land lay open to the spoiler. Southern Italy had suffered less, and Ravenna was still strong and well guarded, but the Transpadane lowlands — destined ere long to change their name to the 'Lombard plain' — were as destitute of civil population as they were of military resources.

The new invaders of Italy were the Lombards (Langobardi), a Teutonic people, who, according to their ancient tribal legends, had once dwelt in Scandinavia, but had descended ten generations before into northern Germany, and from thence had slowly worked their way down to the Danube. They had only come into touch with the frontier of the empire when Odoacer smote the Rugii, in 487. After that tribe had been scattered, they moved into its abiding place on the mid-Danube, and became the neighbours of the Ostrogoths and the Gepidae.

The Lombards were the least tinctured with civilisation of all the Teutonic tribes, even more barbarous, it would seem, than our own Saxon forefathers. Living far back in the darkness of the North, they had been kept from any knowledge of Roman culture, and did not even approach the boundaries of the empire till it had already been broken up and laid desolate. They were still heathen, and still living in the stage of primitive tribal life which Tacitus painted in the Germania. They were divided into many tribal families, or clans, which they called 'faras,' and their subdivisions were ruled by elective aldermen or dukes, but the whole nation chose its king from among the royal houses of the Lethings and Gungings, who claimed to descend from Gambara, the wise queen who had led the race across the Baltic from Scandinavia ten generations back.

During the times of Justinian's Ostrogothic war the Lombards were under the rule of Audoin, whom Narses bribed with great gifts to aid him against Baduila. Five thousand warriors, under the command of their king himself, joined Narses in the invasion of Italy in 552, and took a distinguished part in the victory of Taginae. It must have been in this campaign that the Lombards learnt of the fertility and the weakness of Italy; but they were still engaged in wars with their neighbours on the Danube, and their king was an old man, wherefore we need not think it strange that they waited fifteen years before they turned their knowledge to account.

The Lombards were the close neighbours and the bitter foes of the Gepidae, the Gothic tribe who had remained behind in the Hungarian plains when the other sections of the Goths moved westward to Spain and Italy. The long struggle between Lombard and Gepid only came to an end in 567, when the Lombards called in to their aid the Tartar race of the Avars, and by their assistance almost entirely exterminated the Gepidae, whose scattered remnant only survived as slaves of the conquering horde. By this time Alboin, the son of Audoin, was reigning over the Lombards. He it was who slew with his own hand Cunimund, the king of the Gepidae. The barbarous victor struck off the head of his enemy, and had the skull mounted in gold, and fashioned into a drinking-cup, as the supreme token of his triumph. Yet, but a short time before, ere the last struggle had begun between the Lombards and the Gepidae, he had taken to wife Rosamund, the daughter of the man whom he now slew and beheaded.

Having ended this great national feud by the extermination of the Gepidae, Alboin determined to put into effect a scheme which must have been long maturing in his brain, the conquest of Italy. The Lombard historian of a later day asserted that he had been tempted to the invasion by the treachery of Narses, who, in discontent with Justin II., had urged Alboin to invade the peninsula, and sent him as gifts samples of all the generous fruits and wines that Italy produces. But this is the mere echo of a Lombard saga. Narses, now over eighty years of age and on his death-bed, had other matters to think about than the spiting of his new master. Nor did the Lombards, who had ridden all over Italy in 552, need to be reminded of its existence or its fertility.

Before leaving Pannonia, Alboin made over his old kingdom to his allies the Avars, only stipulating that it should be restored to him if ever he returned from Italy; a rather futile compact to make with such a faithless race as this Tartar horde. Crossing the Carinthian Alps, in the summer of 568, the whole Lombard nation — men, women, and children, with their cattle and slaves — descended into the Venetian plains, and spread themselves over the deserted lands. There was hardly any opposition. In cities that had once been great, like Aquileia and Milan, the scanty population did not even close the gates, but awaited the invader with apathy. Only the places where there was an Imperial garrison offered resistance. Verona, protected by the rushing Adige, Padua in its marshes, and Pavia, the ancient royal city of the Goths, were among the few towns that refused to admit the Lombards. The newcomers spread themselves over the whole valley of the Po, as far as the Tuscan Apennines and the gates of Ravenna, and begun to settle down on the fairest spots among the ruined Roman villages. They divided themselves, like the Franks in Gaul or the East-Angles in Britain, into two folks, the Neustrian, or Western, and the Austrian, or Eastern, Lombards. The former stretched from the Cottian Alps to the Adda, the latter from the Adda to the Julian Alps. Piedmont formed the bulk of Neustria; Venetia the bulk of Austria. Many scattered portions of tribes came to join Alboin in his new conquest. Not only did he grant lands to broken bands of Saxons and Suabians, but even foreigners, such as Bulgarians and Slavs, found shelter with him.

While Alboin was founding the new kingdom of Lombardy, the cities which at first resisted began to drop into his hands. Verona fell early, but Pavia made a long defence. So desperately did it hold out against the host left to blockade it that the king swore, in his wrath, to slay every living thing within its walls. But when, after three years, the starving citizens threw open their gates, he relented of his hard vow, 'because there was much Christian folk in that city,' and made Pavia his capital and royal stronghold.

In the next year, however, he came to his end. The Lombard chronicler, Paul the Deacon, repeating some familiar Lombard saga, tells the grim tale of his death thus: — 'King Alboin sat over long at the wine in his city of Verona, so that he grew boisterous, and he sent for the cup which he had made from the skull of king Cunimund, his father-in-law, and forced his queen, Rosamund, to drink from it, bidding her drink joyfully with her father. Then the queen conceived a deep grief and anger in her heart, and questioned with herself how she might avenge her father by slaying her husband. So she strove to persuade Helmichis, the king's armour-bearer, who was also his foster-brother, to slay his lord. And Helmichis would not, but counselled her to win Peredeo, the strongest champion of the Lombards, to do the deed. Then Rosamund sold her honour to Peredeo, and became his mistress, and said to him, "Now hast thou done a thing for which either thou must kill Alboin, or he thee." So he unwillingly consented to the deed, and at mid-day, when all the palace lay asleep, Rosamund bound the king's sword so tightly to the bed-head that it could not be drawn, and then bid Peredeo go in and slay her husband. When Alboin heard an armed man enter, he sprang from his couch, and strove to draw his sword without avail. For some space he fought hard for his life with a stool that he caught up, but what could the best of warriors do without arms against an armed champion? He was slain like a weakling, and, after passing unharmed through so many battles, died by the counsel of one woman, and she his own wife. So the Lombards took up his body, with much weeping, and buried it beneath the great flight of steps over against the palace, where it lay till my own days.' (May 572.)

Helmichis strove in vain to make himself king in his master's room, but the Lombards would have none of him, and he was forced to fly with Rosamund and the murderer Peredeo, to take shelter with the Romans at Ravenna. There all three of them came to evil ends, 'for the hand of Heaven was upon them for doing such a foul deed.'

Meanwhile the Lombards crowned as king, in the room of Alboin, Clepho, one of the mightiest of their dukes, though not of the royal blood; for Alboin had no son, and was the last of the Lethings. Clepho completed the conquest of all northern Italy, as far as the southern limits of Tuscany and the gates of Ravenna. But ere he had reigned a year he was slain by one of his own slaves, whom he had wronged. After he was dead the Lombards chose no more kings to reign over them for ten years, but each tribe went forth conquering and plundering under its own elective duke. It is said that no less than thirty-five of these chiefs were ranging over Italy at the same time (573-83). Nothing can show better the survival of primitive Teutonic ideas among the Lombards than this period of anarchy. They had not yet learned to look upon the king as a necessary part of the constitution of the tribe, but, like the Germans of the first century, regarded him as a war-chief, to be followed in time of peril alone. The Goths or the Franks, who had advanced to a further stage, could not have borne to live kingless for ten whole years,

Strangely enough, the loss of their supreme head seems to have detracted in no wise from the warlike vigour of the Lombards. In the ten kingless years they went on subduing the land, and pushed their incursions farther to the west and south. Three dukes of Neustria crossed the Alps and harried Provence, then in the hands of king Guntram the Frank, the peaceful brother of the warlike Sigibert and the wicked Chilperich. They took many cities, and were only driven out of the land, after much fighting, by Mummolus, the great Gallo-Roman general, who served king Guntram so well; but for him, Provence might have become part of Lombardy. Meanwhile other Lombard dukes were pressing southward down the Italian peninsula. They did not act on any combined plan of invasion, but each passed on with his war-band, leaving to right and to left many cities held by Imperialist garrisons, till he found a place of settlement that pleased his eye. Hence it came to pass that Lombard duchies and Roman cities were curiously intermixed. In central Italy, Faroald, the first duke of Spoleto, left Ravenna and Ancona to the north, and established himself in the central valley of the Tiber, with Imperialist garrisons all around him. Zotto, the first duke of Benevento, passed even farther to the south, and founded a realm in the Samnite valleys, which was almost entirely out of touch with the other Lombard states. It was hemmed in to east and west by the Roman garrisons of Rome, Naples, and Calabria. The dukes of Lucca and Chiusi, who held the bulk of Tuscany, did not push their limits down to the Tiber, but stopped short at the Ciminian hills, leaving a considerable district north of Rome in the hands of the Imperialists. Even in northern Italy the dukes of Neustria left Genoa and the Ligurian coast alone, and those of Austria did not subdue the marshland of Mantua and Padua, nor follow the fugitive inhabitants of Venetia into the islands where Venice and Grado were just beginning to grow up in the security of the lagoons. All over Italy Lombard and Roman districts were hopelessly confused, and, save that the Po valley was wholly Lombard, and Bruttium and Calabria wholly Roman, there was no part of the land that was not shared between the invader and the old Imperial Government.

Coming into a country already desolate and well-nigh dispeopled, and bringing with them the customs of primitive Germany, untinctured with any Roman intermixture, the Lombards established a polity even less centralised than that of the Visigoths, and infinitely below the standard of government which Theodoric had once set up in Italy eighty years before. When the nation once more chose a king, his power was hopelessly circumscribed by the authority of the great hereditary dukes. Spoleto and Benevento hardly paid even a nominal homage to the king who reigned at Pavia. Only when he presented himself with a large army in central Italy could he hope to win attention for his orders. Even in the valley of the Po, and in Tuscany, his power was very imperfect. The authority of the royal name had been fatally injured by the extinction, with Alboin, of the ancient kingly house of the Lethings. The Lombard monarchs, like their Visigothic contemporaries in Spain, only held their crown, when once they had been, elected, by the right of the sword. In a short history of two hundred years the Lombard kingdom saw nine successive races of kings mount the throne. All represented old ducal families. The rulers of Turin, Brescia, Benevento, Friuli, and Istria all, at one time or another, won the royal crown, besides two or three kings who were not even Lombards by birth, but strangers from the neighbouring land of Bavaria.

In the wasted regions of northern Italy, it would seem that the Lombards formed for some time the large majority of the population. Unlike the Goths in Spain, or the Franks in central Gaul, they did not merely consist of a few scattered families lost among the masses of the old inhabitants. There is a greater breach in the old Roman traditions of municipal and social life in the valley of the Po than in most of the other lands of the Western Empire. In the seventh century Lombardy must have preserved less traces of its ancient imperial organisation than Spain, Gaul, or Burgundy, and must have presented a much more primitive and Teutonic aspect. This is as we should expect, from the fact that the Lombards came from the very back of Germany, and first met with the influence of the older world of Rome when they moved into Italy.

Outside the Po valley, however, Italy was in a very different state; southern Italy and much of central Italy preserved its ancient organisation almost undisturbed; the Exarchate of Ravenna, the Ducatus Romanus, and the southern peninsulas of Apulia and Bruttium remained unchanged down to the ninth century. Records show us in the neighbourhood of Rome the old social organisation of the land, in domains inhabited by coloni, and owned by Roman church corporations, or absentee proprietors, at a time when in the northern plains the feudal system of the semi-independent dukes, each surrounded by their land-holding comites, was in full operation. In organisation, no less than in blood, northern Italy and southern Italy were fatally sundered, and two nations differing in all their usages of life and manners of thought were growing up.

The parts of Italy which remained under the imperial sceptre and preserved their ancient social and political organisation were strangely scattered. In the reign of Maurice (582-602) the emperor was still obeyed in eight regions. First was the Istrian peninsula, and the marsh and lagoon islands of the Venetian coast, with the strong cities of Padua and Mantua thrust inland like a wedge into the side of Lombardy. Second came the Ligurian coast with the city of Genoa, crushed in between the Apennines and the sea; its rugged valleys and cliffs did not yet tempt the Lombards out of their smiling plain to court the neighbourhood of the sea, for the Lombards were essentially unmaritime. Third is found the tract of land round Ravenna, the Exarchate, as it now became called — a title which it shared for a space with Africa, where exarchs also reigned. The Exarchate stretched along the coast of the Adriatic, from the delta of the Po up to the gates of Rimini, reaching as far inland as the Apennines, and comprising the whole southern half of the ancient province of Aemilia. Farther down the coast lay the fourth imperial district, from Rimini to Ancona, which was often called the Pentapolis and the Decapolis, from two groups of five and ten cities respectively which it contained. In Umbria lay a fifth detached district where the emperor was still acknowledged; it centred around Perugia, and was much hemmed in by the Lombard duchies of Chiusi and Spoleto, but it stretched out one horn toward the Pentapolis on the north, and the other toward Rome on the south. The sixth district was the Roman territory, now known as the Ducatus Romanus, from the dux who acted as civil governor in the ancient city in subordination to the exarch at Ravenna. The Roman duchy reached from Civita Vecchia to Terracina, and from the Apennines to the sea, taking in the southern corner of Etruria, and well-nigh the whole of Latium. It was cut off by the Lombard town of Capua from the duchy of Naples, a narrow coast-strip containing the towns of Naples and Amalfi, and ruled by a duke resident in the larger place. Lastly, all the toe and heel of Italy, Calabria Bruttium and southern Lucania, the whole coast line' from Brindisi to Policastro, formed the eighth Roman district. It was evident that the administration of such a number of fragmentary possessions would be a hard task for the exarch, cut off as he was from access by land to the greater part of the regions for which he was responsible. It was not so easy to foresee that the main result of the scission of Italy by the Lombard conquests was destined to be the rise of the temporal power of the Papacy, that most unexpected of the developments of the seventh century.

After the anarchy under the tribal dukes had lasted ten years, the Lombards chose them another king. The election seems to have been made mainly under the pressure of the war with the Franks, which they had brought upon themselves by their reckless invasion and ravaging of Provence in 574-75. Guntram of Burgundy induced his Austrasian kinsman to help him, and the Lombards were attacked by the Austrasians, who descended the valley of the Adige and attacked Trent, as well as by the Burgundians. Moreover, Tiberius II. of Constantinople had sent gifts to the kings of the Franks in order to induce them to aid him in Italy, and had done what he could, while the Persian and Avaric wars still dragged on, to send help to the exarch of Ravenna.

The new Lombard king was Authari, the son of that Clepho whose murder had left the throne vacant in 573. So greatly was the need of providing for the maintenance of the central power felt, that the dukes not only did him homage, and ceded him the royal city of Pavia, but promised him a half of all the lands that were in their hands as a royal domain to maintain him, his comitatus, and his officers. We may doubt if the promise was very exactly kept. Nor did all the dukes unite in the election. The first act of king Authari had to be to subdue and expel duke Droctulf, who had called in the Romans, and fortified himself in Brescello to defend the middle valley of the Po against the king. For the whole of his reign Authari was involved in recurring struggles with the Franks, whose young and warlike king, Childebert II., the son of Brunhildis, was set on resuming the schemes of his cousin Theudebert for conquering Italy. The seven years' reign of Authari was mainly occupied in warding off Frankish attacks on Italy; Guntram and Childebert, stirred up by Smaragdus, the exarch of Ravenna, threatened three or four times to cross the Alps, and twice actually invaded Lombardy. The more dangerous assault was in 590, when two great armies advanced simultaneously, the one from Burgundy over the Cenis against Milan, the other from Austrasia over the Brenner against Trent and Verona. Both forced their way to their goal, and did much damage to the Lombards, but they failed to meet with each other, or with the Roman troops which the exarch had promised to bring to their aid. Famine and pestilence thinned their ranks, and they could not reach the

Lombard king, who had shut himself up in the impregnable Pavia. At last they returned each to their own land, without profiting in the least by their great expedition.

In the intervals between the Frankish invasions Authari had done something to consolidate the Lombard power in north Italy, by capturing the great lagoon-fortress of Commacchio, whose seizure cut the communication between Padua and Ravenna. At about the same time Faroald, duke of Spoleto, took Classis, the seaport of Ravenna, and completely destroyed the city, whose only surviving remnant, the solitary church of St. Apollinare in Classe, stands up in such forlorn grandeur in the Ravennese marshes. Authari is said to have pushed one plundering expedition through Benevento into Bruttium, to have ridden to the extreme south point of the Italian peninsula, and to have touched with his spear a sea-swept pillar near Reggio, crying, 'Here shall be the boundary of the kingdom of the Lombards.' A vain boast, if it was ever made, for Bruttium was not destined to fall at any time into Lombard hands.

Authari married Theodelinda, the daughter of Garibald duke of Bavaria, a pious Christian and a Catholic, whose coming seems to have led the wild Lombards to Christianity, much as the influence of queen Bertha worked on the Jutes of Kent. She had not been long wedded to him when he died; the Lombard witan, who had formed a high idea of her wisdom and virtue, consulted her as to the choice of a new king. She recommended to them Agilulf, duke of Turin, a cousin of Authari. To him she gave her hand, and he was at the same time raised on the shield at Milan as king of the Lombards (590).

Agilulf was led by his wife's persuasion to be baptized, and ere long the greater part of the nation followed his example. The majority of the Lombards, like most of the other Teutonic races, adopted Arianism, and only conformed to orthodoxy in the seventh century. It was Agilulf and Theodelinda who built the famous Basilica of Monza, where the iron crown of Lombardy is even now preserved. In its sacristy are still shown many relics of the pious queen; most curious among them is a hen and chickens of gold of the most quaint and archaic workmanship, a marvellous example of the earliest art of a Teutonic people just emerging from barbarism. With it is preserved the crown of Agilulf, which he dedicated to St. John, and which bears the inscription: AGILULF GRATIA DEI VIR GLORIOSUS REX TOTIUS ITALIAE OFFERT SANCTO IOHANNI BAPTISTAE IN ECCLESIA MODICIAE.

The first three kings of the Lombards had been short-lived, but Agilulf survived for the respectable term of twenty-five years (591-616), and reigned long enough to see his son grow up and become his colleague on the throne. More fortunate than his predecessor Authari, he was delivered from the danger of Frankish invasions by the series of wars between the sons of Brunhildis and Fredegundis, which broke out in 593, and afterwards by the home troubles of Austrasia and Burgundy, caused by the strife between Brunhildis and the great nobles. Agilulf was, therefore, enabled to lop away from the empire several of the detached districts which had hitherto adhered to it. For the greater part of his reign he was in constant war with the Romans, and stripped the exarchs of Sutrium, Orte, Tuder, Perugia, and other south-Tuscan and Umbrian towns (598). By the mediation of Pope Gregory the Great a treaty was, for the first time, concluded between the Lombards and the empire in 599, but the exarch Gallicinus broke the peace, by seizing the person of Agilulf's daughter as she chanced to be passing through imperial territory. This second Lombard war, jwhich fell into the reign of Phocas, proved most disastrous for the Romans. Agilulf began by capturing Padua, the great fortress of the Venetian marshes (602). The fall of Padua cut off Mantua from succour, and that city, the last stronghold of the empire in the interior of Lombardy, also fell in 602. The ministers of Phocas only obtained a final pacification in 605 by promising to pay an annual tribute of 1200 gold solidi, and ceding the south-Tuscan strongholds of Orvieto and Bagnarea.

There was no more fight left in emperor or exarch for many a year; in the throes of the disastrous Persian war, Phocas and Heraclius were unable to send aid to Rome or Ravenna. The opportunity afforded to Agilulf of completing the conquest of Italy was such as never occurred again. But contented with his annual tribute, and perhaps tamed down by approaching old age, the Lombard king remained quiescent. Apparently he preferred to give his realm peace, and to occupy himself in keeping down his unruly dukes. In the course of his reign there were three or four dangerous rebellions of these chiefs, but Agilulf put them all down, apparently without much difficulty. There was also trouble on the north-eastern frontier from the Avars and Slavs, the same foes who were so grievously afflicting the Roman empire at this time. The Slavs made their way into Istria and Cilly, and became troublesome neighbours to Italy, though some of their nearest tribes were reduced to pay tribute by the dukes of Friuli. The Avars were more active and more dangerous; in spite of repeated treaties with Agilulf, their Chagan burst into north Italy in 610, slew Gisulf, duke of Friuli, in battle, ravaged all Venetia, and carried off many captives. Fortunately for the Lombards these invasions were not continued, as the Avars found better prey and less fighting in the Balkan peninsula.

In spite of such troubles, the reign of Agilulf was a time of growth, expansion, and ripening civilisation for the Lombards. They had all, by the end of his reign, received Christianity, had settled down in their new home, and were beginning to build churches and palaces, instead of confining their attention to destroying them. Agilulf had found a modus vivendi with Gregory the Great and the Papacy, and taught his subjects to live in some sort of peace with their neighbours, instead of persisting in the unending war which had filled the first thirty years of Lombard dominion in Italy.

Agilulf was succeeded by his only son, Adaloald, a boy of fourteen, whom he had induced the Lombard witan to salute as his colleague, and raise on the shield some years before. The regency was held by queen Theodelinda, who was both pious and popular, till the young king came of age; but soon after he had attained his majority, Adaloald was stricken with madness, and the nation chose in his stead Arioald, duke of Turin, who appears to have been no kinsman of the royal house, but had married the young king's sister, Gundiberga (626). Little is known of this king's reign of twelve years; we hear neither of wars with the Franks, nor of conquests from the Roman; we only read that he was, unlike his predecessor, an Arian. When he died, however, he was succeeded by a ruler of far greater mark, 'Duke Rothari of Brescia, of the race of Arod, a strong man, and one who walked in the paths of justice, though he was not an orthodox Christian, but followed the deceitful heresy of the Arians.'

Rothari finally completed the conquest of northern Italy, by taking the two districts which had still remained in the hands of the Imperialists down to his day. He subdued the whole Ligurian coast from Nice to Luna, with the great city of Genoa its capital (641). He also took the city of Oderzo, the last mainland possession of the Romans in Venetia. After this time the lagoon islands alone acknowledged the eastern Caesar as their suzerain, and their homage was formal rather than real. Rothari's conquests were not won without severe fighting. His greatest victory was won on the Scultenna, not far from Modena, over the exarch Plato, who had invaded Lombard territory, but was defeated with a loss of 8000 men, and driven back into Ravenna. The new activity of the Romans, to which this battle bears witness, may be attributed to the fact that the Persian and Saracen wars of Heraclius were at last ended, and under his grandson, Constans II., the Eastern empire was beginning to recover some measure of strength (642).

But Rothari is better remembered as the framer of the Lombard Code of Laws than as the conqueror of Liguria. In 643 he published the compilation of the traditional usages of the nation, which had hitherto never been committed to writing. It is noticeable that the code is promulgated, not on the king's personal authority, but, like the English laws of Ine, 'Pro communi gentis nostrae utilitate, pari consilio parique consensu cum primatis judicibus nostris cunctoque felicissimo exercitu nostro' — that is to say, by the king, with the counsel of his witan, and the assent of the armed folk-moot of the Lombard nation. The Edictum Rotharis is a very primitive body of legislation, such as might have been promulgated in the depths of the German forests, instead of in the heart of Italy. It is mainly composed of elaborate lists of weregelds, of laws against armed violence, of rules of inheritance, of statements concerning the obligation of the follower towards his lord, of provisions for judicial duels, per campionem. There is hardly any mention either of things ecclesiastical or of city life, merely a provision against breach of peace in a church, and some rules about magistri comacenses, or skilled Roman artisans. We have from the laws a picture of a people dwelling apart by families, ox faras, each in its own farm-clearing, surrounded by woods or open pasture land. Some are 'free Lombards,' called even thus early 'barones,' others the 'men' of a duke or of the king. Below them are aldii, who correspond to mediaeval villeins, the half-free occupiers of the land of the Lombard master. These, no doubt, are the remains of the old Roman populalation, coloni who had once cultivated the massa of a Roman curialis. The royal authority is found relegated to the local dukes in all military matters, while civil affairs are dealt with by the king's schulthais, or reeve (as the old English would have called him), or to the castaldus, who seems to have been the king's representative in the city, as opposed to the countryside. It is noticeable, as showing the extremely un-Roman character of the Lombard laws, that they are drawn up by a German official, the notary Ansoald, not by a Roman bishop or lawyer, as would certainly have been the case in Gaul or Spain. Their execrable Latin, which makes light of all concords, or rules of government of prepositions, could not have been the work of any educated Italian.

With the death of Rothari in 652, began a time of trouble and confusion for the Lombards, in which they ceased to win ground from the Romans, and fell into civil strife and anarchy. It commenced by the murder of Rothari's son, Rodoald, after he had reigned less than six months. He was a prince of licentious manners, and fell a victim to the dagger of an outraged husband (653).

The eighty years of Italian history during which the Lombards were settling down in the valley of the Po, and along the Umbrian and Samnite slopes of the Apennines, have won their chief importance in the story of the world, not from the doings of Agilulf or Rothari, but from the events that were taking place in Rome. To these years we may ascribe the foundation of the temporal power of the Papacy, and the development of the oecumenical position of the bishop of Rome to an extent which had hitherto been uncontemplated. These movements owe most of their strength to a single man, Pope Gregory the Great.

After the first shock of the Lombard invasion had rent Italy in twain, the Imperial governors resolved to take up their residence in Ravenna, not in Rome — in the capital of the Italy of Theodoric, not that of the Italy of Augustus. They chose the strong marsh-fortress close to the Lombard border, not the decayed city of the Tiber, still scarred by the traces of the Baduila's harrying. The exarch stationed himself at Ravenna, and delegated his civil and military authority in the scattered portions of Imperial Italy to minor officials, of whom the duces of Rome and Naples were the chief. This removal of the seat of the viceroy from the ancient metropolis was destined to have the most far-reaching results. Its first was that the chief lay official in Rome was an individual of far less authority and prestige than the chief ecclesiastical personage there resident. The bishops of Rome had always been men of importance; their claim to a patriarchal primacy over all the Western sees of Europe had already been formulated. In the ancient civil 'prefecture' of Italy — that is, in the Italian peninsula, Africa, and Illyricum — it had much reality. The African and Dalmatian churches referred matters of difficulty to Rome for decision, no less than did the church of Italy. We find Gregory the Great exercising a real influence in places as distant as Salona, Larissa, and Carthage. During the existence of the kingdom of the Ostrogoths, the Popes had obtained a kind of recognition from the Teutonic kings, as the accredited representatives of the Catholic and Roman population of Italy. They were certainly the most important subjects of the realm outside the ranks of the

Gothic conquerors, and were allowed to petition or plead with the king in behalf of all the Catholic Italians. The reconquest of Italy by Justinian had threatened to lower the prestige and power of the Popes, by placing them once more under a master who was both the legitimate ruler of the whole empire and an orthodox Catholic. Justinian had dealt in a very autocratic manner with the Roman bishops, as the tales of the woes of Vigilius and Silverius show. He summoned them to Constantinople, bullied, imprisoned, or tried them at his good pleasure. The continued survival of the Imperial power in Italy would have checked the growth of Papal authority in a great measure.

But the Lombard invasion changed the aspect of affairs. The Imperial governors and garrisons were swept into corners of the peninsula, and the Popes left without any master on the spot to curb them. The unfortunate Eastern wars of Maurice, Phocas, and Heraclius prevented them from turning any adequate attention to Italy. They sent the exarchs over to make what fight they could, without giving them adequate supplies, either of men or money. The exarchs, penned up in Ravenna, could only communicate with Rome with the greatest difficulty: the land-route of communication was almost cut by the Lombards of Spoleto; the sea-route was long and difficult. Hence Rome was left to itself, to fall or stand by its own strength and its own counsel. The Pope and the 'Duke' of Rome were continually thrown upon their own resources, without the power of asking advice or aid, either from the emperor or the exarch. For twenty-seven years, as Pope Gregory once wrote, Rome was continually in imminent peril of Lombard conquest (572-599), and obliged to provide for itself. In this time of stress and storm the Popes won their first secular authority over Rome and its vicinity, and reduced the civil magistrates to a place of quite secondary importance.

The man to whom the increase in the power of the Papacy was mainly due was Pope Gregory the Great, whose sway of fourteen years (590-604) covers the second half of the reign of Maurice and the first two years of Phocas. Gregory was a man of exceptional capacity, and of exceptional opportunities, at once administrator, diplomatist, monk, and saint. He was a noble Roman, who had spent his early manhood in the civil service, and had risen to the rank of prefect of the city. In early middle age he suddenly cast secular things aside, employed his wealth to found monasteries, and entered one himself as a simple monk. He plunged into the most rigid extremes of asceticism, and almost killed himself by his perpetual macerations of the flesh. Ere long he became abbot, and signalised himself by the stringent discipline which he maintained over his monks, as well as by his fiery zeal and untiring charity. It was at this time of his life that there occurred the scene so well known to all English readers. When he found the Northumbrian boys exposed for sale in the market-place of Rome, he conceived pity in his heart for the uncared-for heathen of Britain, and determined to cross the northern seas, and bear the Gospel to the Saxon and Angle. But Pope Pelagius II. interfered to prevent the most able, as well as the most saintly, of his clergy from leaving the service of the Roman See, and risking his life among the Pagans. He forbade Gregory's departure for England, and sent him instead to represent the Papacy at the court of Constantinople. A few years after his return from this mission, which was long enough to enable him to get a clear view of the weakness of the emperor Maurice, and of his impotence to interfere in Italian matters, Gregory was chosen bishop of Rome, when Pelagius died of the plague (590).

Gregory was elected without the Imperial sanction. Rome was so closely beset by the Lombards that there was neither time nor means for asking Maurice's consent, but the emperor afterwards confirmed the elevation of the saintly abbot. All Italy — nay, even the whole of the Christian West — knew of him already as the most prominent of the Roman clergy, and he was able at once to assume a position of great independence and authority. Gregory's most striking feature was his extraordinary self-confidence and conviction in the absolute wisdom and righteousness of his own ideas. The legend, started by his admirers not long after his death, to the effect that he was actually inspired by the Holy Ghost, who visited him in the form of a dove, very adequately represents his own notion of his infallibility. It was this self-confidence which enabled him to take up the line of stern and unbending autocracy which he always adopted. Other men were mute and obedient before the imperious saint, in whom they recognised their moral superior. Few, save the emperor Maurice and the fanatical John the Faster, patriarch of Constantinople, ever ventured to confront or withstand him. Unquestionably he was the most able, and one of the best-intentioned, men of his age. He left his mark on all that he touched, from the conversion of the English and the Lombards down to the official music of the Western Church — the Gregorian chants that still preserve his name. Although posterity enshrined him as one of the four great doctors of the Latin Church, his theological work was the weakest part of his activity. His writings are full of tropes, far-fetched conceits, misinterpretation of Scripture (he was ignorant of Hebrew and even of Greek), and pedantic arguments from analogy.

It was as statesman and administrator, and fosterer of missionary work that Gregory was truly great. In Rome he ruled as a temporal governor rather than a bishop. It was he who provided against the attacks of the Lombards, arrayed soldiers for the defence of the walls, fed the starving people from the funds of the church, and negotiated with the chiefs of the enemy in behalf of the people of the Ducatus Romanus. In 592 he concluded, on his own authority, a truce with the duke of Spoleto, while the exarch was set on continuing the war. Maurice stigmatised this conduct as 'fatuous;' but, as the emperor left Rome to provide for itself, he should hardly have complained. In another crisis, Gregory appointed, on his own authority, a tribune to command the garrison of Naples and a governor for the Tuscan town of Nepi. Finally, it was he who, in 599, negotiated the treaty of peace with king Agilulf, which ended the thirty years of continuous war which had followed the first coming of the Lombards to Italy. When rebuked by the exarch, he claimed to take precedence of him, not only in virtue of his priestly office, but also in place and dignity. In short, for all practical purposes, Gregory made himself the half-independent governor of Rome.

But Gregory's progress in asserting his authority as Patriarch of the West was even more important than his advances toward temporal power. He it was who recovered Spain and Britain for the Catholic Church — the former by the conversion of Reccared from Arianism, the latter by sending the mission of St. Augustine to Kent, and obtaining the baptism of king Ethelbert. Through the influence of queen Theodelinda, he obtained control over the Lombard king Agilulf, and induced him to bring up his son Adaloald as a Catholic. He could claim, in short, that he had reunited Italy, Spain, and Britain to the body of the Church of Christ. He also exercised considerable influence in Gaul, mainly through the influence of the great queen-mother Brunhildis, a favourer of all things Roman, with whom he maintained a long and friendly correspondence. We have already shown how the bishops of the Imperial provinces of Africa and Illyricum deferred to his judgment and decisions. Justly, then, may Gregory be styled the first Patriarch of the united West.

His successors were, for many generations, not men of mark. But by his work he had gained for them a temporal authority and a spiritual precedence which they were never again to lose. When he died, in 604, he left the Roman See exalted to a pitch of greatness which it had never before known, revered by all the Teutonic peoples of Europe, and half-freed from its allegiance to the rulers of Constantinople.

CHAPTER XII: HERACLIUS AND MOHAMMED — 610-641

Distress of the Empire in the early years of Heraclius — The letter of Chosroes — Treachery of the Avars — Heraclius preaches a Crusade — His six victorious Campaigns — Great Siege of Constantinople — Persia vanquished — Triumph of Heraclius — Rise and Character of Mohammed — The Creed of Islam — Conquests of the Caliphs in Syria and Persia — Troubled old age of Heraclius.

When the tyrant Phocas had been handed over to the executioner to pay the penalty for his innumerable misdeeds, the Senate and army joined in offering the crown to the young Heraclius, the saviour whose advent had delivered them from such a depth of misery. He was duly crowned by the patriarch, and acclaimed by the people in the Hippodrome. But when the first rejoicings were over, and he turned to contemplate the state of the empire which he had just won, the prospect was not a very reassuring one. The Slavs were spreading all over the Balkan peninsula, as far as the gates of Thessalonica and the pass of Thermopylae. The Persian, securely established in northern Syria and Mesopotamia, was advancing to permanently reduce the lands of Asia Minor, which he had ravaged so fiercely in the two preceding years. The treasury was empty, and the army scattered and disorganised; for some years it had not dared to meet the Persian in the open field, and the officers whom Phocas had kept in command had never won its confidence.

The first ten years of the reign of Heraclius seemed little better than a continuation of the miseries of the time of Phocas. The empire had gained, indeed, a good man instead of a bad as its ruler, but a change of fortune had not come with the change of sovereigns. It seemed that Heraclius would not be able to cope with the legacy of accumulated ills that had been left him. His predecessor's dying taunt, 'Will you rule the empire any better than I have done?' must often have rung in his ears, when the never-ending tidings of battles lost, towns stormed, revenues decreasing, and starving provinces kept coming in to him. The imperial etiquette which had prevailed for the last two hundred years prescribed that the Augustus should never take the field in person, and this rule seems to have prevented Heraclius from heading his own armies. The generals to whom he delegated his power were uniformly unfortunate, and occasionally disloyal. He was obliged to depose Priscus, the officer who had betrayed Phocas, for arrogant disobedience to his orders. The absence of the emperor from the field was a grave misfortune; for he was much less of an administrator than of a fighting man. His form and face betrayed the warrior. 'He was of middle stature, strongly built, and broad-chested, with a fair complexion, grey eyes, and yellow hair. He wore a bushy beard till he ascended the throne, when he shaved it, and did not let it grow again till he went to the wars ten years later.'

The military disasters of the first eight years of Heraclius' reign were terrible. In 613 the armies of Chosroes began to attack central Syria: Damascus fell, and then the general Shahrbarz pushed southward into Palestine. In 614 the whole Christian world was seized with horror at learning that Jerusalem had been captured. Not only were 90,000 Christians slain in the Holy City, but — what was reckoned far worse — all the treasures of the church of the Holy Sepulchre fell into the hands of the fire-worshippers. Chief of them was the 'Sacred Wood,' the 'True Cross,' which the empress Helena, the mother of the great Constantine, bad discovered in 327, and placed in her magnificent church. It was now carried into Persia, to be mocked by the blasphemous king Chosroes. This was not the end of the disasters of the empire. In 616 Shahrbarz forced his way across the sands of the isthmus of Suez, and attacked Egypt, the one Roman province which had not seen the horrors of war for three centuries. The unwarlike Egyptians submitted with hardly a blow; many of the heretical sects that swarmed in the Nile valley even welcomed the Persians as friends and deliverers. The loss of Egypt seemed a deathblow to the empire. It had been of late the chief source of revenue to the dwindling treasury of Heraclius, and on its corn the multitude of Constantinople had been wont to depend for their free dole of bread. This had now to be cut off, for the State finances did not permit of the provision being purchased elsewhere. In 617 the invasion of Asia Minor was resumed, and a Persian force seized Chalcedon, in very sight of the walls of Constantinople.

The darkest hour had arrived. It is a great testimonial to the popularity of Heraclius that the series of misfortunes which we have related did not cost him his throne. Any sovereign less well-intentioned, and less esteemed, would have lost life and crown. The direst moment of his humiliation arrived when, after the loss of Egypt, the overweening Chosroes sent him a formal letter, inviting him to lay down the sceptre which he could not wield. In language of arrogant condescension, which almost seems to have been borrowed from the letter of king Sennacherib in the Book of Kings, the Persian wrote: —

'Chosroes, greatest of gods, and master of the whole earth, to Heraclius, his vile and insensate slave. Why do you still refuse to submit to our rule, and call yourself a king? Have I not destroyed the Greeks? You say that you trust in your God. Why has he not delivered out of my hand Caesarea, Jerusalem, and Alexandria? And shall I not also destroy Constantinople? But I will pardon your faults if you will submit to me, and come hither with your wife and children; and I will give you lands, vineyards, and olive groves, and look upon you with a kindly aspect. Do not deceive yourself with vain hope in that Christ, who was not able even to save himself from the Jews, who killed him by nailing him to a cross. Even if you take refuge in the depths of the seas, I shall stretch out my hand and take you, so that you shall see me, whether you will or no.'

For a moment it is said that Heraclius contemplated abandoning Constantinople, and taking refuge in his father's old stronghold of Carthage. But the very desperateness of the state of affairs brought its own remedy. Incensed at the arrogance of Chosroes, smarting under the loss of the Holy Cross, and pinched for every necessary of life, the East-Romans were, ready to strike one wild blow for existence. The Church took the lead, and declared the war to be a holy duty for all Christian men, the first of the Crusades. The patriarch Sergius bound the emperor by an oath not to abandon his people, and the clergy offered, as a war-loan, all the gold and silver plate of the churches of Constantinople. Heraclius took heart, and, casting aside the trammels of imperial etiquette, swore that he would himself lead his army in the field. Thousands of volunteers were collected, and the treasures of the Church lavished on their equipment. By the end of 618 this effort of despair had given the empire once more a general, an army, and a military chest.

But an attack on the Persian host in Asia Minor did not turn out to be at once feasible. A sudden danger at home obliged Heraclius to delay his crusade. The Avars concentrated their ravages on Thrace, and their hordes rode up almost to the gates of Constantinople. It was necessary at all costs to free the city from the danger of attack in the rear before the army crossed over into Asia. Accordingly the emperor sent to offer a subsidy to the Chagan of the Avars if he would withdraw beyond the Danube. The Chagan proposed a conference at Heraclea, forty miles west of Constantinople, the point to which he had advanced his army. Heraclius consented to the meeting, and rode out in royal state, with all his court. But the faithless Avar was meditating treachery. He concealed troops of his horsemen in the hills, with the object of waylaying Heraclius on his way to Heraclea, and of holding him to ransom. The emperor was warned just in time to escape from the ambush. Throwing off his long purple robe, and tucking his diadem under his arm, he rode hard for Constantinople, with the Avars close at his heels. Many of his court, and thousands of the Thracian peasantry, who had turned out to witness the meeting, fell into the hands of the enemy. Heraclius had just time to order the gates to be closed before the pursuers swept through the suburbs, and up to the walls.

In spite of this piece of abominable treachery, the emperor was still fain to conclude a peace with the Avars, as an absolutely necessary preliminary before attacking the Persian. In 620 a peace of some sort was patched up, in return for a payment of money, but even then Heraclius Avas not able to start on his projected campaign. Some desultory Persian attacks on Constantinople, and notably an attempt to build a fleet at Chalcedon, and cross the strait, had first to be frustrated.

It was not till 622 that the emperor was finally enabled to take the offensive. But all preparations being complete, after solemnly keeping the Lenten Fast, and receiving the benediction of the Church for himself and his army, he set sail for Asia on Easter Day. He left his young son, Heraclius Constantinus, regent in his stead, und r the charge of the patriarch Sergius and the patrician Bonus, the commander of the garrison of Constantinople.

In the six campaigns which followed, Heraclius displayed an energy and an ability which no one, judging from his quiescence during the last ten years, would have expected him to possess. Historians only doubt whether to praise the more his strategical talents or his personal bravery. From the very first he showed his ascendency over the enemy, taking the offensive, and turning the course of the war wherever he chose to direct it. At his first departure from Constantinople he did not attack the Persian in the front, but boldly sailed round the southern capes of Asia Minor, and landed his army in Cilicia, on the gulf of Issus, a position from which he threatened both Asia Minor and northern Syria. Marching up into Cappadocia, he cut the communications between the Persian army in Asia Minor and the

Euphrates valley. This movement had the result that he expected. Hastily evacuating Bithynia and Galatia, the Persian general Shahrbarz drew back eastward, in order to regain touch with his country. Ere a blow was struck Heraclius had cleared western Asia Minor of the enemy; but he finished the campaign by inflicting a crushing defeat on Shahrbarz in Cappadocia, and thus recovered eastern Asia Minor also (622).

After in vain offering terms of peace to Chosroes, Heraclius took effective means in the next year to bring the Persian to reason. Syria, Egypt, and Mesopotamia were still in the hands of the enemy: he resolved to deliver them in the same manner that he had saved Asia Minor, by striking so hard at the enemy's base of operations that he should be compelled to call in all his outlying troops in order to defend Persia proper. In 623 Heraclius, abandoning his communication with the sea, plunged boldly inland, and fell on Media. For two whole years he is lost to sight in the regions of the extreme East, subduing lands where no Roman army had ever been seen before, where, indeed, no European conqueror had ever penetrated since Alexander the Great. We hear of his winning three pitched battles, and of his storming two great Median towns, Gandzaca and Thebarmes, the latter the reputed birthplace of Zoroaster, the prophet of the Persians. It was some satisfacfaction to the army to destroy their magnificent temples in revenge for the sack of Jerusalem. To defend Media, Chosroes had to draw back his outlying armies from the West, and so far the purpose of Heraclius was served; but the emperor was still too weak to attack Persia proper, or besiege Chosroes' capital of Ctesiphon.

After wintering at Van, in the Armenian highlands, Heraclius dropped southward, in 625, and came into regions more within the ken of Western historians. He recovered the long-lost fortresses of Amida and Martyropolis, the ancient bulwarks of the empire on the upper Tigris, which had been for nearly twenty years in Persian hands, and once more picked up his communication with Constantinople, which had almost lost sight of him during the two last campaigns. The year ended with a fourth crushing defeat of Shahrbarz, who had endeavoured to throw himself between the emperor and his homeward path by defending the passage of the Sarus, near Germanicia.

But 626 was destined to be the decisive year of the war. Before acknowledging himself beaten, the obstinate Chosroes was determined to make one final effort. Drawing every man that he could together, for the Persian empire was now growing exhausted, the old king made two armies of them. While the larger was left in Mesopotamia and Armenia, to endeavour to keep Heraclius employed, a great body under Shahrbarz slipped southward, round the emperor's flank, and marched for the Bosphorus. Chosroes had concerted measures with the treacherous Chagan of the Avars for a combined attack on Constantinople, from both the European and the Asiatic side of the strait. When Shahrbarz appeared at Chalcedon, he found the Avars already masters of Thrace, and preparing to beleaguer Byzantium. The two armies could see each other across the water, but they were wholly unable to communicate with each other: for the Roman fleet kept such excellent guard in the straits that no boat could cross. The patrician Bonus made a most gallant defence, the garrison was adequate, and the population kept a good heart, for they knew that the Persian was striking his last desperate blow. Heraclius himself was so well satisfied with the impregnability of his capital that he only sent a few veteran troops by sea to co-operate in the defence, and kept the greater part of his army in hand for an attack on the heart of the dominions of Chosroes. Meanwhile, the host of Shahrbarz had to look on in helpless impotence, while the Avars, on the other side of the Bosphorus, made their attempt on Constantinople. On the night of the 3d of August 626 the Chagan gave the signal for the assault. A body of Slavs, in small boats, attempted to storm the sea-wall from the side of the Golden Horn, while the main body of the Avars moved against the land-wall. But the galleys of Bonus rammed and sunk the light vessels of the Slavs, and the assault of the Avars miscarried entirely. Thereupon the Chagan hastily broke up his camp, and retired beyond the Balkans. The siege was practically raised, though the army of Shahrbarz still remained encamped at Chalcedon. Thus ended the first of the four great sieges of Constantinople of which we have to tell.

Meanwhile, Heraclius had been retaliating on Persia in the most effective way. In return for the invasion of Thrace by the Avars, he called in from beyond the Caucasus the wild Hunnish tribe of the Khazars, and turned them loose on Media and Assyria. Forty thousand of their horsemen laid waste the whole land, as far as the gates of Ctesiphon, and the emperor took possession of the upper valley of the Tigris, and prepared to strike at his rival's capital in the coming year.

The campaign of 62 7 ended the triumphs of Heraclius. The last army of Persia, under a general named Rhazates, faced him near Nineveh. Charging at the head of the mailed horsemen of his guard, Heraclius slew the Persian chief with his own hand, and scattered his forces to the winds. The victorious army pressed on, and captured Dastagerd, the magnificent country-palace of Chosroes, near Ctesiphon, where they gained such plunder as no Roman army had won for many ages. They burnt Dastagerd, and four palaces more, while Chosroes fled eastward to conceal himself in the mountains of Susiana. The long-suffering Persians were at last growing tired of their arrogant lord. His army rebelled against him, and proclaimed his son Siroes as king. Chosroes himself was thrown into a dungeon, where he perished of cold and starvation. The new king at once sent to ask for terms of peace from Heraclius. The emperor, knowing the exhaustion of his own realm, and its need for instant repose, made no hard conditions. Siroes restored all the Roman territory still in his hands, released all Roman captives, paid a war indemnity, and — greatest of all triumphs in the eyes of the subjects of Heraclius — gave back the 'True Cross,' and other spoils of Jerusalem.

In May 628 the emperor was able to return to Constantinople, bringing peace and plenty with him. He had restored the boundary of the empire, and inflicted on Persia a blow from which she never recovered. His arms had penetrated far beyond the limits of the conquests of Trajan and Severus, and his six years of unbroken victory were a record which no Roman, save Julius Caesar, could rival. Not unjustly did the inhabitants of Constantinople receive him with chants and sacred processions, and hail him by the name of 'the new Scipio.' The crowning moment of his triumph came when the True Cross was uplifted in St. Sophia, and publicly exposed for the adoration of the faithful. Well might the emperor have sung his 'Nunc dimittis' on that day of solemn rejoicing, and prayed that the hour of his triumph might be the last of his life.

But already there was another tempest gathering, which was destined to sweep over the Roman empire, with even greater violence than the Persian storm which had just been weathered. While in the midst of his last campaign, Heraclius had received a letter from an obscure Arabian prophet, bidding him accept a new revelation from Heaven, which its framer called 'Islam,' or 'Submission to God.' A similar missive was delivered at the same moment to Chosroes, then on the eve of his fall. Chosroes tore up the letter, and swore he would, at his leisure, lay the insolent prophet in a dungeon. Heraclius sent a polite letter of acknowledgment and a trifling present to the unknown fanatic, being averse to making enemies of any sort while the Persian war was still on his hands. Little as it could have been foreseen at the time, the followers of the writer of these eccentric missives were fated to tear up the empire of Chosroes by the roots, and to lop off half of its fairest provinces from the realm of Heraclius.

The Arabian prophet was no less a person than Mohammed the son of Abdallah, that strange being, half seer and half impostor, whose preaching was destined to convulse three continents, and turn the stream of history into new and unexpected channels.

The tribes of Arabia had hitherto been of very little importance: their local feuds absorbed all their superfluous energy. They were divided from each other, as well by religious differences as by ancient clan hatreds. Some worshipped stocks and stones, some the host of heaven, some had partly adopted Christianity, others Judaism. They were given over to fetish-worship, human sacrifices, drunkenness, infanticide, bloodshedding, polygamy, and highway robbery. Among these godless tribes appeared Mohammed, a poor man, but born of an ancient and powerful clan, who preached to them a rigid Unitarian creed, accompanied by a reformation in morality. He had been called by the One true God, he said, in a vision on Mount Hira, to proclaim a new revelation to his countrymen, to turn them from idolatry and hatred of each other, to the worship of Allah and the practice of brotherly love. Mohammed was a being of a poetic and visionary temperament, given to high ideals and high enterprises. He was afflicted with long fits, or trances, in which his soul wandered far into the fields of thought: these trances he took for divine inspirations, and his imaginings — which were often noble enough — seemed to him the direct commands of God, though in them good and grand ideas were freely mixed with baser elements, tainted by the ignorance, cruelty, and lust of a seventh century Arab. For long the preaching of Mohammed was of no effect: his own tribe grew weary of his unending exhortations, and chased him away from Mecca (622). It is from this flight to Medina — the famous 'Hijrah,' that all Moslem chronology is dated. But in spite of ill-success and persecution the prophet never swerved from his mission, and at last proselytes began flocking in to him, and he became the head of a powerful sect. Then came the fatal moment which turned his teaching from a blessing to Arabia into a curse for the world. When he grew powerful enough, he bade his sectaries to take up the sword, and impose Islam on their neighbours by the force of arms. His first success in the field, the battle of Bedr (624), was an encouragement to persevere in this evil path, and for the last eight years of his life he went forth, conquering and to conquer, among the tribes of Arabia, till he had built up a little theocratic empire in the peninsula (624-32).

Mohammed's successes were won by unhallowed means, and the desire to extend them at almost any cost gradually led him into compromises with the habits and superstitions of his countrymen which were fatal to the purity of his religion, A strain of cunning, of revenge, of self-indulgence, appeared in a character which, in his years of poverty and trouble, had been blameless. He connived at the ancient fetish-worship of the Arabs, by conceding that the conical black stone of the Kaabah, which they had always worshipped, had been hallowed by Abraham, and should be the central shrine of his new faith. He fostered their vanity by proclaiming them the chosen people of God. He pandered to their craving for lust and bloodshed, by promising them the goods of their enemies to plunder in this life, and a heaven of gross sensual enjoyment in the next. He restricted, but he did not abolish, the evils of polygamy and slavery. In his day of triumph he consigned whole tribes and towns to death, sometimes under circumstances of treachery as well as of cruelty. Worst of all, he foisted into his revelation special mandates of God permitting himself to do things which his teaching forbade to his followers, such as to exceed his own limit of polygamy, and even to take his own foster-son's bride to wife. It is hard to believe that he can have failed to see the horrible blasphemy involved in forging the name of God to special warrants approving his own lust. But this sin he repeatedly committed.

The personal failings of Mohammed seem to have brought into his creed a blight of cruelty, bigotry, and self-indulgence, which has rendered half-useless its higher and nobler features. The religion which legalises the slaughter and plunder of all unbelievers and consigns woman to the harem may have been a comparative blessing to the wild Arabs of Mohammed's own day, or to the Negro of the modern Soudan: to the civilised world it was a mere curse — the substitution of an inferior for a higher creed and life. Even to the Arab of the seventh century it was but half-beneficial: if it stayed him from drunkenness, human sacrifices, and infanticide, it merely directed his bloodthirstiness against foreign instead of domestic foes, and gave a divine sanction to many of his lower instincts. Wherever Mohammedanism has taken root, it has led at first to rapid and enthusiastic outbursts of vigour, but it seems gradually to sap the energy of the nations which adopt it, and leads, after a few generations of greatness, to a stagnation and decay, which the Moslem in his self-satisfied bigotry is too blind to perceive. The creed only thrives while militant. When it has won its victory, it sinks into dull apathy. Islam is a good religion to die by, as its fanatics have shown on a thousand battlefields, but not a good religion to live by. Good and evil elements are too hopelessly mixed in it, just as in Mohammed's Koran, that miscellaneous receptacle of all his revelations: high thoughts about the Godhead or the fate of man are mingled with the mere opportunist orders of the day, or with licences for the personal gratification of the Prophet.

But whatever were the failings of Mohammed and of Mohammed's creed, they had one fearful efficiency, the power to turn their sectaries into wild fanatics, careless of life or death upon the battlefield. Life meant to them the duty of smiting down the Infidel, and the privilege of spoiling him: death, the yet greater joys of a paradise of gross sensual delights. What the first mad rush of a horde of Moslem fanatics, drunk with religious frenzy, was like, modern Europe had half forgotten, though our crusading forefathers knew it well enough. But the generation which has seen the half-armed Arabs of the Soudan face the steadiest troops in the world equipped with quick-firing rifles and artillery, and almost carry the day against them, has had good reason to revise its view about the power of Mohammedan fanaticism.

Before he died, Mohammed had begun to take measures for the spread of his religion by the sword beyond the limits of Arabia. In 629, the year after the end of the Persian war, the troops of Heraclius who garrisoned the fortresses on the desert frontier of Palestine, had been attacked by wandering bands of Arab zealots. But it was not till the Prophet himself was dead that the full storm of invasion fell upon the Roman empire and its Persian neighbours. It was Abu Bekr, the first 'caliph' or 'successor' of Mohammed, who sent forth in 633 the two armies which were bidden respectively to convert Syria and Chaldaea to Islam by the edge of the sword.

Neither the Roman nor the Persian empire was well fitted for resistance at the moment. The twenty years of war brought about by the ambition of Chosroes had reduced each of them to the extreme of exhaustion. Since the end of the war Persia had been a prey to incessant civil strife and revolution: nine princes had mounted the throne in little more than four years. In the Roman empire Heraclius had been doing his best to repair the calamities of the war: his first care had been to repay, by means of the war indemnity paid by Siroes and the imposition of new taxes, the great loan which the Church had made him, in order to equip his troops for the struggle. He had disbanded much of his victorious army in pursuit of the policy of retrenchment for which the ruined state of his empire called. But he could not repair the losses which Syria and Asia Minor had suffered in spending ten years beneath the Persian yoke. The very foundations of society seemed to have been sapped in the provinces of the East by the prolonged Persian occupation. The numerous heretical sects which swarmed in the valleys of the Nile and the Orontes had raised their heads during the Persian rule, and bore with ill-concealed reluctance the restoration of the imperial authority. The Jews, who had often sided with the Persians, were restless and discontented. It was said that half the population of Syria and Egypt wished ill to the empire. It would have required two generations of peace and wise administration to restore to their old condition those Oriental dioceses which had for the last three centuries been the stay and support of the East-Roman Empire; but less than four years after Heraclius had solemnly restored the 'True Cross' to the custody of the Patriarch of Jerusalem the Arabs burst into the land.

While Khaled and one fanatical Saracen horde assaulted the Persian frontier on the lower Euphrates, another, under Abu Obeida, attacked the eastern or desert front of Syria. Bostra, the first city on the edge of the waste, fell by treachery, a small army under the patrician Sergius was defeated, and the governors of Syria and Palestine sent for aid to the emperor. Hardly yet realising the danger of the crisis, Heraclius sent some reinforcements under his brother Theodore to join the local troops. This army checked the Moslems for some months; and it was considered necessary by the caliph to strengthen the Arab host in Syria by sending thither half the force which had invaded the Persian empire, and Khaled, 'the Sword of God,' the most terrible and bloodthirsty of all his fanatical chiefs. In July 634, Theodore was badly defeated by the Saracens at Adjnadin near Gabatha, beyond the Jordan. This ill-success roused the emperor: he poured in further reinforcements, and the Battle of the enemy were attacked in the late summer of 634 Yermuk, 634. by an army of 80,000 men. The fate of Syria was settled by the battle of the Hieromax (Yermuk), where the troops of the Empire, after a long and bloody fight, in which they at one time forced the Arabs back to the very gates of their camp, were broken by the fanatical rush of an enemy who preferred death to defeat. 'Paradise is before you,' cried Abu Obeida to his wavering host, 'the devil and hell fire behind;' and with their last charge the Arabs broke the line of the legions, and rolled the wearied troops in wild disorder back over a line of precipices and ravines, where thousands perished without stroke of sword, by being cast down the lofty rocks.

The army of the East was almost exterminated at the Hieromax, and ere another force could be collected Damascus, the greatest city of eastern Syria, was captured by the enemy, who in spite of accepting its surrender massacred a great part of the population (635).

Heraclius now determined to lead the Roman army in person, but he was no longer the same man who had kept the field with harness on his back for six long campaigns in the. old Persian War. He had now long passed his fiftieth year, and was prematurely broken by the first symptoms of the dropsy which afterwards caused his death. In his private life, too, he had had much trouble of late; he had made an unwise and unhallowed second marriage with his own sister's daughter Martina, and was harassed by disputes between her and the rest of his family, caused by the fact that the young empress wished to induce her husband to leave her own son Heracleonas joint heir to the empire with his elder brother Heraclius Constantinus. But such as he was, Heraclius once more put on his armour, and spent the years 635-6 in Syria endeavouring to keep back the Arabs with the new levies that he had assembled. His failure was complete; city after city, Emesa, Hierapolis, Chalcis, Beroea, fell into the hands of the Moslems, without the emperor being able even to risk a battle in their defence. In 636, completely broken by disease, he returned to Constantinople, having first paid a hasty visit to Jerusalem to take up and remove the 'True Cross' which he had replaced there in triumph only six years before.

After the departure of Heraclius things went from bad to worse; Antioch, the stronghold and capital of northern Syria, and Jerusalem, the centre of the defence of Palestine, both fell in 637. To receive the surrender of Jerusalem, which Mohammed had pronounced only second to Mecca among the holy places of the world, the caliph Omar crossed the desert in person. When the town had yielded, the Arab compelled the patriarch Sophronius to lead him all round the shrines of the city; as they stood in the church of the Holy Sepulchre, the patriarch, torn by grief, could not refrain from exclaiming that now indeed was the Abomination of Desolation, spoken of by Daniel the prophet, in the Holy of Holies. The austere Omar showed more moderation and compassion than his generals had been wont to display, he left the Christians all their holy places, and contented himself with building a great mosque on the site of the temple of Solomon.

While Syria was falling before the Saracens, the lot of Persia had been even worse; after a great battle lasting for three days at Kadesia, the Sassanian empire had succumbed before the Moslem sword. Its capital Ctesiphon was sacked and destroyed, and Yezdigerd, the last of its kings, fled eastward to raise his last army on the banks of Oxus and Murghab (636). Arab hordes working up the Euphrates began to assail the Roman province of Mesopotamia from the south, at the same moment that the conquerors of Syria attacked it from the west. Heraclius made one last attempt to save north Syria and Mesopotamia by sending an army under his son and heir Heraclius Constantinus to endeavour to recover Antioch. After some slight show of success at first, the young Caesar suffered a fatal defeat in front of Emesa, and retired from the scene, leaving Mesopotamia with all its time-honoured strongholds, Daras, Edessa, and Amida, a prey to the irresistible enemy (638-9). With the fall of the seaport of Caesarea in 640 the Romans lost their last foothold south of the Taurus, and Asia Minor itself now became exposed to invasion.

Before he died of the dropsy, which was the bane of his declining years, the unfortunate Heraclius was destined to see one more disaster to his realm. In 640 the Saracens, now headed by Amrou, crossed the desert of Suez and fell upon Egypt. They beat the Roman army in the field, captured Memphis and Babylon, and then received the homage of all upper and central Egypt. The population was very largely composed of heretical sects who received the Moslems as deliverers from orthodox oppression, and Mokawkas the Coptic governor of the province surrendered long ere the situation had grown desperate. It was only about Alexandria, where the Greek orthodox element was strongest, that any serious resistance was made. But the great seaport capital of Egypt held out very staunchly, and was still in Christian hands when Heraclius died on Feb. 10th, 641, in the sixty-sixth year of his age.

Thus ended in misery and failure the man who would have been hailed as the greatest of all the warrior emperors of Rome if he had died but ten years sooner. He had saved the empire at its darkest hour, and won back all the East by feats of arms such as have seldom been paralleled in all history. But he won it back only to lose again two-thirds of the rescued lands to a new enemy, and ungrateful after-ages remembered him rather as the loser of Jerusalem and Antioch than as the saviour of Constantinople.

CHAPTER XIII: THE DECLINE AND FALL OF THE VISIGOTHS — A.D. 603-711

Obscurity of Visigothic History — Sisibut and Swinthila expel the East-Romans — A series of priest-ridden Kings — Chindaswinth restores the royal power — His legislation — Recceswinth's long reign — Wamba and his wars — The rebellion of Paulus — Wamba's weak and obscure successors — Approach of the Saracens — Weakness of Spain — Roderic the Last of the Goths — All Spain subdued by the Saracens.

Few periods of European history are so obscure as the last hundred years of the Visigothic dominion in Spain. The original sources for its annals are few and meagre, and little has been accomplished of late in the way of making the period more comprehensible. The Moorish conquest in 711 seems to have swept away both books and writers, and it was not till many years after that disaster that the composition of historical works in Spain was resumed; the later Visigothic times are as dark and little known as the beginnings of the English heptarchy, and Spain had no Bede and no Anglo-Saxon Chronicle to throw gleams of light across the obscurity. Hence it comes that many of their kings are mere names, and that their acts and policy are often incomprehensible. The tale grows more and more puzzling as the seventh century draws on to its close, and by the beginning of the eighth we have only untrustworthy legends to help us.

The house of Leovigild, after forty years of success, ended disastrously in 603 by the assassination of the young king Leova II. His murderer was a certain count Witterich, a turbulent noble who had joined in the Arian rising of 590, and had been unwisely pardoned by Reccared. The accession of Witterich marked a revulsion against the growth of the kingly power, which had been making such strides under Leovigild and Reccared, and probably also a protest against the ecclesiastical policy of Reccared, who, since his conversion, had given the Catholic bishops such power and authority in his realm. Witterich reigned for seven years, with little credit to himself — it is only strange that he guarded his ill-gotten crown so long. He had some unimportant struggles with the Franks in Aquitaine and the Byzantine garrisons in Andalusia, but won no credit in either quarter. The

Church was against him, his counts and dukes paid him little heed, and no one showed much astonishment or regret when in 610 he was murdered by conspirators at a feast, like his predecessor the tyrant Theudigisel.

The king chosen by the Goths in his place was a certain count Gundimar, who appears to have been the head of the orthodox church party, as the ecclesiastical chronicles are loud in the praises of his piety. Gundimar determined to take part in the Frankish civil war when Theuderich of Burgundy and Brunhildis attacked Theudebert of Austrasia. He naturally sided with the distant Austrasian against his nearer Burgundian brother, with whom the Goths of Septimania had some frontier disputes. But in the year that the war broke out Gundimar died, only twenty-one months after he had been crowned (612).

His successor was king Sisibut (612-20), a prince of some mark and character, who like his predecessor was a great friend of the church party and a foe of the unruly secular nobility. He was not only a great warrior, but what was more strange in a Gothic prince, a learned student and even a writer of books. The modern historian would give much to be able to recover his lost Chronicle of the Kings of the Goths; but the irony of fate has decreed that of his works only an ecclesiastical biography, The Life and Passion of St. Desiderius, and some bad verses, should survive. We learn from his admiring clerical friends that he was skilled in grammar, rhetoric, and dialectic, and that he erected a magnificent cathedral in Toledo.

Bat Sisibut was no mere crowned savant; he took up the task, which had been abandoned since the death of Reccared, of driving the East-Roman garrisons out of Andalusia, and was almost completely successful. The emperor Heraclius, then in the throes of his Persian war, could send no help to Spain, and one after another all the harbours of south-eastern Spain from the mouth of the Guadalquivir to the mouth of the Sucre fell into his hands. Nothing remained to the East Romans except their most westerly possession, the extreme south-west angle of Portugal, with the fortress of Lagos, and the promontory of Cape St. Vincent. After winning the Andalusian coast it appears that Sisibut built a small fleet and crossed the Strait of Gibraltar to wrest Ceuta and Tangier from the exarch of Africa. In 615 Heraclius made peace with him, formally surrendering all that Sisibut had succeeded in gaining from his generals. Sisibut was also successful in taming the intractable Basques; following them into their mountains he compelled them to pay tribute.

A less happy record is preserved of Sisibut in the matter of internal government. As befitted a hot supporter of the intolerant Spanish church, he gave himself up to the promptings of his bishops, and commenced a fierce persecution of the Jews, the first of many tribulations which the unhappy Hebrews were to suffer at the hands of the later Gothic kings.

Sisibut reigned only eight years; he had taken the precaution to have his son Reccared II. elected king by the national council during his own lifetime, and on his death the youth succeeded to the throne without molestation. But less than a year after Sisibut's death Reccared followed him to the grave, and the crown once more passed into a new house.

Count Swinthila, whom the Goths now chose as king, was a general who had distinguished himself in the war with the Basques, and had a great military reputation, but, unlike Sisibut, was not a favourer of the Church party, and had to face its intrigues all through the ten years of his reign. He was equally disliked by the great nobles, whose powers he sought to curb by asserting the rights of the smaller Gothic freeholders, who had for long been lapsing more and more into feudal dependence on their greater neighbours. His care for their interests won for him the title of the 'Father of the Poor,' and their loyalty is no doubt the explanation of the fact that he was able to hold the crown so long when both Church and nobles were against him. Nor was his reign entirely without military successes. He took Lagos and the fort on Cape St. Vincent, the two last Byzantine strongholds in Spain, so that the whole peninsula was at last drawn under a single ruler. He was equally successful against a rebellion of the Basques, and, overrunning their mountain valleys in Navarre and Biscay, built the fortress of Olite, beyond the Ebro and near Pampeluna, to hold them down.

But Swinthila had too many enemies to be allowed to keep his crown. A certain count Sisinand, a governor in Septimania, rose against him, and called in to his aid Dagobert, the king of the Franks. Gaul was now once more united under a single monarch, and the long civil wars of the descendants of Brunhildis and Fredegundis were over, so that the Franks were, after a long interval, able to indulge in foreign invasion. Backed by troops lent him by Dagobert, Sisinand crossed the Pyrenees, and advanced against Saragossa, where the king had marched forward to meet him. No battle took place, for the matter was settled by treachery. The great nobles and bishops, who had obeyed Swinthila's summons to war, seized him in his own camp, threw him into chains, and handed him over to Sisinand. The usurper, more merciful than many Gothic rebels, contented himself with casting Swinthiia into a monastery, and did not put him to death. Sisinand had promised his Frankish friend to surrender to him in return for his help the most splendid treasure in the Gothic royal hoard, a great golden bowl of Roman workmanship, weighing five hundred pounds, a trophy of the old wars of the fifth century. He gave up the vessel to Dagobert's ambassadors, but, when it was seen departing from Spain, the Gothic counts swore that such an ancient heirloom of their kings must never leave the land, and took it back by force. In its lieu Sisinand sent to Dagobert a sum of 200,000 gold solidi (£140,000).

Sisinand was a weak ruler, the tool and instrument of his bishops. Under his impotent hands all the power and authority of the royal name melted away, and the work of Sisibut and Swinthila was undone. The Church and not he ruled Spain. When synods met, the king was seen on bended knee, and with streaming eyes, lamenting his sins, and begging the counsel of the holy fathers. He reigned only for five years (631-36), and was succeeded by Chinthila, another chosen instrument of the hierarchy, of whom we know little more than that 'he held many synods with his bishops, and strengthened himself by the help of the true faith.' He reigned only three years, but was allowed by his clerical partisans to have his son Tulga crowned as his successor before he died. Tulga, another obedient son of the Church, had only reigned two years when he was dethroned by a conspiracy of the great lay nobles, to whom the domination of the clergy in the State became more and more odious under the twelve years' rule of three priest-ridden kings. Tulga was sent to pursue the congenial path of piety in a monastery, while the National Assembly, convened by the conspirators, elected as king count Chindaswinth, whose virtues were recognised by all, while his great age — he was no less than seventy-nine — promised a free hand to his turbulent subjects (641).

But the nobles had erred greatly in their estimate of Chindaswinth, as grievously as did the misled cardinals, who, in a later age, elected the apparently moribund Sixtus V. to the Papacy. The touch of the crown on his brow seemed to give back his youth and vigour to the old man, and the Goths found that a king of the type of Leovigild and Swinthila, a stern repressor of lawlessness and feudal anarchy, was reigning over them. Chindaswinth set himself at once to revindicate the royal prerogative, both against the great nobles and against the ecclesiastical synods. His hand fell heavily upon the traitors who, twelve years before, had betrayed Swinthila; he began to seek them out, and to execute them. At once the majority of the nobles of Spain burst into revolt. Some fled to Africa, and borrowed aid from the Byzantine exarch, others to the kings of the Franks. But Chindaswinth beat down all their risings, and quenched the flame of insurrection in the blood of two hundred nobles, and five hundred men of lesser rank, whom he handed over to the headsman. 'He tamed the Goths so that they dared attempt nothing more against him, as they had so often done with their kings, for the Goths are a hard-necked folk, and need a heavy yoke for their shoulders.' When the revolt was crushed, Chindaswinth compelled the bishops assembled in synod at Toledo to pronounce a solemn curse on all rebeUious nobles — 'tyranni,' he called them — and to decree the penalty of deprivation of orders and excommunication on all members of the clergy who should be found consenting to the plots of the 'tyrants' (646).

Chindaswinth's heavy hand won Spain seven years of peace in the latter end of his reign, and he was able to associate with himself on the throne his son Recceswinth, without any of the Goths daring to murmur. The father and son reigned together for three years, Recceswinth discharging the functions of king, while Chindaswinth gave himself up to works of piety. Their joint rule is marked by one very important incident, showing the completion of the process of unification, which had begun by the conversion of Reccared to Catholicism Goth and Spaniard were now so much assimilated to each other that the kings thought that they might for the future be ruled by a single code of laws. The races were beginning to be completely intermixed. Spanish counts and dukes are as numerous in the end of the period as Gothic bishops and abbots. The one race had no longer the monopoly of secular power, nor the other that of ecclesiastical promotion. Chindaswinth resolved to suspend the use of the old Roman law in his dominion, and to make all his subjects use Gothic law, though he introduced into the latter a considerable Roman element. The advantage of the new code of Chindaswinth was that the counts and vicarii, the king's immediate representatives, had for the future full jurisdiction over the whole native Spanish element, including the clergy; for the Spaniards were deprived of their Roman law-book, the Breviarium Alarici, and of their own courts and judges, and were subjected for legal, no less than for administrative or military matters, to the Gothic count. At the same time the prohibition against marriage between Goths and Provincials, which still nominally existed, though it was frequently broken since the time of

Leovigild, was removed, and all the king's subjects became equal in the eye of the law.

Chindaswinth died in 652, at the great age of ninety, unparalleled among Teutonic kings of his day. His son and colleague, Recceswinth, already well advanced down the vale of years, survived for twenty years more. He had the longest, quietest, and, in a way, the most prosperous reign of any of the Visigothic kings. Unlike his father, he was a devoted supporter of the Church, and, by the aid of the bishops, maintained his rule until the day of his death. But he was gradually letting slip once more all the royal powers which his father had with such trouble regained and restored. As he grew older the entire rule of the State dropped once more into the hands of bishops and synods. Recceswinth was busy all his days in building churches, and making great offerings to the saints. Chance has preserved to us one huge gold crown, with a dedicatory inscription, which he presented to the Virgin; it now forms the pride of the Cluny Museum at Paris, and is the best monument of the rude Teutonic art of the time, except, perhaps, the golden offerings of Agilulf and Theodelinda at Monza. Tradition speaks much of the spiritual blessings that were vouchsafed him. He and Archbishop Hildefuns were privileged to behold with their own eyes a miraculous vision of St. Leocadia, in the cathedral of Toledo. But meanwhile the kingly authority was once more vanishing away, and Recceswinth, provided that he at least enjoyed peace and pious leisure, seems to have cared little for the fate of his successors; he had himself no son to whom he could bequeath the throne. Personally he was popular — 'so mild and unpretending that he could hardly be told from one of his own subjects' — and he did not reap the fruit of the seeds of weakness that he was sowing. One insignificant rebellion alone interrupted the twenty peaceful years of his reign. But meanwhile the elements of dissolution were growing in strength. The nobles were once more reasserting their old claims to feudal independence, and the clergy were growing more and more domineering.

Recceswinth died in 672, leaving no heir, and there was much disputing among the nobles as to the election of his successor. Their choice fell at last upon Wamba, a man of mature age and high reputation, but he refused to take up the burden, in spite of the acclamations with which his name was received. At last, we are told, a certain duke drew his sword, and threatened to slay him, as a traitor to his nation and his duty, if he hesitated any longer to obey the will of the assembly. Wamba bowed to this form of persuasion, and accepted the crown.

We have more knowledge of Wamba's reign than of those of his predecessors and successors, as his biography, written by bishop Juhan of Toledo, has chanced to survive. We learn that he was a stern and hard master to the Goths, modelling himself upon the example of Chindaswinth, and that his reign was spent in a not unsuccessful attempt to recover the powers of the crown, which the pious Recceswinth had let slip. Rebellions were naturally rife when the king began to make his strong hand felt. The untameable Basques took to arms, and, while Wamba was busy in their mountains, a more dangerous rising took place in Septimania, where a certain count Hilderic raised the standard of revolt. The king sent against them a large army, under duke Paulus, a trusted officer of Roman blood. But, instead of attacking the rebels, the treacherous Paulus opened negotiations with them, debauched the chiefs of his own army, and suddenly proclaimed himself king. The challenge which he is said to have sent to Wamba deserves, perhaps, to be recorded for its strange and high-flown style. 'In the name of God,' wrote the usurper, 'Flavius Paulus, the mighty king of the East, greets Wamba, the king of the West. If thou hast traversed the rough, unpeopled waste of the mountains; if thou hast burst through woods and thickets like some strong lion; if thou hast tamed the swiftness of the wild goat, and the bounding stag, and the ravening boar and bear; if thou hast cast out the poison of snake and adder, — then make thyself known to me, thou man of arms, lord of the woods, and lover of the rocks, and hasten to meet me, that we may strive against each other in song, like nightingales. Wherefore, great king, stir up thy heart to strength, come down to the passes of the Pyrenees, and there shalt thou find an athlete with whom thou mayest worthily contend.'

Paulus was taken at his word, the 'lord of the woods' flew down in haste from the Basque mountains, and had thrown himself upon the rebel army before a single week was out. He forced the passes of the Pyrenees, driving the troops of Paulus before him, and then threw himself upon Narbonne, the capital of Septimania. The town was stormed by main force, after a siege of only three days, and, when it had fallen, Wamba recovered most of the other towns between the mountains and the Rhone. Paulus took refuge in the strong town of Nismes, and sent to ask help of the Franks. But the king was too quick for him. The Goths had grown skilled in the art of poliorcetics during their long struggle to expel the Byzantines from

Andalusia, and, by means of his siege-machines, Wamba took Nismes on the second day of its leaguer. Paulus and his chiefs then shut themselves up in the great Roman amphitheatre, which they had turned into a citadel. In a few days they were reduced by famine to throw themselves on the king's mercy. Wamba swore to spare their lives, and Paulus, with six-and-twenty counts and chiefs, gave themselves up to his mercy. The king had their beards and hair plucked out by the roots, and led them in triumph to Toledo, where they were marched through the town in chains and barefoot, clothed in shirts of sackcloth, with Paulus in front, wearing a leather crown, fastened on to his bare scalp by a pitch-plaster. The names of the six-and-twenty have survived. They included one bishop (a Goth), one priest of Roman blood, and twenty-four counts and chiefs, of whom seventeen have Gothic and seven Roman names.

This blow to the unruly Gothic nobles secured Wamba a quiet reign. He sat on the throne for seven years more (673-680), in peace and prosperity, endeavouring to palliate as best he could the diseases of the Visigothic state. Some of his laws show clearly enough the dangers of the times. So far had the class of small freeholders, who should have composed the bulk of the royal host, now disappeared that Wamba ordains that for the future slaves, as well as freemen, are to obey the royal summons to war. He even ordered that the bishops were to head their serfs in the field, a command which was deeply resented by the clergy, though a few generations later we find the practice common enough both in England, Gaul, and Germany.

Wamba lost his throne by a curious chance or, perhaps, by a still more curious plot. He fell ill in 680, was given over by the physicians, and fell into a long stupor. His attendants, in accordance with a frequent practice of the day, clad him in monkish robes and shore his hair to the tonsure, that he might die 'in religion.' Then before the breath was out of his body his most trusted officer, count Erwig, seized the royal hoard and declared himself king. Erwig was a great-nephew of king Chindaswinth, and looked upon himself as the heir of his cousin, Recceswinth, Wamba's predecessor. Yet he was not of pure Visigothic blood; his father Artavasdes was a refugee from Byzantium, whom Chindaswinth had taken into favour and honoured with the gift of his niece's hand. To the dismay of the palace the aged Wamba did not die: he recovered from his long stupor and began to mend. But the new king and the court clergy joined in assuring him that — even though he knew it not — he had become a monk, and could not resume his lay attire or his royal authority. Apparently Wamba was not above the superstitions of his day; he resigned himself to the idea, and retired to the monastery of Pampliega, where he lived to a great old age. It was afterwards rumoured, whether truly or falsely, that his long trance had not been natural, but that Erwig, seeing him on the bed of sickness, had given him a strong sleeping-potion, and deliberately enfrocked him by fraud in order to seize the crown.

Wamba was the last of the Visigoths; the four kings who followed him are mere shadows, crowned phantoms of whom we know little or nothing, for with Wamba's death the history of Spain sinks into the blackest obscurity. Their names were Erwig (680-87), Egica (687-701), Witiza (701-10), and Roderic (710-11). Of the last two we know little more than the names, but a few facts are ascertainable about Erwig and Egica.

The former, though he had nerve enough to seize the throne, had not courage to defend the royal rights. He let the crown sink back into the same state of dependence on the church into which it had fallen in the days of Sisinand and Recceswinth. He was ruled and managed by Julian, the bishop of Toledo, and appears to have been far less truly king of Spain than was that prelate. At Julian's behest he repealed the military laws of Wamba, because they bore hardly on the church, and recommenced the cruel persecution of the Jews, which always accompanied the accession of a priest-ridden king to the Spanish throne.

Apparently because he was tormented by his conscience on account of his dealings with king Wamba, Erwig chose Wamba's nephew and heir Egica as his successor. Having married him to his own daughter Cixilo, and made him swear to be kind to his wife and her brothers, Erwig laid down his crown and followed Wamba into a monastery.

Egica did not keep his vow; the moment that the Gothic assembly had recognised him as king he made the bishops absolve him from his oath, and then repudiated his wife and seized the property of his brothers-in-law, the sons of Erwig. Egica's reign was marked by the last and fiercest persecution of the Jews, in which the Visigothic king and clergy ever indulged. They voted at the sixteenth Council of Toledo (695) that all adult Jews should be seized and sold as slaves, while their children were to be separated from them and given to Christian families to rear in the true faith. Under this wicked law many Hebrews conformed, and still more fled over sea to Africa. The crime which brought down this doom upon them is said to have been a plot to betray Spain to foreign enemies. A new power had just arrived in the neighbourhood of the Visigothic realm; after fifty years of fighting, the terrible and fanatical Saracen had just overcome the Byzantine governors of Africa and stormed Carthage (695), the last stronghold of the East-Romans. It was to them, it would seem, that the Jews had sent messages, to beg them to cross the straits and put an end to the persecuting rule of the Spanish bishops. Nothing came of the invitation at this time; but the very fact that it was possible implied the gravest change in the situation of the Visigoths. For three generations they had been lying between two weak stationary and unenterprising neighbours, the faction-ridden Franks and the exarchs of Africa. How would the decaying realm fare when attacked by a new power in the first bloom of its fanatical youth and vigour?

Egica, however, was not destined to see the day of trial, nor was his son Witiza (701-710), of whom absolutely nothing is known, save that he was 'popular with the people but hated by the clergy.' The details of his evil doings are the mere imaginings of the monkish writers of the tenth century. In his own time they were not written down, for within two years of his death Spain had fallen under the power of the Moor, and no native chronicler had the heart to detail the last hours of the old Visigothic kingdom.

Witiza died young, leaving two sons who were not old enough to wear the crown. The Goths chose, therefore, as their king a certain count Roderic, who is a mere name to us — though the later chroniclers say, what is likely enough, that he was a kinsman of Chindaswinth and Erwig, and therefore hostile to the house of Wamba and Egica.

He reigned but eighteen months, for in his time came the evil day of Spain. The Saracen conquerors of Africa had spent the last twenty years in taming the Moors and Berbers. All the tribes had now bowed to their yoke and accepted Islam: swelled to vast numbers by the new converts, and yearning for fresh fields to conquer, the Arab chiefs were preparing to leap over the narrow strait of Gibraltar, and throw themselves upon the Spanish peninsula.

The romantic legends of a later generation tell a lurid tale of the wickedness of king Roderic, how he violated the daughter of count Julian, the governor of Ceuta, and how the outraged father betrayed his fortress, the key of the straits, to the Moors, and guided them over to the shores of Andalusia. All this is purely unhistoric. There is no reason for believing that Roderic was better or worse than his predecessors; of his character we know nothing: his very existence is only vouched for by a name and date in the list of Gothic kings, and by a few very rare coins.

This much we know, that ere he had been eighteen months on the throne the Moors landed in force at Calpe, thenceforth to be known as Jebel-Tarik (Gibraltar), from the name of their leader. They began to lay waste Andalusia, and Roderic came out against them at the head of the whole host of Visigothic Spain, which must now have been composed — as the laws of Wamba show us — of a few wealthy counts and bishops heading a great multitude of their serfs and dependants. The levy of the Visigoths proved far less able to resist the Moslems than had been the troops of Byzantium. On the banks of the Guadelete, near Medina Sidonia, Tarik gained a decisive victory. Roderic was slain or drowned in the pursuit, the Gothic army dispersed, and without having to fight any second battle the invaders mastered Spain. In less than two years (711-13) Tarik and his superior officer Musa, the governor of Africa, subdued the whole country; a few places, such as Cordova, Merida, and Saragossa, held out for a short space, but the Goths did not choose a new king or rally for any general effort of resistance. By 713 the only corner of Spain which had not submitted was the mountainous coast of the Bay of Biscay, where the untameable Basques and the inhabitants of the Asturias maintained a precarious liberty, preserved rather by their obscurity and the ruggedness of their homes than by the inability of the Moslems to complete their conquest.

So fell Visigothic Spain. The reasons are not far to seek: the kings — chosen from no single royal stock, but creatures of a chance election — had become powerless, the mere slaves of their clergy; the great nobles were disloyal and turbulent; the smaller freeholders had disappeared; the great mass of serfs had no heart to fight for their tyrannical masters. The State combined the weakness of a land under ecclesiastical governance with the turbulence of extreme feudalism. It would have fallen before the first strong invader in any case; if the Moor had not crossed the straits, Spain would probably have become an appanage of the Frankish realm under the mighty Mayors of the Palace, or the still mightier Charles the Great.

CHAPTER XIV: THE CONTEST OF THE EASTERN EMPIRE AND THE CALIPHATE — 641-717

Dynastic troubles after the death of Heraclius — Wars of Constantinus (Constans II.) with the Caliphate — His publication of the 'Type' — His invasion of Italy and war with the Lombards — Reign of Constantine V. — His successful defence of Constantinople — Tyranny of Justinian II. — His deposition — Usurpations of Leontius and Tiberius — Justinian restored — Anarchy follows his murder — Rise of Leo the Isaurian.

At the moment of the death of the unfortunate Heraclius the East-Roman Empire was left in a most disadvantageous position for resisting the vigorous attack which the Moslems were pressing against its remaining provinces. Yielding to the influence of his ambitious wife Martina, the old emperor had left the imperial power divided between Heraclius Constantinus, the offspring of his first wife, and Martina's eldest son Heracleonas. The elder of the young emperors was twenty-nine, the younger only sixteen. Their joint reign opened ill, for Heraclius Constantinus and his step-mother, who acted in all things as the representative of her young son, were at open discord. But before three months had elapsed Heraclius Constantinus died; it is probable that his decease was due to natural causes, but the Byzantine public believed otherwise, and Martina was openly accused of having poisoned her stepson. Her conduct was not such as to render the charge improbable, for she at once proclaimed her son Heracleonas sole emperor, although Heraclius Constantinus had left two young boys behind him.

This was more than the Constantinopolitans would stand. Rioting at once broke out, and the senate, which about this time assumes an independent attitude, very different from its usual obedient impotence, made the most strongly worded representations to Martina and her son, threatening the worst consequences if the sons of Heraclius Constantinus were excluded from the succession. In terror of their lives Martina and Heracleonas bowed to the popular will, and allowed the boy Constantinus to be crowned as the colleague of his uncle; he was no more than eleven years old at his coronation.

The joint rule of the two lads, under the regency of Martina, lasted less than a year. In September 642 the senate executed a coup d'etat; Martina and her son were seized and banished to Cherson. On the accusation that they had poisoned Heraclius Constantinus they were cruelly mutilated: the tongue of the empress and the nose of Heracleonas were slit — the first instance of such a treatment of royal personages, but by no means the last in Byzantine history.

Constantinus IV., or as he was more usually but less accurately styled Constans II., thus became the sole ruler of the East ere he had finished his twelfth year. The real government was, for some time, carried on by the senate — a fact which vouches both for the loyalty of the empire to the house of Heraclius and for the great rise in the power of the senate during the last two or three generations. In earlier days there is no doubt that some powerful general would have seized the throne. But Constantinus, though his minority was not untroubled by revolts, was permitted to grow up to man's estate, and to assume in due course the personal control of the empire.

It is astonishing that more evils did not come upon the State during the boyhood of Constantinus. The energetic caliph Omar was still urging on the Arabs to conquest, and with no firm hand at the helm it might have been expected that the ship of the East-Roman state would have run upon the breakers. But though the Saracens still continued to make way, the rate of their progress was checked. Alexandria, the last Christian stronghold in Egypt, had fallen during the short reign of Heracleonas. The resources of the empire were drained for an attempt to recover it, and in the second year of Constantinus a considerable expedition, under a general named Manuel, fell unexpectedly upon the place and retook it. The Arab governor of Egypt, the celebrated Amrou, had to besiege the place for more than a year before it yielded. Irritated by its long resistance he cast down its walls and massacred many of its inhabitants. It would seem that the Saracen arms were for the next few years more engrossed in the final conquest of eastern Persia than in assaulting the Roman empire. It was not till Yezdigerd, the last of the Sassanian kings, had been defeated and stripped of the farthest corners of his dominion that the Arabs turned once more to the West.

The only point of the Roman frontier which was seriously attacked was Africa. The sandy waste between Egypt and Barca had less terrors for the Arab than for any other invader. Encouraged by the fact that Gregory the exarch of Africa had rebelled and proclaimed himself emperor, so that he could hope for no aid from Constantinople, the Saracen general, Abdallah Abu-Sahr crossed the Libyan desert and attacked Barca. Gregory came out against him, but was defeated and slain: Barca and Tripoli fell to the invaders, but Carthage and the rest of Africa relapsed into allegiance to Constantinus, when the usurper was slain. The Saracen frontier stood still at the Syrtes (646-7), and it took half a century more of fighting before the Romans were evicted from the western half of their African possessions.

Meanwhile the caliph Omar had died, and his weaker successor, Othman, proved less dangerous to the Eastern empire. His generals, however, invaded Cyprus, and overran the island: unable to permanently hold it, because of the preponderance of the Byzantine fleet, they contented themselves with exacting a tribute, and retired (642). But encouraged by the result of this, their first expedition by sea, the Saracens commenced to build a great war fleet, and in a few years they were in a condition to dispute the command of the eastern Mediterranean with the Roman galleys, who since the destruction of the Vandals in 533 had known no rivals on the sea.

Meanwhile Constantinus had grown up to manhood, and, luckily for the empire, proved to be the kind of sovereign required in those days of adversity. He was a stern warlike prince, possessed of no small share of the military ability of his grandfather Heraclius. He was always in the field, headed his own forces by sea no less than by land, and deserved success by his courage and perseverance if he did not always obtain it. Occasionally he was harsh and cruel, but such faults are more easily pardoned in an emperor who had to face such a time of peril than are cowardice and indolence.

In 652 Constantinus sent a second expedition against Alexandria: it was met at sea off the Canopic mouth of the Nile by a great Saracen fleet, gathered from the ports of Syria and Egypt, and defeated with great loss. Three years later the enemy took the offensive, Muavia, the governor of Syria, gathered a great armada to attack the southern coast of Asia Minor, while he himself marched by land to force the passes of the Taurus and invade Cappadocia. Constantinus put to sea with every ship he could launch, and met the Saracens at Phoenix, off the Lycian shore. Here the greatest naval battle which the Mediterranean had seen since the day of Actium was fought: the two fleets grappled, and the crews struggled desperately hand to hand for many hours. Constantinus was in the thickest of the fighting, his imperial galley was boarded, and he only escaped by throwing off his purple mantle, and springing into another ship when his own was captured. At last the Saracens won a decisive victory, and it seemed as if they were about to become the masters of the Aegean (655). Even before the battle Rhodes had fallen into their hands, and the long-prostrate Colossus had been sold for old brass to a Jewish dealer, and exported to Syria to be melted down.

The empire, however, was to be saved from the humiliation of seeing a hostile fleet approach the Dardanelles for yet twenty years. In 656 the caliph Othman was murdered, and his death was immediately followed by a savage civil war among the Saracens. The two claimants for the vacant dignity of 'Successor of the Prophet,' were Muavia, who held Syria, and Ali, Mohammed's son-in-law, who held Mesopotamia and the new Arab capital of Kufa. Engrossed in his struggle with Ali, Muavia was fain to leave the Roman empire unmolested. In 659 he bought peace from Constantinus on the curious terms that he should pay for every day that the peace lasted a horse and a slave. This treaty proved the salvation of the empire: for the first time for twenty-seven years it was free from Saracen war, and Constantinus could pause and take thought for the reorganisation of his much-harassed dominions. In the five years of peace which were now granted to him, he contrived to make a considerable improvement in their condition.

When he took stock of his realm, Constantinus found that in the East five great districts were irretrievably lost: the nearer half of the exarchate of Africa, from Tripoli to the Libyan desert, Egypt, Syria, and the greater part of Roman Armenia had fallen into the power of Saracens. Moreover, in Europe, the troubled years between 610 and 659 had brought about the complete loss of the inland parts of the Balkan peninsula. The Slavs, whose incursions had already grown so dangerous in the reign of Maurice, had now obtained complete possession of the whole of Moesia, and of the inland parts of Thrace and Macedon. Their settlements extended to within a few miles of the gates of Adrianople and Thessalonica, both of which cities they from time to time besieged without success. They had even encroached south of Mount Olympus, and thrust forward their colonies into some parts of Greece. The imperial dominions were restricted to a coast-slip running all round the peninsula, from Spalato in Dalmatia to Odessus on the Black Sea. In the West we have seen, while detailing the history of the Lombards, that the East-Romans now preserved only the exarchate of Ravenna, the duchies of Rome and Naples, the southern point of Italy, and the islands of Sicily and Sardinia. Recognising that he must look to reorganisation rather than to reconquest for restoring the strength of the empire, Constantinus devoted himself to securing his borders. The moment that the civil war of the Arabs broke out, and left him free to move elsewhere, he marched against the Slavs of the Balkans, defeated them, and reduced them to pay tribute. It was hopeless to dream of driving them back across the Danube, and the emperor was contented to accept the existing state of things, and to secure the coast-land of Thrace and Macedonia from further molestation, by imposing a line of demarcation between the Slavonic tribes and the much-reduced provinces (657-8).

The emperor's attention was now drawn to Africa and Italy. His presence was needed there no less than in the Balkan peninsula, if the Lombard and the Saracen were to be finally checked from advancing. In 662 he sailed for the West, and was busy there for the next six years, right down to the moment of his death. Constantinus hated the capital: he was sufficiently autocratic in his notions to dislike the control that the senate had been wont to exercise over him in earlier years, and he cordially detested the mob of Constantinople. He had fallen out with them on the same grounds that had once proved fatal to the popularity of Zeno. The city was torn with the religious feuds between the Orthodox and the Monothelites, and the emperor, to calm the storm, had issued an edict of comprehension called 'the Type,' in which he forbade all mention of either the single or the double will as residing in the person of Our Lord. Without satisfying the heretics, the Type succeeded in irritating the Orthodox to great fury: they persistently accused Constantinus of being a Monothelite himself, and made his life miserable by their clamour. There was yet a third reason for his quitting Byzantium. In 660 he had conceived suspicions, whether true or false we know not, that his brother Theodosius was plotting against him. He promptly condemned the young prince to death, but after the execution his mind had no rest: we are told that his dreams were always haunted by the spectre of his brother, and that the palace where the deed was done grew insupportably hateful to him. If these tales be true, he left Constantinople to seek ease of spirit, no less than to restore the failing powers of the empire in the West.

It was probably in the period 657-662, before his departure from the capital, that Constantinus recast the provincial administration of the empire in accordance with the needs of the times. It seems that the institution of the 'Themes,' or new provinces, must date from this, the only space of rest and rearrangement to be found in a long age of wars. The old provinces, as arranged by Diocletian, and somewhat modified by Justinian, had been small, and in each of them civil and military powers were kept separate, the local garrison not being under the control of the local administrator. The needs of the long Persian and Saracen wars had led to the practical supersession of the civil governors by the military commanders, for it was absolutely necessary that the men trusted with the preservation of the empire should be able to control its local administration and finance. The new provinces were few and large, and ruled by governors, who had civil as well as military authority. They were called 'themes,' after the name of the military divisions which occupied them, a 'theme' being originally a force of some 4000 regular cavalry detailed for the protection of a district. The names of the original Asiatic themes easily explain themselves, 'Anatolikon' and 'Armeniakon' the two largest, were the regions garrisoned by the 'army of the East' and the 'army of Armenia.' 'Thrakesion,' farther west, shows that the original 'army of Thrace' had been brought over into Asia to give aid against the Saracen. 'Bucellarion' was named after the Bucellarii, a corps originally formed of Teutonic auxiliaries. The theme called Obsequium (Opsikion) was held by the Imperial Guard. Only the Cibyrhaeote theme, along the southern coast of Asia Minor, was named from a town, and not from the troops who garrisoned it. In the West, there seem to have been originally three themes in the Balkan peninsula, Thrace, Illyricum, and Hellas, and three beyond it, Ravenna, Sicily, and Africa. Each theme was governed by a strategos, whose military title shows his military character, and was garrisoned by its own local force of regular troops, the core of which was in each case a division of 4000 heavy cavalry. The full force of the twelve themes would give some 48,000 horsemen for the field, in addition to the less important infantry, the local militia used for holding fortresses, and the irregular hired bands of barbarian auxiliaries of many different races.

Constantinus was the only Eastern emperor who ever paid a large and even preponderant share of attention to his Western dominions. The long stay of six years which he made in Italy and Sicily caused his Eastern subjects to suppose that he had designs of restoring Rome to the position of capital of the empire, or even, perhaps, of raising Syracuse to that distinction. Such a project seems so inconvenient from geographical reasons, that we can hardly credit it; probably Constantinus' personal dislike for Constantinople, while sufficing to keep him away from it, did not make him scheme to transfer the seat of empire elsewhere.

There is no doubt, however, that Constantinus was determined to reassert the supremacy of the empire in Italy against the Lombards, and also to take care that the exarchs and the popes should not grow too strong and independent. Even before he sailed for Italy his jealousy of the power of the papacy had been shown by his dealings with Pope Martin I. That prelate had dared to hold a synod at Rome, in which he condemned the 'Type' or Edict of Comprehension issued by the emperor (649). Constantinus never pardoned this: he bided his time, directed the exarch to seize the person of Martin at a convenient opportunity, and had him shipped off to Constantinople. There he was tried for contumacy, thrown into chains, and banished to Cherson, in the Crimea, where he died in exile (655).

Constantinus left the Bosphorus in 662 with a large army, and sailed for Taranto. There he landed, and at once fell upon the duchy of Benevento, the southernmost of the Lombard States in Italy. The time of his attack happened to be unfortunate, for Grimoald, duke of Benevento, had seized the Lombard crown, and his son Romuald was ruling the duchy under him. For once in a way, therefore, Pavia and Benevento were united and ready to act together. The Lombard historian, Paulus Diaconus, has preserved the details of the campaign of Constantinus — whom he usually styles Constans, as do so many other writers. The emperor captured, one after another, all the Lombard cities of south Italy, including Luceria, the chief town of Apulia. He drove Romuald into Benevento, and held him closely besieged there, till he gave up his sister Gisa as a hostage, and promised to pay tribute. He would not have granted such easy terms, but for the fact that he had learnt that king Grimoald, with the whole force of Lombardy, was marching against him.

Departing from Benevento, Constantinus moved on Rome, leaving a part of his army under a Persian exile named Sapor to watch the Lombards. This division was cut to pieces at Forino, and after he had received the news, the emperor seems to have given up his idea of re-conquering central Italy. He contented himself with visiting Rome and receiving the homage of pope Vitalian, who met him at the sixth milestone, at the head of the whole Roman people, and escorted him into the city. But Rome took little profit from the advent of an emperor, a sight it had not seen for two hundred years. Constantinus plundered it of many ornaments, and in particular stripped the Pantheon of its tiles of gilded bronze and sent them to Constantinople (663).

After staying only twelve days in the ancient capital, the emperor turned on his heel, and instead of proceeding against the northern Lombards, led his army through Naples into Lucania and Bruttium as far as Reggio. King Grimoald and his son do not seem to have molested him in this long march. Constantinus then crossed the straits of Messina into Sicily, and established himself at Syracuse, which he made his residence for more than four years [664-8]. His attention was engrossed by the forward movement of the Saracens in Africa. Muavia, having secured the sole caliphate by the death of his rival Ali, had at last recommenced his attacks on the empire in 663. His troops pushed forward in Africa and seized Carthage, from which, however, Constantinus succeeded in driving them out, and once more pushed them back to Tripoli. It must have been in this African war that he spent the treasures which he is said to have wrung out of the people of Sicily, Sardinia, and south Italy by 'exaction such as had never been heard of before,' even tearing the sacramental plate from the churches, and selling as slaves those who refused to pay. These harsh proceedings did as much to weaken the power of the empire in the West as the military successes of Constantinus did to strengthen it.

It was at Syracuse that Constantinus met his end. While he was bathing in the baths that were called Daphne, his attendant Andreas smote him on the head with his marble soap-box, so that the skull was broken, and then fled away.

The blow was fatal, and with this strange death perished that plan of restoring the empire in the West which had been the favourite scheme of Constantinus. His murder was probably the result of a conspiracy, for when it was known, an Armenian officer named Mezecius proclaimed himself emperor in Sicily, and reigned there for a few months.

For the last five years of Constantinus' long absence in the West there had been grievous trouble with the Saracens in Asia Minor, against which the caliph Muavia had launched his hosts for five successive summers. The raids of his generals reached as far as Amorium in Phrygia, which was stormed by the Arabs, and promptly retaken by the Romans in 668. The nominal control of affairs in Asia had been left to the emperor's eldest son Constantine, when his father sailed to the West. On the news of the murder at Syracuse and the Usurpation of Mezecius, Constantine, now aged eighteen, sailed in person to Sicily, put down and executed the usurper, and then promptly returned to Constantinople. He had been beardless when he set out, but returned next year with his face covered with hair, wherefore the people of the capital gave him the nickname of 'Pogonatus,' the bearded, by which he is generally known. Curiously enough the name would have been far better applied to his father whose beard was enormous, while that of Constantine V. did not exceed a very moderate limit.

Constantine Pogonatus was his father's true son, a hard-working, hard-fighting, and somewhat high-handed Caesar, who kept the empire well together, and spent all his energy in holding the Saracens in check, a task in which he won great success. He reigned for seventeen years (668-85), of which the first ten were a time of unbroken war with the Caliphate. The first beginning of this struggle was not very favourable for the empire; in 669-70 the generals of Muavia pushed their way as far as the sea of Marmora, and in 672 the Caliph thought success so nearly in his grasp that he prepared for a formal siege of Constantinople, the second that it had undergone in the century. Using the harbour of Cyzicus as their base, the Saracens, under a general named Abderrhaman, and the Caliph's son Yezid, beleaguered the city for six months (April-September, 673). They were finally forced to retire after a naval engagement in which the Imperial galleys had the better, largely owing, it is said, to the newly invented 'Greek fire,' by which they burnt many of the Moslem ships. When forced away from the Bosphorus, the Saracens fell back on Cyzicus, which they succeeded in holding for no less than four years, making occasional sallies from it towards Constantinople, of which every single one was repelled with loss by the emperor. At last the Arabs, after losing their general, and seeing Abu Eyub, one of the last surviving companions of Mohammed, perish before the walls, raised the siege. Their fleet was destroyed by a storm off the Lycian Coast: their land-army was attacked on its retreat by the East Romans, and defeated with a loss of 30,000 men.

So great was the blow inflicted on the Caliph by the entire failure of his army before Constantinople, that he was glad to conclude an ignominious peace with the emperor, by which he engaged to pay 3000 pounds of gold to Constantine, and to send him fifty Arab horses for every year that the treaty lasted (678).

The fidelity of the East Romans to the house of Heraclius was thus justified by the victory of Constantine; it is a pity that only a very meagre account of his campaign has come down to us, owing to the dearth of chroniclers in the seventh century. We know, however, that the fame of his triumph went all over Europe, and that ambassadors came from the Avars, the Lombards, and even the distant Franks to congratulate him on beating off an attack which had threatened serious consequences to the whole of Christendom.

For the remainder of his reign Constantine enjoyed a well-earned peace, disturbed only by some slight bickering with a new enemy, the Bulgarians. This Ugrian tribe, who had dwelt for the last two centuries beyond the Danube, crossed the river in the end of Constantine's reign, and threw themselves upon the Slavonic tribes who held Moesia. They subdued the Slavs without much difficulty, and defeated a Roman army which Constantine led by sea to the mouth of the Danube. Recognising that it was impossible to reconquer the long-lost Moesia, the emperor made peace with Isperich, the Bulgarian king, and allowed him to settle without further opposition in the land between the Danube and the Balkans, where the Slavs had hitherto held possession (679). A new Bulgarian nation was gradually formed by the intermixture of the conquering tribe and their subjects: when formed, it displayed a Slavonic rather than a Ugrian type, and spoke a Slavonic not a Ugrian tongue.

The later years of Constantine V. were better known to contemporaries as the time of the holding of the council of Constantinople, than as the time of the foundation of the new Bulgarian kingdom. To settle the dispute on the divine and human wills of Christ, the emperor summoned an oecumenical synod, at which the Western churches were well represented. It finally condemned the Monothelite heresy, which for the future ceased to be the great question debated between the churches (680-1). But a new controversy, that on Iconoclasm, was ere long to break out.

To the misfortune of the empire the able and hard-working Constantine died in 685, at the comparatively early age of thirty-six. We hear little that is unfavourable to him from any chronicler: his sole crime seems to have been the cruel act of slitting the noses of his two brothers Heraclius and Tiberius in 680, to disqualify them from holding imperial power. They had hitherto been nominally the colleagues of Constantine, and were honoured with the title of Caesars, but in the interests of his own son Justinian, now a growing boy, the emperor determined to make it impossible for them to aspire to the supreme power. It appears to have been a cruel and unjustifiable act, and unless the Caesars had given provocation, a fact of which we have no hint in any chronicler, it was a grievous blot on the otherwise excellent character of Constantine V.

The young Justinian, second of that name, mounted his father's throne in 685, when only in his seventeenth year. The accession of this prince was a fearful misfortune for the empire. He possessed the qualities of his grandfather Constantinus in an exaggerated form, being arbitrary, cruel, reckless, and high-handed, yet so brave and capable that his throne was not easy to shake. He started on his career too young, and might have come to better things if his father had lived for another ten years; but, abandoned to his own devices ere he was well out of his boyhood, he developed into a bloodthirsty tyrant. The first few years of his reign, ere he had felt his feet and fully realised his own desires, were comparatively uneventful. The Saracens were occupied in civil wars since the death of Muavia, and gave no trouble: the caliph Abd-el-Melik was only too glad to renew with Justinian the treaty that his predecessor had made with Constantine V. Unmolested by the Saracens, Justinian sent armies into Iberia and Albania, the Christian kingdoms under the Caucasus, and compelled them to pay him tribute. Soon after he undertook in person a great expedition against the Bulgarians, designing to push the Roman boundary once more to the Danube. He was very successful, beating the enemy in the field, and bringing back more than 30,000 captives, from whom he organised an auxiliary force for service in Asia.

Justinian's triumph over the Bulgarians emboldened him to undertake the greater scheme of winning back Syria from the Saracens. In 693 he picked a quarrel with the Caliph on the most frivolous grounds: when the annual payment due under the treaty of 686 was tendered to him, he refused to receive the money, because the coins were not the old Roman solidi, which had hitherto circulated in Syria and Egypt, and still formed the bulk of the Saracen currency, but new Arab 'dirhems' with Abd-el-Melik's name upon them, which the caliph had lately begun to strike. But any pretext was good enough for Justinian: he declared war with a light heart, and led his armies in person across the Taurus into Cilicia. At Sebastopolis near Tarsus he suffered a fearful defeat, mainly caused by the desertion to the Saracens of the unwilling recruits whom he had enlisted from among the captives of the Bulgarian War. When he had rallied his army Justinian was cruel and illogical enough to order those of the corps who had not deserted to be put to death — lest they might follow their comrades' example in the next battle (693). In the next year the emperor lost Roman Armenia by the revolt of its Governor, a native Armenian named Sumpad, who deserted to the Saracens. Other disasters followed, and the Arabs harried the 'Anatolic' and 'Armeniac' themes.

Meanwhile the young emperor had been making himself most unpopular at home by the exactions necessary for the support of his unlucky war, and still more by persisting in building expensive and unnecessary palaces in the capital, while the war still raged. His two finance ministers, Theodotus, a lapsed abbot who had quitted his monastery, and the eunuch Stephanus, are reported to have gone to the extremes of cruelty in dealing with the citizens. It is said that Theodotus was wont to torture defaulting tax-payers by hanging them over smoky fires and half stifling them. Stephanus preferred the rod: it is said that he even presumed on one occasion — during Justinian's absence — to seize and beat the empress-dowager Anastasia. The emperor only punished him by ordering him to complete, at his own expense, a building on which he was then engaged.

It was not only by heaping taxes on his subjects that Justinian made himself unpopular. He had a mania for seizing and imprisoning on suspicion senators and other important personages, and he was so merciless in dealing with military officers who met with any defeat, that to accept a command under him was considered the shortest way to the dungeon or the block. Meanwhile his ill-luck in the Saracen war made him as much detested by the soldiery as he was dreaded by their officers. In 695 a distinguished general named Leontius, the conqueror of Iberia and Albania, was ordered by Justinian to take command of the theme of Hellas. Regarding this charge as a mere preliminary to disgrace and execution, Leontius in sheer desperation planned a coup d'etat. At the head of a few dozen followers he burst open the prisons, and made a dash at the palace. Justinian was taken completely by surprise; he fell into the hands of Leontius, who slit his nose, and banished him to the distant fortress of Cherson, in the Crimea. His two detested ministers, Theodotus and Stephanus, were torn to pieces and burnt by the populace.

With the fall of Justinian II. began twenty-two years of anarchy and disaster for the empire. Hitherto Constantinople had been singularly fortunate in escaping the consequences of military revolts and changes of dynasty. With the single exception of the usurpation of the tyrant Phocas, and his deposition by Heraclius, there had been no cases of the transfer of the imperial crown by violence for more than three hundred years. All the earlier emperors of the East had been either designated by their predecessors or peaceably elected by the senate and army. It was now to be seen how fatal was the breaking-up of the rule of orderly succession: in the next twenty-two years there were no less than five revolutions at home, and abroad many grave disasters cut the empire short.

The three-years' rule of Leontius was mainly distinguished by the final loss of Carthage and Africa. Already in Justinian's time the province had been invaded and partially overrun by the generals of the Caliph. In 697 Carthage fell: it was recovered for a moment by an expedition sent out by Leontius, but in 698 it fell permanently into the hands of the Saracens. The Roman generals, however, escaped by sea with the main body of their army. Fearing to face the wrath of Leontius with such a tale of disaster, the returning officers conspired against him. They sailed to the Bosphorus, where their arrival was quite unexpected, caught the emperor, slit his nose, and threw him into a monastery. In his stead they proclaimed the admiral Tiberius Apsimarus as sovereign (698).

Tiberius II., a very capable man, clung to the throne for seven years. He was fortunate in his war with the Saracens: his armies defeated those of the Caliph, recovered Cilicia, and even occupied Antiocb. But this success abroad did not save Tiberius from the wonted end of usurpers. He was overthrown by the banished and mutilated Justinian II., who now reappears upon the stage in a most startling fashion.

Justinian had been consigned by Leontius to the remote fortress of Cherson — the modern Sebastopol — on the north shore of the Black Sea. But being carelessly guarded, he succeeded in escaping, and reaching the court of the Chagan of the Khazars, the Tartar tribe who dwelt on the lower Volga and the shores of the sea of Azoff. In spite of his mutilated nose he succeeded in gaining the good graces of the Chagan, and received the hand of his sister in marriage. Hearing of this Tiberius II. sent a huge bribe to the Tartar, to persuade him to surrender his guest. The treacherous barbarian consented, and despatched an officer to arrest Justinian. But the exile got wind of the plot through a message from his wife, and instead of allowing himself to be seized, slew the Chagan's emissary, and escaped to sea in an open boat, with half-a-dozen attendants. A storm arose, and the little vessel seemed likely to founder. 'Make a vow to God that if you escape you will forgive your enemies,' said one of Justinian's companions to him, as the boat began to fill. 'No,' replied the reckless and inflexible exile, 'if I spare a single one of them when my time comes, may God sink me here and now.' The storm abated, the boat came safe to land, and

Justinian fell into the hands of Terbel, the king of the Bulgarians. Terbel lent him an army with which to try his fortune, and with its aid he advanced to the gates of Constantinople. The city was betrayed to him by partisans within the walls, and he succeeded in getting possession of the palace, and of the person of Tiberius II. Justinian then dragged out of his cloister the deposed usurper Leontius, bound him and Tiberius hand and foot, and laid them before his throne in the Hippodrome. There he sat in triumph with his feet on the necks of the vanquished Caesars, while his partisans chanted 'Thou shalt trample on the Lion and the Asp,' an allusion to the names of the two fallen rulers (Leontius and Apsimarus). The two prisoners were then beheaded (705).

During his first reign Justinian had chastised his subjects with whips, it was with scorpions that he now afflicted them. He had returned from exile in a mood of reckless cruelty; the vow he had made was kept with rigid accuracy. Every one who had been concerned in his deposition ten years before was sought out, tortured, and put to death. Some of his doings rose to a monstrous pitch of inhumanity: the chief men of Cherson, who had offended him during his exile, were bound on spits and roasted: many patricians were sewed up into sacks and cast into the Bosphorus.

It is astonishing to find that the second reign of Justinian lasted for more than five years. His tyranny was such that an instant explosion of popular wrath might have been expected. But if reckless, he was also active, suspicious, and strong-handed, and crushed many plots before they could come to a head. At last he fell before a military revolt: the army, headed by a general named Philippicus, disavowed its allegiance, seized the tyrant, and beheaded him. His little six-year-old son, Tiberius, whom the Chagan's sister had borne him, was torn from sanctuary, and murdered. Thus perished the house of Heraclius. after it had given five rulers to the empire during a century of rule (610-711). It had done much to save the state from the Saracens: all its members, even Justinian, had been men of ability, and Heraclius himself, Constantinus-Constans, and Constantine V. had each borne his part in the long struggle with credit, if not with complete success.

There now followed six years of complete anarchy (711-17), during which the imperial annals are filled by the obscure names of Philippicus(711-13), Artemius Anastasius (713-715) and Theodosius III. (715-17). Each was the creature of a conspiracy, and each fell by the same means by which he had been uplifted. They were all feeble and incompetent sovereigns, far below the rank of the two earlier usurpers, Leontius and Tiberius Apsimarus. The importance of their reigns lies not in their struggle with each other, but in the general collapse of the system of defence of the empire against the Saracen, the natural result of the employment of the whole

army in civil war. The generals of the caliphs Welid and Soliman, the sons of Abd-al-Melik (705-17) burst through the boundaries of the empire on every point. In 711 Sardinia, the westernmost province of the empire since the loss of Africa, was subdued by the Arabs. In the same year they crossed the Taurus, and sacked Tyana in Cappadocia. In 712 they overran Pontus and captured Amasia, in 713 Antioch in Pisidia fell, and with it much of southern Asia Minor. It appeared as if with the downfall of the house of Heracllus the power of self-defence had been taken away from the East Romans. Nor was the lowest depth yet reached.

Emboldened by the easy successes of his armies over those of the ephemeral sovereigns who followed Justinian II., the caliph Soliman at last resolved to fit out an expedition on the largest scale against Constantinople. A hundred thousand men advanced by land from Tarsus, while a fleet of more than 1000 sail gathered in the ports of Syria, and sailed round Asia Minor into the Aegean. The Caliph's brother Moslemah was to head the whole expedition. Cappadocia was already in Saracen hands, and the Caliph's vanguard was occupied with the siege of Amorium, the chief stronghold of Phrygia. That town, indeed, was saved from destruction by Leo the Isaurian, the governor of the Anatolic theme. But soon after, while the Arabs were still advancing, this same Leo, after concluding a private truce with the invaders, proclaimed himself emperor, and advanced against Constantinople, instead of reserving his strength to resist the armies of Soliman (716).

Once more fortune favoured the newest rising against the emperor of the day. The troops of Leo beat those of Theodosius III., and then the latter voluntarily abdicated and sent to offer his crown to the victor. He was a mild and virtuous man, who had been raised to the purple against his will by his military partisans, and longed to return to his obscurity, feeling himself destitute of the power needed to cope with the insurgents, and still more unable to face the impending Saracen invasion.

Accordingly the senate and the patriarch formally elected the rebel Leo as emperor, and set him on the throne which had already changed masters seven times in the last twenty-two years. At length the empire had found a master who could defend what he had won, and was fully able to transmit his power to his heirs. The armament of Moslemah might be awaited without dismay, for the state was once more in the hands of one who could be trusted to use its resources aright. Leo was to dissipate once and for all the Saracen storm-cloud, and to free Constantinople from all danger from the East for more than three hundred years. But his achievements demand a chapter to themselves.

CHAPTER XV: THE HISTORY OF THE GREAT MAYORS OF THE PALACE — 656-720

The Mayor Grimoald unsuccessfully endeavours to make his son king of Austrasia — Decadence of the house of the Merovings — Ebroin and his tyrannical rule in Neustria — Long civil wars — Rise of Pippin the younger and his victory at Testry — The ascendency of Pippin: his successes in consolidating the kingdom — Missionary enterprises in Germany — Civil wars at the death of Pippin — Final triumph of his son Charles Martel.

In 656 died King Sigibert III., the first Meroving king of Austrasia who had been but a puppet in the hands of his Mayor of the Palace. At his death was made, a full century too soon, the first attempt of that great family which had of late held all real power to add the shadow to the substance by assuming the royal name. King Sigibert had only reached the age of twenty-seven when he died: his son and heir, named Dagobert after his grandfather, was but eight. Taking advantage of the boy's youth, the Mayor Grimoald had him stolen away from his country by the hands of a bishop, and lodged him in an Irish monastery, where his head was shorn, and he was consecrated as a monk. Having got rid of the rightful heir, Grimoald induced his partisans to raise his own son Childebert on the shield, and salute him as king of Austrasia. But the times were not yet ripe: Grimoald had many bitter enemies, and the majority of the people were not yet accustomed to the idea of dethroning the ancient house of the Merovings. Within a few days after the usurpation, Grimoald was seized by a band of Austrasian nobles, cast into fetters, and hurried off to Paris, where his captors laid him before the feet of king Chlodovech II. of Neustria, the brother of the deceased Sigibert.

Chlodovech, a cruel and debauched young man, slew Grimoald with horrid tortures. It appeared as if the greatness of the house of Pippin and Arnulf was destined to be extinguished with the life of its chief: but the Fates willed otherwise. Within a few months of the execution of the great Mayor, king Chlodovech died, leaving the diadem to his little son Chlothar III. All the Frankish realms were once more under the nominal rule of a child, and the last chance of the survival of the kingly power was gone, in Neustria now as well as in the Eastern realm. The house of the Austrasian mayors was within a few years to raise its head once more.

Meanwhile the minority of Chlothar III. was destined to be a time of storm and trouble. Before he had been four years on the throne his Austrasian subjects determined that they would once more have a king of their own, and not obey orders from Soissons or Paris. Accordingly they took Childerich, the younger brother of Chlothar, and crowned him as king of the Eastern realm. The joint reign of the boys Chlothar III. and Childerich I. lasted for ten years: at first the kingdoms were kept in a certain measure of peace by the queen-mother, Bathildis, an Anglo-Saxon lady of great virtue and ability. But after four years, worn out by the troublous task of reconciling the opposing factions of the nobihty, she retired into a nunnery, and when her gentle influence was removed, trouble at once broke out.

The man mainly responsible for the evil time of civil strife that followed was Ebroin, Mayor of the Palace in Neustria. He was a cruel, ambitious, vindictive noble, who aspired to much the same position that Pippin the Old and Grimoald had once occupied in Austrasia. Strong by the power of using the royal name, by his numerous comitatus, and by his unscrupulous readiness to strike down all who opposed him, he exercised for several years what the contemporary chroniclers called a 'tyranny.' He was, we are told, so greedy of money, that to him the man with the longer purse always seemed to have the better cause. Nor was greed his worst fault; however small the offence, any crime committed by a man that he suspected or envied brought the invariable penalty of death. His mandates were as capricious as they were harsh, for example he once issued an order that no Frank of Burgundy should approach the king's person without the mayor's express permission. This domination of Ebroin lasted until his young master, Chlothar III., of whose personal influence orcharacter we hear naught, died on the verge of manhood in 670.

The autocratic Mayor of the Palace at once raised on the shield Theuderich, Chlothar's youngest brother. But the majority of the Neustrians saw their chance of getting rid of their tyrant. Rising under the leadership of Leodegar, bishop of Autun, they proclaimed Childerich of Austrasia king of the West, as well as of the East Franks, and called him in to their aid. The personal following of Ebroin was too weak to resist the Neustrian and Austrasian nobles combined. He and his puppet king were made captive, and both compelled to take monastic vows — Ebroin at Luxeuil, Theuderich at St. Denis. It might have been better in the end for the Franks if Leodegar had been less merciful to the vanquished Mayor: he was yet to give much trouble.

For three years Childerich reigned over all the Franks: he reached manhood in this time, but the power of the kingship did not pass into his own hand. The Mayor Wulfoald ruled in Austrasia, while bishop Leodegar administered Neustria with some success 'till the old enemy of mankind, whose wont it always is to foment discord, began to stir up against him the envy of the great men whom he had taken as his fellows at the helm, and to sow the tares of malice between him and the king.' Leodegar was at last thrust by his envious colleagues into the monastery of Luxeuil, where he found his old enemy Ebroin awaiting his company. In the same year king

Childerich was murdered: he had seized a free Frank named Bodolin, and without trial or judgment, bound him naked to a stake, and flogged him in the palace court. No sooner was the furious Neustrian freed from his bonds than he gathered a few friends, and slew the king in his bed.

There followed anarchy all over the Frankish realm, for Childerich had left only an infant son. One party in Neustria took out of the monastery of St. Denis prince Theuderich, who had been Ebroin's candidate for the Neustrian throne three years before, and proclaimed him king. Wulfoald, the Mayor of the Palace of Austrasia, sent to Ireland to find Dagobert, the long-lost prince whom Grimoald had kidnapped and sent over-sea in 656. Sought out by Wilfred, bishop of York, and perhaps guarded by Northumbrian warriors, Dagobert was brought over to Germany, and raised to the throne. But another party, mainly composed of Austrasians, proclaimed a boy named Chlodovech, whom they said was a natural son of king Chlothar III. Ebroin broke from his monastery-prison, let his hair grow, and joined the adherents of Chlodovech. In this three-cornered duel the kings counted for little or naught, the mayors and the nobles for everything. By his superior daring and persistency Ebroin worked himself once more to the front, and on consenting to abandon the boy pretender, whose cause he had feigned to espouse, was made Mayor of Neustria once more by king Theuderich (678). His first care was to send for his old enemy Leodegar, against whom he entertained an unforgotten grudge, in spite of their common captivity at Luxeuil. The good bishop was brought before him, blinded, and afterwards beheaded. Later generations, remembering his well-meaning government and cruel end, saluted him as a saint (St. Leger).

For three years the wicked Ebroin went forth conquering and to conquer: he used the name of king Theuderich to cover his misdeeds, and ordered everything at his own pleasure. Entering Austrasia he crushed its army, and Dagobert, the king from over-sea, was slain by traitors after his defeat. Some of the East Franks, however, refused to lay down their arms, and placed at their head the heir of the house of Arnulf and Pippin, as the most popular chief that Austrasia could find. This was Pippin the Young, nephew of Mayor Grimoald, son of Ansegisel and Begga, and grandson both of St. Arnulf and Pippin the Old.

Ebroin, however, was strong enough to overbear the resistance of Pippin: at Lafaux, near Laon, he defeated the last Austrasian army in the open field, and compelled all the Franks, from Meuse to Rhine, to acknowledge his protege Theuderich as king. He himself became mayor both of Neustria, Burgundy, and Austrasia, and might well have aspired to assume the royal title. But a private enemy, whose death he had been plotting, secretly murdered him in 681, and with his death the ascendency of Neustria came to an end. The Austrasians once more took up arms under Pippin the Young, and after seven more weary years of civil war, a decisive battle at Testry near St. Quentin settled the fate of the Frankish realms (687). Pippin with the men of the East was completely victorious, and Theuderich and the Neustrians were compelled to take what terms he chose to give them. He claimed to be what Ebroin had been, mayor both in East and West, but he chose to dwell himself at Metz, the home of his grandfather, and from thence administered Austrasia almost as an independent ruler; while regents named by him guided the steps of king Theuderich in Neustria. By the fight of Testry the question of precedence between Austrasia and Neustria was finally settled in favour of the former. From this moment onward, the East-Frankish house of the descendants of Arnulf and Pippin is of far more importance in Frankish history than the effete royal family. Warned by the fate of Grimoald, they did not again demand the crown for a space of eighty years, and were content with a practical domination without any regal name. Henceforth we shall find the Franks more Teutonic and less Gallo-Roman than they had hitherto been: the central point of the realm is for the future to be found about Austrasian Metz, Aachen and Koln, not around Neustrian Soissons, Paris, or Laon.

Pippin, the son of Ansegisel, was Mayor of the Palace for twenty-six years (688-714), a period in which he did much to rescue the Frankish realm from the dilapidation and evil governance which it had experienced for the last fifty years. His first task was to endeavour to restore the ancient boundaries of the kingdom; for during the reigns of the sons and grandsons of Dagobert I., the old limits of the realm had fallen back on every side. On the eastern border the homage which the Bavarian dukes owed to the Merovings had been completely forgotten; for all practical purposes they were now independent. Farther north, the Thuringians were in much the same condition; they had been saved from the Slavonic hordes of Samo by their own chiefs, not by their Frankish suzerain, and since they had repulsed the Slavs had gone on their own way, caring nought who ruled at Metz or Koln. The Frisians of the Rhine-mouth, a race whom the Merovings had never subdued, were pushing their raids into the valleys of the Scheldt and Meuse. These were all comparatively outlying tribes, whose freedom is easily explained by their distance from the centre of government. But it is more surprising to find that even the Suabians or Alamanni, on the very threshold of Austrasia, along the Rhine and Neckar and in the Black Forest, had of late refused the homage which for two hundred years they had been accustomed to render to the Merovings, and paid no obedience to any one save their own local dukes. In the south also the Gallo-Romans of Aquitaine had achieved practical independence under a duke named Eudo, who was said to be descended from Charibert, king of Aquitaine, the brother of Dagobert I.

For fifty years Pippin and his son Charles were to work at the restoration of the ancient frontier of the Frankish realm, beating down by constant hard fighting the various vassal tribes who had slipped away from beneath the Frankish yoke. Pippin's chief wars were with the Frisians and the Suabians, against both of whom he obtained great successes. After a long struggle he compelled Radbod, the duke of the Frisians, to do homage to king Theuderich, and cede to the Franks West-Frisia, the group of marshy islands between the Scheldt-mouth and the Zuider Zee, which is now called Zealand and South Holland. To protect this new conquest Pippin set up or restored castles at Utrecht and Dorstadt, new towns destined to become, the one the ecclesiastical, and the other the commercial, centre of the lands by the Rhine-mouth. Duke Radbod was also compelled to give his daughter in marriage to Pippin's eldest son, Grimoald.

Another series of campaigns were directed against the Suabians. Pippin followed them into the depths of their forests, and compelled their duke Godfrid to acknowledge himself, as his fathers had done, the vassal of the Franks.

It is very noticeable that under Pippin's rule and by his aid the conversion of Germany to Christianity was begun. The descendants of St. Arnulf were, as befitted the issue of such a holy man, zealous friends of the Church and patrons of missionary enterprise. The Merovingian kings had been, almost without exception, a godless race. Christian in name alone. They had taken no pains to favour the spread of Christianity among their vassals: it was sufficient in their eyes if their own people, the ruling race, conformed to the Catholic faith; for the souls of Suabians, Frisians, or Bavarians, they had no care. Such missionaries as had hitherto been seen in the German forests, along the shores of the Bodensee, or the upper reaches of the Danube and Main, had been, almost without exception, Irish monks, drawn from the Isle of Saints by their own fervent zeal for the spread of the Gospel, not by any encouragement from the Frankish kings. In the sixth and seventh centuries these holy men overran the whole Continent, seeking for heathen to convert, or planting their humble monasteries in the wildest recesses of the mountains or the primeval forest. They wandered as far as Italy and Switzerland, where two of the greatest of them fixed their homes, St. Fridian at Lucca, St. Gall in the hills above the Bodensee.

But till the time of Pippin no systematic attempt had been made to convert those among the German races who still lay in the darkness of Paganism. It was Pippin who first saw that this duty was incumbent on the Frankish government. He sent to England for St. Willibrord, the first apostle of the Frisians, who with, his twelve companions wandered over the newly conquered West Friesland, preaching to the wild heathen. It was by Pippin's encouragement also that the Englishman Suidbert laboured among the Hessians, till he and his converts were driven away by the invasion of the pagan Saxons. At the same time St. Rupert, bishop of Worms, completed the conversion of Bavaria, and founded there the great bishopric of Salzburg (696). Much about the same date the Irish monk Killian passed up the Main and along the skirts of the Thuringerwald, to preach to the Thuringians, till he met with a martyr's death at Wurzburg. Everywhere the ascendency of the grandson of Arnulf was followed by the arrival of zealous missionary workers, Franks, Irish or English, who strove to bear the standard of the Cross into the German woodlands, where

Woden and Thunor alone had hitherto been adored. What Pippin began, his greater son, Charles the Hammer, and his still mightier great-grandson, Charles the Emperor, were destined to complete. By this work alone the house of the great Austrasian mayors did more to justify their existence in three generations than the wicked Merovings had done in eight.

The years during which Pippin governed the Franks were marked in their regal annals by four obscure names. Theuderich, the weak king who had been drawn from the cloister to sit on his brother's throne,i died in 691: he was followed by his two infant sons, Chlodovech III. (691-5), and Childebert III. (695-711), both of whom were recognised alike in Neustria and Austrasia, but had no real authority. Chlodovech died while yet a boy: Childebert survived to early manhood, begat a son, and then hastened to the grave. Apparently the vices of their ancestors had sapped the vital energy of the later Merovings; scarce one of them survived to reach the age of thirty, and each long minority made the kingly power more and more shadowy, and the authority of the great mayor more and more real. Childebert III. was followed by one more young boy, his son Dagobert III. (711-16), the last of the four puppet kings in whose names the great Pippin swayed the Frankish sceptre.

Pippin lived to a great age, and had the misfortune to lose in his declining years his two legitimate sons, Grimoald and Drogo, whom he had destined to succeed him. The heirs then remaining to him were Theudoald, a young boy, the son of Grimoald, and Carl [Charles Martel], an illegitimate son whom he had by a concubine named Alphaida. The former was only eight years of age, the latter twenty-five , but the old of man designated the boy Theudoald as his successor, hoping that he might be spared to see him grow up to manhood. He died, however, within a few months, and a strange problem was put before the Franks, whether they would tolerate a child-mayor ruling in the name of a child-king. Pippin's widow Plectrudis tried to seize the reins of government in behalf of her little grandson, and some of the Austrasians adhered to her cause. As a precautionary measure she cast her husband's natural son Charles into prison, knowing that many men regarded him as the only possible heir to Pippin's position, since the idea of a child-mayor was preposterous.

Plectrudis' endeavour to rule in the name of her grandson proved, as might have been expected, a complete failure. The counts and dukes of Neustria hastened to take the opportunity of shaking off the domination of the Austrasians. They mustered in arms, chose a certain Raginfred, one of themselves, as Neustrian Mayor of the Palace, and raised an army to invade Austrasia in the name of the young Dagobert III. They did not shrink from allying themselves with the enemies of the state, the Frisians and Saxons, who attacked Austrasia from the rear, while they themselves, advancing through the Ardennes, wasted all the lands between Meuse and Rhine with fire and sword. Plectrudis and her grandson shut themselves up within the walls of Koln.

Before the end of the year, however, two important events occurred to give a new turn to the war. Charles, the son of Pippin, escaped from his stepmother's prison, and was at once saluted as chief by the majority of the Austrasians, who had been driven to wild rage by the ravages of the Neustrian army, and yearned for a leader capable of commanding in the field. Shortly after the young king, whom East and West had both acknowledged, died, as did all his ancestors, just when he had attained manhood, and immediately after the birth of his first child. Like the Grand Lamas of Thibet, these wretched Merovings expired, with hardly an exception, just as they grew old enough to interfere in politics. As with the Lamas, so with the Franks, we cannot help suspecting that there was more in these sudden deaths than appears on the surface: it certainly was not to the interest of those about the persons of the kings that they should ever live long enough to assert their regal power.

On the death of Dagobert, the Neustrians drew out from the monastery, where he had been placed in earliest infancy, the son of Childerich I., the king whom Bodolin had slain in 678. The monk Daniel was saluted by the royal name of Chilperich, and raised on the shield: he was the first Meroving for eighty years who had reached manhood at the moment of his accession, being in his thirty-eighth year. Chilperich, in spite of his monastic rearing — or perhaps in virtue of it — turned out a far more vigorous personage than any of his relatives, and cannot be called one of the 'rois faineants.' He continually took the field at the head of his Neustrians, and did his best to become their national champion. Unfortunately the times were against him.

In 716 the Neustrian king and mayor marched together into Austrasia to make an end of the resistance alike of Plectrudis and of Charles. At the same time Radbod, the Frisian duke, pushed up the Rhine towards Koln. Charles offered battle to the invaders near that city, but was defeated, and forced to take refuge in the mountains of the Eifel. Chilperich then laid siege to Koln, and compelled Plectrudis and her party to acknowledge him as king, give up the royal treasure-hoard of Austrasia, and withdraw the boy Theudoald's claim to the mayoralty. But while the Neustrian army was returning in triumph to its own land, Charles, who had assembled a new force, fell upon it near Malmedy, on the skirts of the Ardennes. At the battle of Ambleve all the work of Chilperich's vigorous campaign was undone, for his army was routed, and he and his mayor, Raginfred, barely escaped with their lives (716).

This was the first blow of Charles the Hammer [Martel], as after generations named him. From henceforth his career was to be one of uninterrupted success against every foe who dared withstand him. Early in the spring he followed up his first stroke by invading Neustria, and defeating Chilperich for a second time at Vincy, near Cambray. Pressing on after his victory he pursued the Neustrians up to the gates of Paris, and when resistance ceased, turned back in triumph to Austrasia. There he compelled his step-mother Plectrudis to give up Koln to him, and dispersed her partisans. Being now undisputed master of the Eastern kingdom, he proclaimed a certain Chlothar king, and named himself Mayor of the Palace. Chlothar IV., whose descent is not certain, but who was perhaps grandson of the Irish exile Dagobert II., was of course a mere puppet in his mayor's hands. After securing for himself a legitimate position in the state, Charles started forth to humble all the enemies who had vexed Austrasia in its time of trouble. He drove the Saxons over the Weser, compelled Radbod the Frisian to surrender West Friesland for the second time, and then turned against Neustria. It was in vain that king Chilperich, who fought hard to maintain his independence, joined forces with Eudo, who in the late troubles had made himself independent duke of Aquitaine. Charles beat them both at a battle near Soissons, and chased king and duke beyond the Loire. This battle of Soissons was the last effort alike of the Merovingian house and the Neustrian realm. After it had been lost they both bowed before the Austrasian sword, and humbly took their orders from the great Mayor of the Palace (718).

At this conjuncture Charles's puppet, king Chlothar IV. died. The victor of Soissons might perchance have chosen to proclaim himself king of Austrasia, but remembering the fate of his grandfather Grimoald, preferred to offer terms to the exiled king Chilperich. On recognising Charles as mayor of East and West alike, the vanquished Meroving was allowed to return to Neustria, and proclaimed King of all the Franks (719). He had deserved a better fate than to sink into a mere name and shadow, and if he had been born eighty years earlier might perchance by his courage and persistence have given a longer lease of power to the Merovingian house. But the times were now too late for his energy to avail.

Chilperich II. died only a year after his submission to Charles. There remain only two more names to chronicle in the ancient royal house, Theuderich IV. and Childerich II. These obscure persons — so obscure that the chroniclers do not even give us the date of Theuderich's death — were too weak even to be used as tools by the enemies of the great mayor. A well-known passage in Einhard describes their wretched position: — 'For many years the house of the Merovings was destitute of vigour and had nothing illustrious about it save the empty name of king. For the rulers of their palace possessed both the wealth and the power of the kingdom, bearing the name of mayor, and had charge of all high matters of state. There was nothing for the king to do save to content himself with his title, and sit with his long hair and long beard on the throne, like the effigy of a ruler, to hear foreign ambassadors harangue him and answer them in words put into his mouth as if speaking for himself. His royal name was profitless and his allowance of revenue was at the discretion of the mayor, nor was there anything he could really call his own save one royal manor of moderate value (Montmacq). There he kept his family and his little establishment of servants. When he had to travel he set out in a covered carriage drawn by oxen, and driven by a rustic retainer. Thus he used to travel up to his palace, or to the national gathering, which met once a year to settle the affairs of the realm, and thus he would return. But the administration of the kingdom, and everything that had to be done either at home or abroad was cared for by the Mayor of the Palace.' Theuderich's name covers the years 720-737, Childerich's the years 742-752. Between the one's death and the other's accession there was a period of six years, in which the great mayor did not even trouble to provide himself with a nominal king, but ruled on his own authority.

The twenty-two years of Charles Martel's rule as mayor of Neustria and Austrasia are the turning-point in the history of Western and Central Europe (719-41). Continuing the policy of his father Pippin the Younger, both at home and abroad, he devoted all his energies to restoring the old boundaries of the Frankish realm, taming its heathen neighbours, spreading Christianity among the more distant German tribes, and restoring law and order among the unruly counts and dukes within the empire. His strong hand was as valuable in ending anarchy at home as in winning victory abroad.

The six years of civil war which followed the death of Pippin the Younger had undone most of the work of that great man, and Charles had to commence once more the task which had busied his father. He was, however, in a position of greater firmness and strength than Pippin had enjoyed, and was able to make his will felt all over the Frankish realms in a much more thorough fashion. It was his task to make the arm of the central government feared all over the kingdom, as much as it had been in the days of the earliest Merovingian kings. The task was hard, because a century and a half of feeble administration had taught the local counts and dukes all the arts of insubordination, more especially the trick of utilising the annual meetings of the great national council — what England would have called the Witan — for the purpose of overawing their ruler. They appeared at the 'March-field,' followed by great hosts of armed followers, and bound themselves together by family or party confederacies to withstand the central government. In this they succeeded as long as the feeble Merovings continued, and were able to elect the officers of state at their pleasure or to distribute the local governorships among each other. The great mayors put an end to this. The house of St. Arnulf had gathered such a great following of faithful partisans in Austrasia that, by their aid, it could face any combination of discontented counts. The other great houses of Austrasia seem to have gradually disappeared, and all the smaller nobility and freemen of the land between Meuse and Rhine had become the enthusiastic followers of Pippin and Charles. In return the great mayors planted Austrasians in office all over the kingdom, and trusted mainly to their aid in all crises. Their system was a domination of the Austrasians over the Neustrians, Burgundians, Aquitanians, and East Germans: their empire reposed on the fact that their own countrymen were loyal, united, and self-confident, while the other races were jealous, divided, and humbled by recent defeat. Yet the struggle was no easy one. It needed the repeated blows of Ambleve, Vincy, and Soissons to crush the Neustrian spirit of separatism. Aquitaine was only kept down by campaign after campaign directed against its disloyal dukes. Neither south Gaul nor south Germany (Suabia and Bavaria) were really tamed till they had been deprived of their native dukes, and cut up into countships or gaus, administered by Austrasian chiefs. But the house of St. Arnulf continued to produce great men for generation after generation, and the taming was finally accomplished.

The work of the great mayors without was no less arduous than within. To subdue those indomitable tribes of northern Germany, from whose pathless woodlands even the iron legions of Augustus had drawn back in despair, was a great work for the tumultuary armies of Austrasia to accomplish. But they carried out the struggle to the bitter end, till they had conquered the very easternmost Teuton, and had looked upon the Baltic and the unknown boundaries of the Slavs. Bavaria and Frisia took many a hard blow ere they were incorporated with the Frankish realm; but at last they relinquished, with a sigh, their heathen independence. Even the Italian kingdom of the gallant Lombards, protected by the great Roman fortresses of Pavia, Verona, and Ravenna could not withstand the Austrasian sword.

But of all the military achievements of the East Franks under the house of St. Arnulf, the grandest, as well as the most enduring in effect, was to be won over a foe unknown to their ancestors, a new enemy who threatened not merely to ravage the borders of the realm like Frisian or Lombard, but to dismember it by lopping away Aquitaine from Western Christendom. Great as were their other feats, the most important of all was the turning back of the wave of Mussulman fanaticism at the battle of Poictiers. For that crowning mercy, if for nothing else, Europe owes an eternal debt of gratitude to the great mayors of the eighth century and the indomitable hosts of Austrasia.

Three years before the death of Pippin the Younger, king Roderic the Visigoth had fallen at the battle of the Guadalete, and Spain had been overrun by the infidel. In 720, — the first year of the complete domination of Charles over the two Frankish kingdoms, — the Saracens had pushed beyond the bounds of the Iberian peninsula, crossed the Pyrenees, and entered Aquitaine, where they laid siege to Toulouse. Their first blow fell on Eudo, duke of Aquitaine, who had just acknowledged himself the vassal of the Frankish king, and given up his claim to reign as an independent prince. The duke obtained aid from the Frankish governors on his borders, attacked the Saracens in their camp at Toulouse, and put them to rout with the loss of their leader El-Samah. But though beaten in battle, the Moslems kept a foothold north of the Pyrenees, by holding to the old Visigothic capital of Narbonne. The danger from them was but postponed, not finally warded off. Ere long Charles himself was to be obliged to take the field, to defend the southern borders of the Frankish realm against expeditions far more formidable than that which duke Eudo had turned back in 721.

CHAPTER XVI: THE LOMBARDS AND THE PAPACY — 653-743

Usurpation and successful wars of Grimoald — Reigns of Berthari and Cunibert — Quarrels of the Papacy and the empire — The exile of Pope Martin I. — Gradual alienation of Italy from the empire — Civil wars of Aribert II. and Ansprand — Successful reign of Liutprand — Leo the Isaurian and Gregory II. — Italy rebels against the Iconoclasts — Liutprand conquers most of the Exarchate,

After the death of Rothari the law-giver the Lombard kingdom entered into its second stage: it had now almost reached the full growth of its territorial extension, and had settled down into its final shape. For nearly a hundred years the main events of its political history are civil wars, or defensive campaigns against its two neighbours, the Roman exarch and the Chagan of the Avars. There is no sustained effort either to expel the Imperialists from Italy, or to extend the boundary of the Lombard realm to the north. It was only in the middle of the eighth century that the estrangement between Constantinople and its Roman subjects in Italy led to such a weakening of the Imperial authority, that the Lombard kings were able to seize the long-coveted Exarchate. The history of the cutting short of the dominions of the eastern Caesar beyond the Adriatic turns much more on the growth of the Papal power, and on the quarrel on the subject of Iconoclasm, which sundered the churches of Rome and Constantinople, than on the ambition or ability of the rulers of Lombardy.

On the murder of Rothari's short-lived son in 653, the Lombards elected as their king Aribert, a nephew of the sainted queen Theodelinda, whose name was still held in kindly memory all over the land. Count Gundoald, Aribert's father, had long been settled in Italy: he had crossed the Alps with his pious sister more than half a century before, so that Aribert himself was counted a Lombard, and not a Bavarian. The new king reigned obscurely for nine years (653-62): he waged no wars and was mainly noted as a friend of the clergy and a builder of churches. He was a fervent Catholic, and did his best to root out the few traces of Arianism yet remaining in Lombardy. The land had peace under his sway, but ere he died he sowed the seeds of future troubles by the unhappy inspiration which led him to induce the Lombard Witan to elect his two sons, Godebert and Berthari, as joint heirs to the kingship.

When their father was dead, Godebert, the elder brother, dwelt as king at Pavia, while Berthari took possession of Milan. Before they had been reigning a year the inevitable civil war broke out, 'because evil-minded men sowed discord and suspicion between them.' They were mustering their followers for a decisive campaign, when Godebert was treacherously murdered by the chief of his own supporters, Grimoald, duke of Benevento, who had left his duchy in the south, and led his men-at-arms to Pavia, under the pretence of helping his suzerain against his unruly younger brother. Grimoald took possession of the crown, and married his victim's sister, in order to connect himself with the house of the holy Theodelinda. He chased Berthari out of Milan, and forced him to take refuge with the Chagan of the Avars, in the far east, by the shores of the Danube.

The unscrupulous usurper reigned for nine years (662-71) over the whole Lombard realm, holding his own court at Pavia, while Romuald, the son of his first marriage, ruled for him at Benevento. This was the only period in the whole history of the Lombards when the king's mandate was as well obeyed in the southern Apennines as in the valley of the Po. It was, therefore, fortunate for the Lombard race that the attack on Italy of the vigorous emperor Constantinus (Constans II.) fell within the years of Grimoald's reign. Though he overran much of the duchy of Benevento, the energy of Constantinus failed before the advent of king Grimoald, and the danger passed away (663.)

His successes against the emperor were not the only triumphs of king Grimoald: he repelled an irruption of the Avars into Venetia, and repulsed a Frankish army which the Mayor Ebroin, who ruled in behalf of king Chlothar III., sent across the Western Alps. His only territorial gain, however, was the capture from the Imperialists of the little town of Forimpopoli, near Rimini, which he stormed by surprise on Easter Day, and harried most cruelly, 'slaying the worshippers at the altar, and the deacons at the baptismal font, while all were engaged in celebrating the Holy Feast.' We might have supposed that the Romans in central Italy would have fared worse after the repulse of Constantinus: but no other city was lost. In the south, however, Grimoald's son Romuald captured Taranto and Brindisi, two of the chief remaining strongholds of the Imperialists in

Apulia. But this was after the death of Constantinus, during the troubles caused by the rebellion of Mezecius in Sicily (668-9?)

In spite of the treachery by which he had attained the throne, Grimoald's victories made him very popular among the Lombards, and many tales survive bearing witness to his generosity and clemency, no less than to his strong hand and cunning. But when he died it was seen that his power rested purely upon his own personal merit: the Lombards did not elect as king either his elder son Romuald, the duke of Benevento, or his younger son, Garibald, whom the daughter of Aribert had borne him. They recalled from exile king Berthari, the son of Aribert, whom Grimoald had driven out of Milan ten years before. This prince had spent an unhappy life in wandering from land to land, from the Danube to the British seas, and was sailing to England when the news of the usurper's death reached him. He returned to Italy, and was received with submission by the whole Lombard race, and solemnly crowned at Pavia.

Berthari reigned for seventeen years (672-88) in peace and quietness, for he loved not war. He was 'a man of religion, a true Catholic, tenacious of justice, a nourisher of the poor; he built the famous nunnery of St. Agatha, and the great Church of the Virgin outside the walls of Pavia.' The kings of this type, whom the monastic chroniclers delighted most to honour, were not those who made history. Berthari never attempted to conquer Rome or the Exarchate, and only took arms once in his reign, when he was assaulted by a rebellious duke, Alahis of Trent, whom he subdued and then pardoned, — as a Christian man should — a pardon which was to cost Lombardy much blood in the next reign.

The reign of his son Cunibert (688-700) was far more disturbed. This king was a man of mixed qualities, brave, generous, and popular, but careless, incautious, and given over to the wine-cup. He was caught unprepared and driven from Pavia by duke Alahis, who now rebelled again, in spite of the fact that his life had once been spared by Cunibert's father. Cunibert was driven for a time from all his realm, save a single castle in the lake of Como, where he stood a long siege. But Alahis, by his tyranny, made himself unbearable to the Lombards, and ere many months had elapsed the lawful king was able to issue from his stronghold and face the usurper in battle. They met at Coronate on the Adda, not far from Lodi, Alahis backed by the 'Austrians' of Venetia, Cunibert by the 'Neustrians' of Piedmont. The men of the West had the better, Alahis was slain, and the son of Berthari resumed his kingship over the whole Lombard realm. This was not the last rebellion that Cunibert had to crush: all through his reign we hear of risings of the unruly dukes, and of the punishments which were inflicted on them when they fell into their master's hands.

There is nothing of first-rate historical importance to relate of the doings of the Lombard kings in this last quarter of the seventh century. But while Berthari was building churches, or Cunibert striving with his rebels, the course of events in the city of Rome was growing more and more important. The papacy and the empire were gradually working up to a pitch of estrangement and mutual repulsion, which was in the next generation to lead to open war between them. We have sketched in an earlier chapter the work of pope Gregory the Great, in raising the papacy to a condition of unprecedented spiritual importance in the Christian world, and no less in building up a position of high secular importance for the Pope in the governance of Rome. For half a century after Gregory's death this state of affairs remained unaltered. The Pope was now firmly established as patriarch of the West, and sent missions to Britain, Gaul, and Spain without let or hindrance. Nor was his secular authority much interfered with, either by the exarch or by the home government at Constantinople. But friction and struggling began under the reign of the stern and ruthless Constantinus (Constans II.) and the hot-headed pope Martin I. We have mentioned elsewhere how the emperor published his 'Type' or edict of Comprehension, forbidding further discussions on the question of the Monothelite heresy. Martin not merely refused to acquiesce in letting the discussion sleep, but summoned a council which declared the 'Type' to be blasphemous and irreverent. Martin wrote to the same effect to the kings of the Franks, Visigoths, and English, thus calling in foreign sovereigns to participate in a dispute between himself and his master. Relying on his remoteness from Byzantium, and on the grandeur of his position as Patriarch of the West, he attempted to defy Constantinus. The emperor's proceedings show that he was determined to assert his power, but that he was fully conscious of the danger and difficulty of dealing with such an important personage as the bishop of Rome had now become. He had to wait for a favourable opportunity for punishing Martin, and it was not by openly arresting him in the face of the people, but by secretly kidnapping him, that he got him into his power. But when once shipped to Constantinople the Pope felt his sovereign's wrath: insulted, loaded with chains, imprisoned, and banished to the remote Crimea, Martin learnt that the emperor's arm was still strong enough to reach out to Rome (655).

But all Italy regarded Martin as a martyr to orthodoxy, and his fate did much to estrange the Romans from their loyalty to the empire. Nor was their wrath diminished by the sacrilegious plunder of the Pantheon and other Roman churches, which Constantinus carried out, when in 663 he deigned to visit his Western dominions. It would seem that Constantinus himself was fully conscious that the Roman see was growing too strong, and deliberately strove to sap its resources, for at this time he granted to the archbishop of Ravenna a formal exemption from any duty of spiritual obedience to the Pope as patriarch of the West, and constituted him an independent authority in the exarchate. For twenty years this schism of Rome and Ravenna continued, but in the end the old traditional prestige of the see of St. Peter triumphed over the ambition of the Ravennese archbishops.

If there had been a strong pontiff at this moment, it is probable that an open rupture might have taken place between the papacy and the empire. But pope Vitalian was a weak man, the fate of his predecessor Martin had cowed him, and the idea of cutting Rome away from the respublica Romana, as the empire was still habitually called, had not yet entered into the minds of the Italian subjects of Byzantium. To disown the Imperial supremacy would have been tantamount to throwing Rome into the hands of king Grimoald the Lombard, and neither Pope nor people contemplated such a prospect with equanimity.

Accordingly the breach between Rome and Byzantium was deferred for another generation. After Constantinus was dead, more friendly relations reigned for a space, for his son Constantine V. was impeccably orthodox. He held the Council of Constantinople in 681 with the high approval of pope Agatho, whose representatives duly appeared at it, to join in the final crushing of the Monothelite heretics. Constantine, in the fulness of his friendship to the papacy, even granted to the Roman see the dangerous privilege that when at papal elections the suffrages of the clergy, the people, and the soldiery, — the garrison of Rome — were unanimously fixed on any one person, that individual might be at once consecrated bishop of Rome, without having to wait for an imperial mandate of approval from Constantinople. As a matter of fact, however, unanimous elections were very rare, and the exarchs of Ravenna are still found interfering to decide between the claims of rival candidates.

Signs of a breach became evident once again in the days of the tyrant Justinian II. When pope Sergius refused obedience to his behests, the emperor bade the exarch seize him and send him to Constantinople. But not only the Roman mob, but the soldiers of the imperial garrison took up arms to resist Justinian's officials when they tried to lay hands on Sergius: the ties of military obedience had already come to be weaker than those of spiritual respect, and the Pope triumphed, for Justinian was deposed, mutilated, and sent to Cherson by his rebellious subjects, ere he had time to punish the Romans.

The twenty-two years of anarchy and dissolution at Constantinople which followed the deposition of Justinian (695-717) were fraught with important consequences in Italy. The ephemeral emperors of those days were unable to assert their authority over the West, and we once more find the popes assuming secular functions, after the fashion of Gregory the Great in the preceding century. John VI. levied taxes in Rome, made treaties with the Lombard duke of Benevento, and even protected and restored the exarch Theophylactus when he had been expelled from Ravenna by a military revolt. Gregory II. went so far in his independence as to refuse to acknowledge the usurping emperor Philippicus; by his advice 'the Roman people determined that state-documents should not bear the name of a heretical Caesar, nor the money be struck with his effigy. So the portrait of Philippicus was not set up in the Church, nor his name introduced in the prayers at Mass.' Gregory only consented to recognise Philippicus' successor Anastasius II. when he heard that the new emperor was a man of unimpeachable orthodoxy. The independent position of the popes had now grown so marked that the next quarrel with Constantinople was destined to lead to the final rupture of relations between the papacy and the empire. It was impossible that things should remain as they were: the breach was inevitable. Its cause was to be the accession of the stern Iconoclast, Leo the Isaurian, and his attempt to enforce his own religious views on the western, no less than the eastern provinces of his empire. The protagonists in the final struggle are Leo, pope Gregory II., and the Lombard king Liutprand, whose position and power we must now proceed to explain.

When king Cunibert died in the year 700, he left his throne to his young son Liutbert, a mere boy, whose realm was to be administered by a regent-guardian, count Ansprand, the wisest of the Lombards. A minority was always fatal to one of the early Teutonic kingdoms. Only eight months after Liutbert had been proclaimed king, his nearest adult kinsmen rose in arms against him, to claim the crown. These were Reginbert, duke of

Turin, and his son Aribert, the child and grandchild of king Godebert, and the cousins of the boy-king's father.

Reginbert was followed by all the Neustrian Lombards, and was able to defeat the regent Ansprand at Novara. He died immediately after his victory, but his son Aribert followed up the success by winning a second battle in front of Pavia, and taking prisoner the boy Liutbert. The victor seized the capital, and was hailed as king by his followers, under the name of Aribert II. The regent Ansprand, who had escaped from Pavia, tried to keep up the civil war in the name of his ward: but the new king put an end to this attempt by ordering the boy Liutbert to be strangled in his bath. Ansprand then fled over the Alps and took refuge with the duke of Bavaria.

Aribert II. reigned over the Lombards for ten troubled years (701-11), fully occupied by the tasks of putting down rebellious dukes, driving back raids of the Carinthian Slavs from Venetia, and endeavouring to assert his power over Spoleto and Benevento. The time was opportune for attacking the imperial possessions in Italy, but Aribert refrained from making the attempt. He was friendly to the papacy, and made over to pope John VI. a great gift of estates in the Cottian Alps: nor did he assist his vassal Faroald, duke of Spoleto, when the latter in 703 made an attempt on the Exarchate. Aribert preferred to live in peace both with the Pope and the Emperor.

Aribert II. had gained his kingdom by the sword, and by the sword he was destined to lose it. In 711 the exile Ansprand, once the regent for the boy Liutbert, invaded Italy at the head of a Bavarian army, lent to him by duke Teutbert. Many of the Lombards still loved the house of Berthari and hated Aribert as a murderer and usurper. The army of Ansprand was ere long increased by many thousands of the 'Austrian' Lombards, and he was soon able to face the king in the open field near Pavia. The battle was indecisive, but when it was over Aribert retired within the walls of the city. His retreat discouraged his army, which began to fall away from him: thereupon Aribert determined to take with him the royal treasure, and flee to Gaul to buy aid of the Franks. While endeavouring to cross the Ticino by night with all his hoard, he was accidentally drowned, and left the throne vacant for his rival Ansprand (712).

The ex-regent was now proclaimed king, but only survived his triumph a few months: on his deathbed he prevailed on the Lombards to elect as his colleague his son Liutprand, who therefore became sole ruler when his father died a few days later.

Liutprand was the most able and energetic king who ever ruled the Lombard realm, and his long reign of thirty-one years (712-43) saw the completion of the long-delayed process of the eviction of the East Romans from Central Italy, and the rise of the Lombards to the highest pitch of success which they ever knew — a rise which was to be closely followed by the extinction of their kingdom.

When Leo the Isaurian commenced his crusade against image-worship, Liutprand had been on the throne for fourteen years. In these earlier years of his reign he was occupied in strengthening his position, and made no attack on the Imperial dominions in Italy, though he is found making war on the Bavarians, and capturing some of their castles on the upper Adige.

But in 726 things came to a head, when Leo issued his famous edict against images, forbidding all worship of statues and paintings. Pope Gregory II. was not in a mood to listen to such a command from Constantinople. He was already in great disfavour with the emperor for having advised the Italians to resist some extraordinary taxation which Leo had imposed to maintain the Saracen war. When he received Leo's rescript, and a letter addressed to himself requesting him to carry out the imperial orders, and destroy the images of Rome, he burst out into open contumacy, and the Romans, with all the other Italians, followed his lead. Exhilaratus, duke of Naples, who tried to carry out the edict in his duchy, was slain by a mob, and many other imperial officials were maltreated or driven off by those whom they governed. The cities elected new rulers over themselves, and would have chosen and proclaimed an Emperor of the West, if Gregory II. had not kept them from this final step. Meanwhile, all the imperial provinces of Italy being in open sedition, and quite cut off from Constantinople, king Liutprand thought the moment had at last come for rounding off the Lombard dominions by seizing the long-coveted Exarchate. He crossed the Po, took Bologna, with most of the other cities of Aemilia, and then conquered Osimo, Rimini, Ancona, and all the Pentapolis. Chassis, the seaport of Ravenna, fell before him, but the exarch Paul succeeded in preserving the great City of the Marshes for a short time longer, till he was murdered by rioters (727). The Lombard king's conquests were made with astonishing ease, for in each city the anti-imperialist faction betrayed the gates to him without fighting.

Soon after, the triumph of Liutprand was completed by the surrender of Ravenna itself: the exarch Eutychius fled to Venice, already a semi-independent city, but one which still preserved a nominal allegiance to the empire. Meanwhile, pope Gregory II. was occupied in writing lengthy manifestos setting forth the atrocious conduct of Leo, and the intrinsic rationality of reverencing images. His letters to the emperor were couched in language of studied insolence. 'I must use coarse and rude arguments,' he wrote, 'to suit a coarse and rude mind such as yours,' and then proceeded to say that 'if you were to go into a boys' school and announce yourself as a destroyer of images, the smallest children would throw their writing tablets at your head, for even babes and sucklings might teach you, though you refuse to listen to the wise.' After completely confusing king Uzziah with king Hezekiah in an argument drawn from the Old Testament, Gregory then proceeded to quote apocryphal anecdotes from early church history. He wound up by asserting that in virtue of the power that he inherited from St. Peter, he might consign the emperor to eternal damnation, but that Leo was so thoroughly damned by his own crimes that there was no need to inflict any further curse on him. A more practical threat was that if the emperor sent an army against Rome, he would retire into Campania and take refuge with the Lombards (729).

As a matter of fact, however, to throw himself into the hands of the Lombards was the last thing that pope Gregory desired to do. He had the greatest dread of falling under the direct authority of Liutprand, for the occupation of Rome by a powerful and strong-handed Italian king would have been fatal to the secular power of the papacy. It was easy to disobey a powerless exarch and a distant emperor, but if Liutprand had become ruler of all Italy, the popes would have been forced to be his humble subjects. Gregory wished to rid himself of the domination of Leo, without falling into the clutches of Liutprand. While disclaiming his allegiance to the emperor, he pretended to adhere to the empire.

Meanwhile an unexpected turn of events had checked the career of victory of king Liutprand. While he was absent at Pavia, the exarch Eutychius had collected some troops at Venice, and aided by the forces of the semi-independent citizens of the lagoon-city had landed near Ravenna. The place was betrayed to him by the imperialist party within the walls, and became once more the seat of imperial power in Italy. At the same time the dukes of Spoleto and Benevento took arms against their suzerain, and allied themselves with pope Gregory (729).

Liutprand determined to conquer the Lombard rebels before resuming the hard task of retaking Ravenna. He even made a truce with the exarch, by which it was stipulated that they should mutually aid each other, the one in subduing the revolted dukes, the other in compelling the Pope to return to his allegiance. Accordingly Eutychius marched against Rome, and Liutprand against Spoleto. On the king's approach the two dukes submitted to him, and swore to be his faithful vassals. He then moved toward Rome, which the exarch was already besieging. But he had no wish that the imperial power should be strengthened by the recovery of Rome, and, encamping his army in the Field of Nero, outside the city, proceeded to claim to act as arbitrator between Gregory and Eutychius. They were too weak to resist him, and the Pope at least gladly acquiesced in the pacification of Italy which Liutprand proposed. The exarch was to return to Ravenna, leaving Rome unmolested, and to be content with the possession of Ravenna only, all his other lost dominions in the Pentapolis and Aemilia remaining in the hands of the Lombards. Gregory, in consideration of being left unmolested in Rome, professed to return to his allegiance, but in reality remained in an independent position. He did not withdraw his opposition to Iconoclasm, and took advantage of the peace to call together a great council of Italian bishops, ninety-three in number, who solemnly anathematised all who refused to reverence images, though they did not curse the emperor by name (730).

Two months later pope Gregory II. died, and was succeeded by Gregory III., as great an enemy of Iconoclasm as his namesake. He had no sooner displayed his views, than the emperor, discontented with the peace which the exarch had concluded, and much irritated by the anathema of the Council of Rome, revenged himself on the papacy by issuing an edict which removed from the jurisdiction of the Pope, as Patriarch of the West, the Illyrian and south Italian dioceses which had hitherto paid spiritual obedience to Rome. For the future, not only Epirus and Sicily, but even Apulia and Calabria, were to look to the Patriarch of Constantinople as their head and chief (731).

In 732 Leo took a more practical step for reducing the Pope to obedience. He fitted out a great armament in the ports of Asia Minor, which was to sail to Italy, to recover by force of arms the lost regions of the Exarchate, and to arrest Gregory III. and send him in chains to Constantinople. But the fates were against the restoration of imperial authority in the West: the fleet was completely wrecked by a storm in the Adriatic, and the fragments of it which reached Ravenna effected nothing. This was the last serious attempt of the empire to recover central Italy. Henceforth the Popes went their own way, while the exarch, penned up in the single fortress of

Ravenna, awaited with trembling the outbreak of the next Lombard war — a war which would certainly sweep away him and his shrunken Exarchate.

But for eight years after the treaty of 730, king Liutprand maintained peace over all Italy. He was a pious prince, and a respecter of the papacy, to which he had even made a grant of territory, ceding the town of Sutri in Tuscany, which he had captured from the exarch in the war of 728-30. His reign was a time of prosperity for Lombardy: the southern dukes were compelled to obey orders from Pavia: the Slav and Avar were kept back from the northern marches, Liutprand also kept up his friendly relations with Charles Martel, the great Mayor of the Palace in Gaul. When Charles was looking about for a neighbour sovereign who should, according to old Teutonic custom, gird with arms and clip the hair of his son Pippin on his arrival at manhood, he chose Liutprand to discharge this friendly office. On the invasion of Provence by the Saracens in 736-7, Charles asked the Lombard for the id of his host, and Liutprand crossed the Alps and joined in expelling the infidels from Aix and Aries.

The peace of Italy was not broken till 738 when Transimund duke of Spoleto rebelled, not for the first time, against Liutprand. The king crushed the revolt with his accustomed vigour, and the duke was compelled to fly: he took refuge at Rome with pope Gregory III. Liutprand promptly demanded his surrender: Gregory refused, and the Lombard army at once marched into the duchy of Rome. The king captured Orte, Bomazo, and two other towns in south Tuscany, and menaced Rome with a siege. Gregory III. could hope for neither help nor sympathy from his master the emperor Leo, whom he had so grievously insulted. Accordingly he determined to seek aid from the one other power which might be able to succour him, the great Mayor of the Franks. He sent to Charles Martel the golden keys of the tomb of Saint Peter, and besought him to defend the holy city against the impious Lombard. He conferred on the Mayor the high-sounding title of Roman Patrician, which was not legally his to give, for only the emperor could confer it. He even offered to transfer to the ruler of the Franks the shadowy allegiance which Rome still paid to the emperor. Thus did Gregory III., first of all the Roman pontiffs, endeavour to bring down upon Italy the curse of foreign invasion. He had drawn upon himself the wrath of Liutprand by his secular policy: the war arose purely from the fact that he had favoured the rebellion of the duke of Spoleto, and sheltered him when he fled. Yet he made the Lombard invasion a matter of sacrilege, complaining to Charles that Liutprand's attack was an impious invasion of the rights of the Church, and a deliberate insult to the majesty of St. Peter. Considering that the king had saved him from destruction eight years before, Gregory must be accused of gross ingratitude, as well as of deliberate misrepresentation and hypocrisy. But the Pope had imbibed a bitter and quite irrational hatred for the Lombard race: the danger that he might lose his secular power, by Rome being annexed to the realm of Liutprand, caused Gregory to view the pious, peaceable, and orthodox king of the Lombards with as much dislike as he felt for the heretical Iconoclast at Constantinople. Considering the amiable character of Liutprand, and the respectable national record of the Lombards when they are compared with their contemporaries beyond the Alps, it is astonishing to read of the terms in which Gregory and his successors spoke of them. No epithet applied to the heathen in the Scriptures was too severe to heap upon the 'fetid, perjured, impious, plundering, murderous race of the Lombards.' And all this indignation and abuse was produced by the rational desire of Liutprand to punish the Pope for harbouring his rebels! It is impossible not to wish that the great king had succeeded in taking Rome, and unifying Italy, a contingency which would have spared the peninsula the curses of the Frankish invasion, of its long and unnatural connection with the Western Empire, and of that still greater disaster, the permanent establishment of the temporal power of the papacy.

Charles Martel did not accept Gregory's offers, or carry out the Pope's plans: he would not quarrel with his old friend Liutprand on such inadequate grounds as the Pope alleged. He chose instead to endeavour to mediate between Gregory and the Lombard king. He accepted the title of Patrician, and received the Roman ambassadors with great pomp and honour, sending them home with many rich presents. But his own delegates who accompanied them were charged to reconcile the Pope and the king, not to promise aid to the one against the other. Both Charles and Gregory, as it happened, were at this moment on the edge of the grave: both died in the next year (741), and it was some time before the first active interference of the Franks in behalf of the papacy was destined to take place.

How uncalled for was the action of pope Gregory is shown by the fact that in the next year Liutprand came to terms with the Roman See. On the accession of pope Zachariah, who promised to give no more aid to the rebel duke of Spoleto, Liutprand restored the cities he had taken from the Roman duchy, and granted a peace for twenty years. He even presented great offerings to the Roman Churches and made a present of some valuable estates to Zachariah. Yet the anger of the popes was in no way appeased: in their hearts they hated the Lombards as if they were still Arians or heathen, and only awaited another opportunity for conspiring against them.

Meanwhile Liutprand died in peace in 743, after a reign of thirty-one years, in which he had added the greater part of the Exarchate to his kingdom, had extended the boundaries of Italy to north and east against the Bavarian and Slav, and had reduced the Beneventan and Spoletan dukes to an unwonted state of subservience. No one, save his enemies the popes, ever laid a charge of any sort against his character, and he appears to have been the best-loved and best-served king of his day. We read with pleasure that he died in peace, ere the terrible invasion of the Franks began to afflict the land he had guarded so well. It would have been better perhaps for Italy if he had been a less virtuous and pious sovereign: a less temperate ruler would have finished his career of conquest by taking Rome, and so would have staved off the countless ills that Rome was about to bring on the whole Italian peninsula.

CHAPTER XVII: CHARLES MARTEL AND HIS WARS — 720-41

Wars with the Saxons and Frisians — Missionary enterprises of St. Boniface — The Saracens in Septimania and Aquitaine — Charles wins the battle of Poictiers — Revolt and subjection of duke Hunold of Aquitaine — Charles and the Papacy.

The name of Charles Martel is generally remembered as that of the victor of Poictiers, but although the defeat of the invasion of the Saracens of Spain was destined to be the greatest of his achievements, his struggle with them was but one of a long series of wars waged against all the races of infidels who surrounded the Frankish realm. It was not till the twelfth year of his mayoralty that he himself took the field to face the invader from the south. Up to that year he had been far more concerned with the heathen neighbours of his own Austrasia, and must have spared comparatively few thoughts for the danger of distant Aquitaine, and its half-independent duke.

Charles had first to deal with the Saxons. To punish them for their interference in the Frankish civil war of 714-20 he led several expeditions into the valley of the Weser, and pushed the Frankish frontier up to the Teutoburgerwald and the head waters of the Lippe and the Ruhr. The Frisians had already submitted to him, but he had come to the conclusion that their homage was worth little until they should have adopted Christianity, and he therefore employed all his influence to make their duke Aldgisl co-operate in the conversion of his subjects. The duke, a just and peace-loving prince, was not averse to the scheme, and under his guarantee missionaries were despatched by bishop Willibrord of Utrecht over all the Frisian districts. In the course of a generation they had christianised the greater part of the country, but the East Frisians were far behind the rest in accepting the gospel, and their conversion was to be reserved till the reign of Charles's son.

Frisia and Saxony having been dealt with, it was the next task of the great mayor to restore the Frankish suzerainty over Bavaria, which had disappeared for more than eighty years. But before he could complete this task he was summoned into the West to suppress a Neustrian rebellion.

The nobles of northern Gaul, in spite of their deep humiliation at Vincy and Soissons, rose once more under Raginfred, the late mayor of Chilperich II. But the rising collapsed at the first appearance of Charles, and the enemy laid down their arms, Raginfred only stipulating that he should retain his countship of Angers on giving up his sons as hostages (724).

The next three years were occupied in the subjugation of south-eastern Germany. Marching eastward through Suabia, whose warriors he compelled to accompany him to the field, Charles advanced against the Bavarians. After severe fighting, lasting over three campaigns, he returned in triumph with much plunder, a troop of hostages, and the submission of duke Hukbert. The allegiance of the Bavarians was still very insecure, but something had been done to enforce the long-forgotten suzerainty of the Franks. Alarmed by the subjection of Bavaria, the Suabian duke Lantfrid rebelled, but Charles slew him in battle, and refused to appoint any duke in his stead, in order that Suabia might more easily amalgamate with the neighbouring districts when it had lost the prince whose title symbolised its separate unity (730).

While Charles worked with the sword against the eastern Germans, he did not neglect the other great means of binding them to the Frankish realm. It was during the time of his Saxon and Bavarian wars that he lent his protection to the zealous West-Saxon monk Winfrith, the indefatigable preacher and organiser who won the name of the 'Apostle of Germany' by his long life-work among the Bavarians, Thuringians, and Hessians. After spending some time with bishop Willibrord at Utrecht, Winfrith had started eastward to find newer and wilder fields for his activity. He fixed himself first among the Hessians where no missionary had been seen since the death of St. Suidbert. Here he met with such success that the whole land was soon reckoned Christian. Pope Gregory II., hearing of his triumphs, sent for him to Rome, and consecrated him missionary bishop of all Transrhenane Germany. After swearing implicit obedience to the Apostolic See for himself and all his converts, Winfrith — or as he is more often called in his later years Boniface — returned to the North with a papal letter of credence recommending him to the Mayor of Austrasia. Charles undertook the support of the new bishop with the greatest zeal: 'without the aid of the prince of the Franks,' wrote Boniface, 'I should not be able to rule my church nor defend the lives of my priests and nuns, nor keep my converts from lapsing into pagan rites and observances.' It was the fear of the wrath of Charles that kept the wild Hessians and Thuringians from murdering the unarmed missionary, when he came among them with his life in his hand, and hewed down the holy oak of Woden at Fritzlar in the presence of thousands of heathen spectators. For the next thirty-one years (723-54) Boniface went forth conquering and to conquer, churches and abbeys rising everywhere beneath his hand, in the regions where the Christian name had never before been known.

While Charles had been busied on the Austrasian frontier a new storm was rising in the South. The Saracens of Spain were once more crossing the Rhone and the Cevennes to overrun southern Gaul. Luckily for the Franks the efforts of the Moslems were most spasmodic; the governors of Spain were, as a rule, more concerned with preserving their own authority against revolted lieutenants than with extending the bounds of Islam. The centre of government at Damascus was so far away that the Caliph's authority was only displayed at rare intervals, and as a rule the various Arab and Berber chiefs who represented the sovereign were busily engaged in deposing and murdering each other. In the first forty years of Mussulman rule in Spain there were no less than twenty viceroys, of whom seven came to violent ends.

We have already related the disastrous issue of the expedition of El-Samah against Toulouse in 721. It was not till 725 that the Saracens stirred again; in that year the Emir Anbasa-ibn-Johim set out from Narbonne with a large army, and subdued Carcassonne, Nismes, and the rest of northern Septimania as far as the Rhone. He placed garrisons in the newly conquered cities, and then crossed the river and executed a rapid raid through Burgundy as far as Autun in the heat of the summer. After sacking Autun he returned with such speed to Spain that the Franks were totally unable to overtake him. But Anbasa died before the year was out, and for seven years his successors were too much engaged in strife with each other to renew the attack on Christendom. Eudo, duke of Aquitaine, employed the respite in conciliating the friendship of Othman-ben-abu-Neza, the Moslem governor of Septimania, whom he won to his side by giving him his daughter in marriage. It was probably in reliance on the aid of his son-in-law that Eudo in 731 rebelled against the Franks, and once more declared himself independent duke of Aquitaine. Charles crossed the Loire, beat Eudo in the field, and ravaged the country up to the gates of Bordeaux. The duke, however, persisted in his resistance, till he learnt that another foe was about to attack him. His son-in-law Othman had rebelled against Abderahman the viceroy of Spain, and had been defeated and slain. After subduing the rebel, Abderahman resolved to march against Othman's ally and father-in-law. This drove Eudo into making an abject and instant submission to his Frankish suzerain.

In 732 the viceroy crossed the western Pyrenees at the head of the largest Saracen army that Spain had yet seen, strengthened by reinforcements from Africa and the East. Eudo stood on the defensive against him and endeavoured to defend the line of the Garonne, but was routed with the loss of almost the whole of his army. He fled beyond the Loire and threw himself on the mercy of Charles Martel; meanwhile the Saracens stormed Bordeaux, and moved slowly forward, ravaging the country on all sides till they drew near to Poictiers. It was for no mere raid that they had come on this occasion, but for the permanent conquest of Aquitaine, perhaps even with the design of attacking Neustria also. Headed by the strongest and most popular viceroy that Moslem Spain had yet known, and mustering not less than seventy or eighty thousand men, they set no limit to their desires.

In the hour of danger the great Mayor of the Palace was not wanting. He did not rush hastily into the field, but drew together the whole force of both the Frankish realms, though his firmest reliance was on his own Austrasians. Leading an army whose like had not been seen since the earliest days of the monarchy — for never had Neustria and Austrasia combined for an expedition of such moment — he crossed the Loire near Tours and advanced to meet Abderahman. It was close to Poictiers 'in suburbio Pictaviensi' that the two great hosts faced each other, though by some freak of the chronicler it is Tours that has given its name to the battle in the pages of many of our histories. Abderahman and Charles both felt that they were about to engage in no common contest. The fate of Aquitaine, possibly of all Gaul, might be largely influenced by the result of the oncoming battle between Christian and Moslem. For seven days the two hosts lay opposite each other, each waiting for the enemy to advance; at last Abderahman took the offensive, and his host poured out from their camp to assail the Frankish line. Hardly a detail of the great struggle has survived: we only know that the Saracen horsemen surged in vain around the impenetrable masses of the Frankish infantry, whose firm shield-wall 'was frozen to the earth like a rampart of ice.' The Austrasians bore the brunt of the fighting; 'the men of the East huge in stature and iron-handed hewed on long and fiercely; it was they who sought out and slew the Saracen chief.' The fight endured till night fell, when the invaders withdrew, leaving Abderahman and many thousands more lying dead in front of the Frankish line. In the darkness the Arabs had time to count up their losses, which were so appalling that they hastily fled rather than face another day's fighting. Their tents, crammed with all the booty of Aquitaine, their baggage and military stores, with thousands of horses and enormous piles of arms, fell into the hands of the victorious Franks. So ended the danger of western Christendom from the Moslem invader, a danger which has not unfrequently been exaggerated, especially by French writers anxious to glorify the Austrasian mayor, whom they have chosen to make into a French national hero. It is probable that even if Abderahman had been victorious nothing more than the duchy of Aquitaine would have fallen into his hands, for this invasion after leaving Bordeaux was degenerating into an incursion for plunder, like that which in 725 had ended with the sack of Autun. The Moslems of Spain had proved themselves during the last forty years so factious and unruly, that we cannot believe that even under a leader of exceptional ability they would have held together long and loyally enough to ensure the conquest of central Gaul. Neustria, and still more Austrasia, were states of a very different degree of vigour from the decrepit Visigothic monarchy which fell in 711. Even if Poictiers had fared as Autun, there was strength and courage enough in the Franks to face many such another blow, and we may doubt the judgment of Gibbon when he draws his gloomy forecast of the probable results of a victory for Abderahman, ending in a picture of the Muezzin calling the True Believers to prayer in the Highlands of Scotland, and the Mollahs of Oxford disputing on the attributes of a Unitarian Godhead.

The remnants of the Saracen host made no attempt to hold Aquitaine, but fled hastily across the Pyrenees, so that duke Eudo was able to reoccupy Bordeaux and Toulouse, and rule once more over the whole of his former dominions as the vassal of the Frank. Meanwhile, Charles returned to Austrasia laden with booty, and was hailed by all western Christendom as the greatest conqueror since Constantine. The Frankish poets and chroniclers continued to celebrate his triumph with such fervour that ere long the world was told and believed that he had slain 375,000 Saracens, with the loss of no more than 1500 men on his own side! If only he had been more of a favourite with the Church he would have been enshrined in history as the equal of his grandson, Charles the Great. But the zeal with which he forwarded the conversion of Germany, and smote the infidel, did not atone, in the eyes of the monkish historians, for the high-handed way in which he had dealt with the Gaulish church. Because he banished bishops, and forbade synods to be held without his leave, and occasionally laid military burdens on church-land, he received a very half-hearted blessing from the annalists of his day.

Charles spent the years that followed his great victory in regulating the government of Burgundy, where he replaced most of the counts and dukes by followers of his own, and in completing the subjection of Frisia. The peaceful duke Aldgisl had been succeeded by a fierce pagan named Boddo, whom the great mayor was soon forced to attack, when he commenced to kill or drive away the missionaries of Willibrord and Boniface. After slaying Boddo in battle, and burning every heathen shrine in Friesland, Charles left the country so tamed that it did not revolt again for full twenty years.

In 735, however, new troubles began in the south. Duke Eudo died, and Charles thought the time was ripe for the complete incorporation of the great southern duchy with the Frankish realm. He rode through the land and forced its inhabitants to do him homage, but their subjection was only the result of fear, and when he had returned home the southerners proclaimed Eudo's son Hunold as their duke. Hunold would probably have been put down had not the Saracens begun once more to stir. Headed by Yussuf-aben-Abderahman, the son of the chief who had fallen at Poictiers four years before, they sallied out of Narbonne, crossed the Rhone, and seized the old Roman city of Aries. The years 736-39 were mainly occupied in driving back three successive Moslem inroads into south-eastern Gaul, and Charles was so engrossed in this strife that he consented to recognise Hunold as duke of Aquitaine, so that he might have his hands entirely free for the greater struggle. Complete success at last crowned his arms: Provence was swept clear of the Arabs; Aries and Avignon, which the Infidels had seized and held for a space, were recovered; Nismes, Agde, and Beziers, which they had possessed since the great invasion of Septimania in 725, were taken, dismantled, and burnt, and a great host was defeated in front of Narbonne. That city, however, did not yet fall into the hands of the Franks; together with the southern half of Septimania it still remained a Saracen outpost, covering the passes of the eastern Pyrenees. For twenty years more it was fated to remain unconquered; not Charles but his son was destined to move forward the Frankish boundary to the foot of the mountains. Meanwhile the Saracens of Spain, cowed by the crushing blows of Charles the Hammer, abandoned their attempt to push northward, and plunged into a weary series of civil wars.

While Charles was engaged in his Saracen war, the puppet-king Theuderich IV., in whose name he had been ruling for the last seventeen years, chanced to die. So little had the royal name come to mean, that the great mayor did not seek out the next heir of the childless king and crown him, but ruled for the last four years of his life without any suzerain. He did not himself, however, take the kingly title, but continued to be styled mayor, prince, or duke of the Franks; he cared not for name or style so long as the real power was in his hands.

The reconquest of Provence and northern Septimania was the last of the great mayor's triumphs. But the four years which he had yet to live were not without their importance. In 738 he compelled the Westphalian Saxons on the Lippe and Ems to do him homage and pay tribute. In 739 the organisation of the south German church was completed by the erection of four bishoprics in Bavaria, which looked to Boniface, now archbishop of all Transrhenane Germany, as their Metropolitan. Thus Bavaria became ecclesiastically an integral part of the Frankish Church, even as politically it had already become an integral part of the Frankish empire. But though Charles was a firm supporter of the Church in his own dominions, he would not interfere in ecclesiastical disputes beyond his frontier. Pope Gregory III. had plunged into a struggle with the Lombard king Liutprand, and invited the pious ruler of the Franks to march against the enemy of the Church. But Charles refused; Liutprand had given him some aid against the Saracens, and he was not minded to attack an old ally merely because the Lombard had fallen out with the Pope concerning the duchy of Spoleto.

In the summer of the next year the great mayor began to feel his health failing, though he had not yet completed his fifty-fourth year. He determined to set his house in order ere yet the hand of death was upon him, and summoned the great council of all the Frankish realms to meet him. With its approval he proceeded to make over the rule of the kingdom to his sons. There was no Merovingian king whose rights needed to be taken into consideration, as Theuderich IV. had died four years back, and had left no successor. Accordingly Charles and the council dealt with the land as if it had already become the rightful inheritance of the house of St. Arnulf. The great mayor had three grown-up sons; two, Carloman and Pippin, were the offspring of his wife Rothrudis, the third, Grifo, was the son of Swanhildis, a Bavarian lady whom he had taken as his concubine during his Bavarian campaign of 725. Their ages appear to have been twenty-seven, twenty-six, and seventeen. Charles handed over the rule of Austrasia and Suabia to Carloman, and that of Neustria and Burgundy to Pippin. It is said that he also contemplated leaving a small appanage on the border of Neustria and Austrasia to Grifo. Bavaria and Aquitaine, the two great vassal dukedoms, were not named in the division, though the former fell under the influence of Carloman, and the latter under that of Pippin.

Shortly after he had accomplished this division of his realms, Charles died at Cerisy-on-Oise on the 21st of October 741. He had completed the work which his father, Pippin the Younger, had taken in hand, for the ancient boundaries of the Frankish empire had now been everywhere restored, Aquitaine and Bavaria had been reduced to vassalage, Christianity was now firmly rooted all over Frisia, Thuringia, and Hesse. The difficulties he had faced were far greater than those which his father had to encounter. He had rescued the fortunes of the house of St. Arnulf from the lowest depths, — though Austrasia had been divided, though Neustria was hostile, and though an energetic king was for once swaying the Frankish sceptre and endeavouring to recover the lost privileges of his ancestors. Having fought his way to power, Charles had then to face the one serious danger from without which the Franks had yet encountered. He had met it without flinching, and smitten the intrusive Moslem so hard that the blow did not need to be repeated. For the future we hear of Frankish invasions of Spain, not of Saracen invasions of Gaul. Charles then had won peace without and within, he had reorganised the Frankish realm, raised it to a pitch of power and glory which it had never attained before, and made possible the triumphant career of his son and grandson. As the champion of Christianity and the protector of the evangelist of Germany, he had won a yet nobler title to honourable memory, and the complaints of the Gaulish bishops, who murmured that his hand was too hard on the Church, may be lightly disregarded when we add up the sum of his merits, and salute him as the inaugurator of a new and better era in the history of Europe.

BOOK III

CHAPTER XVIII: THE ICONOCLAST EMPERORS — STATE OF THE EASTERN EMPIRE IN THE EIGHTH CENTURY — 717-802

Leo and the defence of Constantinople, 718 — Importance of his triumph — Social and economical condition of the Empire — Decay of Art and Letters — Superstition and Iconoduly — The Iconoclast movement — Leo's Crusade against Images — Constantine Copronymus and his persecutions — Successful wars of Constantine V. — Minority of Constantine VI. — Intrigues and triumph of Irene — Restoration of Image-worship — End of the Isaurian dynasty, 802.

In March 717 Leo the Isaurian became master of Constantinople, his predecessor, Theodosius III., having abdicated and refused to continue the civil war which had begun in the previous year. It is probable that his resignation was due as much to fear of the oncoming of the Saracens as to the dread of Leo, for the armies of the caliph Soliman were already ravaging Phrygia and Cappadocia, and slowly making their way towards the Bosphorus. Nothing save the consciousness of his own capacity to stem the rising flood of Moslem invasion could have justified Leo in taking arms against Theodosius in such a time of danger; but fortunately for the empire he had not overvalued his own power, and was destined to show that he was fully competent to face the situation. He was still a young man, but his life had already been full of incident and adventure; he was the son of parents of some wealth, who had migrated from the Isaurian regions in the Taurus to Thrace. He had entered the army during the second reign of Justinian Rhinotmetus, and after serving him well had incurred the tyrant's suspicion, and been sent on a dangerous expedition into the Caucasus, from which he was not intended to return. But he extricated himself from many perils among the Alans and Abasgi of those distant regions, and came back in safety, to be made by Anastasius II. governor of the Anatolic theme. He was an active, enterprising, persevering man, with a talent for organisation, a great power of making himself loved by his soldiery, and an iron hand. His later career shows that he was more than a good soldier, being also one who looked deep into the causes of things, and had formed his own views on politics and religion.

Leo was only granted five months in which to prepare for the long-dreaded advent of the Saracens. He spent this time in accumulating vast stores of provisions, recruiting the garrison of Constantinople, and strengthening its fortifications. On the 15th of August Moslemah with an army of 80,000 Saracens appeared on the Bithynian coast; a few days later a Syrian fleet of over 1000 sail appeared in the Propontis, took the army of Moslemah on board, and transported it into Thrace. The Saracen's land-troops at once commenced the blockade of the capital by land, while part of the fleet moved into the Bosphorus, to post itself so as to block the mouth of the Golden Horn, in which the Imperial navy had taken refuge. Leo delivered his first blow while the Saracen vessels were passing up the Bosphorus; issuing out of the Golden Horn with many galleys and fireships he attacked the enemy as they were trying to pass up the straits, and burnt twenty ships of war. The Saracen admiral then dropped down to the southern exit of the Bosphorus, and left the northern exit free to the Romans, so that Leo was able to continue to draw supplies from the Black Sea.

The blockade of Constantinople was, therefore, imperfect, and we learn without surprise, that while the Saracens in their camp on the Thracian side of the straits suffered severely from the cold of an unusually severe autumn and winter, the garrison within the walls was well fed and also well housed, and continued to grow in self-confidence. Moslemah sent in haste for reinforcements, and the Caliph supported him with zeal; a second land-army marched up from Tarsus to Chalcedon in the spring of 718, and occupied the Bithynian shore of the Bosphorus, while a great fleet from Africa and Egypt joined the blockading squadron, and moored at Kalosagros on the eastern side of the Bosphorus, in order to watch the mouth of the Golden Horn, and stop the communication of the city with the Black Sea.

The preservation of the free waterway to the north was all-important to the defence. Accordingly, Leo determined to make a great effort to destroy the Egyptian fleet. His galleys, many of them fitted with apparatus for discharging the famous Greek fire, sailed out suddenly, and fell on the Saracen ships as they lay moored against the Asiatic shore. Many of the crews of the Egyptian ships were Christians, forced on board against their will; these men either deserted to the Imperialists or fled ashore and dispersed. The Moslem sailors on board made some resistance, but being caught at anchor, and unable to manoeuvre or escape, they were soon overcome. The whole blockading squadron was burnt or towed back in triumph to Constantinople. The rest of Moslemah's fleet made no further attempt to bar the Bosphorus, and allowed the Roman galleys to dominate its waters. Leo then threw a force on to the Bithynian shore, and dispersed the Saracen troops who were encamped there. Thus the army of Moslemah was cut off from Asia, and could draw no further supplies from thence. It had already exhausted those of the nearer districts of Thrace, and by the summer of 718 was reduced to the verge of starvation, living from hand to mouth on what its foragers could procure. Many had already perished of privation, when Moslemah heard that a great Bulgarian army had crossed the Balkans, and was advancing against him. Leo had apparently convinced king Terbel that a Saracen invasion of Europe was as dangerous to him as to the empire. Moslemah detached a portion of his army to hold back the Bulgarians, but near Hadrianople it was completely cut to pieces by the barbarians. The Arab historians confess that 22,000 men fell in the rout.

This decided Moslemah to raise the siege. His fleet took the remains of the land army on board, and put it ashore near Cyzicus. From thence he forced his way back to Tarsus, but of more than 100,000 men comprised in his original army and its reinforcements, Moslemah brought back only 30,000. The fleet fared yet worse; it was caught in a storm off the Lycian coast, and almost entirely destroyed. The Romans captured many of the surviving ships, and it is said that only five vessels out of a thousand got back to Syria.

Thus perished the last Saracen armament which ever seriously threatened the existence of the East-Roman Empire. It was perhaps the most formidable expedition that the Caliphs ever sent forth, far larger and better equipped than the predatory bands which had overrun Africa and Spain with such ease a few years before, or the army which Charles Martel faced at Poictiers a few years later. It was no mean achievement of Leo the Isaurian, that, ere yet firmly seated on his throne, and with all his Asiatic provinces already overrun by the enemy, he should beat off with ease such a mighty armament. His success must be ascribed primarily to his own courage, energy, and skill, next to the impregnable strength of the walls of Constantinople, and lastly, to the inexperience of the Arabs on the sea, which compelled them to use unwilling Christian seamen for their galleys, and prevented them from making any adequate use of their momentary naval predominance. The fleet of Moslemah seems to have been as useless and unwieldy as the fleet of Xerxes. But, however much he may have been helped by the faults of his enemy, Leo the Isaurian deserves the thanks of all future ages for staying the progress of the Saracen invader at a moment when there was no other power in eastern Europe which could have for a moment held back the advancing Moslem. If Constantinople had fallen, it is absolutely certain that the barbarous pagan tribes who occupied all eastern and central Europe would have become the subjects of the Caliph, and the votaries of Islam. There was no capacity for prolonged resistance in the Bulgarian, Avar, or Slav; and if the East-Roman Empire had fallen, the wave of Saracen invasion would have swept all before it up to the borders of Austrasia. Whether the Franks could have stood firm if attacked on the east as well as on the south is very doubtful. It is, therefore, fair to ascribe to Leo the Isaurian an even greater share in the salvation of Europe from the Moslem peril than is given to Charles Martel.

After the failure of Moslemah the victorious Leo had a breathing time granted him, in which to reorganise the shattered realm that had been left him by his predecessor. Although the Saracen war still went on, and border raids never ceased till the very end of his reign, yet there was no very serious danger in these latter bickerings, and Leo was able to turn his attention to the internal affairs of the empire, without the fear of having at any moment a dangerous invasion launched against him from beyond the Taurus.

Leo was a reformer and an innovator in every branch of administration. His dealings with the Church are those which caused most stir and are best remembered, but his activity was as great in secular as in ecclesiastical matters. It is unfortunate that most of the records of his reforms have perished, nothing having been preserved except his Ecloga or new handbook of law. But enough survives to show the character of his administration, and its effects in the succeeding century are very marked.

We have already pointed out in an earlier chapter that the East-Roman Empire had been in a state of rapid decay since the middle of the sixth century. The downward movement that had begun with the wars and taxes of Justinian had been accelerated under his successors, and had threatened the actual destruction of the empire during the reign of Heraclius. That the State struggled through all its troubles, and emerged bleeding at every pore, shorn of many of its members, but still alive, was due to the personal abilities of Heraclius and his descendants Constantinus-Constans and Constantine V. But though the life still lingered in the body of the State, it was yet in the most deplorable condition. Its purely Oriental provinces — Egypt, Syria, and Africa — were gone for ever. Asia Minor was dreadfully wasted by the repeated invasions of the Saracens. The Balkan peninsula was, as regards more than half its extent, in the hands of the Bulgarians and Slavs. In the seventh century Slavonic tribes had made their way even into Hellas and Peloponnesus, there to occupy all the more remote and mountainous corners of the land.

The disasters of the seventh century were accompanied by wholesale displacements of population. In Europe the old Latin-speaking population of Illyricum, Moesia, and Thrace had almost disappeared. Only a few scattered fragments, the ancestors of the modern Roumanians and Dalmatians, still survived, scattered among the Slavs of the Balkans. In Asia the old provincial population had been grievously thinned by Saracen wars, but, on the other hand, it had been recruited by great bands of refugees from all the lands that the Saracen had overrun. Many thousands of Armenians and Persians had chosen to become subjects of the Emperor rather than the Caliph, and in particular the Mardaites or Christians of the Syrian mountains had emigrated wholesale into Asia Minor, after maintaining for many years a struggle in the Lebanon against the power of the Saracens. The European themes were now Greco-Slav, not Greco-Roman, in their population: the Asiatic ones were far more Oriental and far less Greek than in the sixth century. By the time of Leo this change was complete: the empire was now Roman in nothing but name and administrative organisation. On the other hand, it had not yet become Greek, as it was to do in a later age. Its most important element in this and the next two centuries was the Asiatic. Isauria and Armenia and the other mountain lands of Asia Minor supplied most of the rulers of the empire. They were not Orientals of the more effeminate and feeble type — like the Syrians or Egyptians, whose only show of energy for many years had been in the hatching of new heresies and the practice of irrational asceticism — but were a bold vigorous race, hardened by many generations of Persian and Saracen wars, the men who, ever since the fifth century, had been supplying the core of the East-Roman armies. The change in the population of the empire had been accompanied by equally great changes in its social condition. Of these the most important was the disappearance of the old Roman system of predial serfdom, of great estates tilled by coloni or peasants bound to the soil and unable to leave their farms. This tenure, which lasted on in the West till it became the basis of the feudal system, had in the East entirely disappeared between Justinian and Leo the Isaurian. In the time of Leo we find the soil cultivated either by free tenants, who worked the estates of great land-owners at a fixed rent, or by villages of free peasants Occupying their own communal lands. The very healthy outcome of this change was a great growth in the proportion of freemen to slaves all over the empire: of this the most important and beneficial result was that the government could reckon on a much larger and better recruiting ground for the army than in those earlier times, when the peasant was fixed to the soil and absolutely prohibited from serving as a soldier. The cause of the vanishing of the old tenure was, without doubt, the fact that the ravages of Slav, Persian, and Saracen between 600 and 700 had broken up the old landmarks, and either swept away or displaced the former servile population. When many provinces had been, for many years at a time, in the hands of foreign enemies, as happened to the whole of Asia Minor during the first years of Heraclius and to great part of it in the anarchy between 710 and 718, it was not wonderful that old social arrangements which bore hardly on the bulk of the population tended to vanish.

The disappearance of predial serfdom was a change for the better within the empire. But in most other things the changes had been for the worse. The civilisation of the whole realm had sunk to a very low level compared with that which prevailed in the fifth century. Arts and letters had reached the lowest depth which they ever knew in the East. All literature save the compiling of polemical religious tracts had disappeared: between 620 and 720 we have not a single contemporary historian: the story of the times has to be learned entirely from later sources. Poetical, scientific, and philosophical composition had also died off; except the Heracliad — the wars of Heraclius told as an epic — of George of Pisidia, the seventh century produced no single poem. The study of Latin had so far died out that the great legal works of Justinian had become useless to the inhabitants of the empire. They were a sealed book to all save the exceptionally learned, so that systematic law had almost disappeared. In the various themes we find justice being administered according to local customs and usages, instead of by old Roman precept. Leo had to abridge and translate Justinian's Code, in order to render it either useful or intelligible. When doing this he omitted great sections of it, in order to bring the book into accordance with the needs and customs of the day, for both manners and social conditions had been transformed since the reign of Justinian. The decay of art had been as rapid as that of letters: very few remains of the unhappy seventh century have come down to us, but in those which are most numerous, the coins of the emperors, we find the most barbarous incapacity to express the simplest forms. The faces of Heraclius or Constantine V. are barely human: the legends surrounding them are so ill spelt as to be almost unintelligible: the letters are ill formed and ill cut.

But the most painful feature of the time was that the decay of arts and letters had been accompanied by the growth of a dense superstition and ignorance which would have seemed incredible to the ancient Roman of the fourth, or even the fifth century. Although Constantinople still preserved all the great literary works of antiquity, the minds of its rulers were no more influenced by them than were the eyes and hands of its craftsmen inspired by the great works of Greek sculpture that still adorned the streets. It was a time of the growth of countless silly superstitions, of witchcraft and necromancy, of the framing of wild legends of apocryphal saints, and of strange misconceptions of natural phenomena.

Among the most prominent tokens of this growth of irrational superstitions was the great tendency of the seventh century towards image-worship, — Iconoduly as its opponents called the practice. In direct opposition to early Christian custom, it became common to ascribe the most strange and magical powers to representations, whether sculptured or painted, of Our Lord and the Saints. They were not merely regarded as useful memorials to guide the piety of believers, but were thought to have a holiness inherent in themselves, and to be Capable of performing the most astonishing miracles. Heraclius possessed, and carried about with him as a fetish, a picture which he believed to have been painted in heaven by angelic hands, and thought it brought him all manner of luck. The crucifix over the door of the imperial palace was believed to have used human speech. Even patriarchs and bishops affirmed that the hand of a celebrated picture of the Virgin in the capital distilled fragrant balsam. Every church and monastery had its wonder-working image, and drew no small revenue from pious offerings to it. The freaks to which image-worship led were often most grotesque: it was, for example, a well-known practice to make a favourite picture the god-father of a child in baptism, by scraping off a little of its paint and mixing it with the baptismal water.

The act for which the name of Leo the Isaurian is best remembered is the issue of his edict against these puerile superstitions, and his attempt to put down image-worship all through his realm. Leo was not only a man of strong common sense, but he was sprung from those lands on the Mohammedan border where Christians had the best opportunity of comparing the gross and material adoration of their co-religionists for stones and paint, with the severe spiritual worship of the followers of Islam. The Moslem was always taunting the Christian with serving idols, and the taunt found too much justification in many practices of the vulgar. Thinking men like Leo were moved by the Moslem's sneer into a horror of the superstitious follies of their contemporaries. They fortified themselves by the view that to make graven or painted representations of Our Lord savoured of heresy, because it laid too much stress on His humanity as opposed to His divinity. Such an idea was no new thing: it had often been mooted among the Eastern Christians, though more often by schismatics than by Catholics. Of Leo's own orthodoxy, however, there was no doubt: even his enemies could not convict him of swerving in the least from the faith: it was only on this matter of image-worship that he differed from them. Wherever he plucked down the crucifix he set up the plain cross — on the standards of his army, on the gates of his palace, on his money, on his imperial robes. It was purely to the anthropomorphic representation of Our Lord and to the over-reverence for images of saints that he objected.

Leo was no mere rough soldier: his parents were people of some wealth, and he had entered the army as an imperial aide-de-camp (spathiarius), not as one of the rank and file. It is probable therefore that he was sufficiently educated to object to image-worship on rational and philosophic grounds not from the mere unthinking prejudice picked up from Saracens or heretics. This much is certain, that from the moment that he declared his policy he found the greatest support among the higher officers of the civil service and the army. Educated laymen were as a rule favourable to his views: the mass of the soldiery followed him, and the eastern provinces as a whole acquiesced in his reformation. On the other hand, he found his chief opponents among the monks, whose interests were largely bound up with image-worship, and among the lower classes, who were blindly addicted to it. The European themes were as a whole opposed to him: the further west the province the more Iconodulic were its tendencies. Of the whole empire Italy was the part where Leo's views found the least footing.

Leo began his crusade against image-worship in 726, eight years after his great victory over the Saracens. The empire was by this time quieted down and reorganised; two rebellions had also been crushed, one under a certain Basil in Italy, the other under the ex-emperor Artemius Anastasius, who had tried to resume the crown by the aid of the Bulgarians. The heads of Basil and Artemius had fallen, and no more trouble from rebellion was expected. Leo's edict forbade all image-worship as irreverent and superstitious, and ordered the removal of all holy statues and the white-washing of all holy pictures on church walls. From the very first the emperor's commands met with a lively resistance. When his officials began to remove the great crucifix over the palace gate, a mob fell upon them and beat them to death with clubs. Leo sent out troops to clear the streets, and many of the rioters were slain. This evil beginning was followed by an equally disastrous sequel. All over the empire the bulk of the clergy declared against the emperor: in many provinces they began to preach open sedition. The Pope, as we have already seen when telling the fate of Italy, put himself at the head of the movement, and sent most insulting letters to Constantinople. In 727 Rome refused obedience to the edict, and what was of more immediate danger, the theme of Hellas rose in open rebellion. The garrison-troops and the populace, incited by the preaching of fanatical monks, joined to proclaim a certain Cosmas emperor. They fitted out a fleet to attack Constantinople, but it was defeated, and the rebel emperor was taken prisoner and beheaded. It is acknowledged, however, even by Leo's enemies, that he treated the bulk of the prisoners and the rebel theme with great mildness. Indeed, he seldom punished disobedience to his edict with death: stripes and imprisonment were the more frequent rewards of those whom the Iconodules styled heroes and confessors of the true faith. Leo was determined that his edict should be carried out, but he was not by nature a persecutor: it was as rioters or rebels, not as image-worshippers, that his enemies were punished, just as in the reign of Elizabeth of England the Jesuit suffered, not as a Papist, but as a traitor. Leo deposed the aged patriarch Germanus for refusing to work with him, but did him no further harm. In general it was by promoting Iconoclasts, not by maltreating Iconodules, that he worked.

The last thirteen years of Leo's reign (727-40) were on the whole a time of success for the emperor. He succeeded in getting his edict enforced over the greater part of the empire, in spite of some open and more secret resistance; only Italy defied him. From the reconquest of Rome he was kept back by the necessity of providing for the defence of the East, for in 726 the caliph Hisham — hearing no doubt of Leo's domestic troubles — commenced once more to invade the Asiatic themes. In 727 a Saracen host pushed forward as far as Nicaea, where it was repelled and forced to retire, There were less formidable invasions in 730, 732, and 737-8, but none led to any serious loss, and the imperial boundary stood firmly fixed in the passes of the Taurus. The Saracen war practically ended with a great victory won by Leo in person at Acroinon, in the Anatolic theme, where an army of 20,000 Arab raiders was cut to pieces with the loss of all its chiefs. The house of the Ommeyad Caliphs was already verging towards its decline: it never again prepared any expedition approaching the strength of the great armament of Moslemah, which Leo had so effectually turned back in 718, and its later sovereigns were not of the type of those fanatical conquerors who had cut the boundaries of the empire short in the preceding century. Leo had effectually staved off any imminent danger to eastern Christendom from Moslem conquest for three full centuries.

Leo was succeeded by his son Constantine, fifth of that name according to the usual reckoning, sixth if the grandson of Heraclius be given his true name, and not the erroneous title of Constans II. The second of the Isaurian emperors, however, is less known by the numeral affixed to his name than by the insulting epithet of Copronymus, which his Iconodulic enemies bestowed on him — showing thereby their own bad taste rather than any unworthiness on the part of their sovereign.

Constantine was a young man of twenty-two at the moment of his accession. He had long acted as his father's colleague, and was thoroughly trained in Leo's methods of administration, and indoctrinated with his Iconoclastic views. He seems, while possessing a great measure of his father's energy and ability, to have been inferior to him in two respects. Leo had combined caution with courage, and knew how to exercise moderation. Constantine was bold to excess, did not understand half-measures or toleration, and carried through every scheme with a high hand. Moreover, while Leo's private life had been blameless and even severe, Constantine was a votary of pleasure, fond of pomp and shows, devoted to musical and theatrical entertainments, and sometimes lapsing into debauchery. Hence it is easy to see why he has been dealt with by the chroniclers of the next century in an even harsher spirit than his father, and is represented as a monster of cruelty and vice.

Constantine was no sooner seated on the throne than he showed that he was determined to continue his father's policy. He was at once assailed by the rebellion of the Iconodulic faction: they induced his brother-in-law Artavasdus, general of the Obsequian theme, to seize the capital, and proclaim himself emperor, while Constantine was absent on an expedition against the Saracens. All the European themes, where the image-breakers were hated, did homage to Artavasdus. But the Anatolic and Thracesian themes, the heart of Asia Minor, remained true to the son of Leo. He showed his energy and ability by beating the sons of Artavasdus in two battles, and besieging the rebel in Constantinople. When the city was well-nigh reduced by famine, Artavasdus fled, but he was caught and brought before Constantine. The emperor ordered him and his sons to be blinded, and confined them in a monastery. Their chief adherents were beheaded (742).

This sanguinary lesson to the Iconodulic party seems to have cowed them to such an extent that they did not raise another open rebellion in the long reign of Constantine (740-775). But they adhered as fully as ever to their faith: nothing is so difficult to eradicate as a well-rooted superstition, and Constantine's strong hand was better fitted to cow than to persuade. As the years of his reign passed by, and he found image-worship practised in secret by thousands of conscientious votaries, the emperor grew more and more determined to uproot it. After a time he resolved to call in the spiritual sanction to aid the secular arm: in 753 he summoned a general council to meet at Constantinople, but it was oecumenical only in name. The Pope replied by anathemas of contumely to the summons to appear; the patriarchs of Antioch, Jerusalem, and Alexandria, safe under the protection of the caliph, denied their presence. But there assembled an imposing body of three hundred and thirty-eight bishops, presided over by the Constantinopolitan patriarch, Constantine of Sylaeum, and by Theodosius, metropolitan of Ephesus, son of the emperor Tiberius II. This council committed itself fully to Iconoclastic doctrine; it proscribed all representations of Our Lord as blasphemous snares, for endeavouring to express both His human and His divine nature in the mere likeness of a man, and thereby obscuring His divinity in His humanity. At the same time it condemned the worship of images of saints, because all adoration except that paid to the Godhead savoured of heathenism and anthropolatry. The emperor had other scruples of his own, on which he did not press the council to deliver a decision; he denied the intercessory powers of the

Virgin, and scrupled to prefix the epithet ayios, 'holy,' to the names of even the greatest saints. He spoke, for example, of 'Peter the Apostle,' not of 'the holy Peter.' On these awful depths of free thought the Iconodules of his own and the succeeding generation wasted expressions of horror, worthy to be employed on a Herod or a Judas.

Armed with the decree of the council of Constantinople, the emperor proceeded, during the remainder of his reign, to indulge in what was a true religious persecution, for he pursued the image-worshippers as heretics, not as rebels or rioters. He inflicted the death-penalty in a few cases, but the majority of his victims were flogged, mutilated, pilloried, or banished. The most obstinate supporters of Iconoduly were found among the monks, who not only resisted themselves, but never ceased to use their vast influence over the mob in order to turn it against the emperor. After a time Constantine resolved to make an end of the monastic system, as being the strongest bulwark of superstition. To uproot a habit of life founded on the practice of centuries, and highly revered by the multitude was of course an impossibility. Monasteries can only be suppressed, as they were at the Reformation, if the nation sides with the sovereign. Nevertheless, Constantine drove out and harried a vast number of monks. He held that they were over-numerous, that they were men who shirked the ordinary duties of the citizen, and that their profession was a cloak for selfishness and sloth. He aimed not only at breaking up the cloisters, but at secularising their inmates. On one occasion he had all the monks and nuns of the Thracesian theme assembled, and offered them their choice between marriage or banishment to Cyprus. The majority chose the latter alternative, and became in the eyes of their contemporaries confessors of the true faith. On another occasion he exhibited in the Hippodrome a procession of unfrocked monks, each holding by the hand an unfrocked nun whom he was to marry — the Iconodule writers, as might be expected, call the backsliding nuns 'harlots.' The deserted monasteries were either pulled down for building materials or turned into barracks.

But it must not be supposed that Constantine's activity was entirely engrossed in persecuting the worshippers of images. The thirty-five years of his reign were a period of considerable military glory, and the emperor, who always headed his own armies, took the field for more than a dozen campaigns. In Asia the fall of the Ommeyad Caliphs, accompanied by savage civil wars among the Saracens (750), offered an unrivalled opportunity for extending the bounds of the empire. Constantine pushed beyond the Anti-Taurus as far as the Euphrates; in 745 he occupied the district of Commagene, and transported all its Christian inhabitants to Thrace: in 751 he took Melitene on the Euphrates, and the great Armenian fortress of Theodosiopolis. Part of these conquests were afterwards recovered by the first Abbaside Caliph, Abdallah Al-Saffah, but the rest remained to the empire as a trophy of Constantine's wars. Several Saracen attempts to invade Cappadocia and Cyprus were driven back with great slaughter, and in general it may be stated that Constantine effectually protected Asia Minor from the Mohammedan sword, and that the country began to grow again both in wealth and in population.

Nor was his work less useful in Europe. He completely reduced to order the Slavonic tribes south of the Balkan, both in Thrace and Macedonia: they had got out of hand during the troubles of the years 695-718, and required to be subdued anew. Constantine carefully fortified the defiles of the Balkans, which communicate with the valley of the Danube, garrisoning once more the ruined castles which Justinian had built there. This advance northward brought him into hostile contact with the Bulgarians, who had long been accustomed to harry both the Slavonic and the Roman districts of Thrace and Macedon, and could not brook to be walled in by the new fine of forts. Constantine waged three successful wars with the Bulgarians; the first, lasting from 755 to 762, ended with a great victory at Anchialus, after which king Baian sued for peace, and obtained it on promising to keep his subjects from raiding across the Balkans. The second war occupied the years 764-773. Constantine crossed the Balkans, wasted Bulgaria, slew the new king Toktu near the Danube, and was preparing in the next year to complete the conquest of the country, when his whole fleet and army were destroyed by a storm in the Black Sea (765). Long and indecisive bickering on the line of the Balkans followed, and peace was made in 773 on the old terms. The last Bulgarian war, provoked by an attempt of king Telerig to invade Macedonia in 774-5, was notable for a great victory at Lithosoria, but Constantine died while leading his army northward, and his successes had no permanent result. The Bulgarians were not subdued by him, but they were kept at bay, and so tamed that they were compelled to leave Thrace alone, and content themselves with defending their own Danubian plains from the attacks of the East-Romans.

The Saracen and Bulgarian being driven away from the frontier, we are not surprised to hear that the empire flourished under Constantine. He planted many colonies on the waste lands of the borders, settling the emigrant Christians of Armenia in Thrace, and many Slavonic and Bulgarian refugees in Bithynia. We are told that agriculture prospered in his time, so much that sixty measures of wheat sold for a gold solidus. He exterminated brigandage, and made the roads safe for merchants. He furnished Constantinople with a new water-supply by restoring the aqueduct of Valens, broken more than a hundred and fifty years before. When the capital had been devastated by a great plague in 746-7, he more than replaced the lost thousands of its population by new settlers from Hellas and the islands, for whom employment was found by the increasing commerce which followed the growth of internal prosperity. When he died in 775, aged fifty-seven, he left a full treasury, a loyal and devoted army, and a well-organised realm.

Constantine was succeeded by his eldest son Leo IV., often called Leo the Chazar, because his mother Irene had been a Chazar princess. Leo had acted as his father's colleague for many years, and carried on Constantine's policy, though with a less harsh hand. In the beginning of his reign he showed toleration to the Iconodules, but when they commenced to raise their heads again he resumed his father's persecuting manner, flogging and banishing many prominent image-worshippers. He did not, however, object to monks, as Constantine had done, but allowed them to rebuild their convents, and even promoted some of them to bishoprics. It is probable that his resumption of persecution in 777 was connected with the discovery of a conspiracy against him in which his own brothers Nicephorus and Christophorus had leagued themselves with the discontented party. The treacherous Caesars were pardoned by their brother, and their associates suffered banishment and not death.

Leo continued his father's war with the Saracens. In 778 his armies invaded Commagene, defeated a great Saracen host in the open field, and brought back under their protection a great body of Syrian Christians, who were settled as colonists in Thrace. The caliph Mehdy replied in the next year by an invasion of the Anatolic theme: his army forced its way as far as Dorylaeum, but retired in disorder, and much harassed by the Romans, after failing to take that place.

Leo was of a sickly habit of body, and died after a short reign of five years, in 780, before he had attained the age of thirty-two. He left the throne to his son Constantine VI.; for whom the empress Irene was to act as regent, as the boy was only nine years of age. Leo's early death was a fatal misfortune alike for the Iconoclastic cause and the Isaurian dynasty. The empress Irene, though she had succeeded in concealing the fact during her husband's life, was a fervent worshipper of images, and the moment that the reins of power fell into her hands, set herself to reverse the imperial policy of the last sixty years. She began by putting an end to the repression of the Iconodules, and then gradually displaced the old ministers of state and governors of the themes by creatures of her own. This led to a plot against her; the conspirators proposed to crown Nicephorus, the eldest of her brothers-in-law, but they were discovered and banished, while all the five brothers of the deceased emperor were forcibly made priests, to disqualify them from seizing the throne.

When the patriarch Paul died in 784, Irene replaced him by Tarasius, a fervent image-worshipper, and then ventured to call a general council at Nicaea, to which she invited pope Hadrian at Rome, and the Patriarchs of the East, to send delegates. Under the influence of the empress the council, by a large majority, declared the lawfulness of making representations of Our Lord and the Saints, and bade men pay not divine worship, but adoration and reverence to them. The recalcitrant Iconoclastic bishops were excommunicated. The doings of the council caused a mutiny of the Imperial guard in Constantinople, for the greater part of the army still adhered to the views of the Isaurian emperors. But Irene succeeded in steering through the troubled waters, put down the mutiny, and retained her power.

Meanwhile the reign of a child and a woman proved disastrous to the empire. The Slavs of the Balkans burst into revolt, and the Saracens invaded Asia Minor. The want of an emperor to head the army was grievously felt, and Haroun-al-Raschid, the son of the caliph Mehdy, ravaged the whole Anatohc and Obsequian themes as far as the Bosphorus. Irene felt herself unable to cope with the situation, and bought a peace by an annual payment of 70,000 solidi (784). Soon after the Bulgarian king declared war, and ravaged Thrace after slaying the general of the Thracian theme in battle.

Among these disasters Constantine VI. grew up to manhood, but his mother, who had acquired a great taste for power, and feared to see her son reverse her religious policy, long refused to give him any share in the government. She even made the army swear never to receive her son as sole emperor as long as she should live. The young emperor, after chafing for some time in his state of tutelage, took matters into his own hands. In his twenty-first year he repaired to the camp of the Anatolic troops, and there proclaimed himself of age, and sole ruler of the State. He banished his mother's favourites, and confined her for some months to her own apartments in the palace.

When he had firmly seized the helm of power, Constantine was weak enough to take his mother again as his colleague on the throne, and to associate her name with his in all imperial decrees. The ambitious and unnatural Irene repaid his confidence by scheming against him. She had grown so fond of power that she had resolved to win it back at all costs. Constantine was, like his ancestors, a warlike and energetic prince. He won several successes over the Saracens, and then engaged in a Bulgarian war. His popularity was first shaken by a fearful defeat at the hands of the Bulgarian king Cardam, by which he lost much of his influence with the army. Shortly afterwards he entered into a fierce struggle with the Patriarch and the clergy, having divorced, in spite of their opposition, a wife whom his mother had forced upon him in early youth, and espoused Theodota, on whom his own affections were set. Knowing that the Church was wroth with Constantine for this outbreak of self-will, and that the army no longer loved him as before, the wicked Irene determined to strike a blow against her son. She suborned some of the young emperor's attendants to seize their master, and, when he fell into her hands, had his eyes put out. He was then immured in a monastery, where he survived for more than twenty years.

It was by a mere palace-conspiracy, not by an open rising, that the unnatural mother had dethroned and blinded her son. It is, therefore, all the more extraordinary to find that she was able to cling to power for more than five years, in spite of the horror which her act had caused. The gratitude of the image-worshippers to her, for having restored to them the power of practising their superstition, partly explains, but does not at all excuse the impunity which she enjoyed after her cruel deed.

Irene's five years of power (797-802) were disastrous at home and abroad. Her court was swayed by two greedy eunuchs, Aetius and Stauracius, on whom she lavished all the highest offices. Their miserable quarrels with each other are the chief things recorded in the annals of her internal government. Meanwhile the frontiers were overrun by the armies of Haroun-al-Raschid. The Saracens harried the Anatolic and Thracesian themes, and forced their way as far as Ephesus. Peace was only granted when Irene consented to pay a large annual tribute to the Caliph.

In 802 the cup of Irene's iniquities was full. To put an end to anarchy abroad and within, a number of the chief officers of State, headed by the treasurer Nicephorus, seized her by night, and shut her up in a nunnery. No one struck a blow in her defence, for she was loved by no one, not even by the Iconodules, for whom she had done so much. Nicephorus was proclaimed as her successor, and ascended the throne without any disturbance.

Thus ended the house of the Isaurians, after eighty-five years of rule. They had effected much for the empire; for the disasters of Irene's short reign had not sufficed to undo the solid work of Leo III. and Constantine V. The boundaries were safer, the population greater, the wealth largely increased, the armies more efficient than at the commencement of the century. Even the Iconoclastic persecutions, though they had failed to crush superstition, had done some good in rooting out the grosser vagaries of image-worship. The Iconoclastic party still subsisted, and was strong in the army and civil service; we shall see it once more in power during the ninth century.

CHAPTER XIX: PIPPIN THE SHORT — WARS OF THE FRANKS AND LOMBARDS — 741-768

Mayoralty of Pippin and Carloman — Their successful wars — Boniface reforms the Frankish church — Abdication of Carloman — Pippin dethrones Childebert III. and assumes the royal title — Quarrel of Aistulf and Pope Stephen — The Pope calls the Franks into Italy — Pippin twice subdues Aistulf — The Exarchate given to the Papacy — Martyrdom of St. Boniface — Conquest of Narbonne — Long struggle with the dukes of Aquitaine — Death of Pippin.

The events which immediately followed the death of Charles Martel showed clearly enough that the house of St. Arnulf must still depend on the power of the sword to guard its ascendency, and that it could only continue to rule by continuing to produce a series of able chiefs. It was fortunate for the Frankish realm that Pippin and Carloman were both men of sense and vigour, though perhaps they did not attain to the full stature of their father's greatness. Not less fortunate was it that, unlike the kings of the Merovingian house, they dwelt together in amity and brotherly love, and undertook every scheme in common.

The moment that Charles was dead troubles broke out on every hand. Grifo, the younger brother of the two mayors, declared himself wronged in the partition of the kingdoms, seized Laon, and began to gather an army of Neustrian malcontents. Theudebald, the brother of the duke of Suabia, who had been overthrown in 730, raised the Alamanni in revolt in Elsass and the Black Forest. Hunold, duke of Aquitaine, disclaimed the suzerainty of the Frankish crown, while the Saxons refused the tribute which had been laid upon them, and invaded Hesse.

The whole of 742 was spent by Pippin and Carloman in dealing with the storm which had burst upon them. They began with crushing their unruly brother, captured him, and sent him captive to a fortress in the Ardennes. Next they marched against Hunold of Aquitaine, and harried the southern bank of the Loire, but the duke retreated southward without fighting, and other duties called away the two mayors before he was subdued. It was now the dangerous rising in Suabia, in the very midst of their realm, which demanded their attention. They descended upon the Alamanni with irresistible force, and soon subdued the whole land as far as the Bavarian frontier But there was yet more fighting to be done, and, ere they finished their task, the two mayors had determined to legalise their somewhat anomalous position as regents for a non-existent sovereign. They sought out and crowned Childerich III., the last of the Merovingians, as feeble a shadow as his long-deceased kinsman, Theuderich IV. So, after an interregnum of six years, the Franks had once more a king.

It was three years before the authority of Carloman and Pippin had been vindicated in every corner of the realm, but at last Aquitaine had acknowledged once more its vassal obligations, the Saxons had been chastised, and an attempt of Bavaria to make itself independent had been crushed. The struggle had not been without its difficulties, and the two mayors had been so hard pressed for resources, that they had followed in their father's steps by laying hands on Church property, compelling bishops and abbeys to devote a certain portion of their landed estates to the support of the war-expenses of the crown. Other dealings with the Church had been as unpopular though less unorthodox; the Frankish clergy were often irregular in their lives, lax in their spiritual duties, and given over to all manner of secular pursuits. The mayors set the stern missionary enthusiast Boniface to reform these evils. At the great synod of 745, to which all the prelates of both Frankish realms were bidden, the great archbishop entered into a campaign against clerical abuses of all sorts. At his behest canons were passed against immoral life, pluralities, the granting of benefices to unordained persons, the disobedience of bishops to their metropolitans, the light assumption and rejection of the monastic habit and vow, and the favouring of heresy. Boniface had also much trouble with those who, headed by the Irish missionary bishop Clement, refused obedience to the Roman See, a fault which the great archbishop regarded as no less heinous than the open profession of unorthodoxy. In all his doings he received the zealous support of Carloman and Pippin. Ecclesiastical reform within was not unaccompanied by ecclesiastical extension without. In these troubled years of the two mayors, Boniface portioned out the newly-converted lands of central Germany into the three bishoprics of Wurzburg, Erfurt, and Buraburg, to serve respectively as sees for Franconia, Thuringia, and Hesse. At the same time was founded his great abbey of Fulda, the centre of piety and learning in Transrhenane Germany during the succeeding age.

To the great surprise of all his contemporaries, the mayor Carloman, on the completion of his task of re-establishing Order in Austrasia, laid down his sword, and assumed the monk's gown, in the year 747. 'The causes no man knew, but it would seem that he was truly moved by a desire for the contemplative life and for the love of God.' It was certainly no weakness or desire for inglorious ease that led him to follow the example of his ancestor St. Arnulf, and seek out a hermitage. He passed into Italy, obtained the blessing of Pope Zacharias, and built himself a cell on Mount Soracte, in the Sabine hills. We shall hear of his name but once again, seven years after his abdication.

By his brother's retirement Pippin became mayor of Austrasia as well as of Neustria. He had one more struggle to wage ere all things were fully beneath his hand. In 747 his brother Grifo escaped from prison, and fled to Saxony, from whence he tried to stir up trouble. When Odilo duke of Bavaria died, he seized that duchy, claiming it in right of his mother, Swanhildis, who was of the ducal stock. Pippin soon drove him out, and he was constrained to flee to Aquitaine. Bavaria fell to Tassilo, the son of the late duke.

After the rebellion of Grifo we read in the Frankish annals the unusual entry, that 'the whole land had peace for two years' (749-50). Being now in complete possession of the Frankish realm, and fearing no foe from within or from without, Pippin took the step which must always have been present in the brains of his ancestors, since the day when the over-hasty Grimoald had endeavoured to seize the royal power in 656. Warned by Grimoald's fate. Pippin the Younger and Charles Martel had scrupulously refrained from claiming the title of king, and had religiously kept up the series of puppet-princes of the old Merovingian stock. Their descendant was now determined to bring the farce to its end, and would not even wait for the death of the imbecile Childerich III., whose vain name had for the last ten years served to head Frankish charters and rescripts. Early in 751 the national council of the whole realm was summoned, and eagerly approved of the removal of Childerich and the election of Pippin as king. To bestow a still greater show of legal authority on the change, Pippin then sent an embassy to Rome to obtain the approval of the Pope. Its leader, Burkhard, bishop of Wurzburg, demanded of pope Zacharias 'Whether it was well or not to keep to kings who had no royal power?' The pontiff, whose chief desire was to win aid against the Lombards by flattering the ambition of Pippin, made the answer that was expected of him. 'It is better,' he said, 'that the man who has the real power should also have the title of king, rather than the man who has the mere title and no real power.' On the receipt of the Pope's encouraging message, which he regarded as freeing him from any religious obligation resting on oaths sworn to the unfortunate Childerich, Pippin once more summoned the Great Council of the Franks to meet. It assembled at Soissons in October or November 751, and, in the ancient royal city of Neustria, Pippin was first acclaimed as king, and lifted on the shield, after the ancient Teutonic custom, by the unanimous voice of the whole nation, and then anointed, as befitted a Christian sovereign, by the great Austrasian archbishop Boniface. Childerich was shorn of his regal locks, and sent to spend the remainder of his days in an obscure monastery, instead of the hardly less obscure royal manor in which he had hitherto dwelt.

Thus had the house of St. Arnulf at last reached the summit of its ambition, and the Frankish race once more obtained a king whose busy brain and strong right hand could make a reality of the title which for four generations had been but a vain name, while borne by the last effete Merovings. Raised on the shield by the Austrasian counts and dukes, anointed by the Apostle of Germany, blessed by the Roman pontiff. Pippin went forth conquering and to conquer, into lands where the Frankish banner had not been seen for many generations. Charles Martel vindicated the old frontier of the realm, his son was destined to extend its bounds into regions where no Frankish king had ever obtained a permanent footing.

The doings of Pippin the Short during the seventeen years of his kingly rule fall into three main heads. First and most important are his dealings with the popes and the kings of the Lombards, leading to his two great campaigns in Italy. Of secondary moment are his conquests from the Saracens and the Aquitanian dukes in the south of Gaul. His wars against the Saxons are of minor importance only. In giving his blessing to the accession of king Pippin pope Zacharias had kept in view the aid which the Franks might grant him in his quarrels with his Lombard neighbours. Zacharias died ere he had time to demand a return for his complaisance, but his successor Stephen soon claimed the gratitude of the newly-crowned monarch of the Franks. The old Lombard king Liutprand had died in 744, and his nephew Hildebrand, who succeeded him, had held the throne for no more than a few months. The Great Council of the Lombards deposed him for vicious incompetency, and elected in his place Ratchis, duke of Friuli. The new king, a man of mild and pious disposition, kept the peace which

Liutprand had made with the Papacy till 749, when, for reasons to us unknown, he advanced to attack Perugia, one of the few places in Italy which still adhered to the empire. Pope Zacharias visited his camp to plead with him in behalf of peace, with the unexpected result that Ratchis not only raised the siege, but laid down his crown and retired into a monastery, stricken, like his contemporary Carloman, with the sudden horror of secular things which occasionally fell upon the Teutonic monarchs of the seventh and eighth century.

Ratchis was succeeded by his brother Aistulf, an ambitious and restless monarch, who raised the Lombard kingdom to its widest territorial extent by conquering the long-coveted Ravenna. When he attacked the shrunken Exarchate it received no help from Constantine Copronymus, who detested his Italian subjects as obstinate image-worshippers, and was much occupied at the moment by his Saracen war. Ravenna fell with hardly any resistance, and Eutychius, the last exarch, fled to Sicily. Aistulf then busied himself in reducing the independent duchy of Benevento to vassalage. His next project was to annex the towns of the 'ducatus Romanus' — the valley of the lower Tiber — and to make the Pope his liegeman. Although he had concluded a forty-years' peace with the Papacy, yet, in 752-53, he was hovering about the neighbourhood of Rome, and occupying the Umbrian and Sabine borders of the 'patrimony of St. Peter.' At last his ambassadors appeared before Stephen II. to demand the homage of Rome, and the payment of an annual tribute. After trying in vain to scare off Aistulf, first by the terrors of excommunication, and then by empty menaces of applying for aid to Constantinople, which the Lombard derided, Stephen bethought himself of the debt of gratitude which the Frankish king owed to the Holy See. After ascertaining that his presence and demands would not be unacceptable to king Pippin, he left Rome in October 753, and, after making one more appeal to the Lombard king to grant him peace and independence, crossed the Alps, and appeared before the Frankish Court at Ponthion, near Bar-le-Duc.

His reception was all that he could have wished. Pippin met him three miles from the town, knelt before him on the roadside, and walked beside his stirrup to the palace gate, leading his palfrey by the bridle, though the month was January, and the snow lay on the ground. In the royal chapel, when the court was assembled, Stephen, 'with many tears and groans, laid before the king the lamentable state of the Church, and besought him to bring peace and salvation to the cause of St. Peter and the Roman State.

Whereupon Pippin swore an oath that he would grant him all he asked, and use every endeavour to put him in possession of the exarchate of Ravenna, as well as all the cities which belonged by right to the Roman republic'. It was to no purpose that an unexpected guest appeared in Gaul to beg Pippin to swerve from his purpose. This was his brother Carloman, who left his Sabine monastery to pray Pippin not to bring down the horrors of war upon Italy — a request which seemed so strange to the Church historians of the day, that they could only suppose that his mind had been overpowered by diabolic delusions, or that he was yielding to dread of the wrath of Aistulf. Pippin refused to listen to him, and bade him quit the court, and take up his residence at Vienne, where he soon afterwards died.

Meanwhile the Great Council of the Frankish realms was summoned to meet at Cerisy-sur-Oise, and there the king announced to his assembled counts and dukes that he proposed to make war on the Lombards, in order to vindicate the rights of the Holy See. Won over by their king's zeal, and by the great gifts which Stephen II. distributed among them, the Franks eagerly clamoured for war. In return for their goodwill the Pope solemnly crowned Pippin, his wife Bertha, and his young sons, Charles and Carloman, and pronounced a curse on any one who should ever remove the house of Pippin from the Frankish throne.

In the summer of 754 the hosts of the Franks choked the Savoyard passes with their multitudes, and prepared to force their way down into Italy. Aistulf had mustered his army, and was ready to meet them. In the narrow gorge of the Dora, hard by Susa, he fell on the Frankish vanguard; but he suffered such a crushing defeat that he had to fall back on Pavia without striking a second blow. Pippin followed, wasting Piedmont with fire and sword, and soon beleaguered Aistulf in his royal stronghold. Then, with an alacrity which his conqueror should have found somewhat suspicious, Aistulf offered terms of peace. He would do personal homage to Pippin, give him hostages, and engage to restore to the Roman See all that was its due. So a treaty was signed, Stephen was reconducted in triumph to Rome, and Pippin returned beyond the Alps, proud that he had added Lombardy to the list of states dependent on the Frankish crown.

On his homeward journey the king heard of the death of the great archbishop of Mainz, the apostle of Transrhenane Germany. Zealous even in extreme old age for the conversion of every subject of the Frankish realm, Boniface had started on a missionary journey to East Friesland, where paganism still held sway. As he lay encamped at Dokkum a great multitude of wild heathen, indignant at the invasion of their last retreat, fell upon him and slew him with all his companions. His death was not long unavenged; the Christian majority of the Frisians took arms, put down their pagan brethren, slew many thousands of them and compelled the rest to submit to baptism. By his martyr-death the great archbishop completed the conversion of the land for which he had striven so much during his lifetime. He was buried at Fulda in Hesse, where a great abbey was reared over his shrine and became the centre of Christian life in the Hessian lands whose apostle he had been. It would have afforded the keenest pleasure to Boniface if he could have witnessed the zeal with which his patron Pippin went forward with the task of reducing the Frankish clergy to canonical discipline. In the year which followed his martyrdom the Synod of Verneuil passed the most stringent laws against evil-living, simony, the practice of secular avocations, and the other failings of the clergy against which the archbishop had raged in his lifetime.

The easy promises winch king Aistulf had made when he was beleaguered in Pavia had never been intended for keeping. When the Franks had withdrawn from Italy the king found pretexts for delay, and did not restore to Stephen II. a single one of the Sabine or Latin cities which he had occupied in 753, still less the Exarchate of Ravenna, which the Pope had impudently asked and fondly hoped to receive. In the winter of 755-6 he took still more unmistakeable steps of hostility; descending the valley of the Tiber he suddenly laid siege to Rome. The walls of Aurelian were still too strong to be stormed, but three months of blockade brought the citizens near to yielding. The news that king Pippin had once more taken arms restored courage to Pope and people, and ere long Aistulf was forced to raise the siege and hasten north to defend Lombardy. Once more the Franks forced the defiles of the Cenis, and cut to pieces a Lombard force which strove to stop the way. For the second time Aistulf was forced into Pavia, beleaguered, and compelled to sue for peace. This time he was given harder terms. Pippin demanded one-third of the royal hoard of the Lombards, an annual tribute, a larger body of hostages, and the instant surrender of the Exarchate. The unwilling Lombard was forced to concede everything; Frankish envoys received and handed over to the Pope, the cities of Ravenna, Rimini, Pesaro, Forli, Urbino, and Sinigaglia, with all their dependencies. Their keys were brought to Rome and laid in triumph on the sepulchre of St. Peter. Thus did the Pope become an important secular prince, by taking over the old Byzantine dominions in central Italy.

It would seem that the theory by which he justified this usurpation was that the guard of the possessions of the 'Roman Republic' in Italy was incumbent on the emperor, but that Constantine Copronymus being an obstinate heretic his rights fell into abeyance. The Pope then stepped forward as the representative of the 'Roman Republic' in default of a Caesar, and claimed possession of all that the Lombards had lately usurped. Apparently he considered himself as 'Patrician' in the Exarchate, but as a Patrician owing no duty or obedience to a heterodox emperor.

King Aistulf died in the next year, killed by a fall from his horse, and the affairs of Italy troubled Pippin no more, Desiderius, duke of Istria, the new Lombard king, being occupied with strengthening himself against an attempt of the ex-king Ratchis to leave his cloister and resume the crown. The rest of Pippin's reign was mainly devoted to the completion of the Frankish dominion in southern Gaul. Soon after his proclamation as king his officers had recovered for him all the Saracen towns in Septimania north of Narbonne. In 759 Pippin inarched in person to lay siege to that city, the last bulwark of Islam beyond the Pyrenees. The Christian inhabitants of the place rose at his approach, slew the Arab garrison, and opened their gates to the Frank. No help came from Spain, where civil war was — as usual — raging, and the boundaries of the realm of Pippin were advanced to the Pyrenees.

Of far greater difficulty was the conquest of Aquitaine, the last achievement of Pippin. The old duke Hunold, the adversary of Charles Martel, had retired into a cloister, and had been succeeded by his false and restless son Waifer. On being summoned to give up some Frankish refugees, and surrender certain church lands, the new duke took up arms against his suzerain in 760; when Pippin appeared with all the host of Austrasia and ravaged Berri and Auvergne, Waifer asked for peace, and did homage. But the moment that his liege lord had departed home, he flung his fealty to the winds and began to ravage Burgundy. Next year the king returned in force and conquered Clermont and the rest of Auvergne, to which in 762 he added Bourges and the land of Berri. Waifer held out with the greatest obstinacy, and was confirmed in his resistance by learning of the revolt of Tassilo, duke of Bavaria, who judged the time favourable for freeing his duchy from the Franks. This gave Aquitaine a certain respite, but by 766 Waifer had been driven beyond the Garonne, and saw all his subjects except the Gascons compelled to do of homage to Pippin. In 767 his capital Toulouse fell, and soon after his despairing followers ended the war by murdering him and laying down their arms. Aquitaine was now annexed to the Frankish crown, and divided up into counties after the manner of the rest of the realm.

During the seven years of the war of Aquitaine king Pippin had found time to put down Tassilo's rebellion, and to chastise some sporadic raids of the Saxons against whom he had at an earlier date (755) undertaken a more serious expedition, which resulted in all the Westphalian tribes doing homage to him. But the full subjection of this wild race, whose obstinate paganism and unconquerable courage had baffled ten generations of Frankish missionaries and kings, was reserved for Pippin's greater son.

In the last years of his reign Pippin occupied a central place in the affairs of Europe such as no prince had held since the days of Theodoric the Great. Even the Abbaside Caliph of Bagdad sent to solicit his alliance: troubled by the revolt of Spain under the Ommeyad prince Abderahman, he endeavoured to enlist the aid of Pippin for the driving out of the rebel. The Frank wisely allowed the infidels to tear each other to pieces without helping either party. The Eastern emperor Constantine Copronymus sent frequent embassies to Gaul. One was designed to cajole Pippin into restoring the Exarchate to the Byzantine realm. Another brought a proposal for wedding Constantine's eldest son to Gisela, Pippin's only daughter. On a third occasion the communication was on religious subjects, the East-Roman envoys being clerics who were to endeavour to interest the Franks in the Iconoclastic controversy, and induce them to join in the destruction of images. The Byzantines held a discussion with some legates of the Pope in Pippin's presence, but got no assistance from the great king of the West, in whose eyes the dispute was far from having the same importance that it possessed in those of Constantine.

In the fulness of years and honours Pippin passed away on September 24th, 768, at St. Denis near Paris, after a long illness which gave him time to divide the kingdom between his two sons before he died. His character is somewhat difficult to fathom: he possessed all the distinguishing traits of the great men of the house of St. Arnulf, courage, ambition, energy, administrative skill, but showed few special characteristics of his own. It is not easy to detect any ruling passion or foible in his character, but his interference in Italy and his assumption of the royal title show that he lacked the extreme caution of his father. On the other hand his piety is praised by contemporaries not in the half-hearted way in which that of Charles was described, but in the most unqualified terms of laudation.

There are indications that he possessed somewhat of that taste tor literature which we find so well marked in his son Charles the Great. But it is impossible to draw any complete picture of his personality: even his nickname 'the Short' was given him not by his own contemporaries but by the chroniclers of the eleventh century, who speak from tradition and not from knowledge. Our idea of him must be constructed solely from what we know of his life and actions.

CHAPTER XX: CHARLES THE GREAT — EARLY YEARS 768-785 — CONQUEST OF LOMBARDY AND SAXONY.

Charles and Carloman — Final conquest of Aquitaine — Death of Carloman — Character and habits of Charles — State of the Frankish Empire — Charles interferes in Italy on behalf of the Pope — He subdues the Lombard monarchy — His later expeditions into Italy — First conquest of Saxony — Expedition to Spain — Rebellions of Saxony followed by its reconquest and permanent subjection.

The moment that king Pippin had been laid beneath his marble slab near the high altar of St. Denis, his two sons drew apart, and after retiring a few leagues from the place of their father's death hastily had themselves saluted as kings by their counts and dukes, and anointed by their bishops — Charles at Noyon, Carloman at Soissons (Oct. 9th, 768).

Now for the second time it appeared likely that the greatness of the house of St. Arnulf might be wrecked by the old and evil Frankish custom which prescribed the division of the kingdom among the sons of the king. How that custom had worked under the Merovings we have already seen. At the death of Charles Martel it had already threatened to break up the power of his house, a danger which was only averted by the unexpected abdication of the elder Carloman. Untaught by the experience of his own youth Pippin the Short had committed the same mistake: old habit was too much for him. On his deathbed, as we have seen, he divided his realm between his two sons. He had, however, done his best to leave his first-born so superior in strength to his brother, that the younger king should not be able to compete with him. Charles was left the warlike half of the kingdom, all those Frankish lands, both Austrasian and Neustrian, from the Main to the Channel, which supplied the chief fighting element in the Frankish armies. In addition he obtained the western half of the newly conquered Aquitaine. Carloman's share consisted of Burgundy, the Suabian lands on both sides of the upper Rhine, and the whole Mediterranean coast from the Maritime Alps to the border of Spain — the old Provincia and Septimania. Moreover, he took the eastern half of Aquitaine, — the country about Clermont, Rodez, Albi, and Toulouse. Though wellnigh as large as the share of Charles, his kingdom was not nearly so powerful, for the king who could command the swords of the Franks was the one who could give law to the whole realm.

For reasons which we know not, Charles and Carloman had never been friendly — perhaps the younger son as born after his father's coronation may have claimed some precedence over the elder, who was the son merely of a Mayor of the Palace. We know at any rate that throughout the three years of their joint reign they were always on the edge of a quarrel. Nothing but the influence and advice of their worthy mother Bertha kept them from an open rupture. Luckily for the realm both were good sons, and listened to the maternal pleadings: still more luckily for the Franks the life of the younger king was destined to be a short one. If Carloman had been granted many days on earth, we may be sure that the history of the last quarter of the ninth century would have repeated the old fratricidal wars of the Merovings. The historians who wrote the life of the great Charles are never tired of insisting on the many provocations which his brother gave him. If Carloman had chanced to find an apologist we might perhaps have learnt that Charles also gave subjects for offence.

The commencement of the joint reign of the two kings was followed by the prompt revolt of the newly subdued Aquitaine. Duke Waifer, the leader of the Southerners in their long war with Pippin, being dead, his old father Hunold emerged from his monastery to put himself at the head of the insurrection. The country as far north as Angouldme — which was kept down by a Frankish garrison — at once fell away to him, for the Gascons trusted that the two jealous brothers would be too much occupied with their grievances against each other to spare time for the reconquest of the south. Charles immediately marched against the rebels, and invited Carloman to accompany him: the younger king appeared for a moment, but only to hold an angry colloquy with his senior and then to return to Burgundy. He did not, however, take the opportunity to attack Charles, and the latter was able to pursue, unaided but also unhindered, his campaign against the Aquitanians. It was completely successful: he forced his way in arms as far as Bordeaux, built a great fortified camp at Fronsac, which was destined to remain as the central stronghold of the Garonne for many generations, and so thoroughly beat Hunold that the old man fled for refuge to Lupus, duke of the Gascons. But Lupus fearing the wrath of Charles submitted to the conqueror, surrendered the fugitive, and asked and obtained peace. Charles went home in triumph, replaced Hunold in a cloister, and was henceforth undisputably king in Aquitaine. He divided the country into countships on the usual Frankish system, and placed these provinces in the hands not of natives, but of men from north of the Loire whose fidelity he could trust. For the future Aquitaine gave no trouble.

In spite of Carloman's denial of help during the war in the south, Charles was ere long persuaded by his mother to be reconciled to his brother. But he took measures to keep him in check for the future by making alliance with the neighbours of Carloman to north and south. He concluded a treaty with Tassilo, duke of Bavaria, whose dependence on the Frankish realm had of late grown very loose, and allied himself yet more closely with Desiderius, the king of the Lombards, by wedding his daughter Desiderata. This marriage was concluded in spite of the most undignified shrieks of wrath on the part of the Pope, who besought Charles 'not to mix the famous Frankish blood with the perfidious, foul, and leprous Lombard stock — a truly diabolical coupling, which no true man could call a marriage.' The Papacy had learnt so well how to utilise the distant monarch of the Gauls against the neighbouring lord of Pavia, that Stephen III. looked upon an alliance between Frank and Lombard as high treason against the Holy See. The marriage, however, was consummated in spite of Stephen's threats, whereupon, with more prudence than consistency, he suddenly forgot his fundamental objections to the Lombard race, and made his peace with king Desiderius, lest he should be left unaided to feel the weight of the Lombard arm.

Within a year, however, Charles suddenly repudiated his wife, alleging that she was sickly and barren. Whether this was his real motive, or whether political causes also influenced his action, we cannot tell; but as Charles wedded immediately after his divorce a fair Suabian lady, named Hildegarde, we may suspect that his motives were possibly those which guided Henry VIII. of England in a similar circumstance. Be this as it may, he won by this divorce the unrelenting and not unDeath of justifiable hatred of Desiderata's father, the king Carloman. of the Lombards. Trouble was soon in the air. There was again a rumour that war was about to break out between Charles and Carloman, in which Desiderius would have taken part. Just in time to prevent such an outbreak, king Carloman died (December 771). He left an infant son, but the nobles and bishops of Burgundy and Alamannia made no attempt to set the child on his father's throne. Wisely suppressing any particularist yearnings, they betook themselves to Charles at Corbeny-sur-Aisne, and there did homage to him as king of all the Frankish realms. Gerberga, the widow of Carloman, fled with her child and a handful of followers to Lombardy, where Desiderius was now in a state of mind which made him glad to receive any enemy of Charles's, and more especially one who had such a plausible claim to a share in the Frankish kingdom.

Once more, then, all the lands between the mouth of the Rhine and the mouth of the Rhone, and from the Main to the Bay of Biscay, were united under a single king. And this was a king such as none of those realms had ever seen before — a heroic figure, whose like we have not met in all the three centuries with which we have had to deal. Theodoric the Ostrogoth alone deserves a mention by his side, and Theodoric had a smaller task and less success than the great Charles. For the first time since we began to tell the tale of the Dark Ages we have come upon a man whose form and mind, whose plans and method of life, have been so well recorded that we can build up for ourselves a clear and tangible image of him. Charles the Hammer, king Pippin, Leo the Isaurian, and even the good Theodoric himself, are but shadowy figures, whose outlines we can but dimly seize, but Charles stands before us firm and masterful, a living man, whom we can understand and admire.

'He was tall and stoutly built,' writes his chronicler, Einhard; 'his height just seven times the length of his own foot. His head was round, his eyes large and lively, his nose somewhat above the common size, his expression bright and cheerful. Whether he stood or sat his form was full of dignity; for the good proportion and grace of his body prevented the observer from noticing that his neck was rather short and his person rather too fleshy. His tread was firm, his aspect manly; his voice was clear, but rather high-pitched for so splendid a body. His health was excellent; only for the last four years of his life he suffered from intermittent fever. To the very last he consulted his own goodwill rather than the orders of his doctors, whom he detested, because they bade him give up the roast meats that his soul loved.'

Charles was always of an active habit of body. He delighted in riding and hunting, and was skilled in swimming above other men. One of the chief reasons that induced him to make Aachen his capital was that he loved to take his sport in the great swimming-bath that was supplied by its hot springs.

He always used the Frankish costume, and loved not foreign apparel. Next his skin he wore a linen shirt and drawers, over these a woollen tunic, with a silk border, and breeches. He wrapped his calves and feet with the linen bandages that were worn ere stockings were invented, and drew high boots over them. In winter he wore a coat of the fur of otter or ermine, and over that a bright blue cloak. A sword with a golden hilt was always at his side. On great days of state he assumed a tunic and cloak embroidered with gold and clasped with gold buckles, girt his head with a jewelled crown, and carried a sword with a jewelled hilt. But for every-day wear his clothes were not more splendid than those of his courtiers.

He was temperate in food and drink, more, however, in drink than in food. No one ever saw him drink more than three cups at his dinner, and he hated drunkenness, and chastised it among his suite. But eating he loved in moderation, and would often say that church fasts were bad for his health. There were never more than four dishes on his table, besides a roast, which was brought him hot from the kitchen on its spit, and this was his favourite food.

At dinner he used to listen to a reciter or a reader. He loved histories and tales of the ancients, and also the works of St. Augustine, whose De Civitate Dei delighted him especially. He caused to be written out and committed to memory the ancient Frankish epics about the deeds and wars of the kings of old. He himself was well skilled in reading aloud and singing to the harp, and took much pains in instructing others in those accomplishments. All the liberal arts were dear to him, and he loved learned men, and summoned them from all quarters of the world. To study grammar he sent for the deacon Peter of Pisa. In most other arts he had as his preceptor Alcuin, the Englishman, the most learned of all men, with whom he studied rhetoric and dialectic, and spent much time in acquiring a knowledge of astronomy; for he was curious about the times and motions of the stars. He invented German names for the twelve months of the year, and the twelve winds. He tried, too, to learn the art of the scribe, and used to keep paper and notebooks under his pillow in bed, to practise his fingers at odd moments in forming the characters; but he began too late in life to get very forward in this undertaking. Moreover, he loved building, and designed the splendid cathedral of Aachen, glorious with lamps and candlesticks of gold and silver, and doors and railings of solid bronze. When he was erecting it, and could not get marble columns near at hand, he had them brought all the way from Ravenna and Rome. He was a great churchgoer, and always took care that the service in his presence should be conducted with decorum. He used to pray both in Frankish and in Latin, being equally skilled in both tongues. For he had a great power of acquiring languages, and spoke Latin excellently. Greek he learnt, but understood it better than he spoke it He had a free and fluent power of speech, and always expressed his meaning in the clearest way.

He slept lightly, and would often rise three or four times in the night. When he was dressing for the work of the morning he would have not only his friends in his chamber, but would bid the count of the palace bring in litigants before him, and give a decision from his chair just as if he was in a court of law.

Charles had one lamentable failing — he was too careless of the teachings of Christianity about the relation of the sexes. He divorced his first wife over-lightly, and when his third wife died he took to himself three concubines at once, who bore him many bastard children. There were scandals at his court, and two of his own daughters were known to be living in open sin with two of his courtiers. Charles treated their offence lightly, and never visited them with any rebuke. Not so his son, Lewis the Pious, who regarded his sisters' shame as so heinous that he banished them when he came to the throne. It was the shortcomings of the great king in respect of sexual morality which prevented the Church from decreeing the beatification of its protector after his death. The spirit of the times was well shown by the strange vision of the monk Wettin of Reichenau, who, falling into a trance and wandering through the other world, saw Charles in Purgatory, kept in purifying flames for a space, till this sin should be purged from his soul.

So much do the chronicles tell us concerning the person and the manner of life of Charles the Great; but there are other points which impress us more than they did the contemporary observer. Considering that he was so far in advance of his age in the cultivation of literature, art, science, and architecture, that in administration and organisation of his realm he so far surpassed all that had lived before him, and that he rose in most of his conduct to such a high conception, alike of his kingly office and of his personal responsibility for all his actions, it is disappointing, though not surprising, to find that in some matters he was not above the standard of his time. We have already alluded to his loose living, but a worse failing was his occasional liability to outbursts of inhumanity. The most savage of them was his massacre of 4500 unarmed prisoners of war at Verden, in 782. If the majority of his wars were defensive, or at least necessary, there were a few — notably the Lombard war — in which aggressive ambition was the main operating cause, but this was a small failing in the unscrupulous eighth century. On the whole we stand amazed at the magnanimity of the man, and are so much struck with his splendid qualities, that we are perhaps in danger of doing him wrong by judging him from our own moral standpoint. He rises so far above that of the Dark Ages, that it scarcely occurs to the historian to judge him by their low standard. Yet it is by remembering what was the spirit of those times that his greatness is most readily recognised.

We shall have to deal with Charles in three main aspects, as conqueror, as organiser, and as the introducer of new theories of political life into the mind of Christendom. It is difficult to keep the three lines of activity clearly separate; for all through his reign, from first to last, Charles was equally busy in each of these capacities. To make clear the logical sequence of his doings it is sometimes necessary to override their chronological order.

At the first glance the most extraordinary of the achievements of Charles appear to be his huge additions to the territory of the Frankish realm by the annexation of the Lombard kingdom, the Spanish march. Saxony, and the Slavonic lands of the Elbe and the Drave to the inheritance that he had been left by his father. These conquests represent a plan of operations deliberately undertaken, carried out with an unswerving hand, and brought to a successful finish. Charles had inherited from his father and grandfather the duty, which they had undertaken, of protecting Christian Europe from the Saracen, the Slav, and the heathen Saxon, the three enemies whom his ancestors had driven back, but had not crushed. Closely connected with this duty was the obligation to convert to Christianity the new subjects whom he might subdue, to deal with Saxon and Slav as Charles Martel had already dealt with Frisian and Thuringian, and so to push the outer defences of Christendom into those parts of central Europe which had hitherto been sunk in savagery and paganism. The Saracen alone it was impossible to convert. He might be expelled, but then, as now, it was found easier to exterminate the Moslem than to make him abandon Islam. To these altogether useful and salutary tasks, which Charles inherited from the great Mayors of the Palace, another was added, the less happy plan of cementing a close union with the Papacy by crushing the nation of the Lombards. Pippin had committed the Franks to this scheme, and Charles did but carry out his father's pledges. But by his action he destroyed a healthy and vigorous Christian state, the possible base for a strong Italian nationality, and committed the Frankish kingdom to a profitless union, which was to bring forth seven centuries of discord. What was worst of all, he firmly established the temporal power of the Papacy, a curse to blast Italy for a thousand years. The gains which he received in return, — the religious sanction bestowed on his royal power by the Pope, and the imperial title, were but doubtful boons. It was to be seen, ere the ninth century had expired, that the house of St. Arnulf, like all the dynasties that succeeded it, lost more than it gained by putting itself under obligations to the Roman See, and consenting to accept from the Pope's hands the style of emperor, and the vague commission to protect the unity of Christendom, — a commission which to the Roman pontiff meant little more than the duty of giving the Church all that she chose to crave.

Before proceeding to relate the earlier conquests of Charles the Great, it is necessary to explain the boundaries of his realm as it stood at the moment of the death of his brother Carloman. In Germany the border to north and south was held by the two vassal peoples of Frisia and Bavaria, both now Christian, and both reduced during the last fifty years to a more strict obedience to the Franks than they had ever known before, but still possessing their own native rulers, and not completely united to the monarchy. East of Frisia lay the Saxons, the race whom the Merovings, and the great mayors who succeeded them, had alike failed to tame. After three hundred years of hard fighting the boundary of the Frank and Saxon remained where it had stood in the year 500. To the east of Saxony lay races hardly yet known to the Franks, the Slavonic tribes of the Abotrites, Wiltzes, and Sorbs.

The duchy of Bavaria had as its eastern neighbours another group of Slavonic peoples, the races who had once formed the ephemeral kingdom of Samo, Czechs and Moravians on the upper Elbe, Carentanians on the Drave. Beyond these Slavs lay the realm of the Avar Chagan, now in a state of decadence owing both to civil wars and to rebellions of its Slavonic subjects.

Between Frisia and Bavaria the frontier of the realm of Charles was held by the Thuringians, now no longer under the rule of native princes, but divided up into Frankish counties, as the adjacent Suabia had also been, and forming like Suabia an integral part of Charles's monarchy. The neighbours of the Thuringians beyond the border were the Slavonic Sorbs.

The south-east frontier of the Frankish empire was formed by the main chain of the Alps, beyond which lay the Lombard realm of king

Desiderius. Its south-western limit was the main chain of the Pyrenees, beyond which lay the Saracens of Spain, over whom at this moment Abderahman the Ommeyad had just succeeded in establishing his power, and had formed a state independent of the Abbaside caliphate (755).

Of all the neighbours of king Charles, it was Desiderius the Lombard who was first destined to feel the weight of the Frankish sword. He had not only received Carloman's widow Gerberga, when she fled from Burgundy, but had shown some intention of proclaiming her son king of the Franks. Yet it was not this machination against Charles that was the actual cause of war, but the relations of the Papacy with Desiderius. Hadrian I. had just been raised to the Papal throne. He was a Roman by birth, and a great hater of the Lombards. He refused the friendship and alliance which Desiderius proffered, and very shortly after he was consecrated began to pick a quarrel with the unfortunate king. He demanded from him the important towns of Ferrara and Faenza, as part of the Exarchate of Ravenna. They had been promised to St. Peter, he said, in 757, while Desiderius was struggling for the crown with king Ratchis, and must be handed over at once. Desiderius, thinking that Charles would be too much occupied beyond the Alps in settling the newly-annexed dominions of his brother to allow of his appearance in Italy, replied to the Pope's challenge by sending a host into the Pentapolis, and seizing Sinigaglia and Urbino. Shortly afterwards he raised the full force of the Lombard realm, and marched against Rome. Hadrian had expected this. He fortified and strongly garrisoned the city, and sent in haste to bid the lord of the Franks to come to the help of St. Peter, and force the unrighteous Lombards to carry out in full the treaty that king Pippin had imposed upon them. The news of the despatch of this embassy seems to have frightened Desiderius. He drew back to Viterbo, and, instead of pressing the siege of Rome, sent an embassy to Charles, to explain that the Pope's charges were unfounded, as he was not keeping back anything that really belonged to the Exarchate (772, autumn).

Desiderius, when he first attacked Rome, was not wrong in thinking that Charles was already occupied in the affairs of his own kingdom. He had that summer commenced the great undertaking of the conquest of Saxony, a task which was to tax his energies for the next twenty years. In the summer of 772 he had entered the land, compelled the Mid-Saxons or Engrians to give him hostages, and cut down in token of triumph the Irminsul, a holy tree reverenced by all the Saxon tribes, which stood in a grove near Paderborn, and was adorned with many rich offerings. On his return to Austrasia, Charles met the ambassadors of Hadrian and Desiderius at Thionville. He did not swerve for a moment from his father's policy of supporting the Papacy through thick and thin. He sent off ambassadors to bid Desiderius give up all the cities belonging to the Holy See that he was unlawfully occupying, and told him to do justice to St. Peter without delay. The Lombard king was far too angry at this interference to grant the Frank's demands. He swore that he would restore nothing. This drew down Charles into Italy. Marching from Geneva he crossed Mont Cenis with one division of his army, while his uncle Bernard with the rest followed the route of the Great St. Bernard. Desiderius on their approach fortified the Alpine gorges by Susa and Ivrea, and stood upon the defensive. But a chosen band of Franks turned his position at Susa by climbing over the hills, and when he saw himself outflanked, the Lombard king abandoned his lines, and fell back on Pavia, exactly as his predecessor Aistulf had done in the war with king Pippin. Charles followed in haste, and laid siege to Pavia, which held out for many months. Meanwhile Adelchis, the son of Desiderius, raised a second Lombard army, and took post in front of Verona. Leaving part of his army to maintain the blockade of Pavia, Charles marched against Adelchis, compelled him to fly, and captured Verona, and afterwards Brescia and Bergamo. The Lombard prince took to the sea, and sought Constantinople, where he endeavoured to obtain help from Constantine Copronymus, then in the midst of his Bulgarian war.

As king Desiderius held out in Pavia with the greatest obstinacy, and the siege was protracted for many months, Charles resolved to spend the spring of 774 in visiting Rome, and coming to a complete understanding with pope Hadrian. He reached the city in Holy Week, and celebrated the Easter festivities with great splendour: his communings with Hadrian ended in his confirming his father's grant to the Papacy of the whole Exarchate of Ravenna, from Ferrara and Commachio on the north, to Osimo on the south, including all the places that had been in dispute between the Pope and the Lombard king. Later Roman writers pretended that Charles had even increased Pippin's liberal gift by adding to it north Tuscany, Parma and Modena, Venice, and even the island of Corsica. But there is no trace of this in contemporary authorities: the Frank never made over to the Pope the sovereignty of Tuscany or Aemilia, much less of Venice — which was not his to give, — or the distant island of Corsica.

On returning from Rome to the valley of the Po, in the early summer of 774, Charles found Pavia ready to submit: Desiderius and his men of war were wasted by famine and opened the gates on condition that their lives should be spared. The king was sent as a prisoner to Neustria, and died many years after as a monk in the abbey of Corbey. His royal treasure was divided among the Frankish army. Adelchis, the heir of the Lombard throne, had, as we have already mentioned, escaped to the Byzantine court, and died there many years afterwards as a 'patrician.'

Instead of following Pippin's example, and allowing Lombardy to survive as a vassal state, Charles had himself proclaimed as king in Italy, and compelled all the Lombard dukes and counts to do homage to him at Pavia. Only Arichis of Benevento, the son-in-law of Desiderius, persisted in maintaining his independence. For the future Charles styled himself 'King of the Franks and Lombards, and Roman Patrician.' Except that he left a garrison in the capital, and handed over some of the more important Italian cities to Frankish counts instead of leaving them in the hands of their old Lombard governors, he made little change in the administration of Italy. His rights of conquest were used with such moderation, that Italy gave him very little trouble for the rest of his reign. The only serious disturbance that took place was in 776, when the dukes of Friuli, Spoleto, and Benevento conspired to send for Adelchis from Constantinople, and proclaim him as king of the Lombards. Hearing of their plot, Charles descended upon Italy, slew the duke of Friuli in battle, and compelled the duke of Spoleto to do him homage. Arichis of Benevento was not subdued: he maintained his southern duchy intact, though the Franks sent more than one expedition against him. Apparently Charles regarded the homage of this distant state as too small a thing to be worth his attention till 787, when he made another descent into Italy in person, besieged Arichis in Salerno, and finally compelled him to become his vassal. But in 792, Arichis being dead, his son Grimoald shook off the Frankish yoke, and maintained a precarious semi-independence for the future, though he was several times attacked, and saw more than one of his chief towns stormed by the armies of Charles. The great king himself, however, never entered Beneventan territory again, and it was only his presence that could have sufficed to subdue the unruly duke.

But we must return to the doings of Charles after his first conquest of the Lombards in 774. During his absence the Saxons had once more taken arms, and it was now high time to recommence the campaign against them, which had been interrupted by the great expedition to Italy. The year 775 saw the first of the many subjections of Saxony which Charles was to carry out during his long reign.

The Saxons were divided into four great divisions. Nearest the Frankish frontier were the Westphalians, who dwelt on the Ems and Lippe, and about the Teutoburger Wald. Beyond them to the east, the Engrians occupied the valley of the Weser, from its mouth as far as the borders of Hesse. East of the Engrians again, lay the Eastphalians, on the Aller and Ocker and Elbe. The latter-named river separated them from the Slavonic tribes of the Abotrites, who lived in the modern Mecklemburg. The fourth division of the Saxons were the Nordalbingians, who dwelt in Holstein, beyond the Elbe, on the borders of the Danes, and were the least accessible and most savage of their race. Saxony was a land of wood, heath, and morass: only on its southern Saxony. border was there a hilly tract, the spurs of the Harz mountains. The chief obstacle in the way of conquering the country was the fact that the Saxons had no towns and very few fortified posts; they took refuge in woods or swamps when the king's army appeared, and came forth again when he was gone. The land was quite roadless, so that the pursuit of the flying tribes was very difficult. If surrounded and compelled to do homage to Charles, they gave hostages, and paid great fines in cattle, but the moment that the Franks had left their neighbourhood took arms again. Nine times did one or other section of the Saxon race rebel, and any will less strong than that of the inflexible Charles, would have yielded before their intractable obstinacy. But he persevered to the end in leading expedition after expedition against the rebels, punished their revolts by fire and sword, transplanted incorrigible tribes across the Rhine, built towns and castles all over the land, erected bishoprics, and sent forth countless missionaries, till in the last ten years of his life he had the satisfaction of seeing Saxony both submissive and Christian.

The expedition of 775 began by the invasion of Westphalia; after dispersing its inhabitants, and storming their great entrenched camp at Sigiburg, Charles passed on into Engria, defeated the Mid-Saxons and crossed the Weser. This brought him into EastphaHa, which he ravaged as far as the river Ocker. The Eastphalians, though the furthest of the Saxons from the Frankish border, were the first to submit to Charles, and their chief Hessi eagerly accepted Christianity, and did homage. Soon after the Engrians also came in to the king's camp, and gave up hostages for their fidelity. The Westphalians held out last, and only submitted when Charles, on his return towards Austrasia, ravaged their land from end to end, and made a great slaughter of their warriors. The king left garrisons in two great camps at Sigiburg and Eresburg, to hold down the Westphalians and Engrians respectively. The hostages whom he brought back were mostly boys of noble family, whom he sent to be brought up as Christians in various Austrasian monasteries. Three-fourths of Saxony had thus done homage to Charles, but their adhesion was of the most unstable sort. They hated the Franks as ancestral enemies, and detested Christianity as a Frankish device for subduing them body and soul. It was only the presence of Charles and the fear of his return that kept them in order for a moment.

No sooner had Charles started in the next year for his second invasion of Italy, to put down the dukes of Friuli and Benevento, than the Westphalians and Engrians at once took arms. They stormed the Frankish camp at Eresburg, and slaughtered the garrison, but failed in a similar attempt at Sigiburg. The moment that Charles heard of this rebellion, he hastened back from Italy with such speed that he was already on the Lippe before the Saxons suspected that he had crossed the Alps. So great was their fear of him that the whole race at once asked for peace, and sent their local chiefs to do him homage, 'promising that they would all be baptized, and hold their land as true vassals of the king.' Only one chief, named Witikind, refused to submit, and fled northward, to take refuge with the Danes (776). Charles replaced his garrison in the fort of Eresburg, and built another entrenched camp at Karlstadt. That winter he remained in Austrasia, close to the Saxon border, in order to watch these untrustworthy subjects. In the next spring he summoned the great national council of the whole Frankish realm to meet at Paderborn, in the heart of Engria, in order to mark the fact that Saxony had now become an integral part of his dominions (777). 'Then were a great multitude of the Saxons baptized, and following their national custom, they swore that they would forfeit their freedom and their lands if ever they revolted again, according to their old habit, and unless they kept their Christianity and their loyalty to king Charles and his heirs.'

To this great diet at Paderborn came some ambassadors from Spain, bearing an unexpected offer of homage to the king. Abderahman, the Ommeyad, had finally succeeded in conquering well-nigh the whole of the Spanish peninsula from those of the Saracens who refused to accept him as king. The last survivors of his opponents, in desperate straits, sent to offer to become the vassals of Charles if he would preserve them from the conqueror. These chiefs were Soliman Ibn-al-Arabi and Kasmin Ibn-Yussuf, who were holding the towns of Barcelona, Gerona, and Huesca, in the extreme north-west of Spain, on the Frankish border. Charles determined to accept their offer, and so to thrust forward his frontier beyond the Pyrenees, as to protect Septimania from Saracen raids by interposing a new line of fortresses between it and the dominion of the ruler of Cordova. He believed that Saxony was fully subdued, and might be safely left alone to settle down into loyalty and Christian ways.

Accordingly, in 778, Charles led his first great expedition into Spain. He himself crossed the Western Pyrenees with the host of Neustria, while the levy of Austrasia, Burgundy, and Lombardy, passed the Eastern Pyrenees. The two armies met in front of Saragossa, and Charles there received the homage of the rebel Saracen chiefs of Barcelona and Gerona. Saragossa, however, did not fall, in spite of the great army that had been concentrated against it, and Charles then wheeled about, and returned to Aquitaine by the same way that he had come. His expedition had not proved a great success. The Saracen rebels were untrustworthy vassals, nor was the only other result of the campaign, the homage paid to Charles by the Spanish Basques and Navarrese, after he had stormed their town of Pampeluna, a more solid gain. Indeed, while the Prankish army was returning through the passes of the Pyrenees, the Basques fell upon the king's rearguard and waggon-train, in the famous defile of Roncesvalles. They captured much booty, and slew three great officials — Eggihard, the seneschal; Anselm, the count of the palace; and Hruotland (Roland), the warden of the Breton marches. The last named, of whom history knows nothing save his untimely fall at Roncesvalles, must have been a great man among the Franks, for within a short time after his death he had become the hero of many legends, which ultimately took shape in the famous Chanson de Roland, wherein the Breton Margrave appears as second only to Charles the Great among the hosts of Christendom (778).

The king had not long reached Aquitaine when the unwelcome news arrived that the Saxons had broken their oaths, and were once more up in arms. The exile Witikind had returned from Denmark, and called the turbulent youth of Saxony into the field. The greater number of the tribes had risen at his call, and a great Saxon host had stormed the new fort of Karlstadt, and harried Hesse and the right bank of the Rhine, as far as Deutz and the mouth of the Moselle, burning churches, and slaying the peasantry of the country-side in revenge for the destruction of the Irminsul and the ravages of Charles in 775-76. On receiving this disturbing news the king made his way to Austrasia, sent out some troops to clear the Rhine-bank of the Saxon plunderers, but put off the general muster of the hosts of the Franks for a third conquest of Saxony till next year. In the summer of 779, however, he again started on his endless task, and marched through Westphalia with fire and sword. The Westphalians once more surrendered, after a defeat in the open field; the Engrians and Eastphalians yielded without fighting. In the next spring he returned again, held a great diet at the headwaters of the Lippe, and divided all Saxony into missionary districts, each to be worked by a colony of monks from Austrasia, the first step towards the partition of the land into the later bishoprics. This activity was rewarded by the conversion and baptism of many thousand pagans. Charles assisted in person on more than one occasion, when whole thousands of Saxons were simultaneously passed through the waters of the Ocker and the Elbe (780).

He then turned off towards Italy. For the first time his departure was not followed by an immediate outbreak of rebellion. The land remained quiet for more than two years (780-82), and when he next passed that way Charles thought it had advanced so far in the paths of peace that he divided it up into countships, after the model of the rest of his empire, and gave the charge of many of them to native Saxon chiefs, whom he honoured with the title of count; the rest were placed under officers of Frankish blood. He also published a code of laws for Saxony, in which the harshest punishments were denounced against all those who still clung to paganism. Such offences as sacrificing to Woden, burning instead of burying the dead, openly deriding church ceremonies, or robbing a church, were to be punished with instant death. Even those who obstinately refused baptism, or who after baptism refused to fast in Lent, and conform to church discipline, were threatened with capital punishment.

It was perhaps in consequence of the issue of this cruel code that the Saxons once more flew to arms in the autumn of 782. The rebel Witikind returned from Denmark to put himself at their head, and most of the northern tribes rose at his call. The news quickly brought Charles back into the country. Once more he came in overwhelming force, and many of the Saxons at once laid down their arms and submitted. But now for the first time the king showed signs of violent wrath against the unruly race. He could not pardon them for slaying priests, burning churches, and washing off in mockery their marks of baptism. He bade each tribe send to him in bonds those men who had been most prominent in casting off Christianity and fomenting the last rising. Four thousand five hundred captives were brought before him by their submissive countrymen in his camp at Verden, on the Aller. Yielding to an impulse of revenge, Charles had the whole of this great body of helpless prisoners beheaded. But, instead of cowing the Saxons, this cruel execution only roused them to wild wrath. Every man in the nation had lost some friend or relative in the great massacre, and even the tribes which had hitherto been most submissive flew to arms. There followed more than two years of unbroken fighting (783-85). Charles marched twice through the land, burning and slaughtering over the face of every Saxon gau, from the Ems to the Elbe, but the infuriated rebels closed in behind him after he had passed, and still held out in the woods and marshes. But the king only hardened his heart. He refused to quit the land, and wintered, with all his army, near Minden, in the heart of Saxony. At last, in the spring of 785, the perseverance of the rebels began to quail; it was impossible to drive off the inflexible king of the Franks, and they once more bethought them of submission. The rebel chief Witikind obtained a promise of his life if he would surrender and be baptized, and, when he, with his chosen warriors, submitted, the great rising was at last an end. Once more the counts received charge of their old districts, the missionaries returned to rebuild their ruined churches, and the surviving Saxons submitted in despair to the yoke of the Frankish warrior and the Frankish priest.

It was seven years before any further trouble arose in Saxony, though there were to be four more partial risings between 792 and 804. But none of these threatened seriously to shake Charles's domination; they were merely the last throes of Saxon despair, and cannot be compared to the great struggle of 783-85, in which the fate of Saxon independence and Saxon heathendom was really settled.

It was shortly after the final annexation of the Germans of the Elbe and Weser that Charles fully incorporated the Germans of the upper Danube with his empire. His vassal, Tassilo, duke of Bavaria, had been a somewhat unruly and disobedient subject. He was pardoned for more than one outburst of disloyalty, but when he was treated with kindness and consideration he behaved no better than before. At last, in 788, he was deprived of his duchy, which was cut up into countships and put under

Frankish governors, while he himself was sent to end his days HI the Neustrian monastery of Jumieges.

CHAPTER XXI: THE LATER WARS AND CONQUESTS OF CHARLES THE GREAT — 785-814

Wide scope of the later conquests of Charles — Outlying provinces governed by his sons — Conquest of the Baltic Slavs — Subjection of Bohemia — Wars with the Avars and their final subjection — Hostilities with the Eastern Empire — Conquest of the Spanish March — Later revolts of the Saxons — Wars with the Danes.

King Charles had now come to the end of the first of the stages of his conquests, and the nearer enemies of the Frankish kingdom had been reduced to subjection. With comparatively little trouble the fertile Lombard plain had been won; after long toil and exertion the pathless woods and moors of Saxony had been taken within the boundary of his realm. But his schemes of conquest had a much wider scope than the annexation of Lombardy and Saxony. Before Christendom could be reckoned as safe from all foes without, there were more realms to be won, more marches to be made secure. By pushing his frontier up to the Elbe and the Julian Alps, Charles had taken up the ancient feuds of the Lombard and the Saxon with their eastern neighbours, the Avar and the Slav. Moreover, there was still the Spanish border to be made firm, for the expedition of 778 had resulted in no permanent gain; the unstable allegiance of Barcelona and Gerona was once more being paid to the Ommeyad king at Cordova, not to the lord of the Franks.

The second period, therefore, in the record of the conquests of Charles the Great includes the history of the making firm of his new eastern and south-western borders. But this is not, like the first fifteen years of his reign, a time of complete conquest and incorporation of races who were near akin to the Franks. All the Teutonic peoples of central Europe were already gathered beneath the sceptre of Charles; the tribes with which he had now to do were strangers to the Franks, not only in religion, but in blood and language. The work of Charles in the East in the second period of his reign was to make the Slav and Avar harmless, by compelling their princes to pay homage and tribute, not by occupying their realms with Frankish garrisons, or carving them up into countships and marches. In the

West, on the other hand, his task was to build up a strong border against the Moor, by conquering, one by one, the fortresses between the Pyrenees and the Ebro. The Moslem had to be driven out, since there was no hope of converting him. In the towns from which he was expelled a new population grew up, neither purely Spanish nor purely Frank, but the mixed race of the Catalans, in whose veins Romano-Spanish, Visigothic, Aquitanian, and Frankish blood was mingled in various proportions, so that they have always differed very considerably, both in character and in language, from the inhabitants of the rest of the peninsula. But the history of the foreign policy of Charles during the second period of his reign contains much more besides his dealings with the Slav, the Moor, and the Avar. He had frequent troubles with the East-Roman Empire, arising from their disputed boundaries in Italy. In the very end of his reign he met and turned off the first assault of the Danes on the Frankish realm, an attack insignificant in itself, but portending the gravest dangers in the future. We find him interfering beyond the British sea with the affairs of Northumbria, and at the same time extending his hand far to the south to seize the Balearic Isles. Even to the distant Abbasside Caliph at Bagdad his fame was known, and Haroun's ambassadors sought the court of Aachen to concert an alliance with him.

In the second half of his reign Charles very frequently took the field in person, but was not so constantly at the head of his armies as during the period 773-85. He had now three growing sons, whom he intrusted with the charge of three important sections of his realm, and he looked to them to guard each that portion of the frontier of the Frankish empire which bordered on his own sub-kingdom. Charles, the eldest of the three, ruled in western Neustria (Anjou, Maine, Touraine); Pippin, the second, in Lombardy; Lewis, the youngest, in Aquitaine. Charles would thus be specially concerned with the unruly Bretons of Armorica, who twice made unsuccessful risings in his father's reign (786 and 799). Lewis was in charge of the Saracen frontier along the Pyrenees. Pippin had to keep watch over the duke of Benevento, as well as to turn his attention to the Avars on the north-east of Italy. But the three princes were not strictly confined each to his own sphere. Charles was occasionally sent against the Saxons; Lewis conducted at least one campaign in southern Italy; Pippin more than once took charge of an attack on the Slavs of Bohemia. Whenever, in short, the great king could not march in person against a rebel or a foreign enemy, he would send one of his sons to take his place.

He did not allow them to become completely localised and engrossed with the affairs of their respective governments, but often kept them with him at Aachen for many months at a time.

In reviewing the later conquests of Charles the Great it will be most convenient to follow the geographical order from north to south, rather than the chronological order of each campaign, for his arms were engaged in so many quarters at once that an attempt to tell his doings in a purely annalistic form leads to dire confusion.

On the North-East the Frankish border, after 785, was fringed by Slavonic tribes, all ancient enemies of the Saxon. These were the Abotrites in the north — in the modern Mecklemburg — the Wiltzes beyond them in western Pomerania, and the Sorbes in Brandenburg, on the Havel and Spree. These tribes, like their kindred whom we have already met in the Balkan peninsula, were rude peoples, and not very formidable enemies, owing to their subdivisions under petty princes, and their incapacity for union. Though numerous and not unwarlike, all the Slavs between Elbe and Oder were subdued by Charles in a single campaign. He crossed the Elbe in 789 with an Austrasian army, strengthened by levies of Frisians and of Saxons, who served gladly against their ancestral foes. The terror of his name seems to have stricken the Slavs with dismay. After a very slight resistance, first the Abotrites and their chief king Witzin, then the Wiltzes and their chief king Dragovit did homage to Charles, gave him as many hostages as he chose to demand, and consented to pay him a tribute and to receive the Christian missionaries whom he prepared to send among them. The Frankish army marched through moors and woods till it saw the Baltic at the mouth of the Peene in Pomerania, and then returned with some booty and no loss to the banks of the Rhine. So thoroughly were the Slavs subdued that during the next revolt of the Saxons they did not take the opportunity of disowning their homage to Charles, but came to help him against the rebels (795). Witzin, prince of the Abotrites, was actually slain by the Eastphalians while in arms for the Franks, and his death was well revenged by the king, who harried the lands along the Elbe with exceptional severity to atone for his ally's slaughter. In a later Saxon rising (798) we again find the Abotrites taking arms at the bidding of Charles. Their new king Thrasuco reconquered the Nordalbingians without Frankish aid, and brought their chiefs in bonds to the king's feet, 'whereupon Charles honoured him marvellously, and gave the Slavs great gifts.' Ten years later the same prince and people fought valiantly against the Danes when they invaded the northern frontier of Charles's realm, though their neighbours the Wiltzes on this occasion deserted to the enemy. The latter people, however, were subdued again in 812, at the very end of the great king's reign, so that he left his eastern boundary undiminished at his death. On the whole the Slavs of the North were not by any means the most difficult to rule of the many races with whom Charles had to deal.

With their fellow Slavs more to the south, the Czechs of Bohemia, the Franks had comparatively few relations. The vast uninhabited tract of forest and mountain called the Bohmerwald seems to have long kept them apart. But in 805-6 the king sent against them his son and namesake Charles the Younger, who twice wasted all the valley of the upper Elbe, and finally compelled the chiefs of the Czechs to acknowledge their dependence on the Frankish empire by paying tribute.

South of Bohemia, along the Danube and the Raab and Leithe, the realms of Charles bordered on the Tartar tribe of the Avars, ancient enemies both of the Lombards and of the emperors of Constantinople. The Avars had of late years fallen on evil times. They were vexed with civil wars so much that none of their princes any longer ruled the whole race, or could call himself by the title of Chagan, the old name of their supreme ruler. Yet, though wasted by their own dissensions, and by the revolts of the Slavonic tribes who were their vassals, the Avars could not keep from their old habit of making descents on their neighbours. They drew down their doom on themselves by invading, in 788, at once the Lombard march of Friuli and the vassal duchy of Bavaria. When next he had leisure, two years later, Charles planned an invasion of their land on the largest scale. He himself marched down the Danube with an Austrasian and Saxon army, burst through the long line of fortifications with which the Avars had strengthened their border, and wasted their lands as far as the Raab. At the same moment a great Lombard host entered the valley of the Drave, pushed into the heart of Pannonia, beat the Avars in the field, and stormed their great circular camps. The complete subjection of the whole tribe would have followed in the next year if Charles had not been called away by a Saxon revolt, which kept him employed during the two next campaigning seasons. The king himself never again took the field against the Avars, but his son Pippin and Eric duke of Friuli continued the war on his behalf. Twice they captured the great 'ring,' or royal camp, between Danube and Theiss, the central stronghold of the Avar race, and sent its spoils to Aachen in such quantities that Charles was able to send Avaric trophies as gifts to all his friends, even to such distant kings as Offa of Mercia. At last the spirit of the Avars was so much broken that their chiefs, or 'Tuduns,' came of their own accord to Aachen to do homage to Charles, and offered to receive Christianity. Their submission was accepted. The king appointed one of them to rule the whole race as his vassal, and bade him assume the ancient title of Chagan (805). This prince was baptized by the name of Abraham, paid a regular tribute to the Franks, and kept his subjects for the future from the dangerous temptation of meddling with the Lombard or Bavarian border. The Avars were, however, in a state of decay at this time, and their race and kingdom were ere long to be swept away by the invading Magyars.

The same fate which befell the Tartar Avars fell also upon their southern neighbours and former vassals, the Slavs of the Save and Drave. These Carantanians (Carinthians) and Slovenians were subdued by the arms of Charles's Bavarian and Lombard subjects, and became dependants of the Prankish empire, forced to pay tribute and do homage, but not wholly incorporated with the realm.

We have already spoken in a previous chapter of the dealings of Charles with Italy. He never succeeded in fully subduing the duchy of Benevento, though its dukes were several times compelled to do him homage when he marched in person against them. Italy was finally put under charge of Pippin, the king's second son, who was given the royal title and authority there as his father's delegate. Pippin, besides the task of striving to hold down Benevento, had also to cope with the intrigues of the East Romans in Italy. The Constantinopolitan emperor had still a foot-hold in the peninsula at Naples, Reggio, and Brindisi, and still enjoyed the homage of the half-independent peoples of Venice and Istria. Luckily for the Franks the Eastern realm was during the most important years of Charles's reign, under the weak hands of the empress Irene (780-90 and 797-802) and the usurper Nicephorus I. (802-11.) They bitterly resented the establishment of a new power in Italy, and the assumption of the imperial title by the Frankish king, which they regarded as the worst insult that could be put upon the majesty of the Eastern Empire, which claimed to be the sole and legitimate heir of Augustus and Constantine. But their efforts went little further than endeavouring to stir up trouble in Italy by means of the Lombard prince Adelchis, the son of king Desiderius, who had fled to Constantinople and become a Byzantine patrician. He tried to make more than one descent on Italy, but met with uniform ill-success. The only serious fighting between Frank and East Roman was in the years 804-10, when Nicephorus I. undertook several expeditions against Italy to avenge the revolt of Venice. In the first-named year, a party among the Venetians, who were torn by civil strife, called in the Franks and transferred their allegiance to Charles. Nicephorus sent out a fleet which harried the coasts of Tuscany and the Exarchate, but could make no solid impression on the Lombard kingdom. A little later the East Roman party in Venice got the upper hand, and once more handed the city over to the Byzantines. Contented with the recovery of his vassal-state, Nicephorus then made peace with Charles. The only net result of the war had been that the Franks got permanent possession of Pola and the other coast-cities of Istria, which had hitherto been East Roman. Michael Rhangabe, the successor of Nicephorus, went so far in allying himself with Charles, that he consented to recognise him as Emperor of the West, a concession accepted with pride by the Franks, and regarded as a lamentable token of weakness by the Constantinopolitans (812).

One of the consequences of the conquests of Charles in Italy was to bring the Franks into collision with the Saracen pirates, who infested the central Mediterranean, making their harbourage in the ports of the islands which face the western coast of the peninsula. At a date which cannot be accurately fixed, the Franks took possession of Corsica and Sardinia, hunting out the Saracen colonists who had conquered the islands from the East-Romans some fifty or sixty years before. In 799 the Franks also took possession of the Balearic islands. These distant dependencies were attacked and ravaged by fleets from Spain on more than one occasion, but they were held down to the close of the reign of Charles. They were given in charge to the counts of Genoa and Tuscany, who seem to have been able to raise a considerable fleet, and more than once gained naval victories over the plundering Moor.

But the most serious struggle between Charles and the Moslems took place in Spain, where during the whole of the second period of his reign the fighting was almost continuous. The permanent advance of the Christians beyond the Pyrenees began with the capture of Gerona in 785. The conduct of the war fell mainly into the hands of Lewis, the third son of Charles, whom his father had named king of Aquitaine, and trusted with all the affairs of the south-west. He and his chief captain and councillor William, count of Toulouse — a great hero in the Frankish romances — had to deal with the two first Ommeyad kings of Cordova, Abderahman

(755-88) and Hisham (788-897), both strong and capable rulers, from whom it was by no means easy to win territory. Nevertheless the Christian border slowly advanced, owing to the seditious and turbulent Moslem governors, who were always rebelling against their masters, and calling in Frankish aid. In 795 the newly-won land beyond the Pyrenees — around the towns of Gerona, Cardona, Urgel, and Ausona — was made into a separate government, the March of Spain, and intrusted to a Margrave of its own, instead of forming a dependency of the duchy of Septimania. Barcelona, the greatest town of Catalonia, was added to the March in 797, by the treachery of its governor Zeid, who, failing in a rebellion against his master at Cordova, handed the place over to the Franks. The Moors recovered it for a moment in 799, but king Lewis then came over the Pyrenees with the whole levy of Aquitaine, and laid siege to the town. It held out for nearly two years, but fell in 801, conquered by famine, after the Franks had walled it in with a circumvallation, and sat before it in their huts for the whole winter of 800-801. The Moorish population departed en masse after the surrender, and the great city was re-populated with 'Goths' from Septimania. The Franks were now firmly established beyond the Pyrenees, and in the last ten years of Charles's reign subdued the whole southern slope of the mountains from Pampeluna as far as the mouth of the Ebro. Tarragona, the second town of Catalonia, fell in 809, and Tortosa, the great fortress which commanded the lower course of the Ebro, in 811. After this the Franks were able to cross the river, and ravage the wide plains of Valencia; it was probably their advance in this direction that induced Al-Hakem, the third Ommeyad ruler of Cordova, to sue for peace in 812, ceding to the Christians all that they had gained beyond the Pyrenees. The Franks were not destined to hold permanently the entirety of their conquests, but Barcelona and all the towns north of it were lost to Islam and won for Christendom: these strongholds guarded the Aquitanian frontier against Saracen inroads with success, and were ultimately to form the nucleus of the more important half of the Christian kingdom of Arragon.

Such were the foreign conquests of Charles the Great. But his offensive campaigns were not the only wars in which blood was shed during the later years of his reign. There were also troubles, though of comparatively insignificant scope, within the interior of his realm. We have already alluded to two fruitless attempts of the Bretons of Armorica to resume their ancient independence. These were easily crushed, but not so the later

Saxon rebellions. It was seven years after the pacification of 785 before the unruly dwellers by the Elbe and Weser rose again, but in the eighth summer some of the districts of the extreme north took arms again and relapsed into their ancestral heathendom, 'returning like the dog to his vomit,' in the words of the contemporary chronicler. The insurrection spread widely among the Eastphalians and Nordalbingians in the following year (793), and was not finally put down till 794, though it never extended over the whole land, as did the great risings of the early part of the reign of Charles. Ere two years more were passed there were new troubles among the Engrians and Nordalbingians, which required the presence of Charles: but it says much for the growing strength of his power in the country that he was able to suppress them by means of armies composed partly of Christian Saxons, and partly of the loyal Slavs of the Abotrite tribe. The last outbreak in the land was as late as 804: it extended only over the northern tribes, and was suppressed by the summary transportation to Gaul of the whole of the unruly Nordalbingian race, the greatest offenders among the rebels. Charles settled 10,000 of their families in small colonies among the Neustrians, and gave their vacant lands as a gift to his vassal, the king of the Abotrites. This was the last Saxon rebellion: henceforth 'they abandoned the worship of evil spirits, and gave up the wicked customs of their fathers, and received the sacrament of Christian baptism, mingling with the Franks till at last they were reckoned one race with them.' The complete subjection and conversion of Saxony is marked by the creation of the first bishoprics in the country at this period. Charles established bishops at Bremen, Munster, and Paderborn in 804-6, to serve respectively as the religious centres of northern, western, and southern Saxony. Others were afterwards added at Hamburg, Osnabruck, Verden, Hildesheim, Minden, and Magdeburg, but these foundations belong to the next generation. Round these bishops' sees grew up the first towns of Saxony, for hitherto its inhabitants had lived a purely rural life, and never gathered within walls.

The possession of Saxony brought Charles in the end of his reign into hostile contact with a race almost unknown to his ancestors, but destined to be only too well known to his sons — the Danes of the Jutland peninsula and the Scandinavian isles, who dwelt beyond the Eider on the Nordalbingian border. The advent of a new and militant Christian power into the recesses of the unknown North seems to have stirred up the Danes to unwonted activity. They must have heard from Witikind, and the other

Saxon exiles who took refuge with them, many tales of the untiring energy and unrelenting severity of the great king of the Franks, and feared lest his strong hand would be stretched out beyond the Eider to add them to the list of his tributaries, and force them to accept his religion. To guard against the further advance of the Franks, king Godfred built in 808 all along his frontier, at the narrowest point of the isthmus of Schleswig, a great earthwork from sea to sea, long known as the Dannewerk, and famed in wars down to the last conflict of German and Dane in 1863. But Godfred did not confine himself to defensive works; he began to make piratical descents all along the Frisian and Flemish coasts as far as the mouth of the Seine, and at the same time attacked the Abotrites and Wiltzes, the Slavonic vassals of Charles on the Baltic. Godfred did much damage in Frisia, and actually succeeded for a moment in crushing the Abotrites and subduing the Wiltzes. He gave the Franks much trouble, since he ravaged all the coast where it was unguarded, but took to his ships again when a large army was sent against him. In 810 he penetrated so far into Frisia, that he spoke, in boasting mood, of paying Charles a visit at Aachen. But in the same year he was murdered by his own people, and his nephew and successor Hemming made peace with the Franks. The peace was ill-kept, for we hear of isolated Danish raids in the last years of Charles's reign and a fleet of war-ships, which were built in the ports of Neustria for the defence of the coast, does not seem to have protected the Frisian waters very efficiently.

But Charles did not survive to see the serious development of the Danish attack: he died before his realm had suffered any serious loss from their ravages, and must have been far from suspecting that ere he was fifty years dead these half-known and somewhat despised foes would pierce through the Frankish empire from end to end, and even sack his own chosen dwelling, the royal palace of Aachen.

CHAPTER XXII: CHARLES THE GREAT AND THE EMPIRE

Survival of the Theory of the Empire in Western Europe, and especially in Italy — Its influence — Troubles of Pope Leo III. — He crowns Charles on Christmas Day 800 — Consequences, immediate and remote, of the coronation — The Papacy and the Empire — Charles as administrator and legislator — His encouragement of Literature, Architecture, and Science — His later years and death.

While narrating the never-ending wars of the great king of the Franks, we have barely found time to mention the internal changes which he wrought in the condition and constitution of his realms. Of these the first and foremost was his introduction of a new political theory into the government of Western Christendom, when he caused himself to be crowned emperor by Pope Leo III. in the memorable year 800.

We have had occasion to remark in an earlier chapter that the theory of the universal dominion of the Roman Empire had long survived the extinction of any real power of the emperors in most of the countries of Western Europe. Theodoric the Ostrogoth and Chlodovech the Frank had been proud to acknowledge themselves as the first subjects of the Constantinopolitan Caesar, and to receive from his hands high-sounding titles and robes of honour. Till the middle of the sixth century Gaul, Spain, and Italy had all owned a nominal allegiance to the empire, and their homage had only been denied when Justinian by his bold attempt to recover the whole of the West had forced the Teutonic kings to take arms against him in their own defence. Then Baduila, Leovigild, and Theudebert had disclaimed their allegiance, and banished the imperial name from their coins and their charters. The last practical traces of the old Roman connection had been lost in Spain when the soldiers of Heraclius were driven out by Swinthila (623), and in Gaul when the encouragement and the subsidies of Maurice had failed to sustain the pretender Gundovald (585). Yet there still lingered on in the minds of the educated classes a memory of the ancient empire; curious turns of expression in chroniclers of the seventh century often show us that they still remembered the old theory of the world-wide rule of Rome. A Spanish chronicler writing in the seventh century can still call the East Roman armies 'the soldiers of the respublica.' Subjects of the Frankish kings in Gaul still dated their letters by Constantinopolitan indictions.

In Italy, of course, the tradition of the unity of Christendom under the emperors was in no danger of being forgotten. Appeals to the ancient temporal and spiritual supremacy of Rome were the most powerful items in the Pope's stock of arguments, when a Gregory or a Zacharias stated his pretensions to patriarchal authority in the West, or denounced the wickedness of the intrusive Lombard. The personal ambition of the Popes was always leading them to indulge in fond reminiscences of the ancient glories of the Empire. The vanity of the degenerate populace of Rome sometimes found vent in futile claims that they, 'the Roman senate and people,' really were the heirs of Augustus and Constantine, while the Caesar at Constantinople was nothing more than a mere Greek. When, by the rupture between Leo the Isaurian and Pope Gregory II., Rome practically passed out of the hands of the Eastern Augustus, it was easy enough for an Italian to maintain that Constantine Copronymus or Leo the Khazar had no longer any true right to use the Roman Imperial title. And the Italian malcontent would add, not, of course, that Rome had ceased to form part of the Roman Empire, but that the title of emperor had passed away from the heretical Isaurian house, and fallen into abeyance, while the empire itself still existed, for its cessation had grown to be inconceivable to the Italian mind.

The Italians, and to a less extent the Franks, were sorely puzzled by the long continuance of the anomalous condition of affairs, when for sixty years the titular emperors had remained heretics, and had failed to maintain their hold on Rome. Nor was the position improved when the Eastern Empire relapsed into orthodoxy indeed, but at the same time passed into the hands of an empress-regnant, a thing repugnant to all those who remembered the ancient Roman horror of a woman's reign. Irene herself, too, had obtained the crown by such a series of crimes against her son, that not merely constitutional jurists, but all right-minded men shrank, in spite of her extreme orthodoxy, from the idea of recognising in her the legitimate ruler of Rome.

More than once during the long quarrel between the Popes and the Isaurian emperors there had been some talk of electing a separate Augustus to bear rule over Roman Italy, — those districts of the peninsula which were not in the hands of the Lombards. The scheme had not been carried out, mainly because the Popes opposed it, but it had not been forgotten. Now that the greater part of Italy, both Lombard and Roman, was under the rule of a single king, and one well liked both by the Pope and by the Roman people, it would have been strange if the idea of completely repudiating the ignominious dependence of Rome on Constantinople had not been once more mooted. For as long as there remained but one person bearing the Imperial style, — the ruler of the East, — the Pope and his Roman and Italian contemporaries had an uneasy consciousness that their homage ought still, perhaps, to be paid to that person, Greek and heretic though he or she might be.

We may suppose that these doubts hardly troubled the Frankish vassals of Charles the Great, but to his Italian subjects they were a constant source of vexation of spirit; while practically they were liegemen of the Frankish king, they were not quite sure whether in theory they might not still be considered the liegemen of the hated Caesars at Constantinople.

Such thoughts must have been running through the heads of all the Popes who held the Roman See from 773 to 800. But it would seem that it was Pope Leo III. who first bethought him of the easiest way of settling the situation — to declare the king of the Franks Roman emperor, and not merely Roman patrician. A barbarian Augustus would be unprecedented, but not more so than the female ruler of the Empire who now swayed Constantinople. It was evidently the sight of a woman — and a very wicked woman — on the Byzantine throne that gave the final impulse to the desire of the Italians to cut off the last thread of connection with the Imperial line in the East. Their desire must have been well known to Charles himself, but it would seem that he for some time shrank from granting it. Perhaps he feared the responsibilities of the title; more probably he did not see how it legally could be conferred upon him: there was no precedent to settle what person or body in the West could claim to give it, and it was most certain that the court of Constantinople would utterly refuse to grant it, and would view its assumption by a 'barbarian' king of the West as a gross piece of insolence.

It would seem that the fervent gratitude of Pope Leo III. for his deliverance by the hand of Charles from certain domestic enemies in Rome, was the active cause of the great ceremony of Christmas Day 800. Leo had been cruelly maltreated by personal enemies in Rome, the kinsmen of his predecessor Hadrian I.; they had seized his person and tried to blind him. But he escaped, fled over the Alps, and took refuge with the great king at his camp near Paderborn, in Saxony. Charles investigated the dispute between Leo and his enemies, and he determined that he would come to Rome and decide the matter in person; meanwhile he sent Leo home under the protection of some Frankish ambassadors. Late in the year 800 Charles moved down into Italy, and held a synod at Rome in which he carefully investigated the conduct of Leo, and pronounced him blameless, while his enemies were executed or thrown into prison. The Pope then purged himself by an oath from all the charges that had been made against him, and was reinstated in his place with much solemnity.

It was only a few days after Charles had thus restored and commended Leo, that the Pope paid the debt of gratitude by crowning his saviour as emperor. The details of this all-important ceremony are curious. The royal and papal courts were thronging St. Peter's basilica to celebrate the festival of Christmas. When the service was ended, and while the emperor was still kneeling before the altar in silent prayer, Leo advanced with a diadem in his hand, and placed it upon the bowed head of the great king, crying, 'God grant life and victory to Charles the Augustus, crowned by God, great and pacific Emperor of the Romans.' Frankish warriors and Italian clergy and citizens joined in the cry, and all present, including the Pope himself, bent their knees to Charles as he rose, and saluted him with the fashion of adoration paid to the ancient emperors.

Charles himself was wont to declare that the ceremony took place without his consent having been obtained, and that he would never have entered St. Peter's that day, if he had known of the Pope's intention. Yet there is no doubt that he had seriously taken the matter into consideration long before; it is probable that Leo in his outburst of gratitude for his restoration did no more than force Charles's hand, by sweeping away by his sudden act the king's lingering objections to the coronation. He knew that the act would be hailed with joy both by Frank and Roman, and that Charles himself was rather doubtful as to the proper form for assuming the title than opposed to its actual adoption. The way in which the coronation was viewed by the majority of his subjects may be gathered from an extract from the Frankish chronicle of Lauresheim: — 'The name of emperor had ceased among the Greeks, for they were enduring the reign of a woman, wherefore it seemed good both to Leo the apostolic Pope, and to the holy fathers (bishops) who were in council with him, and to all Christian men, that they should hail Charles king of the Franks as emperor. For he held

Rome itself, where the ancient Caesars always dwelt, and all these other possessions of his own in Italy and Gaul and Germany. Wherefore, as God had granted him all these dominions, it seemed just to them that he should accept the imperial title also, when it was offered him by the consent of all Christendom.'

That there was much to be said against the legality of the assumption by Charles of his new style, cannot be disputed. Certainly the Pope had no right to give it: nor had there been a precedent for many centuries for the conferring of the imperial title by the decayed body of nobles and the miscellaneous gathering of citizens who might still call themselves 'the senate and people of Rome.' Apparently the Pope, when he saluted Charles as 'crowned by God,' claimed that the impulse to hail him by the great name of emperor, descended by a direct inspiration from heaven upon the multitude gathered in St. Peter's. But such a plea would hardly appeal with much force, either to the Byzantine Court or to the modern historian. In truth, there was much to be said for the assumption of the imperial style by Charles, as recognising an accomplished fact, but little for the particular forms by which it was carried out. Most especially did the fact that the Pope seemed to confer the title, by his own act and impulse, prove of incalculable harm in future years. If the coronation of the great king had taken some other form, it would have been impossible for the Popes of later generations to bring forward their preposterous claim to have the power of giving or taking away the imperial crown. The successors of Charles would have been spared many a weary journey to Rome, and many a bitter wrangle with the Holy See, if there had been a formal election-ceremony in which all the nations of the West could have taken part, or if Charles, like Napoleon in a later age, could have placed the crown on his own head instead of receiving it from the pontiff's hand.

The assumption of the imperial title by the great king had many practical consequences at the moment, and many and yet more important influences upon the history of Europe for long centuries to come.

The most notable of the immediate results of the coronation was that Charles and all his subjects regarded his regal authority as being reaffirmed in a new and more hallowed shape by the ceremony. Formerly his power rested on his election as king by the Franks, and afterwards by the Lombards: now he was 'crowned by God' as well as chosen by the people. For the future he showed an increasing tendency to insist on the omnipotence of his authority in things ecclesiastical and moral as well as in civil matters. As Heaven's anointed he claimed to be the guardian of morality and the reformer of Christendom, as well as the protector of the Church. Charles had always shown a deep interest in the spiritual welfare of his dominions. We have seen already what energy he displayed in enforcing the conversion of Saxony, of the Slavs, and of the Avars. He had presided at innumerable councils and synods, stirring up his bishops to enforce strict discipline and sober life among the clergy, and to root out heathen survivals and immorality among the laity. Now that he had become emperor he insisted even more than before on the moral side of his authority: he thought of himself not only as the successor of Constantine and Theodosius, but even as inheriting the theocratic powers of the ancient kings of Israel — of David or of Josiah. When Charles recrossed the Alps after his coronation and held his next great council in Austrasia, he took the opportunity of bringing home his views to his liegemen. He made all his subjects, lay and secular, swear allegiance to him for a second time under his new name of emperor: every person above the age of twelve was to have the oath administered to him by the local clergy, and to be warned 'that his vow of homage was not merely a promise to be true to the emperor and to serve him against his enemies, but a promise to live in obedience to God and His law according to the best of each man's strength and understanding. It was a vow to abstain from theft and oppression and injustice, no less than from heathen practices and witchcraft: a vow to do no wrong to the Churches of God, nor to injure widows and orphans, of whom the emperor is the chosen protector and guardian.' Much more followed to the same effect: Charles formally claimed that the defence of all law and morality was involved in the imperial name, and warned his subjects that any offence against him and his ordinances was a direct crime against the anointed of God.

It was not only in the mind of Charles that this high and holy view of the duty and power of the emperor found a place. He succeeded in impressing it on his own contemporaries and on long centuries to come: with him starts the idea of the 'Holy Roman Empire,' which affected so deeply the whole secular and religious life of the Middle Ages. The Frankish kingship, a mere rule of force, had no exalted and spiritual meaning: the new empire represented a close and conscious union of Church and State for the advantage of both. It started with the conception that the emperor should be the protector and overseer of the Church: by an unhappy development it ended in making the Pope the overseer of the State. But the generation which had seen Pope Leo on his knees 'adoring' the majesty of the great Charles, could not have foreseen the day when the successor of Charles should humbly wait for hours before the unopened door of the successor of Leo, or beg as a favour the privilege of holding his stirrup.

A new age then commences in Europe with the coronation of Charles the Great. The reign of pure barbaric force is ended: there follows a time when the history of Europe is complicated by the strife of ideas no less than by the strife of armed nations. For the future we must always be on the watch to detect the influence on politics of the ideal conception of Christendom as a great empire, under a single ruler chosen by God to sway the sword, and the rival conception of it as a great Church under a single Patriarch at Rome, appointed to hold the keys of heaven and hell, and to guide kings in the way they should go.

The internal government of the vast realm of Charles was a difficult problem. In his own lifetime the great king provided for it by delegating his authority in certain large sections of it to his sons: we have already spoken of his nomination of Charles, Pippin, and Lewis to be kings in Neustria, Italy, and Aquitaine. Charles contemplated the possibility of a single empire existing while yet many of its parts should be governed by vassal sovereigns. In his own time the plan worked well enough: he did not, perhaps, foresee that the problem would be far harder in the next generation, when the homage and obedience of the lesser kings would have to be paid to a brother, an uncle, and at last to a mere distant cousin.

Charles publicly issued in 806 the scheme on which his realm was to be ruled after his death: the title of emperor and all the Frankish lands, both Neustrian and Austrasian, were to go to his first-born Charles; with them went Saxony, Thuringia, and Burgundy. Pippin, the second son, had Italy, together with Bavaria and eastern Suabia. Lewis, the youngest child, was to take Aquitaine, Provence, and the Spanish March. This division, however, was rendered fruitless by the unexpected decease of the two elder kings: to the great grief of their father. Pippin died in 810, and Charles in 811. This necessitated a new division of the empire: Lewis was now the only grown man in the family: to him, therefore, was left the imperial name and all the realm save Italy, which was to be a vassal-kingdom for Bernard, the young son of Pippin.

Charles, while all his sons yet lived, gave over the charge of large sections of his realm to them. Beneath their authority the kingdoms were ruled by the same hierarchy of dukes and counts who had existed in

Merovingian times. When any new land, such as Saxony or Lombardy, was added to the empire, it was ere long cut up into countships on the same pattern that already served for Austrasia and Neustria. Thus a regular ascending scale of grades lay between the count and the emperor. The count obeyed the duke, the duke the sub-king, the king his father the suzerain of all. In the conquered lands Franks were, as a rule, intrusted with the most important provincial governments: but Charles often gave countships in their own native districts to Lombards, Aquitanians, or even Saxons who had served him well and truly.

The best security for the unity and peace of the empire was the never-ceasing activity of Charles himself, who incessantly perambulated his realm from end to end so long as life was in him. It was his own frequent visits to Saxony, Italy, or Bavaria, that were the best means of keeping those outlying provinces in loyalty and obedience. But he had also a regular system of travelling commissioners who were always moving round the realm, and reporting to him on the needs and requirements of the different provinces. The circuits of these Missi Dominici, or royal legates, as they were called, were fully settled by him only in 802, but he had been employing them less systematically at a far earlier date. His father and grandfather, Pippin the Short and Charles Martel, had been wont to send out occasionally travelling commissions (Missi discurrentes), but it was Charles the emperor who multiplied and systematised their activity. By his arrangements his emissaries, who were sometimes clerics, sometimes laymen, were appointed for a year's duty over a certain number of countships. They visited the assemblies of the inhabitants of the district, summoned to the count's Mallus. and inquired into the state of the provinces. Complaints against the count himself or the local bishop were brought before them, and they would send them up to the king or take account of them on the spot. We sometimes find Missi charged with other duties, such as the conduct of an embassy or a warlike expedition, but this terminal inspection of the local governors was their primary duty. As long as men of probity and strength were chosen, no better machinery for keeping together the wide empire of the Franks could have been devised.

We have already mentioned in an earlier chapter the interest which Charles always showed in art and letters, an interest which had been very rare among the Frankish kings, whether of his own house or of the Merovings. Of all the two dynasties the ruffian Chilperich I. is — curiously enough — the only one who is recorded to have shown any literary tastes.

Charles, however, atoned for the neglect of his predecessors. He collected learned men from all quarters: the Northumbrian Alcuin and the Lombards Peter of Pisa and Paul the Deacon were the best-known names among them: at first his scholars were mostly foreigners, but by the end of his reign he had seen a generation of learned Franks arise in response to his encouragement. Two of his proclamations, the Epistola de litteris colendis and the Encydica de emendatione librorum, set forth his purpose. He complains that the letters addressed to him by bishops and abbots from all parts of his realm are 'very correct in sentiment but very incorrect in grammar,' so that he has begun to fear whether his clergy have enough knowledge of Latin to understand the whole sense of the Scriptures. Wherefore he will have schools established in every monastery for the perfect teaching of the Latin tongue, 'because it is useful that men of God should not only live by the rule and dwell in holy conversation, but should devote themselves to literary meditations, each according to his ability, that they may be able to give themselves to the duty of teaching others.' Under the fostering hand of Charles all the greater monasteries became centres of learning: we owe to his care the preservation of many of the classical authors, for he was incessantly causing the old volumes, 'almost worn out,' as he says, 'by the carelessness of our ancestors,' to be fairly copied out and multiplied. Each monastery was urged to have its own treasures preserved by several copies, and to interchange them with those of its neighbours. He paid special attention to the books of the Old and New Testaments, was shocked at the diverse readings which he found to exist — due, as he asserts, to the extreme ignorance of copyists — and set Paul the Deacon to construct a new lectionary, corrected according to the best texts, and destined to be used in all the Churches in his realm. It was not only to religious books that he turned his attention: he had the old heroic epics of the Franks — the prototypes, we may suppose, of such works as the Nibelungenlied — collected and written out: unfortunately his pious son Lewis destroyed this invaluable corpus of Frankish poetry, because he deemed it heathenish. He is also found setting his scholars to work on the compilation of grammars — both Latin and German — biographies, and even of works of secular history. It is, no doubt, to his inspiration that we owe the sudden expansion and multiplication of the Frankish chronicles. Our historical sources, down to his time, are few, bald, and jejune; soon after his accession they become full, satisfactory, and numerous. The ninth century, in spite of all its troublous times, is far better known to us than the eighth.

Charles kept the best of his scholars about his Court, and treated them as familiar friends. When he was settled down at Aachen for the winter, and was at rest from wars, he gathered them about him to discuss all manners of subjects, from astronomy to logic. The literary circle assumed old classical names. Alcuin called himself Flaccus, Charles was addressed as King David, other scholars styled themselves Homer, Mopsus, and Damaetas. Their discussions were often fruitless, and sometimes childish, but it was something new in Western Christendom to find a whole group of scholars busied in discussions of any sort whatever. After looking back at the blank darkness of the seventh century, we find the court of Charles the Great a very centre of light and wisdom. In it lay the promise of great things in the future, a promise for which we have looked in vain in any period of the preceding ages.

It was not only in literature that Charles busied his leisure hours. He was a great admirer of music, both secular and ecclesiastical. His ear was charmed by the Gregorian chants which he heard at Rome, and he took back with him Italian choirmasters to teach the churchmen of the north the sonorous cadences of the sainted Pope.

He was also a mighty builder. At Aachen he reared a great palace for himself and a magnificent cathedral. The former has perished, but enough survives of the latter to show the exact extent to which Romanesque architecture had developed by his time. So much was he set on making it the most magnificent basilica to the north of the Alps, that when he found his own workmen unable to carry out his ideas, he sent for ancient columns and marbles from distant Rome and Ravenna. His own coffin was a splendid Roman sarcophagus, probably procured from Italy. He constructed palaces in two other Austrasian towns besides Aachen, the old royal seats of Nimuegen and Engelheim, for he was Austrasian to the core, and always made the land of his ancestors his favourite dwelling. He built a bridge at Mainz five hundred yards long, the first effort of Frankish engineering in that class of structure. Unfortunately it was destroyed by fire in 813, and never renewed. Another piece of work which testifies to his interest in engineering was a canal to join the Rhine and Danube, by means of their tributaries, the Altmuhl and the Rednitz.

But to follow Charles into every department of his activity, during his long life and reign would require many volumes. Here it must suffice to say that after all these achievements he died at his chosen abode at Aachen, on the 28th of January 814, carried off at a ripe old age by a pleurisy caught in the winter cold. He was buried in the cathedral that he himself had built, and over his tomb was placed a golden shrine, with his image and the inscription: — 'SUB HOC CONDITORIO SITUM EST CORPUS KAROLI MAGNI ET ORTHODOXI IMPERATORIS, QUI REGNUM FRANCORUM NOBILITER AMPLIAVIT, ET PER ANNOS XLVII FELICITER REXIT.'

It was but a short epitaph considering the mighty deeds of him who lay beneath, but no length of words could have done justice to his greatness. A far better memorial was left to him in the hearts of his subjects; his name survived in the mouths of all the races that had served him, as the type of power, wisdom, and righteousness. All Western Europe looked back to him for seven hundred years as the common pride of Christendom, the founder of that 'Holy Roman Empire' which satisfied their ideal of governance. His figure looms out, though often with outlines blurred and distorted, from dozens of the legends and romances which shadowed forth the aspirations of the Middle Ages. Within a hundred years of his death it was currently believed that he had conquered Spain and Byzantium, and carried his arms as far as Palestine. So great was the impression he had left behind him, that the world thought nothing too impossible for him to have achieved. Perhaps the notion that his reign had been a kind of Golden Age was partly produced by the contrasting years of trouble and civil strife that followed his death. But the tendency to look back to his time as a period of unexampled splendour and righteousness was no delusion, but a just recognition of the fact that he had given the Western world a glimpse of new and high ideals, such as it had never known under the brutal rule of twelve generations of barbarian kings, nor in those earlier days when it was still held together in the iron grasp of the Caesars of ancient Rome.

CHAPTER XXIII: LEWIS THE PIOUS — 814-840

Character of Lewis the Pious — He reforms the Frankish court — His ecclesiastical legislation — After a narrow escape from death he divides his kingdom among his sons — The partition of Aachen — Rebellion and death of Bernard of Italy — The second marriage of Lewis and its consequences — Second partition of the empire followed by rebellion of Lewis' elder sons — Their repeated risings — The 'Lugenfeld' — Lewis twice deposed and restored — Continued troubles of his later years — He dies while leading an army against his son Lewis — Disastrous consequences of his reign.

Charles the Great left his throne and his empire to his only surviving son born in lawful wedlock, Lewis the Pious, as his own age named him, though later chroniclers style him Lewis the Debonnair. The heir of the great emperor was a devout prince, who proved — like our own Edward the Confessor — 'a sair saint for the crown.' He was a weak, good-natured man, no longer in the first flower of his youth, whose meek virtues were far more suited to adorn a monastery than a palace. Utterly wanting in self-respect and determination, the slave of his wife, his chaplains, and bishops, a doting father and husband, and an over-liberal giver, he had one of those natures which are entirely unfit to bear responsibility, and are only happy when placed under the rule of a stronger will than their own. Lewis had before him the problems that had taxed his father's iron nerve, — the task of ruling each of the nations that dwelt beneath the Frankish sceptre in the way that it needed, with the additional trial of being sorely vexed by the incursions of the Danes, whose first ravages Charles the Great had hardly lived to see. Enough was there to occupy his every moment, even had he been a man of ability. But he chose to add to his troubles the needless trial of a disputed succession and a spasmodic civil war. The main feature of his reign of twenty-six years is the weary tale of his unwise dealing with his undutiful sons, and of the evils that ensued therefrom.

The great realm which now fell to Lewis had been built up in despite of three main difficulties — the enormous extent of the conquered lands, and the slowness of communication between them, the national differences between the various peoples which inhabited them, and the old Teutonic custom which favoured the partition of a kingdom among all the sons of its ruler, just as if it were a private heritage. The first two dangers had not proved fatal. The personal energy and never-ending travels of Charles the Great had vanquished space and time. Racial divergences were less formidable than might have been expected, for true national feeling was not yet fully developed in Western Europe. It was neither the enormous extent of the Frankish empire nor the heterogeneous character of its inhabitants that proved the direct cause of its ruin, but the baleful practice of the partition of heritages among all the heirs of the reigning sovereign. Hitherto the empire had been fortunate in escaping the consequences of this evil. Charles the Hammer had broken up his realm, but the voluntary abdication of the elder Carloman had ere long reunited the Neustrian and Austrasian lands. Pippin, again, had divided his kingdom, but the co-heir, whose survival would have thwarted the life-work of Charles the Great, died young. And in the next generation, too, death had stripped the king of all his lawful issue save one, and Lewis the Pious received an undivided heritage.

But Lewis, unhappily for himself and for the empire, had already three half-grown sons when he succeeded to the empire, and was destined to see a fourth reach manhood ere he died. The custom of partition was now destined to have a fair trial and develop to its utmost extent.

Lewis was at Doue, in his kingdom of Aquitaine, when he received the news of the death of his aged father. Making such speed as he could, he arrived at Aachen after a journey of thirty days, and took possession of the reins of power. Without sending for the Pope to assist at his coronation, he celebrated his accession by taking the imperial crown off the altar in the cathedral of his capital city, and placing it on his own head, while the assembled counts and bishops shouted Vivat Imperator Ludovicus! The magnates also saluted him by the title of 'the Pious,' an appellation which he placed upon his coins, on whose other side appeared the legend, 'Renovatio Regni Francorum.' The 'renewing' of the kingdom found its first expression in the expulsion from office of the ministers who had administered affairs during the declining years of Charles the Great. Lewis came to Aachen with his own trusted servants at his back, and was determined not to put himself in the hands of his father's favourites. There had been much in his father's life and court which his own scrupulous conscience could not approve. As a man who led a singularly virtuous life himself, he could not abide the bishops and abbots who had connived at his father's immoralities. The Frankish court, though teeming with ecclesiastics, had not been a model of soberness or chastity, and the old emperor himself had not set the best of examples. Lewis was determined that this should cease.

The moment that he was firmly seated on the throne the new monarch dismissed from his court his sisters, whose life had been nothing less than scandalous during his father's later years. Their paramours were banished or imprisoned — one was even deprived of his eyes. His next step was to send away the three chief ministers of Charles the Great. The Chancellor Helisachar, Abbot of St. Maximin, was relegated to his monastery. The two brothers, count Wala and abbot Adalhard, had harder measure dealt out to them. The emperor sent Adalhard to dwell in the lonely monastery of Hermoutier, on an island by the Loire mouth. Count Wala was stripped of sword and armour, shorn, and immured as a monk in the cloister of Corbey.

These councillors were replaced by men whom Lewis had learnt to know while he was yet but king of Aquitaine. The chief were Ebbo, his own foster-brother, abbot Hildwin, and count Bernard of Septimania. Ebbo, though but the son of a serf, was dear to the emperor from early association; he had taken orders, and was made archbishop of Rheims by his patron at the earliest opportunity, amid the murmurs of many high-born Frankish ecclesiastics, who exclaimed that such preferment was not the meed of a man of servile extraction. Hildwin, the new chancellor, was a shameless pluralist, three abbots rolled into one, and ever seeking more preferment. Bernard, however, a clever, restless, intriguing Gascon, provoked even greater jealousy and bitterness among the old courtiers of Charles the Great, and seems to have been the best-hated man in the realm. But perhaps the most influential of all the advisers of Lewis was his wife, Hermengarde, the daughter of the count of the Hesbain, an ambitious and unscrupulous woman, who exercised such an influence over her uxorious spouse that she was even able to drive him once and again to deeds of ill-faith and cruelty very foreign to his mild and righteous disposition.

Charles the Great had left the frontiers of his great realm so well secured that in the earliest years of Lewis the Pious there was no foreign war to call the emperor into the field. It was a characteristic sign of the new regime that things ecclesiastical took precedence of all others at the first meetings of the magnates of the empire. We hear of legislation against carnally-minded bishops and abbots, who shocked the pious by riding with cloak and sword and golden spurs like secular nobles. A modus vivendi was established between clerics of servile birth and their former lords, providing that on due compensation being paid the villein might go free. The emperor took the keenest interest in this question. Not only his favourite Ebbo, but several others of his counsellors had been serfs, and he was most anxious to defend them alike against claims of their ancient masters, and insults at the hands of the free-born clergy. Another decree of Lewis' dealt with the tenure of the lands of monasteries. After stipulating that fourteen great houses owed both military service and aids in money to the empire, and sixteen more the financial duty alone, he declared that all the other monastic establishments in his wide dominion should hold their property on the simple undertaking that they should 'pray for the welfare of the emperor and his children and the empire.' This threw a vast quantity of estates into tenure by what later ages called 'frank almoin,' and relieved of its natural responsibility to the State more land than could prudently be suffered to go scot-free.

Another sign of Lewis' extreme regard for the Church was given at the very commencement of his reign. When pope Leo III., the aged pontiff, who had crowned Charles the Great, died in 816 the Romans elected, in great haste, Stephen IV. as his successor. The new Pope was consecrated without the imperial sanction being sought, but Lewis made no objection, and showed no wrath at this disregard of his prerogative. So far was he from resentment that he allowed Stephen to represent to him that his coronation at Aachen had lacked the Church's blessing, inasmuch as he had taken the crown from the altar with his own hands. To render Lewis' position more like that of his great father, the Pope proposed to cross the Alps and recrown his master. Lewis took no offence at the slur thrown on the form of his election to the empire, but received Stephen in great state at Rheims, and was there crowned for the second time (816). Thus he loosened his own grasp on the Papacy in one year, and allowed the Pope to tighten his grasp on the empire in the next.

In 817 happened an accident which was to have the gravest consequences on the emperor's character and fate. He was passing with all his train over a wooden gallery which connected the cathedral and the palace at Aachen, when the whole structure came crashing to the ground. Many of the courtiers were killed, and the emperor himself received injuries which confined him to his bed for many weeks. The shock and the narrow escape from death set Lewis meditating on the instability of life and the necessity for being always prepared for the grave. He had never been anything but sober and self-contained, but he now fell into a morbid and lugubrious frame of mind, which never left him till his dying day. If he had only hitherto been a daring sinner he might have salved his conscience by turning to a new manner of life: but being already a man of blameless and virtuous habits, his conversion only led him into an exaggerated asceticism. He abandoned the study of profane literature, which had hitherto soothed his leisure hours, and would for the rest of his life read nothing but theology. We are even told that he destroyed the collection of Old-Frankish heroic poems which his father had made, because of the many traces of heathenism which he found in them. It was with difficulty that his councillors prevented him two years later from laying down his crown and retiring to a monastery.

One of the first effects of Lewis' morbid brooding over his latter end was that he determined to make a settlement of the inheritance of his wide dominions in view of his own possible death. He was now only forty-three, and his eldest son was but seventeen, but he resolved to take the untried boy into partnership and associate him with himself, so that his succession might be assured at his own death. At the same time he determined to give his younger sons appanages in the realm which would be their brother's. The old German instinct for dividing the paternal heritage was still too strong to be resisted.

By this Partition of Aachen, the first of many partitions that we shall have to bear in mind, Lothair, the eldest of Lewis' three sons, became co-emperor, and was allotted as his special province, during his father's life, the kingdom of Italy. Pippin, the second son, was to inherit Aquitaine, his father's original portion. Lewis, the third son, was assigned Bavaria, and the wild marches to its east along the Danube. Thus it was provided that at the emperor's death his successor should hold the great bulk of the realm, containing both its capitals — Aachen and Rome — and including all the oldest Frankish lands, Neustria and Austrasia alike. The kings of Aquitaine and Bavaria would be far too weak, even if united, to trouble him by rebellions, but Lewis ended his deed of gift by a solemn exhortation to the younger sons to obey their brother, visit his court once a year, and be his helpers in peace and war. In spite of the experience of elder generations of his house he hoped that his children might dwell together in amity.

There was one clause in the Partition of Aachen which was certain to cause instant trouble. It named Italy as the special portion of the young Lothair. Now, Italy was, and had been for seven years, under the government of the emperor's nephew Bernard, son of that Pippin of Italy who died in 810. Charles the Great had placed him there, and while obeying Lewis as a loyal subject he looked upon the Cisalpine kingdom as his own appanage, and expected to retain it through all changes in the imperial succession. Bernard was determined not to be ousted from his realm; the moment that the news of the Partition of Aachen reached him he flew into rebellion. His rule had been popular, and the Lombards gladly took arms in his behalf and seized all the passes of the Alps. He even tried to stir up trouble in Gaul by the aid of his friend Theodulph bishop of Orleans.

Having gone so far, Bernard would have done wisely to abide altogether by the arbitrament of the sword. Instead of doing this he held back and negotiated. Relying on the emperor's well-known character for justice and moderation Bernard left his army and went to a conference at Chalons-sur-Saone. He soon found that he had made a fatal mistake. He was treated as a criminal on trial, not as a prince who came to negotiate terms of peace. The conference adjoined to Aachen, and there Bernard and his chief adherents were judged and condemned. The council doomed the accused to death, but Lewis, half-mindful of the safe-conduct that his ambassadors had promised, commuted the sentence to blinding. The cruel order was executed, but so clumsily was it carried out, that Bernard died of the shock. Rumour added that it was the empress Hermengarde who had bribed the executioners to do their work so badly. The remorse that seized the emperor for his broken safe-conduct and the death of his nephew never ceased to vex his soul for all his remaining years. It was the only grave moral offence that he had ever committed, and his tender conscience would give him no rest.

Within a few months after Bernard's death Lewis was visited by a calamity which he considered the first instalment of the divine vengeance for the deed. On his return from an expedition to Brittany he was met by the news of the death of his wife Hermengarde. It was whispered that she had been largely guilty in the matter of her nephew's death, and that she was now paying the penalty. Lewis at any rate seems to have had this idea. He had been deeply attached to his imperious wife, and leant much on her guidance. Deprived of her he fell into a state of morbid melancholy, far worse than any he had yet experienced. He shut himself up with his grief, neglected state affairs, and talked of retiring into a cloister. After some months his ministers found the situation growing so impossible that they took every means to rouse him. It was, we are told, his bishops who took the strange step of urging on him that he must marry again as a public duty; his seclusion injured the realm, and he must remember that man was not meant to live alone. When the emperor would neither go to seek a wife nor take a princess whom he had not seen on another's recommendation, his ministers brought to his court all the fairest of the daughters of the counts and nobles of his realm. The same scene was rehearsed that was a few years later to be seen at Constantinople when the widowed Theophilus took his second wife. Among the crowd of ladies presented before him, the eye of Lewis fixed upon Judith, a noble damsel from the Suabian Alps, daughter of Welf, count of Altdorf. Pressed hard by his courtiers he consented to take her to wife, and rued it all his remaining years. Judith was fair, wise, witty, and learned above all the women of her day, and soon acquired an empire over her melancholy spouse, not less than that which her predecessor had exercised. Two years later she presented him with a son, whose birth was to cause unending evils to the empire. The boy was named Charles, after his great grandsire. (A.D. 822.)

For a space things seemed to be going well with Lewis, but three years after his second marriage the black shadow closed in again over the unfortunate emperor. Some cause, to us unknown, suddenly plunged him once more into a fit of misery and contrition. He remembered first that he had not pardoned all his enemies as a good Christian should. Forthwith all whom he had ever injured were recalled from exile. The brothers Wala and Adalhard were drawn out of their monasteries. The partisans of Bernard of Italy who had suffered Winding and imprisonment were sent back to their homes. So anxious was the emperor to atone for his harshness that he most unwisely proceeded to place the most important of the exiles in high posts of trust. He made Adalhard master of his household, and sent Wala to his son Lothair to be his first councillor. He had forgotten that others might not forgive as he could himself; these appointments placed in power men who at the bottom of their hearts could never pardon their years, of weariness and cloistered seclusion.

After doing what he could to recompense his victims for the indignities they had suffered, Lewis took another and a more startling step. He summoned a great council at Attigny, hard by the royal city of Soissons, and proceeded to do penance for his sins before the face of his magnates. Coming forth crownless and robed in sackcloth he recapitulated all the faults and misdeeds that had ever been committed, from the execution of Bernard of Italy down to many trifling transgressions, which most men counted as harmless failings, and all had long forgotten. He even rehearsed, with a somewhat unnecessary scrupulousness, all the crimes and short-comings of his great father the emperor Charles. Then he besought his bishops to lay on him such a meed of penance as might fit these many and grievous sins. Not unwilling to take advantage of their sovereign's humiliation, the prelates prescribed to him a course of stripes and fasting and vigils, of prayer, almsgiving, and building of churches, all of which he conscientiously carried out. The astonished counts and courtiers saw their monarch baring his back to the lash, and discharging with exactitude all the humiliating burdens that the clergy laid upon him. It was the act of a saint, but not of an emperor.

Nothing could have done Lewis more harm than this outburst of laboured penitence. While his subjects marvelled at his Christian humility, they drew from his conduct the conclusion that as a sovereign he was no longer to be feared or obeyed. The Frankish nobles who remembered the high-handed Charles the Great, and had loved him in spite of all his harshness, felt more scorn than admiration for an emperor who wept and grovelled in public over deeds which few in that age considered sins at all. They muttered that Lewis was no better than a brain-sick, self-torturing monk. For the future there was an under-current of contempt for the emperor passing through the minds of most of his lay vassals. It needed but some small encouragement to turn this feeling into active disloyalty.

The year of the council of Attigny was the last year of good fortune for Lewis. It was followed by premonitory symptoms of evil all over his realm. The Moors of Spain, quiescent for more than twenty years, sent a sudden invasion into Septimania. The Danes drove out their king Harald, a protege of Lewis and a favourer of Christianity, and began to ravage the Frisian coast. But there were worse foes than Saracen or Dane awaiting Lewis in his own household. His eldest son Lothair, under the tutelage of the unforgiving Wala, had begun to display an alarming amount of self-will and disregard for his father's wishes and the common weal of the empire. He bore himself like an independent king at his court in Pavia.

In 829 the fatal civil wars of the ninth century began. Charles, the young son of Lewis and Judith, had now attained his seventh year, and his future had become the greatest concern of his father and mother. The emperor, always brooding over his own latter end, was convinced that he had not long to live: he was filled with fears as to the fate of the Joseph of his old age when he should fall into the hands of his brethren. Urged on by his wife he determined to make some provision for the boy in the event of his own early death. He set aside the duchy of Alamannia and the Swiss and Burgundian Alpine lands to the south of it, as a kingdom for his youngest son.

Lewis declared his purpose of erecting the kingdom of Alamannia at a great council held at Worms, to which no one of his three elder sons vouchsafed his presence. The moment that the edict was published murmuring and conspiracy began. The new kingdom was carved out of territory which would have ultimately fallen to Lothair, but his two brothers showed themselves quite as resentful at the partition as was the heir of the empire. Their wrath found vent in slanderous rumours: they did not shrink from asserting that Charles was no brother of theirs. Bernard of Septimania, they said, had betrayed their father and seduced the old man's wife. The accusation was absolutely without foundation, but it met with wide belief. The chiefs of the higher clergy joined themselves to the royal princes; Wala found an opportunity of revenging himself by aiding the conspiracy; the ministers Ebbo and Hildwin, who had found themselves superseded in favour by count Bernard, had the ingratitude to join in the plot against the man who had raised them from the dust. The two chief prelates of Gaul, Agobard of Lyons and Jesse of Amiens, were also of the conspirators. A general revolt was planned before the unsuspecting Lewis had any notion that aught was amiss.

It burst out in the next spring. A new rising of the Bretons had called the emperor off into a remote corner of his realm. He summoned a small force to follow him, and was soon lost to sight on the distant western moors. But the very moment that the emperor was gone his enemies set to work to stir up rebellion. The implacable Wala harangued the west Frankish nobles, and sent letters to the chief ecclesiastics of Gaul in which he accused the emperor of ruining the unity of the Church and the empire, the one by his interference with things sacred, the other by his neglect of things secular. Lewis had become a mere tool in the hands of an adulterous wife and an unfaithful servant, and it was the duty of good Christians and patriotic Franks to rescue the empire from its shame. Pippin of Aquitaine soon gave point to the harangues of Wala by leading a Gascon army to Paris, where all the counts of Neustria joined him in arms, Lothair sent word from Italy that he was approaching at the head of a great host of Lombards. Presently Lewis came back from Brittany to find the land in arms behind him: he penetrated as far as Compiegne before he was surrounded by the forces of Pippin. Beset by an overwhelming host of enemies, the army of the emperor dispersed, and he himself fell into the hands of the rebels. His sons put him in confinement, pending the meeting of a grand council. The empress Judith they dragged from sanctuary and forced under the terror of death to take the veil at Poictiers. But when the great council of the empire assembled at Nimuegen in the next spring a reaction had followed the first success of the rebellion. The meeting was in the heart of the old Frankish land, where the rebels had few sympathisers, and the counts of the Rhineland and northern Germany came up to it with such a following of armed men and such a truculent aspect that the Neustrians and Lombards who accompanied Pippin and Lothair were quite overawed. Without a sword being drawn or a blow struck the tables were completely turned, and the old emperor found his rebel sons at his feet. He showed himself merciful — all too merciful — in the moment of his triumph. Lothair was despoiled of his imperial title, but permitted to keep his kingdom of Italy, and sent back unharmed to Pavia. Pippin returned to Aquitaine pardoned also. The rancorous Wala, the soul of the conspiracy, was sent back to his cloister at Corbey and bidden to live according to his rule, till his disloyal murmurings provoked the emperor into banishing him into a less comfortable seclusion on the shores of the Lake of Geneva. The discomfiture of the rebels released the empress Judith from her nunnery; but Lewis thought it necessary to make her clear herself by compurgation from the cruel charges that had been brought against her, before she was released from her monastic vows.

Lewis was once more emperor, but the mercy with which he had treated his conquered enemies was destined to breed him unending troubles. His undutiful sons had been left as powerful as before, and instead of feeling grateful for their pardon, were only vexed at the mismanagement which had ruined their well-planned conspiracy. When they had returned to their kingdoms they merely took breath for a space, and then recommenced their intrigues. This time Lothair and Pippin took pains to enlist their younger brother, Lewis of Bavaria, in the plot. By his means they hoped to divide Germany, for the young king was very popular in his own realm, and counted many adherents beyond its bounds. His brothers promised him the Suabian lands of the boy Charles if he would join them in a fresh rebellion.

The new troubles broke out in the spring of 832. The first signal was given by Pippin of Aquitaine, who fled from his father's court, refused to attend the Easter great council, and began to arm his Gascon subjects. The emperor determined to take warning by the events of 830 and not to be caught again unprepared. He summoned the whole force of the empire to meet for an invasion of Aquitaine. But next came the news that Lewis of Bavaria had raised an army, called in the Slavs of the Danube to his aid, and conquered Suabia. For once provoked to righteous wrath by his sons' misdoings, the emperor proclaimed that Pippin and Lewis of Bavaria had forfeited their kingdoms. He announced that his favourite Charles should be crowned king of Aquitaine, and that Lothair — who had not yet made any hostile move, though he was really in secret agreement with Pippin and Lewis — should be the heir of the whole of the rest of the empire.

This new project of partition only did harm. It did not win the aid of Lothair; it provoked the Bavarians and Gascons, both of whom were much attached to their young kings; worst of all, it caused the whole empire to exclaim that it was the emperor's unreasonable fondness for his youngest son that was at the bottom of all the trouble. Why should the whole empire be upset merely in order that Charles might add Aquitaine to Suabia?

Matters soon went from bad to worse. Lewis the Pious lay at Worms gathering the levies of Austrasia and Saxony, when it was announced not only that Pippin and Lewis of Bavaria were approaching, but that Lothair had taken the field with the forces of Italy, and had crossed the Alps, bringing in his train pope Gregory IV., a pontiff whose election he had confirmed without his father's leave some years before.

Lewis marched southward to meet his rebellious sons. The hosts faced each other in the plains of the Rothfeld, and a battle appeared imminent. But the pious emperor was still loth that blood should be shed in the quarrel: he held back from the fight and offered to treat with his sons. The princes knew their father's weakness, and learnt that his army was much discouraged and demoralised. They determined to try fraud rather than force, and assented to the proposal to negotiate. Pope Gregory lent himself to their plans, and presented himself before the emperor in the character of an impartial mediator. But he had not been long in the old man's camp before the imperial army began to melt away. To all appearance the Pope had sold himself to his patron king Lothair, and used his opportunities to persuade the counts and bishops who still remained loyal that they were adhering to a doomed cause. There soon were agents of all kinds passing between the two camps, and their influence was fatal. One after another the chief leaders of the emperor's host fled away by night to their homes, or with still greater baseness took their soldiery over to the hostile encampment. At last a mere handful mustered under the imperial banner. Looking round on their scanty ranks the emperor exclaimed, half in sarcasm, half in Christian resignation, 'Go ye also to my sons: it would be a pity if any man lost life or limb on my account.' The counts wept, but they departed, and Lewis was left standing alone in the door of his tent, with his wife at his side and his son Charles clinging to his hand. From that day the plain of the Rothfeld was called by the Franks the Field of Lies — the Lugenfeld, the 'Campus Mendacii ubi plurimorum fidelitas extincta est.' (June 833.)

At once the sons of the emperor swooped down on their helpless prey. They promptly rode over to the empty camp of Lewis, and after saluting their father with feigned respect set a guard over his tent. Judith was reinvested with the veil, and sent over the Alps to Lothair's fortress of Tortona. The boy Charles was consigned to the monastery of Prum: his extreme youth saved him both from blinding and ordination. The old emperor was forwarded to the abbey of St. Medard at Soissons, and placed in confinement in its tower. The most strenuous efforts were made to induce him to abdicate and take the monastic vows. But though he would have been willing enough to do so if unconstrained, Lewis refused to lay down his crown when force and threats were employed. Failing to induce him to resign, Lothair and archbishop Ebbo assembled an ecclesiastical council of the bishops of Gaul and formally declared the emperor deposed for incapacity and evil government. The unthinking Lothair was indeed preparing a rod for the back of all future emperors when he allowed the clergy to usurp such power!

Though Lewis would not acknowledge that he was legally dethroned, to do penance he was now, as always, only too ready, and Lothair at last resolved to be contented with this. His father's humiliation could not have been greater if he had formally resigned the crown. The old emperor came before the altar of St Medard with his sword and wearing the jewelled imperial dalmatic. Then laying the weapon and robe upon the altar he cast round himself a cloak of sackcloth and read a declaration in eight articles, whereby he accused himself of being, by his sins, the sole cause of the disorders of the empire. He began with deploring the death of Bernard of Italy, the sole crime of which he can fairly be held guilty. Then he went on to accuse himself of many futile offences — such as that of summoning an army to meet during the holy season of Lent. He was even mean enough to own that he had of done evil in permitting his wife to throw off the monastic veil, and clear herself by compurgation from the charges brought against her: in so doing, he confessed, he might have abetted perjury.

Having read this humiliating document, the old man laid the parchment on the altar, and retired again to his prison-tower. But the degrading scene had not the effect that Lothair had hoped. Men felt more indignation against the son who could force his father to such humiliation, than contempt for the father who could submit to it. The crowd outside the church tried to mob Lothair. The counts of Austrasia and Saxony began to gather armed bands against him. Scared at their approach the younger king fled away into Burgundy. The German counts at once drew Lewis out of his confinement, girt him once more with the sword of empire, and proclaimed him sole ruler of the Frankish realm. A considerable army set out to pursue Lothair, and though he checked its pursuit at a skirmish near Chalons-sur-Saone, he none the less withdrew from Gaul, and took refuge in his own kingdom of Lombardy. This was the first blood actually shed in battle in the civil war.

The vengeance of Heaven seemed to pursue the undutiful son and his adherents. Soon after he had reached Italy a pestilence smote his army, and slew his chief councillors, the aged Wala and Jesse of Amiens together with Matfrid, count of Orleans, the chief of his men of war. Lothair himself was stricken down, and lay for many weeks at the gate of death, but he struggled through to give many more troublous years to the empire. The two great ecclesiastics who had shared with Wala the guilt of the illegal deposition of the old emperor, Ebbo of Rheims and Agobard of Lyons, fell into the hands of the partisans of Lewis. Both were deposed from their archbishoprics, and Ebbo the ungrateful foster-brother of the emperor was put into solitary confinement in the abbey of Fulda in the heart of Germany.

Still untaught by his misfortunes, Lewis now took the one step most certain to alienate his newly recovered popularity. He summoned a diet at Cremieux, near Lyons, and proposed in it a new division of his realm. Lothair was to be punished by being deprived of all his dominions save Italy. The greater part of the confiscated land — Burgundy, Provence, and the old Austrasian realm about Metz and Trier — was to go to the dearly-loved Charles, now a boy of fourteen years of age.

This project pleased nobody. It rendered Lothair desperate, did not please Lewis and Pippin, and disgusted the whole of the Franks, who exclaimed that the sole cause of the wars was to be found in the emperor's doting affection for his youngest son. It is probable that another war would have broken out, if a new disaster had not fallen upon the realm. The first great Viking invasion was just about to descend upon the empire. The men of the North had seen its forces turned aside into fratricidal civil war, and took the opportunity to make havoc of the undefended coastland. In 835 when Lothair was being driven back towards Italy, they landed in great force in Frisia and sacked Utrecht, its metropolitan city, and Dorstad, the great harbour and mart of the province — the predecessor in commercial history of Rotterdam. In 836 while Lewis had been planning the redivision of his empire to the prejudice of Lothair at the diet of Cremieux, the Danes harried Flanders and burnt the new city of Antwerp. Now in 837 they fell upon the island of Walcheren, wasted it, and worked up the Rhine mouth with fire and sword as far as Nimuegen. Relinquishing his plans against Italy, Lewis the Pious turned against the heathen of the North, and marched rapidly towards the scene of their ravages. But the Danes did not yet dare to face the full imperial army of Frankland, and fled away to their ships leaving nothing in front of the emperor but ravaged fields and burning villages.

Lewis returned at once to his unwise schemes for endowing his well-beloved Charles. At a great council at Aachen in 837 he girt the boy, now aged fifteen, with the royal sword, crowned him with his own hands, and bestowed on him not only the Suabian and Burgundian lands that he had been promised at the diet of Cremieux, but a great tract of German land up to the borders of Saxony, which had been previously allotted to Lewis of Bavaria. The counts and prelates of the new realm were bidden to do homage to their young ruler, and become his men.

Lewis of Bavaria, however, was determined not to give up his promised inheritance in Germany, and found support among all the Teutonic peoples east of the Rhine, who had no wish to be handed over to the boy Charles. He mustered an army, sent to beg the help of his brother Lothair, and stood on the defensive. The old emperor replied by summoning a great council at Cerisy-sur-Oise, at which he declared Lewis deprived of all his lands save Bavaria, and conferred them on the young Charles. Immediately afterwards

Pippin of Aquitaine died, and the emperor put the finishing touches to his unwisdom by handing over the whole of Pippin's realms to his darling. If this plan had been carried out, Lewis would have left all the Frankish empire north of the Alps, save the single duchy of Bavaria, to his youngest child. The worst point in the project was that Pippin left sons, and the eldest of them — his father's namesake — was a growing boy of about the same age as Charles. The majority of the people of Aquitaine would have nothing to say to the transfer of their allegiance, and proclaimed Pippin the younger king in his father's room. The emperor, with transparent injustice, declared the boy too young to reign, and bade the Aquitanians send him to Aachen to be trained up at his court and learn the art of government — an art which Lewis was so competent to teach! When the young Pippin did not appear, Lewis threatened his southern subjects with invasion.

At once the civil war burst out in East and West and South. Lewis of Bavaria broke into Suabia; the Gascon followers of Pippin the Young marched on the Loire. At the same time the Danes who had been narrowly watching their opportunity returned to the Frisian coast, destroyed Dorstad for the second time and harried all the lands about the Rhine mouth. (Spring of 839.) At his wit's end to know which foe he should first attack, the emperor resolved to seek aid in the only place where it might still be found. Consigning to oblivion all memories of the Lugenfeld, and the humiliations before the altar of St. Medard, he besought the help of his eldest son. Lothair on his side was anxious to recover his birthright, and to be recognised once more as heir to the empire. He hurried from Pavia to Worms, to place himself at his father's disposition. Kneeling before the old man in full meeting of the great council, he confessed his ingratitude and repeated treasons, and asked for pardon. But while ostensibly craving for forgiveness only, he had secretly stipulated for reward. Accordingly Lewis the Pious now proclaimed the last of the many partitions of the empire which had been the bane of his life. The Placitum of Worms stated that Lewis of Bavaria should retain his original Bavarian duchy alone, that the younger Pippin should be wholly disinherited, and that Lothair and Charles should divide the empire. The eldest son and heir took Italy, Saxony, Suabia, all the Frankish lands on the Meuse and Rhine, and the Burgundian and Provencal realms along the Rhone. The dearly-loved Charles was given Neustria and Aquitaine, the two kingdoms whose union roughly represents the modern land of France.

The year 840 saw the commencement of the civil war, with a new arrangement of combatants. Lewis the elder, Lothair, and Charles, against Lewis the young, and Pippin. Fortune favoured the old man for once. He first marched into Aquitaine, drove the rebels before him, and forced the bishops and counts of the land beyond the Loire to do homage to Charles at Clermont in Auvergne. Contrary to his usual custom the emperor did not pardon all his enemies, but beheaded several of the chief partisans of the young Pippin.

Aquitaine was no sooner overrun, than Lewis, with a vigour which he had never shown before — it was the dying flash of his life's energy — wheeled his army northward and marched against his son the king of Bavaria. So rapid was the attack that the younger Lewis was driven out of Suabia, chased along the Bavarian bank of the Danube, and forced to take refuge in the far Ost-Mark on the Slavonic border. The emperor had now vindicated by the force of arms the partition of Worms: Pippin was disinherited, and Lewis driven back into a narrow corner of Germany. A great council was summoned to meet in July, and the emperor came back by slow stages towards the Rhine to preside over it. But the double campaign of the spring had been too much for him. For some years his lungs had been affected, and the chills of a March and April spent in arms in the open field brought on a rapid consumption. At Frankfort-on-Main he dismissed his army and took to his couch. His strength dwindled as the weeks passed away, and at last he bade his attendants place him in a boat and row him down to the Rhine, to a spot which he loved well, the island in mid-stream hard by his palace at Ingelheim, where the tower of the Pfalz now rises from the rapid rushing waters. Then it contained only a rough hunting lodge thatched with reeds, and in that poor shelter the dying emperor lingered out the midsummer weeks, lying for hours motionless on his couch with a little cross clasped to his breast. His wife and his son Charles were far away at Poictiers, in Aquitaine, and did not arrive in time to receive his dying blessing. But a crowd of bishops and monks mustered around the emperor's deathbed, to watch over his edifying end. On June 25th the old man's last agony seized him; he started up in bed, cried in a loud voice 'Out! Out!' and fell back dead, leaving the clerical throng around to debate whether his last words bade some evil spirit depart from his presence, or referred to his own setting out for a better world. So ended king Lewis,

Rex Hludovicus, pietatis tantus amicus,

Qui Pius a populo, dicitur et titulo.

He left the empire which he had done so much to dismember to be fought for by his three sons and his grandson. He left the imperial dignity fatally injured by his grovelling penances at Attigny and Soissons. He had allowed the Danes to spy out the nakedness of the land in the North; while the Saracens had already landed in Italy to the South. He had suffered the clerical power again and again to usurp authority over secular things, as none of his predecessors of the Frankish race, Meroving or Karling, had ever done. Yet in spite of all, his piety and conscientious desire to do right — often as it was misled — gave him a greater claim to the respect of his subjects than did the personal character of any of his successors. Ere long men came to look back to the time of Lewis the Pious as to an age of comparative quiet and prosperity.

CHAPTER XXIV: DISRUPTION OF THE FRANKISH EMPIRE — THE COMING OF THE VIKINGS — 840-855

Wars of the sons of Lewis the Pious — Battle of Fontenay and Peace of Verdun — The Vikings and their ships and methods of warfare — All Western Europe subject to their incursions — Their invasion of Neustria and Austrasia — Intermittent civil wars of the Franks — Charles the Bald and his policy — Death of Lothair.

At the moment of his death Lewis the Pious had been at enmity with his son Lewis of Bavaria and his grandson Pippin the young of Aquitaine, while he had by his last partition-statute provided for the division of the bulk of his realm between his eldest-born Lothair, and his youngest-born Charles. It seemed natural, therefore, that when, after the old man's death, the succession troubles broke out with renewed vigour the Franks of Neustria and Austrasia and the Lombards would be ranged in battle against the East Germans and the Aquitanians.

Such, however, was not to be the case; the governing force in the future course of events was to be, not the dying will of Lewis the Pious, but the dispositions of his three sons, and still more the unwillingness of the various kingdoms in their heritages to abide by the unnatural partition — last among so many — which Lewis had left behind him.

The first question to be settled was whether the empire, in the shape in which Charles the Great and Lewis in his earlier years had ruled it, was to continue. There was no doubt as to the succession to the imperial title. Lothair had been crowned co-regent emperor many years before, and before his father's death had been restored to favour, and acknowledged as heir to the imperial throne. But would he be strong enough to sustain the burden which had been too much for his father, to combine a strong hand and a conciliatory policy, and hold the various races of his subjects together, without driving any one of them to discontent and revolt? Lothair was brave, unscrupulous, active, troubled by none of the morbid scruples and ill-placed tenderness which had been so fatal to his father. But he was full of faults of the opposite extreme, as dangerous to a ruler as his parent's over-great mildness and long-suffering. He was quite destitute of natural affection, as his doings at the penance of St. Medard and the Lugenfeld had shown, and was not merely wanting in tenderness for his kith and kin, but unable even to pretend to a reasonable regard for brother, father, or nephew. Even in that rough time his unfilial conduct had shocked his own subjects and followers. His ambition and pride were the only sentiments to which an appeal could be made with success. He was filled with an overweening idea of the greatness of the imperial position, though he had done so much himself to cause its degradation in the eyes of all the nations of the empire, by his cruel and offensive treatment of his father. He had taught the Franks that an emperor could be imprisoned, preached at, dictated to, publicly chastised, deposed, and he foolishly supposed that his own imperial dignity would not suffer from the precedent. The moment his accession was proclaimed it was known that harsh unbending rigour would reign all over the Frankish realm.

Yet Lothair's situation in 840 was not disadvantageous; his enemies Lewis and Pippin had been driven into remote corners of the empire. He was loyally supported by the Lombards of his old Italian kingdom and by the Austrasians, the old ruling race, whose imperialist tendencies had been shown by their constant fidelity to Lewis the Pious throughout all his troubles. But Lothair wasted his strength by a strange combination of arbitrary claims and dilatory action. He began by showing the most reckless disregard for his father's dying wishes. He made no secret of his intention of stripping his young brother Charles of the Neustrian dominions which had been left him, though the child of his father's declining years had been specially commended to his protection. But he did not follow up his threats by any prompt action against the young king, but went off to Germany to conclude the campaign against his brother Lewis of Bavaria, which his dead father had left half finished. But on arriving in Bavaria he did not strike down his enemy, but made a six months' truce with him, and returned to Neustria. There he made a feeble attempt to put down Charles, but finally returned to Aachen, where he spent the winter in pomp and feasting, while his two brothers were repairing their strength and raising large armies. Lewis and Charles had determined to combine, for they saw that strict union was needful against their common enemy.

In the spring of 841 the king of Neustria and the king of Germany each drew towards the Rhine, with the purpose of joining their armies. The emperor was frightened by the strength which they displayed, and thought it necessary to add to his own forces by enlisting in his cause his only possible ally. He hastily promised to confirm the young Pippin in his kingdom of Aquitaine if he would lead the men of the south to his aid. Pippin accepted the offer, and brought an army of Gascons across Burgundy to join his uncle. Meanwhile Charles and Lewis had successfully united their hosts at Chalons-sur-Saone in such force that Lothair feared to fight them. He held them off by disloyal negotiation for some weeks, till he heard that his nephew had arrived with all the forces of Aquitaine, and then suddenly declared that nothing could be settled without a battle, and proceeded to attack his brothers. The armies met in the valley of the Yonne, and there followed the decisive and disastrous battle of Fontenay, the greatest fight that Europe had seen since Charles Martel smote the Saracens at Poictiers. The whole of the nations of the empire were arrayed against each other. On the hill by Bretignolles Lothair, with the host of Austrasia, faced the Bavarians and Saxons of king Lewis. In the plain by Lefay the Neustrians of Charles were drawn up against the Aquitanians of the young Pippin. After much hard fighting the Neustrians gave way before the onslaught of their southern countrymen, but on the other flank the Germans of Lewis won a far more decisive advantage over the emperor's Austrasian followers. Lothair was driven down from the hill with fearful slaughter, the flower of the nobility of the land between Meuse and Rhine lay dead on the field. It was a blow from which Austrasia never recovered. Her ancient supremacy over the rest of the empire, won six generations back at Testry and Ambleve, was gone for ever. The swords of the Teutons of the east had shattered the reputation of her invincibility, and the balance of power was permanently transferred eastward (June 25th, 841). The slaughter was long remembered, and the evils which the empire was to pass through during the next forty years were often ascribed to the result of this fatal fight. 'By that day,' says the chronicler Regino, 'the strength of the Franks was so cut down, and their fame and valour so diminished, that for the future they were not merely unable to extend the bounds of their realm, but even incapable of protecting their own frontiers.'

Lothair drew back the wrecks of his army to Aachen, while Pippin fled southward to Aquitaine. The victorious brothers, Charles and Lewis, succeeded before the year was out in subduing all the partisans of the emperor, both in Neustria and in Germany. It was in vain that Lothair tried to stir up trouble against them by supporting a rebellion in Saxony, where, in the wilder corners of the land, a rising of the servile classes, and the few surviving adherents of paganism, was troubling king Lewis.

In the next spring the kings of Neustria and Germany united their armies to drive Lothair from Austrasia. They met at Strasburg, where they swore to each other the solemn oath, whose wording is so precious to us as giving the first monument of the new French and German tongues that were just developing in their realms. When they marched on Aachen Lothair was compelled to take his wife and children and the royal treasure-hoard, and fly southward into Burgundy. It was long remembered how on his retreat he broke up the great silver globe, which had been the pride of his grandfather Charles the Great, 'whereon were represented the divisions of the world, and the constellations of heaven, and the courses of the planets,' and distributed its fragments as pay among his discontented soldiery. He halted at Lyons, and there his proud spirit at last bowed to the necessity of asking for peace from his brothers. The two kings showed themselves willing to treat, and the final result of the negotiations was the famous Partition of Verdun. It was indeed no time for civil wars. While the brothers were fighting, the Danes had sacked Quentovic, a great port on the English channel, and the Moors had landed in Provence and harried Aries, while the Slavs beyond the Elbe had shaken off the Frankish yoke.

The Partition of Verdun finally broke up the empire. Though Charles and Lewis restored to Lothair his capital of Aachen, and consented to recognise him as emperor, and to respect him as elder brother, yet for the future they were for all practical purposes independent sovereigns. The scheme which Charles the Great had worked so successfully, and Lewis the Pious so feebly, for conducting the government of Western Christendom by an emperor assisted in certain outlying regions by subject-kings of his kindred, now definitely disappeared. Lothair had no power or authority outside the district which his brothers consigned to his direct sovereignty.

Examining the boundaries fixed by the treaty of Verdun, we find the Frankish empire divided into three long strips running from north to south. In the east Lewis of Bavaria took all the Teutonic lands east of the Rhine — Saxony, Thuringia, Bavaria, Suabia, and the suzerainty over the Slavs of the Elbe and Save. He had also one small tract of Austrasian territory west of the Rhine, the gaus of Speier, Worms, and Mainz. Lothair kept his old kingdom of Italy, together with a long narrow strip of territory reaching from the mouth of the Rhone to the mouths of the Rhine and Yssel. This strip consisted of Frisia, the bulk of Austrasia, the most of Burgundy, and Provence. Charles took the western kingdoms of Neustria and Aquitaine, with the Spanish March and western Burgundy, for his kinsman Pippin was abandoned to his mercy by the emperor, and the lands south of the Loire, as well as those north, were put into his share of the empire.

Two of these realms, those of Charles and Lewis, roughly corresponded to national unities. The eastern kingdom comprised all the Teutonic districts of the empire, except Austrasia. The western, formed by the union of Neustria and Aquitaine, was the first foreshadowing of the modern kingdom of France, comprising as it did the bulk of the Romance districts of the empire, where the Teutonic element had always been small, and was of late growing less and less prominent. But Lothair's kingdom was an unnatural and unwieldy aggregation of districts connected neither by blood, by language, nor by historical ties. Its shape seems to have been determined merely by the wish to give the emperor both the imperial cities — Rome and Aachen — together with a strip of soil conveniently connecting them. The Teutonic Austrasians, the Romance-speaking Burgundians, and the Italian Lombards were in no wise fitted for union with each other, and were certain to drift apart, alike from geographical and from national reasons. They only adhered to each other for one man's life, and fell asunder the moment that he died.

For the future we shall find the wide realm of Charles the Great constantly tending to minute sub-division. The connection between east and west, north and south, grows constantly less, and ere long we shall be compelled to tell of the fortunes of the different fractions of the empire in separate chapters, since the central cord of connection formed by the kingly power has finally snapped. But as long as the generation of the sons of Lewis the Pious survives, there is still a certain interdependence between the history of the Eastern and Western Franks, and it is not till the deposition of Charles the Fat, in 887, that the elements of dissolution finally triumph, and all ideas of the reunion of the empire are finally discredited.

In 843 commences the tripartite government of Lothair the emperor, and his two brothers, whom we may for the future style by their well-known names of Lewis the German and Charles the Bald, though the latter style can hardly yet have been appropriate to the Neustrian king, who had only just celebrated his twenty-first birthday. His elder brothers were now much older men, Lothair having attained his forty-fourth and Lewis his thirty-eighth year. Both of them had now growing sons whom they were ere long to take as colleagues in part of their realm.

The period from the Peace of Verdun, in 843, down to the deposition of Charles the Fat, in 887, is the most chaotic and perplexing portion of the history of Europe with which we have to deal. For the fortunes of the various fractions of the Frankish empire are bound up with the fortunes of the members of a much-ramified royal house which — with a lamentable want of originality — the same four names are continually recurring. We have hitherto been confronted only with the three brothers — Lothair, Lewis, and Charles. Now each of these brothers had three sons, and with a perversity which the reader and the writer of history must alike deplore, each christened his boys after their uncles. Lothair's three sons were Lewis, Charles, and Lothair; Lewis named his offspring Lewis, Charles, and Carloman; and Charles, when at a later date he became a father, followed the evil example by christening his children Lewis, Charles, and Carloman also. The genealogical table must be kept carefully before us, lest from the similarity of names we confuse the imperial, the German, and the Neustrian houses of the Karlings.

The dates of the reigns of the three contentious brothers were, for Lothair 843-855, for Lewis 843-876, for Charles 843-877. When they had settled down after the Peace of Verdun, they found two problems before them. The first was that of keeping the peace with each other, in spite of all the grudges which the events of the last fifteen years had raised between them. The second was that of defending Western Christendom from the assaults from without, which were daily growing more and more dangerous. The Danes, whose first ravages we have related under the reign of Lewis the Pious, were now becoming no longer a mere pest to the coastland, but a serious danger to the whole empire. The Saracens were commencing a series of daring piratical descents on Provence and Italy. The Slavs beyond the Elbe were gradually throwing off their allegiance to the empire, and recommencing the raids on Germany, from which they had been stayed by Charles the Great.

For ten years (843-53) the three kings succeeded — contrary to all expectation — in keeping the peace with each other. But in spite of their temporary freedom from civil strife, they did not succeed in defending their realms with success from the outer barbarian. As the chronicler observed, 'the slaughter of Fontenay seemed not only to have thinned the ranks of the Frankish host, but to have robbed them of their ancient invincibility in war.' The only one of the three kings who showed the slightest power to defend his borders was Lewis the German: his two brothers suffered one continual series of checks and disasters.

The main problem which now confronted the Frankish rulers was the necessity for dealing firmly with the invasion of the Scandinavian pirates. The peoples on both shores of the Cattegat had now thrown themselves heart and soul into the occupation of harrying the lands of their southern neighbours. They were a group of kindred tribes, some of whom dwelt in Jutland and the Danish isles, others on the southern and south-eastern shore of the Scandinavian peninsula, others along the fiords which face the German Ocean. Western Christendom often styled them indiscriminately by the name of Danes, though in truth the Danes were only the most southern of the four races which joined in the invasions. A better common appellation was that of Northmen, which would include the Swede, the Goth and the Norwegian as well as the Danish dwellers in Jutland and Zealand.

From time immemorial the dwellers on the Cattegat and the southern Baltic had been a sea-faring race. Tacitus, in the second century of our era, speaks of Scandinavia as powerful by its fleets. The Jutes and Angles who joined in the conquest of Britain had sprung from these seas. The Danes had been addicted to piracy from the earliest times. Far back in the sixth century, we have heard of Viking chiefs, like king Hygelac whom Theudebert the Frank slew, as occasionally descending on the Austrasian and Frisian shores. But it was not till the end of the eighth century that western Europe began to be seriously troubled by the Northmen. The cause of the sudden increase of activity among races who had so long spared the feeble realm of the later Merovings is difficult to ascertain. Perhaps their constant wars with the Saxons, tribes as fierce and untameable as themselves, had kept them quiet. But it is certain that down to the time of Charles the Great they were mainly expending their energy on wars with each other, and were seldom heard of in the North Sea or the British Channel till the Frankish empire with its wealth, its commerce, and its Christian propaganda came up to meet them by subduing the Saxon and Frisian, and stretching forth its boundary to the Eider.

It was just after Charles the Great had conquered Saxony that the Vikings began to make themselves felt. The earliest trace of them in western waters was a petty raid on the English town of Wareham in 789. Within a few years, however, the scope of their expeditions enlarged; in 793 they sacked the great Northumbrian monastery of Lindisfarn; in 795 they are heard of in Ireland for the first time. In 799 they began their assaults on the Frankish empire by a transient raid on Aquitaine. From this time forward their activity grew incessantly; every year their fleets discovered some new and rich field for plunder, till no creek or estuary of western Europe was unknown to their pilots. We have already told how Charles the Great was so vexed by their first ravages that he endeavoured to establish a defensive flotilla in all the ports of Neustria, and how in the last years of his reign the Danish king Godfred had given him serious trouble both in the south Baltic and on the Frisian shore. We have mentioned the far more important descents of the Vikings on the lands about the Rhine mouth in the days of the feeble government of good king Lewis. But now the evil was still growing: the emperor Lothair and his brothers were to find the Northmen no longer a nuisance but a real danger.

Nothing could have been more daring than the enterprise of the Northmen in setting out from their distant homes to undertake the long voyage to Ireland or Aquitaine. Their vessels were merely long narrow open boats, generally some seventy-five feet long by fifteen broad, but drawing only three-and-a-half feet of water. They relied on rowing more than on Sailing, and their one mast could easily be lowered, and generally was taken down before a naval engagement. When the wind was favourable they used a single large square sail, but it was always in the strength and endurance of the oarsmen that they placed their main confidence. The ordinary Viking vessel seems to have carried about one hundred and twenty men, so that to transport any large body an enormous number of ships was required. But even in small numbers the Vikings were very formidable; they were all professional warriors, who had taken by choice to the trade of sea-robbers, and were individually far superior to the forced levies whom English aldermen or Frankish counts could hurry into the field against them. They were far better armed than their opponents, almost every man being well equipped with the shirt of ring-mail and steel helmet, while among the Franks and English only the nobles and chiefs were as yet wearing armour. They were also fighting for their lives: the pirate defeated in a strange country was completely at the mercy of the people of the land, and always doomed to death; hence he fought with a far greater fury than his enemies. But at first the Viking came to pillage rather than to fight: he was better pleased to plunder some rich undefended port or monastery and then put out to sea, than to win precarious spoil after hard handstrokes with the levies of an angry country-side.

By this time the Vikings were operating on every coast in western Europe. It was not only the Franks who were suffering from their inroads: the English kingdoms and the Celts of Scotland and Ireland were faring even worse. The expeditions of the Northmen were now taking two well-marked courses; one was the voyage past Frisia and the Rhine-mouth to the Neustrian and south English coasts. The other was a longer and bolder adventure, the open sea voyage from the western capes of Norway to Orkney and Shetland, and thence south-west, past the Hebrides, to Ireland, Wales, and western England. The former line of plunder was mainly in the hands of the Danes; the latter was more frequented by the Norwegians. The other two northern peoples, the Swedes and Goths of the Scandinavian peninsula, were almost entirely engrossed in cruises eastward, against the Slavs and Finns of the Baltic.

In the earlier years of the Viking raids, Ireland suffered more than any other country; its tribal kings could give no protection to their subjects. There was not a town in the island defended by a stone wall, and the numerous and wealthy monasteries, protected by their sanctity alone, lay open to the spoiler. The Norwegian pirates ranged at their good pleasure over the face of the land, and ere long commenced to winter in it, instead of returning home at the end of their summer ravages. It was in Ireland that they first bethought them of seizing the whole country and turning it into a new Norse kingdom. It was in the very year of the Partition of Verdun that a great chief named Thorgisl gained full possession of the northern half of the island, and established himself as king therein. He reigned for two years (843-45) with great success, till he fell by chance into the hands of Malachy, king of Meath, who drowned him in Loch Owel. With his death, his kingdom fell to pieces, and the Irish recovered much that he had conquered from his divided followers. But the Norwegians still clung to all the ports and headlands of Ireland: at Dublin, Wexford, Waterford, Limerick, they built their towns and waged continual war against the Irish of the inland parts.

England fared at first better than the sister isle. The great over-king Ecgbert of Wessex was well able to defend his realm; most of the Viking attacks were beaten off with loss as long as Ecgbert lived (802-838), But under his weaker son Ethelwulf the invasions grew more and more desperate and persistent, till in 850 we find the fatal sign that the Vikings succeeded for the first time in wintering in the land, fortifying themselves in the Kentish isle of Thanet, and defying the fyrd of Wessex to force the narrow waterway that separated it from the mainland.

The Danes in the Frankish empire had a far harder task than their Norwegian brethren had found in Ireland, and for a long time they showed much greater caution in venturing inland, or accepting battle in the open field. They fled before the face of Lewis the Pious when he marched against them in force, and it was only when the empire was distracted by civil war that they began to strike boldly up the great rivers and plunder the towns of the interior. It was of evil import for the empire that just before the fight of Fontenay they had sailed up the Seine and taken Rouen (841), and that just before the pacification of Verdun they had entered the Loire and burnt the great port of Nantes.

But when at last the Frankish kings had made peace, the Vikings had grown so bold that they persisted none the less in their attacks on the empire, and in the years that followed the new partition, their successes were even greater than before. All the three brothers were sorely beset by the Northmen, and two of them met with an unbroken series of disasters. Lewis the German fared best; the tough Saxon tribes on his frontier always made a good fight against their hereditary enemies the Danes. But the king saw the new town of Hamburg burnt in 845, so that its bishop had to fly to Bremen, and in 851 a great expedition sailed up the Elbe, defeated the Saxon counts in the open field and returned in triumph to Jutland after ravaging the eastern half of Saxony.

Lothair and Charles fared far worse. The emperor saw his coastland in Frisia ravaged every year. It was in vain that he tried to gain peace by giving the island of Walcheren to Rorik the Dane, on the condition that he should hold it as a fief and guard the coast from his brethren. Other greedy adventurers followed Rorik, till the whole Frisian coast was dotted with their palisaded forts, and their ravages penetrated farther and farther inland, till Lothair in his palace at Aachen began to tremble for his own safety.

But the lot of the young king Charles and of the Western Franks was still less happy. His realm had a far greater length of exposed coastland than those of his brethren, and he was vexed by a lingering civil war, for Pippin of Aquitaine had never acquiesced in the Partition of Verdun, and did his best to maintain himself among his partisans south of the Loire. After much fighting he was compelled for two years to do homage to Charles, but he soon rose in arms again, and though his uncle had the better in the contest he was still able to keep up an obstinate resistance. Charles thought more of subduing Pippin than of warding off the Danes, and while he was engaged in Aquitaine the northern parts of his realm were fearfully maltreated. As early as 843 the Vikings found courage to winter in Neustria, seizing and fortifying the monastery of Noirmoutier on an island at the Loire-mouth. Next year they were enabled to strike far inland, for Pippin, overborne by his uncle Charles, madly called in Jarl Oscar to his aid, and brought the Vikings up the Garonne as far as Toulouse. Thus introduced into the very heart of the land, they were able both to spy out its fertility and wealth, and to judge of the weakness and unwisdom of its rulers. It was not Aquitaine, however, that first felt their heavy hand. In 845 they boldly entered the Seine-mouth, plundered Rouen for the second time, and then ascended the river far higher than they had ever mounted before, up to the very walls of the city of Paris. Charles dared not face them, but fortified himself on the heights of Montmartre and the abbey of St. Denis, while the Vikings entered Paris and plundered part of the city, till, stricken by an inexplicable panic, they returned to their boats and dropped down the river again. It was certainly not the army of Charles that they need have feared, for he was thinking of paying tribute rather than of fighting. Indeed he paid 7000 lbs. of gold to this particular horde to induce them to quit Neustria altogether.

From this time onward things went from bad to worse for king Charles, largely owing to his own faults as we may guess, for he was a fickle unsteady prince, always taking new enterprises in hand and dropping them suddenly for some fresh plan before he had half carried them out. Nor was his courage beyond suspicion; more than once in his reign he fled out of danger with an alacrity that savoured more of fear than of prudence. After the sack of Paris we find the Vikings hovering around Neustria on every side; one band had established itself at the Loire-mouth, another under Jarl Oscar watched the Garonne, another devoted itself to the harrying of Flanders, and got succour when required from the emperor Lothair's Danish vassals on the isle of Walcheren. Spasmodically hurrying about from one scene of Viking outrages to another, king Charles protected nothing, and always arrived too late to be of use. In 847 even Bordeaux, the greatest city of southern Gaul, was beleaguered by the Vikings of the Garonne. This drew him for some time into Aquitaine, where he for once won a success, by subduing his nephew Pippin, who had lost his former popularity among the Gascons by his drunken and dissolute habits, and still more by his unwisdom in calling in the Danes to his aid. But while Charles lay in Aquitaine he suffered a greater disaster than any he had yet sustained, by the loss of Bordeaux, which was betrayed to Jarl Oscar by a discontented party among its citizens. It was to be held for some years by the Vikings.

The plunder of such a wealthy place was well calculated to draw more Danish hordes into Gaul. The condition of the country grew progressively worse, and we trace every year the advance of the ships of the invaders farther and farther up the great rivers. In 850 they grew so bold that they fortified themselves high up the Seine at Givald's dyke (Jeufosse), where they abode many months and harried all the country about Beauvais and Mantes at their leisure. Charles the Bald, engaged in a luckless campaign against the rebellious duke of the Bretons, brought no succour to his subjects. Nor was he on the spot when in the following year Ghent, Terouanne, and all Flanders were wasted. But probably the capture of his old enemy Pippin of Aquitaine atoned in his eyes for many such disasters: the pretender was taken prisoner by the count of Gascony, who handed him over to the king. In accordance with old Frankish custom Pippin was shorn and thrust into a monastery.

The year 852 saw the kingdom of the West Franks sink to a worse degradation than any it had yet known. When the Danes again came up the Seine and settled down in their former camp at Givald's dyke, Charles called out the whole force of Neustria m such overwhelming strength that the Vikings retired behind their palisades and stood on the defensive. Presently the emperor Lothair with his warlike Austrasians marched up to help his brother, and the doom of the Danes seemed settled. But after a siege which lasted many months, Charles suddenly made peace with Godfred the Danish chief and granted him a great sum of money and a tract of land at the Loire-mouth to settle in. Lothair and the Austrasians went home in wrath, and never aided the fickle Neustrian king again.

When the Franks were faring so badly, only one more evil was wanted to make their position unbearable, and this was soon added. In 853 the ten years' peace between the brothers, which had lasted since the treaty of Verdun, was broken. The restless people of Aquitaine, though they had lost their old leader Pippin, had determined to try a new revolt. They secretly sent to ask aid of Lewis the German, and he, though much vexed at home by Danish raids and Slavonic rebellions, was unwise enough to grant their petition. He sent his second son Lewis the Saxon, with a Suabian and Bavarian army, into Aquitaine, and declared war on his brother Charles.

The emperor Lothair, with more sense than he usually showed, tried to keep his brothers from the mad struggle. But it was not owing to his efforts that the Germans finally consented to retire from southern Gaul, but merely because the younger Lewis met less support than he had expected from the Gascon rebels, and found himself not strong enough to resist the full force of Neustria, when his uncle took the field against him. But while this wholly unjustifiable civil war was in progress, the Danes had made worse havoc than ever in the midst of the kingdom of Charles. They burnt Nantes and Tours, harried the districts around Angers and Blois, and only checked their course before the walls of Orleans, which made a sturdy and successful resistance (853-4).

In the next year the last formal link which still held together the Frankish empire was snapped by the death of the emperor Lothair. Old before his time, and feeling himself utterly unable to cope with the evils of the day, he retired into the monastery of Prum, and died there only a few weeks after he had taken the cowl. His heterogeneous empire at once fell to pieces: his eldest son Lewis, who had already been crowned as his colleague in the empire by pope Sergius II., was left nothing but the kingdom of Italy with Death of which to support his imperial title. To Italy he Lothair, 855. was a good king, but beyond the Alps he met with neither respect nor obedience. His younger brothers Lothair and Charles divided between them the northern parts of their father's heritage. Lothair took Austrasia, Charles took Provence, and the intermediate Burgundian territory was parted between them.

Thus the unity of the Empire had already become a mockery, and the realm of Charles the Great was split into five kingdoms, owing each other neither love nor homage nor succour in time of need.

CHAPTER XXV
THE DARKEST HOUR — A.D. 855-887

FROM THE DEATH OF LOTHAIR I. TO THE DEPOSITION OF CHARLES THE FAT

Civil Wars following the death of Lothair I. — King Lewis and his rule in Germany — Troubles of Lothair II. — The Vikings in Neustria — The

Edict of Pistres — Charles the Bald invades Austrasia — Treaty of Mersen — Charles made Emperor — Death of Lewis the German — War of his sons with Charles the Bald — Charles's successors in Neustria — Disastrous reign of Charles the Fat — He unites Germany, France, and Italy — The siege of Paris — Charles the Fat dethroned.

Evil as had been the years which followed the fight of Fontenay and the Partition of Verdun, there were yet worse to come. It was the miserable peculiarity of the second half of the ninth century that it saw Christendom, for the first time since the commencement of the Dark Ages, begin to sink back towards primitive chaos and barbarism. After four hundred years of vacillating but permanent progress towards union, strength, and civilisation, it began to relapse, and to fall back into disunion, weakness, and ignorance. The reign of Charles the Great was to be for long years the high-water mark of progress. The succeeding age rapidly sinks away from it, and it is not till the middle of the tenth century that a rise is once more perceptible.

But of all the evil years those between 855 and 887 were to be the worst. The civil wars of the descendants of Lewis the Pious grew yet more numerous and ruinous; the raids of the Viking and the Saracen spread wider and wider; the rulers of the Frankish empire were struck by a blight, dying young or sinking into imbecility long before they attained middle age, till the race seemed destined to disappear from history with the fall of the cowardly, unwieldy, incompetent Charles the Fat in 887.

The new troubles began immediately on the death of the emperor Lothair. His three sons could not agree in the partition scheme which divided their father's realm. Lewis thought that his share — the kingdom of Italy — was far too small for the eldest son and the bearer of the imperial title; Lothair II. grudged the share of Burgundy which fell to his youngest brother Charles, and tried to seize the young man, in order to tonsure him and confine him in a monastery. Before any actual blow had been struck, pope Benedict III. succeeded in patching up a truce between the brothers, but they drew apart and sought alliances against each other, Lothair leaguing himself with his younger uncle Charles the Bald, while Lewis became the friend of his elder uncle and namesake Lewis of Germany. Two years later the family grudge led to war under the most disastrous circumstances. Charles and Lothair II. had united their forces for a decisive campaign against the Danes, whose main army, under a certain

Jarl Biorn, had concentrated itself in central France, and burnt Paris, Chartres, and Blois (857). Before the united strength of Neustria and Austrasia the Vikings drew back, and stockaded themselves in a great camp on the Seine-island of Oissel. Charles blocked their way down the river by bringing up a fleet, which he had lately built, to the next reach, and determined to starve them out. After a siege of three months it seemed likely that he would achieve his purpose; the Danes could neither beat him nor escape him. But just as they were about to yield there came to the king of Neustria the dire news that his brother Lewis with the whole host of Germany had crossed the Rhine, and was marching against him. Charles straightway raised the siege of Oissel, allowed the Danes to burn his fleet and to escape, and turned eastward to resist king Lewis. Their armies met at Brienne-sur-Aube, but when Charles saw the overwhelming numbers of the Germans his heart failed him — as it often did in such a crisis — and he deserted his men and fled away into Burgundy. Deprived of their leader his vassals laid down their arms, and most of the Neustrian counts and bishops did homage to king Lewis. The German monarch was able to take possession of his brother's realm, and to proclaim himself king of the West Franks. His nephew Lothair II. sent to beg for peace from him, and it seemed that Lewis would become the suzerain of all the realms north of the Alps. But when he had sent away his German troops, and prepared to winter near Laon among the Neustrians, the instability of his power was suddenly shown. Charles the Bald had secretly raised a new army in Burgundy. He marched on Laon at mid-winter. The Neustrians refused to take arms against their old king, and Lewis, with a very small following, had to flee away into Germany, and abandon his lightly-won dominion over the West Franks. Eighteen months later the brothers made peace (860), but no treaty could undo the harm that the reckless ambition of Lewis had brought on all the Frankish realms. While the war was raging the Danes had swept unresisted across the land. One army had harried the Rhine-mouth and Flanders, another had sacked Amiens and Noyon; a third had entered the Mediterranean, sailed up the Rhone, and devastated the distant kingdom of Charles of Provence, the younger brother of Lothair II., a weakly youth racked by epileptic fits, who showed no power to defend his fertile land from the pirates. The last-named band had even extended their ravages to Italy, and sacked the flourishing port of Pisa in the realm of the emperor Lewis II.

From the time of his wicked invasion of Neustria onward, king Lewis the German, who had hitherto been the most fortunate of the Karling kindred, began to meet with troubles to which he had as yet been a stranger. While his attention had been directed to the West, his Slavonic vassals in the East, the Abotrites, rose in rebellion: when he led a host against them in 862, he encountered defeat and disaster. But a far worse blow came from the bosom of his own family: his eldest son Carloman, whom he had made governor in Carinthia and the Bavarian Ostmark, rose in rebellion against him. Twice conquered and twice pardoned (861 and 863), the ungrateful prince took arms for a third time in 864, and compelled his father to grant him a share in the kingdom. Feeling old age closing in upon him, and hoping to conciliate all his sons, Lewis the German now took the unwise step of dividing his realm in his own lifetime, just as his father Lewis the Pious had done. He made Carloman king of Bavaria and Carinthia, designated his second son and namesake Lewis to be ruler of Saxony, Thuringia, and Franconia, and his youngest born Charles the Fat to reign in Suabia and Rhaetia (865). He must have felt that the hand of Heaven was laid upon him in punishment for his own unfilial conduct to his father Lewis the Pious, for his sons dealt with him just as he had dealt with the old emperor thirty years before. They murmured about the boundaries of their heritages, and often took arms both against him and against each other. Four separate rebellions of one or another or all of the princes are recorded between 865 and 876. But Lewis the German was made of sterner stuff than his pious father. Time after time he beat down the risings of his undutiful sons, and after each victory had the constancy or the feebleness to restore them to their former honours.

In spite of these rebellions, and in spite of the successful revolt, first of the Abotrites, and then of the Moravians, both of whom succeeded in shaking off their dependence on the empire, Germany was yet the most fortunate of the five Frankish realms. The subjects of the three sons of Lothair I., who were now ruling the fragments of their father's 'middle kingdom,' all had evil times to endure. Of the troubles of Lewis the emperor in Italy we shall speak elsewhere. His two younger brothers fared even worse. The epileptic Charles of Provence was vexed by Danish and Saracen pirates, as well as by the intrigues of his greedy uncle Charles the Bald, who tried to add Provence to his own Neustrian dominions, though he was entirely unable to protect even Neustria from the Danes. Lothair II. in Austrasia — or Lotharingia, as men now began to call it, after its ruler's name — was sore vexed by the Vikings, who pushed up the Rhine as far as Neuss and Koln. But he was far more incommoded by a trouble for which he was himself entirely responsible. He drove from his court his wife Teutberga, and openly married his concubine Waldrada. Not only did this bigamy lead to the rebellion of Teutberga's brother Hukbert, abbot of St. Maurice and duke of Transjurane Burgundy, but it brought on a quarrel with the Papacy which embittered all Lothair's remaining years. Pope Nicolas I. set his face against the king's unrighteous dealings with his wife, and repeatedly summoned him to take her back to his couch. He induced the nobles of Lotharingia to compel their king to dismiss Waldrada for a season; but Lothair was passion's slave, and soon chased away his wife and again sent for his mistress. This brought on him fresh thunders of ecclesiastical censure, and for the last ten years of his life he lived under the ban of the Pope, till in 868 he was so far humbled that he came in person before Hadrian II. and made a complete surrender — one of the greatest triumphs that the Papacy had won since the days of Gregory the Great.

But though the other Frankish kingdoms fared ill, it was, as usual, the realm of Charles the Bald which bore the brunt of the troubles of Christendom. There were now permanent hosts of Danes established at the mouth of each of the great rivers of France, the Somme, Seine, Loire, and Garonne — the chronicles call them 'pagani Sequanenses' or 'pagani Ligerenses' as a matter of course. Settled on islands or headlands at the mouths of these rivers, each band devoted itself to the harrying of the district which lay inland from its camp. Meanwhile, Charles the Bald left the defence of his realm to the local counts, and busied himself in futile schemes for seizing the realms of his nephews, Charles of Provence and Lothair of Austrasia. He was not without his family troubles; his children — like those of Lewis the German — were very unruly: his second son Charles, who ruled Aquitaine for him, tried to make himself an independent king, and his youngest son Carloman was detected conspiring against his life, for which he was condemned to blinding and perpetual imprisonment. But neither domestic troubles nor Viking raids could keep Charles from his unending intrigues against his brother and his nephews. When he did turn his attention to his own proper business, his methods of dealing with the problems that lay before him were not generally wise. No man of real intelligence would have conceived the plan that Charles invented in 861 for getting rid of the Vikings by bribing them to fight each other. The wily pirates took the king's subsidy, and then all united against him, as might have been expected.

There were, however, two schemes for organising resistance against the Danes which were broached at Charles's council board that are worthy of note, as foreshadowing the methods by which the invaders were ultimately to be checked. The great difficulty which the Franks had hitherto found in dealing with the Vikings came mainly from two reasons — the power of rapid movement which the enemy possessed, and the fact that walled towns were still very rare, and castles quite unknown in the Frankish realms, so that the inhabitants of the countryside had no secure shelter to seek. In the Edict of Pistres (864) Charles shows some appreciation of these two difficulties, and endeavours to dispose of them by very well judged measures. To cope with the swiftly moving Vikings, he determines to make the Frankish army more mobile also. He endeavours to substitute cavalry for the unwieldy masses of local levies by ordering that 'omnes pagenses Franci qui equos habent aut habere possunt cum suis comitibus in hostem eant.' The day of feudal cavalry was indeed just beginning, and from the military point of view this expedient was perfectly correct; unhappily for the monarchy, the day of the feudal horseman was also to be the day of feudal separation and disunion. The second measure ordered by the Edict of Pistres was one for the strengthening of the kingdom by means of fortifications. The particular plan which Charles most favoured was that of blocking the great rivers by fortified bridges. Towns lying beside the water were to throw a bridge across, with a fortified bridgehead on the opposite bank. Thus the Vikings would find their advance up the lines of the rivers completely checked, since their boats would not be able to pass under the bridges till the forts at either end of them were taken, a long matter in those days, when the art of poliorcetics had sunk so low. As the first fruits of this edict, a strong bridge was built at Pistres itself, low down the Seine, where the Eure flows into the great river. It was at the same time that the island on which old Paris lay was furnished with two fortified bridges, across the northern and southern branches of the Seine, joining it to the mainland. It was mainly owing to these defences that, when next attacked by the Vikings, Paris, though twice plundered before, held out successfully, and did not suffer capture and desolation after its third siege.

In 863 died Charles, king of Provence, the youngest son of the emperor Lothair I., carried off by the epilepsy that had always afflicted him. His little kingdom was divided between his brothers Lothair II. and Lewis the

Emperor, to the great discontent of Charles the Bald, who would have liked to have a hand in the partition. But Charles was vexed for the moment not only by the Danes, but by his nephew Pippin the Younger, who had escaped from his monastery and raised a new rebellion in Aquitaine. While the king was dealing with his nephew, the Vikings of the Loire made the widest sweep round central France that any horde had yet carried out — burning Poictiers, Angouleme, Perigueux, Limoges, Clermont, and Bourges in one single incursion. The rebel Pippin joined himself to them, and is actually said to have cast aside his Christianity and worshipped Woden in their camp — ex monacho apostata factus, ritum paganorum servavit. He fell into his uncle's hands before the year was out, and with the general approval of the Franks was condemned to perpetual solitary confinement.

For a short time after these events the West Frankish kingdom was destined to have a time of comparative respite from the inroads of the Northmen. In 867 all the Vikings of the West massed themselves for an attack on England, which had hitherto suffered comparatively little at their hands. From the capture of York in 868 down to Alfred's great victory at Ethandune in 878, the main strength of the Danes was spent in winning a kingdom beyond the channel. The invasion of England was not for plunder but for conquest, and 'the Great Army,' led by two kings and five jarls, was composed of all the hordes who had been harrying the Continent for the last ten years. If they did not succeed in subduing the whole of England, they yet won the great Danelagh, the eastern half of the island, and settled down in the land they had subdued.

But the comparative immunity from Viking raids which the Franks obtained between 868 and 878 was not of much profit to them. In 869, Lothair II. died, as he was journeying home from Italy in a disconsolate mood, after making his peace with the Pope. From that time there was unending trouble between his two elderly uncles, as to which of them should inherit Austrasia, the old Frankish land between Scheldt and Rhine, the ancestral home of their race. At this moment began the struggle between France and Germany for the inheritance of the 'middle kingdom' which Lothair had ruled, a struggle which was to last for a thousand years. Who can say even yet if the final fate of Aachen and Trier and Metz and Liege and Strasburg has been settled?

The moment that Charles the Bald heard of Lothair's death, he crossed the Meuse at the head of the levies of Neustria, and had himself crowned at

Metz as king of Lotharingia. The Bretons were in open revolt that year, and a stray Viking band was levying contributions on Tours and Angers, but for such minor distractions Charles cared little. Lewis the German was bedridden at the moment, and his sons were absent on an expedition against the Slavs. But next spring he took the field with all Germany at his back, whereupon always better at seizing than at fighting, drew back, and offered to negotiate. Then followed the Partition of Mersen, by which Lotharingia was divided between the brothers: Charles took the Burgundian part of his deceased nephew's realm, and western Austrasia as far as the Meuse; Lewis had Frisia and eastern Austrasia. To Charles, therefore, fell Lyons, Vienne, Besancon, Toul, Verdun, Cambrai, Liege, Tongern, Mecheln; to Lewis, Aachen, Koln, Trier, Strasburg, Utrecht, Nimuegen, and Maestricht. (870.)

But the Treaty of Mersen was only to patch up matters for a short time. Five years of comparative rest followed, while the Vikings were still employed in England against the gallant kings of Wessex. But in 875 died the emperor Lewis II., the last of the three sons of Lothair I. Like his two brothers, he left no male heir, and there followed one more struggle between his aged uncles Lewis the German and Charles the Bald for the imperial title and the Italian realm. Now, as always, Charles moved with rash and inconsiderate haste, and was first in the field. Leaving Neustria to shift for itself, he posted into Italy at the head of a small army, and swooped down on the diet of the Lombard kingdom, which was sitting at Pavia, and disputing about the choice of a successor to their late monarch. He was acclaimed as king by some of the Lombards, and then made ready to march on Rome, where he knew that the Pope was ready to give him the imperial crown. But, meanwhile, Lewis the German was preparing to interfere. He first sent his youngest son Charles of Suabia — better known as Charles the Fat — to oppose the Neustrian king. But Charles, who always throughout his life consistently mismanaged everything that was intrusted to him, was easily scared by his uncle, and fled back into the Alps. Then the king of Germany sent down into Lombardy his unruly eldest born, Carloman the king of Bavaria, with an imposing array of Bavarian and Franconian levies. Charles the Bald feared to face this army, and proposed to Carloman that both the Neustrian and the German forces should withdraw from the peninsula, and allow the disputed succession to be settled by peaceful negotiation. The Bavarian prince was beguiled by his uncle's specious offer, and betook himself homeward over the Brenner.

But, instead of making a corresponding retreat towards the Cenis, Charles the Bald turned southward and made a dash for Rome. He reached it, and was duly crowned emperor by his friend John VIII. But he did not linger in Italy to help the Pope against the Saracens, as the latter besought him, but returned at once to Neustria to exhibit his new imperial crown at home.

At this moment died Lewis the German, now an old man of seventy-six; it was sixty years since he had been appointed king of Bavaria by his father, and thirty-three since he had obtained sway over the whole of Germany by the award of the Treaty of Verdun. He had been on the whole a successful ruler, in spite of the many revolts of his sons, and in spite of the fact that he had not been able to retain all his Slavonic vassals under his hand. To him more than to any other king Germany owed her organisation as a unified national kingdom. His long reign gave Saxon and Franconian, Bavarian and Suabian, time to grow together and to learn to regard themselves as a nation apart, not merely as provinces of the Frankish empire. But if to Germany his reign was one of unqualified good, history can not pardon him the two occasions in 854 and 858 when he deliberately sacrificed the general welfare of Christendom to private ambition, and attacked his Neustrian brother while Charles was in the thick of his Viking wars. These are the darkest spots on the reputation of the first king of Germany.

We have already related how Lewis, following the evil custom of his family, had divided his realm among his three sons Carloman, Lewis, and Charles, the kings of Bavaria, Saxony, and Suabia. They were not destined, however, to inherit their father's realm in peace. No sooner did Charles the Bald hear that his elder brother was dead, than he made another vigorous attempt to seize Lotharingia, arguing that as emperor he was entitled to the imperial city of Aachen, and openly asserting that the oaths of Mersen had been 'sworn to the father but not to the sons.' At the head of a large army Charles entered Austrasia, and occupied Aachen and Koln. Of the three young kings of Germany Lewis alone came out against him. Carloman was away far in the East fighting with rebellious Slavs, and Charles the Fat was, or purported to be, on a bed of sickness. The fate of the lands between Rhine and Scheldt was settled by a battle at Andernach, in which the Neustrians, though superior in number, were completely defeated by the Franconians and Saxons of Lewis of Saxony. Charles the Bald was — as usual — the first to fly, and arrived in safety at Liege, though the greater part of his army was cut to pieces. He returned to his home to find a

Danish fleet up the Seine, for the Vikings were just beginning to drift back from England. But such troubles moved him little, and though his Austrasian expedition had fared so ill, he started off with hardly a moment's pause on an equally rash and ill-judged descent into Italy, where the imperial crown that he had so lightly gained in 875 was now in jeopardy. He sent the Vikings 5000 lbs. of silver to induce them to transfer their ravages from Neustria to his German nephew's land, and hastened to Lombardy with a small and hastily equipped army, for the best of his men had been slain or captured at the battle of Andernach. Charles met his friend pope John VIII. at Pavia, and was about to proceed to Rome when he heard that his eldest nephew, Carloman of Bavaria, who possessed many supporters among the eastern Lombards, had crossed the Alps and was marching against him, eager to revenge the treachery to which he had been subjected in the preceding year. Charles hastily fled before the approaching forces of the Bavarian, but as he was crossing the Cenis he was stricken down by dysentery, and died suddenly in a miserable hut at the foot of the pass (877).

Charles the Bald was still below the age of sixty, but he had been a king from his boyhood, and had reigned over the West Frankish realm which the treaty of Verdun gave him for thirty-four disastrous years. Of all the Karlings he was the man who wrought the empire the most harm: his birth had been a misfortune: the endowment of his youth cost the state a long civil war: his manhood was flighty, unscrupulous, eager, yet unstable. He started four several wars by reckless snatching at the heritages of his kinsmen, but when withstood and faced he always slunk away in rapid retreat. The condition of Neustria was a disgrace to his name: if half the bribes and subsidies that he had spent to buy the Danes' departure, had been used in military preparations against them, they might easily have been driven off. But Charles was always busied with fantastic schemes of foreign conquest; and while his eyes were fixed abroad he allowed his realm to fall to pieces at his feet. History can find nothing to praise in the first king of France,

In the ten years which followed the death of Charles the Bald, a blight seemed to fall upon the house of the Karlings. King after king was swept away by an untimely death, some by accident, more by disease. In France and in Germany six reigning monarchs died without leaving a single child of legitimate birth, and by 887 the royal house was represented by one solitary male heir, and he a boy of only eight years old. Meanwhile the

Danes had returned from England in full force, and the whole empire of these short-lived kings was enduring the worst crisis that had yet fallen upon it.

Charles the Bald was succeeded in Neustria and Aquitaine, or France, as we may now call the Western realm, by his son Lewis II., better known as Lewis the Stammerer. The new king was a prudent and circumspect ruler, very unlike his flighty parent. He at once gave up all pretension to the kingdom of Italy and the imperial crown, though John VIII. urged him to reassert his father's claims. He promptly made peace with his German cousins, renewing with them the terms of the Treaty of Mersen, by which eastern Lotharingia fell to Germany and western Lotharingia to France. He then took the field against the Danes, who had just returned once more to the mouth of the Loire, but while engaged with them he was stricken down by disease, and died a few months later, long before he had completed the second year of his reign (879). He left two sons, Lewis and Carloman, and a third child was born to him just after his death, and christened Charles. The counts and bishops of France, following the invariable and unhappy custom of the times, crowned both Lewis and Carloman as kings. The two lads — they were but seventeen and sixteen — were not to enjoy a quiet heritage. Alfred had just expelled from England those of the Danish 'Great Army' who had refused to settle down in the Danelagh and do him homage. The swarm of Vikings fell on Flanders, and burnt Ghent and St. Omer before the young kings' reign was two months old. At the same time Lewis of Saxony, on whom the Spirit of greed that had possessed Charles the Bald seemed now to have descended, invaded Neustria — summoned, it would appear, by some disloyal counts. But the West Franks rallied around their young masters, and Lewis the Saxon consented to retire on condition that Western Lotharingia — the lands that Charles the Bald had acquired by the Treaty of Mersen ten years before — should be ceded to him. So Liege, Namur, Cambrai, and Tongern became for the moment German and not French.

In another part of the West Frankish realm an equally serious loss was at the same time taking place. Since the death of the good emperor Lewis II. Provence and southern Burgundy had been united to Neustria (875-79). But Lewis' only daughter, the princess Hermengarde, had now found a strong and ambitious husband in Boso, count of Vienne, one of the governors of Burgundy. Taking advantage of the crisis in Neustria, this count Boso resolved to assert his wife's claim to her father's heritage. In

Italy he failed to win success, though the Pope would gladly have helped him, but in Provence and Lower Burgundy the nobles rallied to his standard. He was proclaimed king in October 879, and afterwards crowned at Lyons. His new realm of Aries, Provence, or Lower Burgundy — for it is found styled by all these names — was the first fraction of the empire of Charles the Great to pass away from the male heirs of the great royal line. Boso's dominions nearly coincided in size with the kingdom of Provence as it had been held by Charles the son of the emperor Lothair I. They included the whole valley of the Rhone, from Lyons to the sea and the borders of Italy.

While the West Frankish kingdom was being cut short to north and south, Germany was on the whole in better condition. The three sons of Lewis the German, unlike most royal brothers of the time, dwelt together in harmony. The two elder brothers had come to an agreement that Carloman should prosecute his fortunes in Italy, while Lewis sought to aggrandise himself in Lotharingia. But Carloman, after driving Charles the Bald out of Lombardy, and mastering most of the land north of the Po, was stricken down with a fever which terminated in a paralytic stroke. He was carried back to Bavaria, and survived for two years, but never rose from his couch again. Feeling the hand of death upon him, he handed over the administration of his realm to his brother Lewis, only stipulating that the frontier duchy of Carinthia should be given to his own illegitimate son Arnulf, the child of a Slavonic princess whom he had taken as his concubine. Carloman lived out another year, and died in 880 before he had passed the limits of middle age.

Meanwhile, his place in Italy had been taken by his shiftless younger brother, the king of Suabia. Charles the Fat entered Italy in the autumn of 879, was everywhere recognised as king, and solemnly received the Lombard crown from John VIII. at Ravenna. But his new kingdom saw little of him: though he was earnestly besought to oppose the Saracen invaders of the south he did nothing of the kind, but went ingloriously home to Suabia.

The Danes were by this time mustering in greater strength than ever for an assault on the Frankish empire. They had gathered together from all the shores of the West, and this time threw themselves on the Eastern realm, not on their old prey in Neustria. The year 880 was long remembered by the Germans for the awful defeat suffered on the Luneburg Heath near Hamburg by the levies of Saxony and Thuringia. Bruno, duke of Saxony, two bishops, with no less than twelve counts, were left dead upon the field, and the victorious Vikings ravaged the whole valley of the Elbe without further resistance. Almost at the same moment another Danish army appeared in Austrasia, fought an indecisive battle with king Lewis, and though they left him the field were able to establish themselves permanently on the Scheldt, at a great camp near Courtray, threatening Neustria and Austrasia alike.

In the spring of 881 they made up their minds that the Western realm should first be their spoil. Marching on Beauvais, they met at Saucourt the young king of France and his levies. To the joy and surprise of all Western Christendom Lewis III. inflicted a crushing defeat on the invaders, slew 8000 of them, and chased them as far as Cambrai, beyond the borders of his own kingdom. This was the only pitched battle of first-rate importance that the Franks had won over the Vikings, and great hopes were entertained that in Lewis III. Europe might find a saviour from the sword of the pagans. But ere a year was out the gallant young king met his death in a foolish frolic, and left the Neustrian throne to his brother Carloman.

The Danish army which had been defeated at Saucourt retired to Ghent, where it was strengthened by newly arrived bands under two famous sea-kings, Siegfred and Godfred. Then the host threw itself on Austrasia as the autumn was closing. The levies of the old royal land of the Franks were beaten: their king, Lewis of Saxony, was far away, and the winter months of 881-2 saw the whole countryside harried, from the Scheldt-mouth to the Eifel. The inland parts of Austrasia had hitherto been exceptionally fortunate in escaping the Danish sword, but in this fatal winter Liege, Maestricht, Tongern, Koln, Bonn, Neuss, Zulpich, Malmedy, Nimuegen, and every other town in the district was pillaged. Most heartrending of all was the sacking of the royal city of Aachen: the Danes plundered the palace, stabled their horses in the cathedral, and broke the shrine and image above the tomb of Charles the Great.

To the despair of all Germany, king Lewis the Saxon, whose task it should have been to attack the invaders in the next spring, died on January 20th, 882 — the fourth Carolingian monarch who had been carried to the grave within three years. His subjects found nothing better to do than to elect his only surviving brother, Charles the Fat, the king of Suabia and of Italy, as his successor.

Thus began the unhappy reign of Charles, the last Carolingian emperor of the full blood. He was at this moment in Italy, where he had been visiting Rome and receiving the imperial crown. Making a leisurely journey homeward, — the Danes were meanwhile sacking Trier and Metz, — he reached the Rhine in July, and summoned to him the levies of Saxony, Suabia, Bavaria and Franconia: he had brought a Lombard army in his train. With this great host, the largest that had been seen since the death of Charles the Great, he moved against the Danes. Godfred and Siegfred retired before him to a great camp which they had built at Elsloo on the Meuse. The faint-hearted emperor faced them for twelve days, and then instead of ordering his vast army to assault the camp, began to negotiate with the enemy. A few days later his soldiery heard to their dismay and disgust, that Charles had consented to allow the Vikings to withdraw with all their plunder, to pay them 2000 lbs. of silver, and to grant king Godfred a great duchy by the Rhine-mouth, with the hand of his cousin Gisela, an illegitimate daughter of king Lothair II. In return the Dane consented to be baptized and to do homage to the emperor. This expedient for buying off Godfred was probably suggested by the way in which Alfred of England had dealt with Guthrum four years before at the peace of Wedmore. Unfortunately Charles forgot that while Alfred was strong enough to compel Guthrum to keep faith, his own character was hardly likely to have a similar influence on Godfred.

King Siegfred, with those of the Danes who did not wish to settle down by the Rhine-mouth, took their way from Elsloo into Neustria. Charles the Fat had merely stipulated for the evacuation of his own kingdom, and cared nought for what might happen to his cousin Carloman. The winter of 882-3 was as disastrous for northern France as that of 881-2 had been for the Rhineland. From Rheims to Amiens and Courtray, the whole countryside was harried: king Carloman and his nobles, instead of copying the conduct of Lewis III., and remembering the triumph of Saucourt, followed the miserable example of Charles the Fat, and paid the invaders the enormous bribe of 12,000 lbs. of silver to induce them to transfer themselves to Austrasia, England, Ireland, or any other realm that they might choose. In the moment of rest obtained by the temporary departure of the pirates, Carloman died, ere yet he had reached his twentieth year. He was accidentally slain by one of his companions, while hunting the boar in a forest near Les Andelys (884). The Carolingian line was now well-nigh spent: five kings had died in five years, and the only males surviving were the shiftless emperor Charles the Fat, and Carloman's younger brother, a child of five, the posthumous son of Lewis the Stammerer, the prince whom the next generation was to know as Charles the Simple.

Rather than face the horrors of a minority, the West-Franks sent to the emperor and besought him to take up the kingship of Neustria. All the empire that had obeyed Charles the Great was therefore united once more beneath a single sceptre, save the little realm of king Boso, in Provence. But Charles the Fat was a sorry substitute for his great namesake. The three years of his reign over the whole of the Frankish kingdoms (884-7) were fated to shatter the last remnants of loyalty in the breasts of the subjects of the empire, and to cause them to cast away the old royal house in despair, and seek new saviours and new kings.

The history of these three evil years is easily told. Hearing of the death of Carloman, the Danes flocked back to Neustria: 'oaths sworn to a dead man,' they said, 'did not count.' But their return was chiefly caused by a thorough beating which their main body had suffered at Rochester from the strong hand of king Alfred. At the same time the converted Viking Godfred rose in rebellion on the Lower Rhine. He impudently bade the emperor give him the rich lands about Bonn and Coblenz, 'because his duchy had no vineyards to yield him wine.' Charles did not take arms against him, but sent ambassadors to lure him to a conference. When the Dane appeared, the counts Henry and Eberhard treacherously cut him down, and massacred his retinue. The army of Godfred broke up; some of his warriors went plundering in Saxony, where they were cut to pieces, the rest joined king Siegfred, who was just about to invade Neustria (885).

The great host of the Vikings had once more united itself under Siegfred, and entered north France, as if designing to subdue the whole country and settle down therein. But they met with an unexpected resistance at Paris, where the local count and bishop, Odo and Gozelin, had gathered together all the best warriors of Neustria. The defence of Paris was the bravest feat of arms which the Franks had wrought since the battle of Saucourt. They maintained the isle of Paris, with its two fortified bridge-heads over the two branches of the Seine, for more than eleven months, against all the assaults of the Northmen (Nov. 885-Oct. 886). Seven hundred Viking keels were drawn ashore on the flat land where the Champ de Mars now lies, and 40,000 Vikings beset the city on all sides. But though shamefully abandoned by the emperor — who chose the time as suitable for a journey to Italy — Odo and Gozelin refused to despair, even when the northern bridge-head was cut off from the city by an inundation, and burnt by the besiegers.

At last, in the summer of 886, Charles the Fat so far bestirred himself as to raise the national levies of the whole empire, and march to the relief of Paris with an army not less than that which he had led four years earlier against the camp of Elsloo. But when his vanguard received a check, and its leader, Henry., duke of Franconia, was slain, the emperor refused to risk an attack on the Danes. Once more the disgraceful scene of Elsloo was renewed: Charles paid the Danes 700 lbs. of silver, and gave them permission to pass up the Seine into Burgundy, and work their will there. He was angry with the Burgundians for refusing him obedience and leaning to the cause of Boso, the king of Aries, and chose this despicable means of wreaking his vengeance on them.

Paris was saved, and the reputation of its gallant defender, count Odo, raised to the highest pitch. But the emperor had thrown away his last chance, and forfeited the respect of even the meanest of his subjects. His remaining days were few and evil. Attacked by softening of the brain, and burdened by an ever-increasing corpulence, he retired to Germany after the disgraceful treaty of Paris. There his doom was awaiting him: the counts and dukes of the East Frankish realm conspired against him, headed by his illegitimate nephew Arnulf, duke of Carinthia, the son of king Carloman. In 887 the young duke took up arms, openly announcing that he was about to march on Frankfurt and depose his uncle. Charles tried to raise an army, but none of his vassals would lend him aid: in sheer despair he sent his royal crown and robes to Arnulf, abandoning the kingdom, and craving only five manors in his native Suabia to maintain him for his few remaining days. This boon the duke granted, and the unwieldy ex-Caesar dragged himself away to a royal villa at Neidingen, where he died less than three months after, worn out by the bodily ills which form the only possible excuse for his shiftless and cowardly conduct during the last three years.

Meanwhile Arnulf entered Frankfurt, and was there hailed as king by all the counts and dukes of Germany. He was known as a brave and able young man, and though he was but a Karling of bastard blood, the East Franks gladly intrusted themselves to the protection of his arm. But the other parts of the empire did not consider themselves bound to follow the lead of Germany. In each of the kingdoms a noble of great local note and power stepped forward to claim the crown of his native land.

In Neustria there still survived one Karling of the direct line, the boy Charles the Simple, Carloman's youngest brother; but he had only reached the age of eight, and when Paris was but just saved, and the Danes were still on the Seine, it was no time to give the crown to children. Two claimants appeared for the Neustrian throne, Wido duke of Spoleto, an Italian noble whose mother had been a daughter of the emperor Lothair, and Odo count of Paris, the hero who had saved his city from the Danes in the past year. Though he could boast of no Carolingian blood in his veins, Odo easily carried the day against his rival; he was crowned king at Compiegne by Walter, archbishop of Sens, and soon forced Wido to leave France and retire to Italy.

We shall relate in another chapter how Berehgar of Friuli was chosen king of Italy, and how he was obliged to fight hard for his crown with Wido, when the latter returned from his unsuccessful expedition to France.

A fourth kingdom was established in the Jura and the western Alps by count Rudolf, one of the governors of Upper Burgundy. He first got himself crowned at St. Maurice by the counts and bishops of Helvetia, and then, pushing beyond the Jura, was again proclaimed king at Toul. But Rudolf never got any firm footing in Lotharingia: his realm was limited to the lands north of the Alps, west of the Aar, and east of the Saone. The chief towns of this — the smallest of the fractions of the Carolingian realm — were Lausanne, Geneva, St. Maurice, and Besancon.

Boso's kingdom of Aries or Lower Burgundy was now in the ninth year of its existence; its founder had died in 887, but his son Lewis — a Carolingian on the female side through his mother Hermengarde, the daughter of the emperor Lewis of Italy, had succeeded without trouble to his father's throne.

Thus the Frankish empire was cut up into five states, not ephemeral creations of a heritage-partition, like the many kingdoms which we have seen rising and falling from the days of the Merovingians onward, but more permanent divisions, three of which represented real national differences, while even the other two — the Upper and Lower Burgundy — had a certain national coherence and individuality of their own, and were destined to last for several generations. One of the five realms was ruled by a bastard Carolingian; two by two princes who boasted a Carolingian descent on the spindle side: only France and Upper Burgundy were in the hands of monarchs who could lay claim to no drop of the ancient royal blood.

CHAPTER XXVI: ITALY AND SICILY IN THE NINTH CENTURY — (827-924)

Invasion of Sicily by the Moors: the Western half of the island conquered — Civil wars in Southern Italy — The Moors invade Italy — Pope Leo's victoiy at Ostia — Quarrels of the Eastern and Western Churches — The False Decretals — Campaigns of the Emperor Lewis II. against the Moors — Anarchy in Italy after his death — The Byzantines reconquer Southern Italy — The Moors in Campania — Civil wars of Wido and Berengar — King Arnulf's invasion of Italy — Long period of anarchy after his departure.

On the fortunes of the kingdom of Italy, that is, of the old Lombard realm, which had now become a province of the empire of Charles the Great, we have already had occasion to touch on more than one occasion. But while northern Italy with its king established at Pavia, and central Italy with its pontiff and its turbulent Roman mob, have from time to time claimed our attention, we have had little necessity to mention the southern third of the peninsula, or the great island which faces it across the straits of Messina.

In the ninth century the bulk of southern Italy, all those valleys of the Apennines, which had in ancient days bred the warlike Samnite race, was still in the hands of the dukes of Benevento. We have mentioned that they had more than once been forced to pay homage to Charles the Great, but since his day the empire had left the duchy alone. Two dukes, Sico and Sicard, had held Benevento during the reign of Lewis the Pious, and had to do with his son Lothair, the sub-king of Lombardy. Luckily for them the heir of the empire was more set on maintaining a hold north of the Alps than on completing the Frankish supremacy in Italy.

But it was not the whole of south Italy that the Beneventan dukes ruled. The East Roman emperors had never lost hold of the 'toe and heel' of the peninsula (if we may use the familiar phrase that describes so well the shape of Italy). In Brindisi dwelt a strategos, whose authority extended over the southern part of the ancient Apulia. In Reggio another governor ruled the ancient land of Bruttium, now known by the name of Calabria.

Beyond the straits of Messina a third military ruler had the hard task of preserving from the Saracen the half-lost 'theme' of Sicily, where since 828 an unending struggle with the Moslem invader had been raging.

Beside the Beneventan duchy and the Byzantine themes, there were yet more states in south Italy. Naples preserved a precarious independence under a series of hereditary consuls: it still paid a shadowy allegiance to the Eastern Empire, as did also the neighbouring Amalfi and Gaeta, which, like Naples, had never fallen into the hands of the Lombards. But these cities were rather allies than subjects of the Byzantines, and paid no obedience to the governors of the neighbouring themes.

The one important element in the politics of southern Italy during the ninth century must be sought in the approaching peril of conquest by the Saracen. At first it was only the Byzantine possessions that were endangered, but very soon the whole of the Christian states were involved in the same trouble. The storm-cloud from the south, which had threatened Constantinople in 720 and Gaul in 735, had now shifted its position. The new attack was in the centre, not on the eastern or the western flank of the line of defence of Christendom. For twenty years Italy was to be in deadly peril, and there appeared every prospect that Naples and Benevento, if not Rome also, would share the fate that had fallen on Carthage and Toledo a hundred and fifty years before.

The trouble began with the landing of a Mussulman army in Sicily during the year 827. They had been called in by a traitor named Euphemius, a turmarch in the Sicilian theme, who rebelled against the emperor Michael the Amorian. Euphemius had carried off a nun from a convent, and the emperor had ordered the strategos of Sicily to punish him by cutting off his nose. But the soldier, instead of submitting, slew the governor, induced his troops to rebel, and seized Syracuse. His rising was put down by a fleet sent from Constantinople, but Euphemius himself escaped by sea, and took refuge with Ziadet-Allah, one of the Aglabite monarchs who ruled in northern Africa since that land had shaken off its allegiance to the Caliph at Bagdad.

The Moor consented to lend Euphemius his aid, not in order to replace him on the Sicilian throne, but in the hope of winning Sicily for Islam, and adding it to his own dominions. He proclaimed the holy war, and named as general Ased-ibn-Forat, an aged doctor of law, who was worshipped as a saint by all Africa. The preaching of Ased gathered a multitude of fanatical adventurers — Arabs, Berbers, and Moors — to join the regular troops whom his master placed under his orders. Taking Euphemius with them, in the hope that the Sicilians would rise in his behalf, the Saracens landed at Mazara, on the south coast of the island early in Moors. June 827. The natives execrated the traitor, and refused to join him, but when the strategos Photinus led the army of Sicily against the invaders he was completely defeated. The fanatical fury of the Mussulmans swept all before it; we are told that the aged Ased himself charged in the front rank in spite of his seventy years, and slew so many Christians that the clotted blood glued his lance to his hand. The army of Sicily was almost exterminated, and its commander fled to Calabria, and died there.

The Mussulmans then seized Girgenti and marched to besiege Syracuse. But before its walls, while they camped in the marshes of the Anapo, they were smitten by the same deadly marsh-fever which has struck down so many other besiegers of that ancient city. Ased died of the pestilence, and his army fled from their plague-stricken camp, and fell back on Castrogiovanni (Enna), to which they laid siege. Here the traitor Euphemius fell — as he well deserved — himself the victim of treachery. He was tampering with the officers of the garrison, to induce them to surrender the place, when two brothers, who pretended to listen to his offer, enticed him to meet them under the walls, and promptly cut off his head when he came to the secret interview. The siege of Enna was soon afterwards raised by a force sent from Constantinople, and the Mussulmans fell back on the fort of Mineo, where they were beleaguered by the Byzantines.

But just as victory seemed about to crown the East Roman banners, the whole aspect of the war was suddenly changed by the arrival of two new Saracen hosts. A force despatched by Ziadet-Allah to aid his first army fell upon Palermo and took it. A second force, composed of Moors of Spain, a band of exiles driven out of their own land by civil war, landed on the south coast, relieved their besieged co-religionists at Mineo, and defeated the strategos of Sicily in the open field.

For some time the emperor Theophilus, who had just succeeded his father Michael on the Byzantine throne, continued to send succour to Sicily. But in 832 he became involved in a desperate war with the caliph Motassem, which distracted all his attention to the East. This war in Asia proved the ruin of Sicily. The African Moors kept pouring in fresh fanatical hordes, and gradually subdued all the cities of the western half of the island. For a moment it seemed likely that Sicily would be permanently divided between Greek and African, just as it had been twelve hundred years before, in the days of Dionysius and Hiero II. But at last the stubborn defence of the Byzantines was broken down by two fatal blows, the fall of Messina in 842, and that of Enna, the strongest post in the centre of the island, seventeen years later, in 859. This drove the East Romans back to the eastern coast, where they retained no more than the sea-girt city of Syracuse and the strong towns about the roots of Mount Etna — Taormina, Catania, and Rametta. The Moslems, masters of the bulk of the island, were now at leisure to turn their arms farther afield, and to cross the Straits of Messina to invade the mainland.

In south Italy all the elements of disaster were ready and prepared. Sicard duke of Benevento, a ruffian and an oppressor, had been assassinated by his outraged subjects in 839. The Beneventans then proclaimed a certain count Radelchis as their prince. But the important towns of Capua and Salerno adhered to Siconulf, the brother of the deceased tyrant. A civil war broke out between these two pretenders, which was destined to last, with many variations of fortune, for no less than twelve years. In the second year of the struggle (840) Radelchis, hard pressed by his rival, had the unhappy inspiration of asking aid from the Moslems of Sicily. The chance was too good to be lost, and a Moorish army was landed at Bari, where it was received by the partisans of Radelchis, and allowed to take possession of the town. Then Siconulf, as mad as his enemy, answered evil with evil by sending to Crete to call in to his aid the Saracen pirates of Candia. They came, and the same sight was seen which occurred six hundred years later, when the rival emperors of Constantinople called in the Turks. The auxiliaries of each prince sacked the towns held by his rival, and generally ended by garrisoning them, and holding them on their own account. Apulia and Lucania were overrun by the Moors and Cretans, while, at the same moment, the Sicilian Saracens crossed the straits — Messina had just fallen — and swept all over the Byzantine possessions in Calabria. Between 843 and 851 the whole of Italy, from Reggio to the gates of Rome, was overrun by the Moslem marauders, and it seemed as if Christendom was to lose the southern part of the peninsula. Half its towns, Bari, Taranto, Reggio, Brindisi, even the castle of Misenum at the very gates of Naples, had now become Saracen fortresses. In 846 a great fleet from Africa appeared at Ostia, and the pirates overran the Roman Campagna, and even sacked the rich churches of St. Paul outside the Walls and St. Peter on the Vatican. But for the solid ramparts of Aurelian they would have entered the eternal city itself, and the town of Romulus and Gregory might have become a Moslem stronghold.

But already the man to whom, above all others, Italy was to owe her salvation, had crossed the Alps and taken up his life's task. Lewis, the eldest son of the unwise emperor Lothair, was appointed king of Italy by his father in 844, soon after the Partition of Verdun, and appeared in the next year before Sergius II., to be solemnly crowned at Rome. The Pope made the young Frankish prince swear to protect the Church and all its privileges, but when once crowned Lewis made Sergius and all the nobles of Rome do him homage, and when in 847 Sergius died, and Leo IV. followed him, the imperial right of confirmation was duly acknowledged.

Lewis and Leo, who lived in concord and amity, were the first to discomfit the Saracens, and give some hope of salvation to Italian Christendom. In 849 the African and Sicilian Moslems sent a second and larger expedition against Rome. Pope Leo took the field himself with the forces of the Roman and Latin counts and barons, while the fleets of Naples and Amalfi, under the consul Caesarius, guarded the harbour of Ostia. When the infidels appeared battle was joined at sea, but a tempest arose, and drove most of the African fleet ashore. Caught between the Neapolitan ships and the Pope's army, the Moors were crushed: the few who escaped death by the sea and the sword became the slaves of the Romans, and were set to labour on the wall which Leo built to protect the Vatican and St. Peter's — the new quarter of Rome, which got from him the name of the Leonine city. The great fresco of Raphael representing this victory has made pope Leo's triumph the one ninth century event in Italy which is well remembered by the world.

In the next year the emperor Lewis compelled the rival Beneventan dukes to come to terms. He marched into Samnium and threatened to attack Radelchis if he refused to make peace with his enemy Siconulf. Under this pressure a partition of the duchy was made: Radelchis kept the capital and the eastern half of the principality: Siconulf became 'prince of Salerno,' and ruled the Campanian and Lucanian half. The conclusion of peace was celebrated by the massacre of the Saracen auxiliaries of Radelchis, whom the duke quietly betrayed to the sword of Lewis, now that he had no further need for their aid (851).

But though the civil war in south Italy was ended, the situation was still perilous. The whole coast from Bari to Reggio was still in the hands of the Moslems, who were coalescing into a single state under Mofareg-ibn-

Salem, the pirate-king who governed Bari. He had taken the title of Sultan, and the majority of his countrymen had done homage to him. For eighteen years (853-71) he was the terror of south Italy, and might have founded a kingdom and a dynasty, if he had not been opposed by a warrior as active and obstinate as himself in the person of the emperor Lewis.

The young Frankish Caesar was already making his power felt in Italy as neither his sire nor his grandsire had done. Unlike most of his race, he concentrated his mind on one kingdom, and devoted himself to its defence. It resulted that he was an excellent ruler for Italy, but that he never gained such a footing beyond the Alps as he might have claimed in virtue of being the eldest heir of Charles the Great. Though a crowned emperor he never reigned at Aachen, or held a foot of land outside the peninsula, except the single county of Provence. But in Italy his power was very real. He dealt most firmly with the Papacy. When Benedict III. and Anastasius contested the Papal throne in 855, the emperor's legate held a court of inquiry in the Lateran and adjudged the former to be the true successor of St. Peter. Nicolas I., the next pontiff, was nominated by Lewis in opposition to the majority of the Roman clergy; when he ventured to oppose his creator he saw his city occupied by a Lombard army, and soon had to make his peace.

Hadrian II. who followed Nicolas was no less content to keep on good terms with the emperor, whom he praised as 'the sovereign who wars not, like other kings, against Christians, but only against the sons of Belial, the enemies of the Christian faith; wherefore the hand of the Apostolic See will always be strong on the side of this most pious emperor, and the great Dispenser of battles, through the intercession of the chief of the apostles, will ensure his triumph.'

The success of Lewis in keeping the Papacy in hand was all the more notable because the three popes Benedict, Nicolas, and Hadrian were all men of mark, who left their impress for ever on the history of the Roman See. It was Benedict who began that quarrel with the patriarch Photius of Constantinople which brought about the final schism between the Eastern and the Western Churches. Starting with a mere dispute as to the validity of the election of Photius, it was soon complicated by wrangles about the supremacy of the Roman See over the Illyrian and Macedonian bishoprics, a supremacy which had ceased to be real since Leo the Isaurian had declared them to owe no obedience save to Constantinople. Benedict died in 858, but his successor Nicolas kept up the struggle with vigour, styling Photius an intruder and usurper, because his predecessor had never legally resigned the patriarchate, and finally declaring him deposed from his metropolitan throne. That one patriarch should venture to remove and excommunicate another without the aid of a general council, and merely in virtue of his power as the successor of Peter, appeared monstrous to the Byzantine clergy. They paid no attention to the letters of Nicolas, and the emperor Michael the Drunkard threatened to make his arm felt in Italy, and to reclaim by the sword the right of the successor of Justinian over Rome. Nicolas replied by comparing the Byzantine ruler to Sennacherib, and by taunting him with the loss of Sicily and Calabria to the Saracens, which had deprived him of any opportunity of exercising his power west of the Adriatic. After seven years of wrangling the division between East and West was finally formulated by the Synod of Constantinople (866), where the patriarch, the emperor, and a thousand bishops and abbots drew up the eight articles which declared the Roman Church to have departed from the orthodox faith and discipline. Six of the articles only dealt with small ritual matters, such as the observance of Lent and the shaving of the clergy. But the third, which denounced the enforced celibacy of the priesthood as a snare of Satan, and the seventh, which condemned the Roman doctrine as to the procession of the Holy Ghost, were all-important. The Eastern Church now formally stated that the Western Church, by declaring that the Holy Spirit proceeded both from the Father and the Son, fell into 'a heresy so awful as to deserve a thousand anathemas.'

Photius was soon afterwards deposed, but his fall did not heal the breach between the churches, for the Byzantine emperors and clergy all adhered to the statements of doctrine contained in the decree of the Synod of Constantinople. To this day they are held by the Eastern Church.

Nicolas I. was not only the pontiff who precipitated the quarrel with the Eastern Church; he will also be remembered as the protector of the injured queen Teutberga, and the chastiser of the adulterous king Lothair of Lorraine, whose fortunes we have related in another chapter. But he has won his greatest fame from being the first Pope who used the famous 'Forged Decretals.' Up to his time the collection of the letters and edicts of the bishops of Rome, which all the Church knew and used, extended no further back than those of Siricius. (A.D. 384.) But there was brought to Rome about the year 860 a collection of fifty-nine decretals, which purported to be those of the Popes of the second and third centuries, and thirty-nine more which were interpolated among the real documents extending from Siricius down to Gregory II. (384-731.) There was also in this precious collection the celebrated donation of Constantine and the acts of several councils. This wonderful series of documents, it was said, had been discovered in Spain by Riculf, archbishop of Mainz. It was at once incorporated in the authentic series of Acts of Councils, edited by the great Isidore of Seville, and the new as well as the old documents were in future called by his name.

To any one with a competent knowledge of early church history, or with a turn for textual criticism, the False Decretals would have betrayed their character at once. But these accomplishments were rare in the ninth century, and the few who could have exposed the new decretals were precisely the persons most interested in proving them to be authentic. For, as was natural considering their origin, they were full of authoritative decisions on the points in which the ninth century clergy were interested. What could be more delightful than to find St. Clement or St. Felix giving just such decisions on the questions of church lands or clerical celibacy as would have been given by the reigning pontiff? To inquire whether the Church had any lands in the first century, or whether the idea of clerical celibacy had then been broached, would have been not only impious but unwise. So the False Decretals with all their anachronisms and confusions of persons and impossibilities of style and form were greedily swallowed by the Pope and the whole clerical body, and promptly turned into weapons of war against the civil power, the Eastern church, and any other enemy for whose discomfiture they were suited. It is impossible not to suppose that Nicolas I. knew what he was doing in accepting the Decretals: he had in his own hands the genuine decrees of the Popes from 384, preserved with care and accuracy; how was it possible that more should exist in a corner of Spain than in the papal chancery? Would the most important title-deeds of the Roman See, which proved that from the days of the apostles downward the Popes had exercised the power of legislating for the whole Western Church, have been suffered to pass into oblivion? On such points Nicolas must have had his own views: but the documents were too tempting to be neglected, and from henceforward they were freely used as a basis for the monstrous claims of the mediaeval papacy.

Who forged the Pseudo-Isidorian Decretals we shall never know. They were first heard of at Mainz, and it would seem that it was either at Mainz or at Rheims that they were composed. Rome, though she used them, did not have the shame of framing them. Indeed they were originally intended to serve the ends of the local bishops rather than those of the Pope. The first time that they were used in a case of importance was in 866. Hincmar, archbishop of Rheims, had deposed Rothad, bishop of Soissons, for incompetence. Rothad appealed to Nicolas I., on the plea that according to the Decretals the power of deposing a bishop lay with the Pope alone, and not with the archbishop. Nicolas then restored the bishop of Soissons to his see to the great wrath of Hincmar, who would have repudiated the decretals but for the unfortunate fact that he himself had used them in the previous year. He had to content himself with the cautious saying that the documents were 'a mousetrap for archbishops' — circumposita omnibus metropolitanis muscipula — because they threw all power into the hands of the Roman pontiff.

But we must return to the secular affairs of Italy. In 853 the emperor Lewis made the first of his attempts to expel the Saracens from the peninsula; it failed owing to the slackness or treachery of the duke of Benevento, who bought a private peace for himself from the Sultan of Bari, and rejoiced to see the worst of the Moslem raids turned off against his neighbours of Salerno. Naples also long remembered the day when Mofareg forced his way to its very gates, and sat in triumph on a heap of corpses by the bank of the Sebeto, while his soldiery laid the heads of their victims at his feet.

Some years later Lewis began a second series of campaigns against the infidel. At first he met with many checks, but in 867 he forced the dukes of Benevento and Salerno to do him homage and to join his Lombards in the field. He took one after another many of the towns of Apulia, and at last in 868 laid siege to Bari itself. The leaguer lasted no less than three years, but while it was in progress Lewis was clearing Lucania and Calabria of the enemy. Yet as long as the sea was open Bari never failed to obtain provisions and reinforcements, and Lewis was forced to find some naval power to back him. He asked the aid of the emperor Basil the Macedonian, who had just succeeded Michael the Drunkard on the Byzantine throne. Accordingly the admiral Nicetas Oriphas swept the Adriatic with a hundred ships and drove the Moslems out of its recesses. He then blockaded Bari for a space, but soon quarrelled with Lewis and withdrew. The Sultan, however, deprived of the command of the sea, had been driven to extremity, and in February 871 the emperor succeeded — even without Byzantine aid — in storming the city. The garrison was put to the sword, all save the Sultan, whom duke Adelgis of Benevento had captured in the citadel.

Lewis now turned to seize Taranto, the last Saracen stronghold in Apulia, and spoke of completing his work by clearing Calabria and attacking Sicily. But treachery frustrated this grand and salutary scheme. While the emperor was paying a visit to Benevento, in company with his wife and daughter, the new duke Adelgis treacherously seized him and threw him into a dungeon. The traitor is said to have been persuaded by his prisoner the Sultan of Bari that the further success of Lewis would mean the annexation of all Italy to the imperial domain and the extinction of all the southern principalities of the peninsula.

But punishment was at hand. On the news of the fall of Bari the Aglabite monarch in Africa had resolved that Italy should not be lost to Islam, and had prepared a vast expedition against southern Christendom. Duke Adelgis had only kept his suzerain forty days in bonds when he heard to his dismay that 30,000 Moors under a general named Abdallah, who styled himself the Wall oi Italy, had landed at Taranto. In terror at this approaching storm the duke liberated his august prisoner, after making him swear to bear no rancour for his captivity. It was felt that Lewis alone could save Italy, and the armies of the Lombards would be needed to drive out the African. Meanwhile the Wali Abdallah laid siege to Salerno, which its duke Waifer defended with great courage

The moment that he was released the emperor summoned the hosts of northern Italy to Rome: they mustered in great strength, eager to avenge Lewis on the treacherous duke, and pope Hadrian II. at once declared the oath that had been sworn at Benevento null and void, because extorted by force. But before punishing the traitor, Lewis was magnanimous enough to resolve to drive away the Moors who lay before Salerno. His vanguard under count Gunther defeated, near Capua, the covering army with which the besiegers were protecting their main operation. Then the emperor himself came down on the Moorish camp: after a short struggle the invaders fled to their ships. A tempest swept down on them ere they had well got out to sea, and the whole armament was engulfed. (Aug. 872.)

It was now time to deal with the traitor duke of Benevento. In the spring of 873 Lewis, supported by the solemn blessing of pope John VIII., marched into the duchy, overran it, and forced his way to the gates of the capital. But his successful campaign did not end, as might have been expected, by the annexation of Adelgis' dominions. At the intercession of the Pope the duke was admitted to pardon, and on doing homage and penance was reinvested with the sovereignty of Benevento.

Lewis had now leisure to undertake his great scheme for expelling the Moors from Calabria and Sicily. But to the grief of all his subjects, and the eternal misfortune of Italy, he died in 875. To crown the disaster he left no male heir, but only a daughter, and the princess Hermengarde was not yet married to any stalwart count who could have championed her claim to her father's realm.

Lewis was by far the best of the later Karlings. Just, pious, and forgiving like his grandfather and namesake, he was no weakling as the elder Lewis had been, but a mighty man of war from his youth up. If he had succeeded his father Lothair in all his kingdoms, the fall of the empire of the Franks would have been stayed for another generation. If he had lived longer and left male issue, a strong and compact kingdom of Italy would probably have come into being. But when they bore him to rest in the old basilica of St. Ambrose at Milan the hope of a united Italy was buried in his grave, and the 'Age of Iron,' as it was afterwards styled, set in for all the provinces of the peninsula.

We have narrated in another chapter the troubles which were brought upon Italy and all the other kingdoms of the Frankish empire by the extinction of the eldest line of the descendants of Charles the Great and the vacancy of the imperial throne. Charles the Bald became the nominal successor of Lewis II., but while he was absent in Neustria, the Saracens recovering from their fearful defeat of 872 began once more to infest Apulia and Campania. They thrice defeated Adelgis of Benevento in the open field, and it was in vain that he and pope John joined to beg Charles the Bald to return and deliver them.

Deliverance, however, came not from the West but from the East. While the Frankish emperor failed to appear, Basil the Macedonian had resolved to take up the task of driving the Moors from Italy. His armies crossed the Ionian Sea, and seized Bari in 875. They met with unbroken success. The Apulian towns opened their gates one after another in order to get succour from the infidel. Two splendid naval victories annihilated for a space the piratical fleets of the African and Sicilian Moors. Their stronghold of Taranto was stormed, and then, m three years, the great general Nicephorus Phocas, grandfather of the emperor of the same name, overran Calabria, and left not a single Saracen on the eastern side of Italy (884-87). The Byzantines then went on to attack the duchy of Benevento. They swept over it with ease, and forced duke Urso to fly into exile. For four years East Roman governors ruled at Benevento itself; but in 894 Wido king of

Italy drove them out of that city, and reconstituted the Beneventan state on a smaller scale. Its south-eastern half, the provinces which got from the Greeks the names of the Basilicata and Catapanata, remained permanently in the hands of the eastern emperor. It is strange to find that while the Byzantines were faring so well in Italy, their fate in Sicily had been disastrous, unless, indeed, it was success in one quarter that led to the neglect of the other. In 877 a great horde of African and Sicilian Moslems laid siege to Syracuse, the main post of the East Romans in the island. It was defended stubbornly by two forgotten worthies, John the Patrician and Nicetas of Tarsus, and held out for ten months. By May 878 the besieged were reduced to feed on grass, nettles, and unclean animals, and the fainting troops could no longer man the walls. The Moors burst in, and massacred the patrician and the remains of the gallant garrison. Nothing now remained to the empire in Sicily save a few forts among the roots of Etna and the single town of Catania. These were held throughout the war, and only fell in the beginning of the next century.

While the Byzantines were maintaining their struggle in south Italy and Sicily with the Aglabite monarchs of the Moors, Lombardy and Rome had troubles of their own. Much vexed by Saracen inroads on Campania, pope John VIII. summoned Charles the Bald to return to Italy. The king of Neustria did for once appear to vindicate his imperial claims in 877. But it was only to fly in haste, and to expire while crossing the pass of Mont Cenis.

The title of emperor and the kingdom of Lombardy were both now vacant; several princes stepped forward to claim them. The majority of the North Italians, headed by the bishop of Milan, chose to rule them Carloman, the eldest son of Lewis the German, though the Pope tried to support the claims of count Boso, a Burgundian noble, who had just married the princess Hermengarde, the heiress of the good emperor Lewis II. But Carloman never was able to make good his rule over Lombardy; soon after his election he lost his health, and fell into a lethargy, which obliged him to abandon all State affairs. Yet till his death in 880 he held the title of king of Italy.

Meanwhile the peninsula fared very ill without the hand of a ruler to guide it. While the East Roman armies were evicting the Moors from the Adriatic shore, the expelled infidels kept throwing themselves upon Latium and Campania. Aided by new swarms from Africa they infested the regions about Naples, Capua, and Gaeta, till, in despair, the Neapolitan republic made a private peace with them, and bought immunity from their ravages by allowing its harbour to become a base of operations for the plunder of the neighbouring lands. A veritable colony of Mohammedans was soon established on the banks of the Garigliano, and from 882 till 916 the central Italian powers were quite unable to drive them out. Their ravages extended far and wide into the Samnite Apennines, and even as far as Tuscany. Yet, strangely enough, the adventurers never succeeded in capturing Gaeta or Capua or any other of the strong towns around them. They were purely predatory, and showed no signs of settling down into an organised state.

In his despairing search for an emperor who should save Rome and Italy, pope John finally crowned Charles the Fat, the most unpromising candidate upon whom he could possibly have pitched. But the incapable and unwieldy monarch soon returned to Germany, and even took with him for northern wars the Lombard levies which John had fondly hoped to use for the extirpation of the Campanian Moslems (881).

Next year John VIII. died. He was the last of those able pontiffs of the ninth century who did their best to defend Italy from the infidel, and to strengthen and extend the Papal power over the Frankish kings and the Frankish church. After his decease the same blight which had already fallen on the house of Charles the Great seemed to descend on the bearers of the Roman keys. Three Popes died in eight years, and men of mark ceased to appear on the papal throne. The last fifteen years of the century saw the first of those scandalous prelates who were for a century to be the disgrace of Christendom.

The inglorious reign of Charles the Fat was no less fatal to Italy than to the rest of the Frankish realms. The Moors of Sicily and their colonists on the Garigliano sent their expeditions farther and farther afield; their vessels were seen as far north as Pisa and Genoa. Another band from Spain descended on the Provencal coast at the same moment, and seized the sea-girt fortress of Fraxinet, where they established a strong colony, which lasted nearly a hundred years (888-975). The raids of the Moors of Fraxinet reached far inland, in despite of the kings of Aries and Upper Burgundy. We read, to our surprise, of incursions which devastated the whole valley of the Rhone, and reached as far as Lausanne and St. Maurice in Switzerland. On one occasion a band of Provencal Saracens and a band of Magyars from the Danube met and fought at Orbe in the land of Vaud. It seemed as if the enemies of Europe had met at her central point, and that Christendom was doomed to succumb.

After the deposition of Charles the Fat no more Karlings of legitimate blood survived. Italy, like the other Frankish realms, had to seek a new royal house. Two princes courted the suffrages of the Lombard Diet and the blessing of the Pope — Wido, duke of Spoleto, the most powerful and the most turbulent of the nobles of central Italy, and Berengar, margrave of the march of Friuli, the Italian borderland toward the Slavs of Illyria. Both claimed Karling blood on the spindle side. Berengar was the son of Gisela, a daughter of Lewis the Pious and the empress Judith; Wido's mother was a daughter of Lothair I. and a sister of the good emperor Lewis II. At first there appeared some chance that the two competitors might not come to blows, for Wido had the bold idea of crossing the Alps to seize the Lotharingian dominions of his grandfather Lothair, in the general break-up of the empire which followed the deposition of Charles the Fat. He agreed to allow Berengar to be crowned king of Italy if he himself was aided in his Transalpine schemes. The margrave of Friuli, therefore, was duly elected by the Lombard Diet, and anointed king by the archbishop of Milan, while duke Wido entered Burgundy, and got himself crowned at Langres. But after a short struggle with Odo of France the Spoletan prince abandoned his hopes beyond the Alps and fell back on Italy. Then, disregarding the oaths he had sworn to Berengar, he commenced to intrigue with the counts of central Italy, and soon laid claim to the crown. There followed four years of bitter war between Berengar and Wido, the former supported by Lombardy, the latter by Tuscany and all central Italy and backed by the Pope. Pretending that the archbishop of Milan ought not to have crowned Berengar, the privilege belonging to the Papal See alone, Stephen V. anointed Wido, and proclaimed him Emperor as well as King of Italy (891). The struggle between the rival kings ended in the victory of Wido, who took Pavia, drove Berengar back into his own duchy of Friuli, and ruled all the Lombard realm for three years. He made pope Formosus crown his son Lambert as co-regent emperor with him, and thought that his dynasty wag firmly established.

But a new competitor for the imperial throne now intervened. The humbled Berengar sent over the Alps to ask aid from Arnulf, king of Germany. That prince had always claimed the primacy among the various rulers who now shared the empire of Charles the Great between them, and was only too glad of an Opportunity to interfere in Italy. He crossed the

Alps in 894, was joined by Berengar, and laid siege to Bergamo, the strong cliff-built city which dominates the Lombard plains from the last spur of the Alps. The Germans stormed the town, and Arnulf hung count Ambrosius, the governor, in his armour before the gate, after massacring the whole garrison. The terror of this deed cowed the partisans of Wido, and all Italy north of the Po did homage to Arnulf. The Spoletan emperor retired southward to prepare to defend the line of the Apennines. There he died, leaving his claims to his son Lambert.

Next year Arnulf returned in force, passed triumphantly through Tuscany, and though disease much thinned the ranks of his army, appeared before the walls of Rome. Not Lambert of Spoleto, but his mother Engeltrud defended the Eternal city. Inspirited by her the Romans held out for some days, but when Arnulf had stormed the 'Leonine City,' the new quarter beyond the Tiber, the empress and her warriors fled, and the Pope opened the gates. Formosus, who had always opposed the Spoletans, looked on Arnulf as a deliverer, and crowned him emperor with joy; but the violence and rapine of the conquering soldiery disgusted the populace of Rome, whose confidence had not been won by Arnulf's first act — the beheading of thirty citizens who had favoured the cause of Wido and Lambert.

Attacked by fever and a paralytic stroke, Arnulf returned to Germany without having conquered Lambert's hereditary duchy in the Umbrian Apennines. The moment he was gone all central Italy rose in favour of the Spoletan. Pope Formosus, Arnulf s chief supporter, died at this moment, and the new pope, Stephen VI., a rabid supporter of the faction of Lambert, violated his predecessor's sepulchre, declared him an antipope and usurper, and cast his corpse into the Tiber (896).

Arnulf, stricken down by disease, returned no more to Italy, and in his absence Berengar of Friuli once more became master of Lombardy, while Lambert of Spoleto was acknowledged in Rome, Tuscany, and Umbria. Fortunately for Italy, Lambert died eighteen months later, killed by a fall from his horse, and his mother Engeltrud sent to recognise him as sole king, making no claim in behalf of her young grandchild, the son of Lambert. Arnulf died a year later, and thus in the last year of the century (900) Berengar was left without competitors.

That his reign was not likely to be happy may be gathered from the preceding pages. The Saracens of Campania were still in the field; a new scourge, the Magyars from the Danube, appeared for the first time in Italy in 899, and raided as far as Verona, showing by their brutal cruelty that Christendom might have even worse foes than the Moslem. Rome meanwhile was a prey to anarchy; six Popes died in four years, nor was their loss much to be deplored. Boniface VII. had been twice deposed from the priesthood for profligacy. For Stephen VI., who showed his disposition by his horrid treatment of the corpse of Formosus, we need not much grieve, when we read that his enemies caught him and strangled him in prison. Of the other Popes, creatures of a few months' reign, we know so little that it is hard to take any interest in their fate. They represented nothing more than parties among the citizens of Rome or the barons of Latium.

So closed the ninth century, with prospects as black for Italy as for the other kingdoms which a hundred years before had joined in saluting Charles the Great as emperor. The only favourable point in the outlook was the hope that a national Lombard kingship might be once more restored in the person of Berengar.

It was the unfortunate connection between the Pope, the Italian crown, and the imperial title that was still to be Berengar's bane. He had hardly reigned a year in peace (900) when Pope Benedict IV. and the remains of the party of Lambert of Spoleto found a new competitor to pit against him. This was Lewis, king of Provence (or Aries), the son of king Boso and the Italian princess Hermengarde, and therefore the grandson of the good emperor Lewis II. Lewis won several successes over Berengar, was crowned king of Lombardy at Pavia, and then received the imperial crown at Rome in February 901. But he could not permanently hold his own. After a year's fighting Berengar succeeded in chasing him beyond the Alps. He returned in 905, again called in by the rebellious counts of central Italy, and once more won some fleeting advantages over the native king of the land. But as he lay in Verona he was suddenly surrounded by an army of Berengar's partisans; the citizens of the place threw open the gates at night, and the young Provencal emperor fell into his rival's hands. Berengar bade his servants blind the captive, and sent him back in sorry plight to abide in his kingdom by the Rhone. 'And so at last he firmly held the Italian crown, which had cost so many princes their lives.' But it was only a precarious empire over the Lombard plain that Berengar enjoyed. The Pope and the counts of central Italy, even when they did not raise up any rival against him, systematically set his commands at nought. The imperial title he either did not covet or could not obtain from the Pope, till in 915 John X. bought his support against the Saracens of the Garigliano by conferring on him the long-withheld dignity. In the following year Italy was happily relieved from that band of marauders. The troops of Berengar, of the dukes of Spoleto and Benevento, and of the Pope were all for once united in the holy war, and when united they proved invincible. The forts of the Mussulmans were stormed, their armies beaten in the field, and the whole colony finally rooted out.

But after this triumph Berengar was not fated to die in peace. In his old age his enemies stirred up against him yet another king from beyond the Alps, Rudolf II. of Upper Burgundy. Berengar was once more deserted by many of his followers, and once more saw the greater part of Lombardy overrun by a Transalpine army. But this time he was not destined to survive his troubles. While besieged in Verona in the year 924, he was murdered by traitors, and lost his life, as well as the royal and imperial crown, for which he had so often contended.

CHAPTER XXVII: GERMANY — 888-918

Arnulf, king of Germany — His victory at Louvain over the Danes —
His expedition to Italy — His troubles with his son Zwentibold —
Approach of the Magyars — Reign of Lewis the Child — Internal anarchy,
and disasters from Magyar invasions — Reign of Conrad of Franconia —
His troubles and death.

Arnulf of Carinthia was base-born, the son of the Slavonic mistress of
king Carloman, but he possessed a considerable share of the strength and
vigour of his ancestors. For the twelve years of his reign the German realm
made head against its enemies to north and east, and held the primacy
among the states of Christendom. The Frankish empire had now fallen
apart into five states: but the kings who held the other shares all came to
seek out Arnulf and obtain his recognition of their rights. Odo the ruler of
the West Franks was the first to appear before the German monarch and
crave his friendship. It would almost appear that he recognised Arnulf as
his superior and liege-lord, for on his return to Neustria he had himself
crowned for a second time at Rheims in the presence of German
ambassadors, and with a diadem which Arnulf had given to him. Rudolf
the ruler of Upper Burgundy was the next to visit the German court: he
came to Regensburg, obtained recognition from Arnulf, and returned in
peace. Berengar of Lombardy, already threatened with war by his
competitor Wido of Spoleto, met the king of Germany at Trent, on the
border of his realm, and promised to be his faithful supporter in all things.
Lastly Hermengarde, the widow of Boso of Lower Burgundy (Aries),
placed her young son Lewis under Arnulf's protection, and besought him
to undertake the regency of the Provencal realm. Though Arnulf had not
obtained the imperial title he was for all practical purposes far more of a
general suzerain and ruler of the whole Frankish realm than any of his
relatives had been for the last fifty years. The best sign of his strength was
that he succeeded in checking the inroads of the Vikings in a manner which
made them for the future the least dangerous of the many enemies of
Germany. In 891 the Danes came flooding into Austrasia in great force,
and harried all the lands on the Meuse and Moselle. The local levies of

Lotharingia were beaten, and Sunderold archbishop of Mainz, who had led them, fell on the field. But Arnulf, who had been far away in Bavaria, came flying westward on the news of this disaster, and chased the Danes as far as their great fortified camp at Louvain on the Dyle. There they had entrenched themselves with the river at their back and a marsh in their front, which rendered it impossible for the Frankish horsemen to approach them. But Arnulf bade all his warriors dismount, and taking axe in hand led them through the swamp and up to the Danish palisades. The Germans hewed down the breastwork, broke into the camp, and drove the Danes into the river, where most of them perished. This was the last first-class engagement which the Danes ever fought in the East Frankish realm. They continued to come on plundering excursions to Frisia and the lower Rhine, but never attempted again either to penetrate deep into the land or to set up any independent principality upon its borders.

After defeating the Danes and putting down some risings of his eastern Slavonic vassals, the Czechs and Moravians, Arnulf undertook the unwise enterprise of conquering Italy, whence his friend and vassal Berengar had of late been expelled by Wido of Spoleto. Of the details of his two invasions of 894 and 895-6 we have spoken at length in our Italian chapter. Arnulf returned from Italy wearing the imperial crown, whose splendour seemed to ratify the primacy that he already possessed over his brother-kings; but he was broken in health by the fever that he had caught in the Roman campaign, and he left Italy behind him in a state of complete disorder, and mainly in the hands of Lambert of Spoleto.

After his Italian expedition Arnulf s reign was much less fortunate. A fatal succession-difficulty arose in his own house, and caused endless trouble. For many years he had no lawful issue born to him: so he persuaded the national council of the Germans to allow him to designate his bastard son Zwentibold as his heir (889). Four years later he made this prince sub-king in Lotharingia. But the same year (893) his wedded wife Ota bore him a son, known in history as Lewis the Child, who was therefore recognised as the lawful heir to the empire, to the great grief and anger of the new king of Lotharingia. From this time forward Zwentibold, an unruly and turbulent young man, was a perpetual thorn in his father's side. He grudged his infant brother the heritage of the German kingdom, and persistently stirred up strife. He fell into a long and bloody feud with some of the chief nobles of Lotharingia, and notably with Reginald-with-the-Long-Neck, count of Hainault and the Maasgau. In revenge for his tyranny Reginald and many others of the Austrasians called in to their aid Charles the Simple, the monarch of Neustria, and did homage to him as king of Lotharingia, handing over to him the old royal towns of Aachen and Nimuegen. The attempt to tear away Austrasia from Germany failed, not because of Zwentibold's arms, but because Charles the Simple feared to face the whole force of the East Frankish realm, when Arnulf took up his son's cause (898). He agreed to retire into his own states, and evacuated Austrasia.

Of even greater import of evil to Germany than Zwentibold's unruliness was the arrival on the eastern frontier of the kingdom of a new race of enemies. These were the Ugrian tribe of the Magyars or Hungarians who appeared in 896 on the middle Danube and Theiss, where the decaying remnant of the Avars were now dwelling mixed among the Slavonic Moravians. The Magyars had been driven westward by another wild horde, the Tartar Petchenegs, who thrust them out of South Russia and forced them to find new homes. They were a race of light horsemen, mighty with the bow, skilful in sudden onsets and feigned retreats, but wanting the perseverance and steady strength in pitched battle which would have rendered them invincible. Their raids were even more rapid and destructive than those of the Northmen, but they were not such formidable foes to meet as the Vikings, for they never could learn to besiege a fortified place, or to defend themselves in entrenched camps, or to fight in regular line of battle. All their attacks were mere ambushes or sudden surprises, and they seldom allowed the heavy horsemen of Germany to fight them on equal terms and in the open field. Their custom was to ride through the open country burning defenceless monasteries and villages, but avoiding walled towns and always escaping in haste if the levies of the district came out against them in full force.

Arnulf himself was responsible for the first visit of the Magyars to the empire. During his Moravian war he hired some of their warriors to follow him to the field as auxiliary light horse. Thus they learnt the way into Moravia and Germany alike: during Arnulf's own life they do not seem to have seriously molested his kingdom, for they were mainly occupied in evicting the Slavs from the plains by the Danube. But no sooner was the emperor dead than they began to extend their ravages into Bavaria and Thuringia. At an even earlier date they are found already harassing north Italy, and vexing the soul of king Berengar by ravaging his native duchy of Friuli (899).

In December 899 Arnulf died, old before his time, and was buried in his favourite city of Regensburg. Then the dukes, counts, and bishops of Germany met at Forchheim and chose as king Lewis the Child, the six-year-old son of their deceased monarch. The reign of a minor was always dangerous to the old Teutonic kingdoms, and that of Lewis was no exception to the rule. The eleven years during which he nominally ruled as king of Germany were almost the most disastrous ever known in the history of the East Frankish realm. Hitherto the land had been fortunate in its rulers; of all the descendants of Charles the Great the German line had been by far the most able and vigorous; save the unhappy Charles the Fat, — who only reigned for five years — they had all proved strong and capable rulers. But now under the nominal sway of Lewis the Child all the evils that had been kept down by his father's strong hand came to a sudden head. Germany was deprived of all central authority, and exposed to two evils at once, invasion by the enemy from without and civil war at home.

The first troubles came from Lotharingia, where king Zwentibold had made himself so hated that many of the Austrasian nobles determined to disavow their allegiance to him, and to acknowledge his boy-brother as immediate ruler as well as suzerain. While waging war on his rebellious subjects Zwentibold fell in battle; as he very happily left no male issue, his kingdom was at once reunited with the main body of the Germanic realm.

But worse was to come: in 902 there burst out the first of the great family feuds which were to be such a curse to Germany. During the last generation the succession to the posts of duke, count, and margrave throughout the land had been tending more and more toward hereditary right. It was growing quite usual to continue the son in the father's office, and to give to brothers countships in each other's close neighbourhood. Under a strong government this had not led to any danger. Arnulf had been powerful enough to keep all his vassals in order. But his son was a mere child without any grown relative at his side to act as protector, and not even provided with a strong Mayor of the Palace to vindicate the royal authority. So far as there was any central government at all, it was worked by two great bishops, Adalbero of Augsburg and Hatto of Mainz — the wicked prelate of German tales, of whom posterity persisted in believing that he was devoured alive by rats in divine punishment for his sins. But Hatto and Adalbero were not even formally acknowledged as regents by the national diet, and had no authority to use the royal name save to execute the behests of that council.

In the third year of Lewis two powerful family-groups of counts in Franconia began to wage open war on each other, not under any pretence of serving the crown but purely to settle a personal feud. Adalbert of Bamberg and his two kinsmen, who governed the land of the Saal and upper Main, fell upon Conrad and Eberhard, two brothers who ruled in Hesse and on the Lahn, and for four years central Germany was torn by their intermittent struggles. The meeting of the national council, and the anathemas of the bishops proved quite unable to bring the feud to an end. Presently the quarrel spread into western Lotharingia, where two other counts, Gerhard and Matfrid, espoused the cause of Adalbert and attacked his enemies in Hesse. It was only after four counts had fallen in battle, and the whole Main valley had been miserably ravaged, that a diet, summoned by bishop Hatto at Tribur, finally put its ban on Adalbert of Bamberg, as the fomenter of the war, and raised a great army against him. He was beleaguered by the national levy in his castle of Theres, captured and executed, while his friends Gerhard and Matfrid were exiled. But it had taken four years to induce the nation to move, and meanwhile other great counts and dukes had learnt the lesson that they might enjoy a long impunity, whatever turbulent enterprise they might take in hand. A few years later we find Burchard margrave of Rhaetia endeavouring to make himself duke of all Suabia by coercing the small governors in his neighbourhood; when he was put down and executed, by counsel of the bishops who surrounded the young king, popular sympathy was decidedly in favour of the feudal usurper and not of the central government. In Lotharingia too troubles never ceased; they culminated in a second attempt of count Reginald-with-the-Long-Neck to make over the Austrasian countries to the king of Neustria, Charles the Simple.

But serious as were these civil broils, their importance was as nothing compared with the greater disasters caused by the Hungarians' ravages on the eastern frontier. From the first year of king Lewis onward their attacks knew no intermission. They began by raids on Bavaria and Carinthia; a little later, while the Franconian civil war was in progress, we find them penetrating into Suabia and even into the distant Saxony. In 907 they defeated the whole levy of Bavaria, and slew its duke Luitpold together with the archbishop of Salzburg and the bishops of Freising and Seben. The consequence of this disaster was the temporary loss to Germany of its eastern frontier, the Bavarian 'Ostmark,' which we now know as Austria; the Magyars overran the whole of it as far as the Enns. In the very next year the victorious horde entered Thuringia and slew its duke together with the bishop of Wurzburg. In 910 the young king himself, now sixteen years old, took the field against them for the first time, and for once Bavarians, Suabians, and Franconians were found united under him for a common campaign against the invader. But the first fight of king Lewis was a disaster: his army was caught in an ambush and routed with great slaughter, only the Bavarian troops escaped the panic and succeeded in checking the outset of the victorious enemy.

How Lewis might have fared in future warfare against the Magyars we cannot say, for a year later, ere yet he had attained the threshold of manhood, he was carried off by disease. With him was extinguished the German line of the Carolingian house, for he left no male heir of any kind, whether brother, uncle, or cousin, to take up the heavy heritage of the Teutonic crown. (911.)

The only alternatives that now lay before the German nobles were either to elect as king one of the French branch of the Carolingian line, or else to follow the example of the Burgundians, Italians, and Provencals and choose one of themselves as the new ruler. After much hesitation the latter course commended itself to the diet, and at Forchheim the Franconians, Saxons, Suabians, and Bavarians joined in elevating to the throne Conrad, a count of lower Franconia, the son of that Conrad who had fallen in the war with Adalbert of Bamberg five years before. Only the Austrasians, faithful now as ever to the house of Charles the Great, refused to acknowledge the new king, and once more did homage to Charles the Simple, the weak but ambitious monarch of Neustria. Conrad seems to have been remotely descended in the female line from the house of St. Arnulf, but could not pretend to represent the old traditions of Frankish royalty. He was simply the most powerful, or almost the most powerful, man among the German noble houses, and was chosen purely for his military abilities.

Conrad's reign of seven years (911-918) was one continuous story of rebellion and disaster. Under a ruler of a new line, whom they regarded merely as one of themselves, the local governors became even more insolent to the central power than before. They made war on each other at their good pleasure, and each endeavoured to put down his weaker neighbours and make their possessions his own. Each of the ancient divisions of the German realm, the original tribal unities of Suabian and Bavarian, Saxon and Frank, showed a tendency to draw apart from its fellows. Each sought to reassert its individuality under some new ruler of its own, to hail its strongest noble as duke and follow him even against the king. It required a strong and persevering monarch to keep this separatist tendency under, and to prevent it from splitting up the realm.

Conrad I. was deficient neither in energy nor in perseverance. His whole reign was filled with struggles against the usurpations of the greater nobles, but he was still far from having won a victory when he died. Except from his fellow-countrymen in Franconia, and from the higher clergy, he got little assistance in the strife, and his own last words were a warning to the Germans that they must choose a stronger king than himself if their kingdom was to survive.

It would be wearisome to relate the many campaigns of Conrad against his too-powerful subjects, to tell how the Palatine count Erchanger tried to make himself duke in Suabia; how Arnulf, the son of that Luitpold whom the Hungarians had slain, claimed the ducal power in Bavaria; how the great Saxon Henry, son of duke Otto — to be better known a few years later as king Henry the First — defied his liege lord to drive him out of Saxony. Conrad was generally unsuccessful in his strife against the rebels; it is true that he defeated, captured, and executed the would-be duke of Suabia, and that he drove Arnulf the Bavarian into exile for a time. But he utterly failed in his attempt to win back Austrasia from Charles the Simple, and his expedition into Saxony against duke Henry came to a disastrous end, so that he was compelled to make peace and to recognise Henry's ducal power over the whole country. It is said that Hatto, the great archbishop of Mainz, died of sheer anger and disgust on hearing of the triumph of the Saxon, against whom he had a personal grudge. Hatto had been the chief supporter of the central government in the reign of Conrad, as in the reign of Lewis the Child, and could not bear to see the forces of disunion finally victorious.

It need hardly be added that while civil war raged all over the German kingdom, the foreign enemy was more active than ever Instead of afflicting Only the eastern border of the land, the Magyars came flooding in over its whole extent. They even reached the Rhine: in 913 we find them before the walls of Coblenz: in 917 they surprised and burnt Basel, the south-westernmost of all the cities of the realm. Meanwhile the Suabians and Bavarians were too much occupied in resisting the king to be able either to unite or defend themselves.

In this melancholy position of affairs Conrad I. died on the 23d of December 918. His last act was to assemble his brothers and his chief councillors at his bedside, and to warn them that if Germany was to be saved they must find a stronger man than himself to crown as king. He advised them not to look within his own family, but to elect his rival the powerful duke Henry of Saxony. Though Henry was an obstinate enemy of his own, Conrad considered him the strongest and most capable statesman in the realm, and putting aside all personal enmity gave his vote in the Saxon's favour. His advice was taken and the happiest results ensued.

Here then we must leave Germany, still in evil plight, but on the eve of better things. She had yet to solve the question whether the work of Charles the Great — the blending of Frank, Saxon, Suabian, and Bavarian into a single nationality — was to endure, or whether the disruptive tendencies were still too strong. Fortunately for her there were two great forces at work in favour of unity. The Church owed her rise and growth in Germany to the protection of the great Frankish kings, and in gratitude always fought upon the side of royalty and union. But even more important was the pressure of hostile neighbours from without: it had become evident since the death of king Arnulf to even the most turbulent of the Suabian counts and the most unruly of the Saxon tribes, that if Germany was to survive she must submit herself to a single ruler. If the reigns of Lewis the Child and Conrad the Franconian had been disastrous failures, it was because the one was too young and the other too destitute both of heriditary claims and of personal followers. When a strong man with one of the great duchies at his back took Conrad's place, the problem of saving Germany was found not to be insoluble.

CHAPTER XXVIII: THE EASTERN EMPIRE IN THE NINTH CENTURY — 802-912

Nicephorus I. and his wars — He is slain by the Bulgarians — Short reign of Michael I. — Leo V. defeats the Bulgarians — His ecclesiastical troubles — Michael the Amorian dethrones him and reigns nine years — His policy — Reign of Theophilus — His wars with the Caliphs — He persecutes image-worshippers — Long minority of Michael III. — Restoration of image-worship — Orgies and end of Michael — Basil I. and the Macedonian dynasty.

The East Roman Empire was always at its best when it was subject for several generations to princes of the same family; it was always at its worst in the periods between the fall of one dynasty and the rise of another, when the crown had become for the moment a prize that could be grasped by every successful general or intriguing statesman. In such times attempts at usurpation grew so frequent that civil war became an endemic disease, and while the empire was troubled within, foreign enemies were always ready to take their opportunity to assail it from without. We have already noted one of these anarchic and disastrous intervals, that between 695 and 717, when the house of Heraclius had fallen, and that of Leo the Isaurian had not yet come to the front. We have now to record a second period of short reigns, and of troubles both at home and abroad, between the deposition of the empress Irene and the establishment on the throne of Michael the Amorian, the founder of the next dynasty. This period, which filled the years between 802 and 820, was by no means so disastrous as that which followed the fall of Justinian II. in the earlier century, but, nevertheless, it was distinctly a time of decline and decay, from which the empire took many years to recover.

The wicked empress Irene was dethroned, as we have already had occasion to relate, by a palace-conspiracy, headed by her high-treasurer, Nicephorus. The new monarch was a man of mature years, who was known merely as a capable finance minister, and had never been suspected of any great ambition. When he had seized the reins of government he proved that he had more character, more self-will, and more energy than his contemporaries had credited him with. He put down with success two rebellions of discontented military chiefs, who thought that they had as good a right to the throne as he, and established himself so firmly on his seat that none could shake him. In matters ecclesiastical he reversed the policy of the superstitious Irene, and showed a perfect tolerance for the Iconoclasts, as well as for all the other dissident sects in the empire. He kept a firm hand over the patriarch and clergy, who would have been glad to persecute these schismatics, a fact which probably explains the bitterness with which the chroniclers of the succeeding age write of him, — a bitterness which nothing in his actions seems to justify. He was neither cruel nor arbitrary in his rule, and the only accusation against him which seems to have the least foundation, is that after his accession he still remained too much of the high-treasurer, caring more for a good balance in the exchequer than for the welfare of his subjects.

Nicephorus's reign was not untroubled by wars. Haroun-al-Raschid still sat on the throne of Bagdad, and the caliphate was still a dangerous neighbour to the empire. Nicephorus refused to pay the tribute which Irene had promised to the Saracen, so Haroun renewed the intermittent war with the East Romans, which had dragged on, with short intervals, ever since the days of Constantine Copronymus. The emperor was not favoured by fortune in the war; it would seem that the maladministration of Irene's eunuch-ministers had caused the army to deteriorate, and matters went so ill that Nicephorus was glad to buy a peace when Haroun offered to grant him one. The emperor was to pay 30,000 solidi annually, beside — a curious detail — six large gold medals of greater weight for himself, and one for his son and heir, Stauracius.

In spite of this humiliating treaty it was not the Saracen war that was to prove Nicephorus's direst trouble; nor did he fare very badly in his struggle with Charles the Great. The long and desultory war with the new western empire terminated in a treaty which left Frank and East Roman exactly where they started. Not even Venice, which was now completely surrounded by the dominions of Charles, and which had been for a time in his hands, was sacrificed. Nor did Nicephorus find himself compelled to take what he would have regarded as the degrading step of recognising Charles as his equal and colleague in the administration of the empire.

It was a war with the comparatively insignificant power of the Bulgarians which was to be the worst of the disasters of Nicephorus. Since the failure of the great expedition of Constantine VI. in 796, the predatory tribe behind the Balkans had been growing more and more venturesome. Under a new king, the cruel but able Crumn, they were making raids far into Thrace, which at last drove Nicephorus to take the field against them in person. At the head of a great army, drawn from all the European and Asiatic themes, and accompanied by his son Stauracius, he crossed the Balkans in 811. Victory at first crowned his arms; he defeated the Bulgarians in the open field, and took and plundered their king's palace. But a few days later, as his victorious army lay carelessly encamped and paying no heed to the defeated enemy, it was beset by a fierce night-attack. In the confusion and panic which followed the emperor was slain, and his son Stauracius desperately wounded. Left without a leader the Byzantine army broke up, and retired in great disorder, leaving the body of the emperor with those of many of his chief officers upon the field. The Bulgarian king cut off the head of Nicephorus, and made his skull into a drinking-cup, as Alboin had done with the skull of king Cunimund three centuries before.

The wrecks of the imperial army rallied at Adrianople, whither the wounded Stauracius was borne. He was at once proclaimed Augustus in his father's room; but he never rose from his couch, for his hurt was mortal. It was evident that his end was near, and that his crown would soon be the prize of some usurper. Seeing this, his brother-in-law, Michael Rhangabe, who had married the only daughter of Nicephorus I., bribed the guards of his dying master, and had himself saluted as emperor before the breath was out of Stauracius's body (812).

Michael Rhangabe owed his rise purely to the chance that had connected him with the family of Nicephorus. He was personally insignificant, superstitious, and cowardly. But his accession had some importance from the religious point of view; he was a European Greek — the first of his race that had yet worn the imperial crown — and, like most of his countrymen, was a strong Iconodule, and wholly opposed to his father-in-law's tolerant ecclesiastical policy. He surrounded himself with fanatical monks, and set to work to reverse the doings of Nicephorus, and to remove all Iconoclasts from high office in state and army.

These actions might have been popular if Michael had been a man of strength and energy; but he was a weak and incapable ruler. He refused for some time to enter the field against the Bulgarians, who were ravaging Thrace far and wide, and when he did at last head an army, it was only to suffer a crushing defeat. He took what his subjects considered the degrading step of conciliating the Franks, by formally recognising Charles the Great as a legitimate emperor, and treating with him as an equal. In everything that he did indecision and want of courage was to be traced.

The army was fated to be the instrument of Michael's fall. It was deeply leavened with Iconoclastic feeling, and highly discontented with a master who sent it neither encouragement nor orders. At last, when Michael allowed king Crumn to penetrate so far into Thrace that he actually approached the walls of the capital, the army concentrated at Adrianople openly threw off its allegiance, and took the decisive step of saluting as emperor one of its generals, Leo the Armenian. Priests and courtiers could give Michael Rhangabe little support when the whole military caste turned against him; he was deposed with little trouble and sent into a monastery, while the rough soldier who had headed the revolt became emperor in his stead (813).

Leo the Armenian was a capable man, not destitute of good qualities, who might have founded a dynasty had fortune played him fair. He successfully discharged the task for which he had been chosen emperor — the ending of the Bulgarian war. Immediately after his accession the king of Bulgaria marched up to the very walls of Constantinople and camped over against it. Leo at first strove to get rid of Crumn by the dishonourable expedient of attempting to seize or slay him at a conference — much as Charles the Fat dealt with king Godfred. This attempt failed, but the Bulgarians, after plundering the suburbs, retired from before the walls, and in the next year when they again advanced into Thrace, Leo met them at Mesembria and inflicted on them a bloody defeat. So crushing was the reverse that the new Bulgarian king instantly asked for peace, and the empire was not troubled by another Bulgarian invasion till a whole generation had gone by.

Leo reigned for six years more, unvexed by wars without, and swaying the sceptre with a very firm hand. He reorganised the army and the finances, and did much to repair the harm caused by the depredations of Saracen and Bulgarian in the reigns of Nicephorus I. and Michael Rhangabe. But unfortunately for himself and the empire, he soon became involved in the old Iconoclastic controversy, and had no peace thereafter. Leo was, like most of the inhabitants of the Eastern themes, and most of the higher officers in the army, strongly imbued with the doctrines of his great namesake the Isaurian. For the first two years of his reign he kept his opinions to himself, and endeavoured to maintain a strict neutrality between the image-worshippers and the image-breakers. But the Iconodule clergy were too vehement, and Leo himself too conscientious for such a truce to endure for very long. In 815 the struggle broke out: Leo had requested the patriarch Nicephorus to order certain images, which were especial stumbling-blocks to the Iconoclasts, owing to the grovelling popular devotion which they attracted, to be raised so far from the ground that devotees should no longer be able to kiss and embrace them. The patriarch refused, bade all his clergy commence special prayers for deliverance, because the church was in danger, and excommunicated a bishop whom he suspected of having counselled the imperial order. Leo replied by deposing Nicephorus, and substituting for him a successor of decided Iconoclast views. The new patriarch at once held a council which declared image-worship superstitious, and re-affirmed all the decrees against it which had been passed in 754, by the synod held by Constantine Copronymus. But Leo did not plunge into persecution as his Isaurian predecessor had done: beyond removing a few church dignitaries from office, and banishing an abbot who made an open display of images in the streets of the capital, he took no repressive measures against the Iconodules. His moderation profited him little, for the image-worshippers hated a heretic as much as a persecutor, and his mildness only gave them the better opportunity of intriguing and conspiring against him. The last years of his reign, though full of outward prosperity, were a time of discontent and unrest beneath the surface, and it was felt that he had offended too many of his subjects for his life to be safe, or his throne secure. Knowing of this, unquiet spirits among his generals and courtiers began to draw together and plot against him.

The chief of these malcontents was Michael the Amorian, a turbulent soldier who had been the emperor's close friend when both were private persons, and who had been promoted to high office when Leo gained the crown. His conspiracy was detected, and he was thrown into prison, but when his confederates learnt that they were in danger of discovery, they resolved to strike at once before they were arrested. Leo was attending matins on Christmas Day in his private chapel, when the conspirators fell upon him. Snatching the great cross from the altar he fought desperately with it against his assailants, but before help could arrive he was cut down, and fell dead in the sanctuary.

The murderers hastened to the cell of Michael the Amorian, and saluted him as emperor. He was drawn from his dungeon and presented to the people in the imperial robes, before the fetters had been struck from his feet, and ere the day was ended the patriarch had crowned him in St. Sophia (December 25, 820). Michael was very inferior to the man whom he had dethroned: he had nothing to back him save his military talent and a certain measure of unscrupulous ability. He was quite uneducated, and his provincial dialect and ungrammatical expressions were the jest of the court and capital. But he knew how to strike hard, and his harshness cowed his enemies more than Leo the Armenian's mild policy. His accession was the signal for rebellion all over the empire: a certain Thomas raised the heretical sects of Asia Minor and the Iconoclast partisans of the late emperor in rebellion, and for three years made Michael's throne insecure. He even beleaguered Constantinople, and might have taken it, had not his followers alienated public sympathy by their ravages in its neighbourhood. He was ultimately put down and slain, but his rebellion caused a serious loss to the empire. While the whole of the imperial fleet and army was acting against him, a horde of Saracen pirates descended on the great island of Crete, and overran it from end to end (825). After peace had been restored, Michael made two attempts to expel the adventurers, but both failed, and for a hundred and thirty five years the 'island of the hundred cities' remained a Saracen outpost, and a sad hindrance to the commerce of the Aegean. Hardly had the expeditions sent against Crete returned with loss and disgrace, than Michael heard that a new province was being assailed by the same enemy. In 827 the Moslems of Africa, summoned by the traitor Euphemius, landed in Sicily, and began the conquest of that island. We have described its slow but steady progress in another chapter.

The loss of these two outlying provinces does not seem to have troubled Michael. He was perhaps content that he was preserved from a greater Saracen war with the whole force of the caliphate, owing to the civil strife of the descendants of Haroun-al-Raschid. Nor did the peaceful Lewis the Pious stir up the Franks against him. The conquest of Crete and Sicily was a vexatious incident, not a pressing danger.

In dealing with the thorny ecclesiastical questions which had proved so dangerous to his predecessor, Michael the Amorian showed caution rather than zeal. His accession had been supported by the image-worshippers, who cordially detested Leo the Armenian. But when safe on the throne he refused to put himself into their hands, or to commence a persecution of the Iconoclasts. He was probably at heart a contemner of images himself, and his son and colleague Theophilus had a fierce hatred for them. His line of policy was to proclaim complete toleration of both parties, and to recall and replace the prelates whom Leo had banished. But in public worship he maintained the condition of things that he found existing, and refused to restore the images which his predecessor had removed or mutilated. On the other hand he allowed such figures and pictures as had escaped Leo's hand to remain, and permitted the monks to practise as many superstitions as they pleased within the walls of their monasteries. Neither party was satisfied; both accused Michael of time-serving and lukewarm service of God, but they kept fairly quiet, and the controversy was for a time quiescent.

Michael reigned for nine years only, and at his death in 829 left the throne to his eldest son Theophilus, a man of much greater mark and individuality than himself. The new emperor was an active warlike prince, with a great love of splendour and pomp, and a strong determination to have his own will in all things. Moreover — and this was certain to give the empire troublous times — he was a firm and conscientious Iconoclast: it had been with great difficulty that his father restrained him from taking harsh measures against image-worship, while he was still only his junior colleague on the throne. The chroniclers bear strong witness to his courage, his personal virtues, and his even-handed justice, but his meddling in things ecclesiastical has sufficed to blacken his character in their pages.

The greater part of the reign of Theophilus was taken up with a long struggle with the caliphate. The Abbasside empire had been much weakened since the death of Haroun-al-Raschid, first by the civil strife between his sons, and then by the religious wars excited by the heterodox caliph El-Mamun. Theophilus thought that the ancient enemy was so reduced by the loss of many outlying provinces, and by long strife at home, that the empire would be able to win back some of the lands lost two centuries before by Heraclius. Accordingly he provoked a war with El-Mamun by sheltering the many refugees from Persia and Syria, who fled before the persecutions of the caliph. Unfortunately for Theophilus, the troubles of his adversary were just at an end, and the Saracens had their hands once more free for a struggle with the empire. The long war which set in revealed that the forces of the caliph and the emperor were now so evenly balanced that it was impossible for either to deal the other any deadly blow, but quite possible for each to harry and molest the other's frontiers for an indefinite time. With some trifling interruptions of truce and armistice, it lasted more than thirty years. The caliph began the struggle by invading his neighbour's Cappadocian borders, and overrunning the land as far as Heraclea (831). His fleets at the same time made some descents on the Cyclades and the Mysian coast. El-Mamun led three expeditions in person into Asia Minor, and after getting possession of the passes of Taurus, took the great town of Tyana at their northern exit, and fortified it as a base for further operations. Fortunately for Theophilus the caliph died at this moment, and his armies retired to Tarsus, abandoning their conquests beyond the mountains. The emperor was more fortunate against the new Saracen monarch, El-Motassem, the brother of El-Mamun. Theophilus was able to invade Syria and Mesopotamia, and to capture the important town of Samosata, where the Byzantine banners had not been seen since the time of Constantine Copronymus. But the ravages of Theophilus on the Euphrates, and especially his sack of Zapetra, a place for which El-Motassem had a special regard, provoked the Saracens to greater efforts. In 838 the caliph took the field at the head of a vast army: he had sworn to sack the emperor's birthplace, Amorium, in revenge for the plundering of Zapetra, and it is said that 130,000 men marched out of Tarsus, each with the word 'Amorium' painted on his shield. Theophilus hastened forth to defend his ancestral town: but one division of the Saracen army defeated him with great slaughter at Dasymon, while another, under the caliph's personal orders, stormed Amorium and slew the whole population — men, women, and children — to the number of not less than 30,000.

Such a disaster, and the sight of the caliph's troops advancing as far as the centre of Phrygia, seemed to portend danger to the empire. But having satiated his wrath and vengeance, El-Motassem retired, and the generals of Theophilus recovered the whole of the lost lands as far as the line of Taurus. Intestine troubles kept the caliph busy at home, and after the East Romans had recommenced their invasions of Syria and taken Laodicea, the port of Antioch, a truce was patched up, which lasted, with some intermissions, down to the death of the emperor and the caliph, both of whom expired in 842.

When not employed in the field against the Saracens, Theophilus had been busy at home against the image-worshippers. In 832 he issued an edict against all kinds of representations of our Lord and the Saints, whether in the form of statues, pictures, or mosaics, and had them sought out and destroyed not only in public places, but in monasteries and private dwellings. His especial wrath was reserved for the painters whom he found working in secret to reproduce the prohibited figures; he mutilated their disobedient hands with hot irons, and branded their foreheads with words of contumely. The patriarch John the Grammarian aided the emperor by excommunicating all the clergy who refused to abide by the decrees of the synod of 754. Theophilus then laid hands on the recalcitrant monks and bishops, and imprisoned or banished them. His wrath, however, did not lead him into the extremes that the Isaurian emperors had countenanced; he did not inflict the penalty of death for disobedience, nor did he endeavour to suppress the monastic system, like Constantine Copronymus. Those who bent before the storm met no harsh treatment: it was only open disobedience that moved Theophilus to anger. His very palace was full of secret image-worshippers, chief among whom was his own wife, the empress Theodora.

Like his western contemporary Lewis the Pious, the emperor yielded to the unhappy inspiration of choosing a second wife by public competition. When his childless empress died in 830, he summoned all the fairest daughters of his nobles to his Court, and passed them in review. His eye was caught by the young Theodora, the child of the high-admiral Marinus, and he espoused her without taking the trouble to discover that she was a fervent and bigoted image-worshipper. During her husband's life she concealed her views, and contented herself with protecting all the Iconodules whom she could shelter. But after Theophilus's death she was destined to undo all his religious schemes, and to bring up his children to loathe their father's creed.

In spite of the Saracen war and the ecclesiastical quarrels which rendered his life unquiet, the reign of Theophilus — like that of his father — was not an unprosperous time for the empire. His strict and exact justice benefited far more of his subjects than his bigotry harmed. The revenue was in such good condition that even in war-time he was able to execute many great public works — such as the strengthening and embellishing of the walls of the capital, and the building of many palaces and hospitals. His care for the fostering of trade was shown by the conclusion of commercial treaties, not only with Lewis the Pious, but even with the distant caliph of Cordova; and Constantinople became in his day more than ever the centre of the whole trade of Europe, because the Italian ports, which were her only rivals, were now suffering greatly from the occupation of the central Mediterranean by the Moors of Sicily.

To the great loss of the empire, Theophilus died in 842, while still in the prime of his life, leaving a son and heir of only four years of age. We have already spoken, more than once, of the dangers of a long minority in that time, and the youth of Michael III. was not to be an exception to the rule. For fourteen years a council of regency governed in his behalf to the small profit of the empire. The chief place in it was taken by the empress-dowager, whose interests were mainly religious. Almost before the breath was out of her husband's body Theodora set to work to undo his policy. Calling to her aid the whole image-loving party in the palace, she deposed the patriarch, drove into exile the chief Iconoclastic bishops, and summoned a council at Constantinople, which anathematised the enemies of images, and re-affirmed all the doctrines which had been condemned in 830 by order of Theophilus. Only thirty days after the new reign had begun Iconoduly had once more become orthodox, and Iconoclasm was proscribed. Active persecution against heretics followed; the Paulicians and other dissidents of Asia Minor were so maltreated that they migrated en masse to the dominions of the caliph, and from thence revenged themselves by making incursions into the empire.

The two men who shared the chief power with Theodora were her worthless brother Bardas, and the count Theoctistus: they were bitterly jealous of each other, and Bardas ultimately procured his rival's death. Each of these personages believed himself to be a great general, and their ambitious but ill-managed expeditions against the Saracens ended in uniform disaster. It was fortunate for the empire that the caliphate had now passed into the hands of two incapable bigots and debauchees, Wathek and Motawakkel, who were quite unable to profit by their neighbour's weakness (842-861). Indeed the Byzantine arms won some success when neither Bardas nor Theoctistus were present, and one daring expedition even seized and held Alexandria for a year. The long, weary war dragged on, but neither empire nor caliphate got any advantage from it.

In 856 the young Michael attained his eighteenth year, and took the government into his own hands. He at once sent away his mother, whose long domination he had secretly resented, and confiscated most of her treasure and estates. Michael was an ill-disposed youth, but owed much of his evil character to his uncle Bardas, who had brought him up in the worst of fashions, and taught him to plunge, while yet a mere boy, into drinking, gambling, and debauchery. Michael and his uncle were sworn companions in all kinds of ribaldry and evil-living, and their court was a scene of perpetual scandals. Bardas was made Caesar in 862, and for the next four years had as much to do with the government of the empire as his nephew. But he was unwise enough to take too much upon him, to treat Michael as a drunken boy, and to assume a superiority over him which the young emperor could not brook. After they had reigned together four years Michael caused his uncle to be slain, and took another associate in the empire (866).

His new colleague was Basil the Macedonian, a young man of Slavonic descent, who had long been one of his boon-companions. When Michael was still a boy he had been impressed by the courage and strength of Basil, who had entered his service as a groom. The young emperor promoted him from one office to another, till he became Protostrator, or Count of the Stables — Marshal as he would have been called in a western monarchy. The new favourite was bold, ready-witted, and hard-headed; he could drink down the emperor himself at their feasts — a power which inspired Michael with the greatest respect. So trusting to the faith of the friend of his youth, Michael preferred him to the place of the murdered Bardas.

When not under the influence of the wine-cup, Michael the Drunkard — as his subjects named him — was a warlike and energetic sovereign. He often took the field against the Saracens and the Bulgarians, and sometimes met with success when courage could take the place of strategy. After a successful campaign beyond the Balkans he forced the Bulgarian king not only to do him homage, but to become a Christian, a change which did much in later years to make relations easier between the empire and its northern neighbours.

Michael sometimes busied himself about things ecclesiastical: his mother had brought him up as a fervent image-worshipper, and he distinguished himself when he came to years of discretion by the disgraceful outrage of exhuming and burning the bodies of Constantine Copronymus and the patriarch John, the chief representatives — lay and spiritual — of Iconoclasm. Another of his doings had a graver consequence: it was he who, offended by the austere morals of the patriarch Ignatius, deposed him and nominated Photius in his stead. The preferment of Photius was, as we have already stated when dealing with the Papacy, the original cause of that breach between East and West which has never yet been healed.

Michael had attained the age of thirty-one, and seemed destined to rule for many more years, when he was suddenly cut off. His friend and boon-companion, Basil, whom he had raised from a groom to be a Caesar, was the murderer. At the end of one of their debauches the Macedonian rose and bade some of his friends slay his benefactor, Michael was stabbed as he lay in a drunken sleep, and the crown passed away from the Amorian house (867). Basil had already, as colleague in the empire, got the reins of power in his hands, and the murder of Michael passed unrevenged. No one raised his voice in behalf of the dead man's infant sons, and the new dynasty was inaugurated without a struggle or a civil war.

The Macedonian, though he had shown himself an ungrateful traitor, was a man of great ability. He held firmly to his ill-gotten crown, and founded the longest dynasty that ever sat upon the Byzantine throne. It was not till 1056 that his house was extinguished. As emperor he did all that he could to make his subjects forget that he had once been the deep-drinking favourite of Michael III. He proved himself a hard-working sovereign, economical, prudent, and judicious, and the empire flourished under his rule. Some of his work was destined to be permanent; his code, a new revision of the laws of Justinian, superseding Leo the Isaurian's Ecloga, remained the text-book of the eastern empire down to its last days. His financial arrangements, which seem to have been excellent, were also destined to endure for nearly two centuries. In matters ecclesiastical he did his best to patch up the breach with the Roman church; he reinstated the deposed patriarch Ignatius, and sent Photius into private life; but though the cause of offence was removed the quarrel remained, and the exorbitant claims of the Popes prevented any reunion of the East and West. Finding this to be the case, Basil restored Photius when Ignatius died, and allowed things to take their inevitable course.

Except in Sicily the wars of Basil were generally successful. The empire of the caliphs was rapidly breaking up; the dynasty of the Saffarides had lopped off the eastern provinces of their realm, and Egypt had fallen into the hands of Ahmed-ibn-Tulun. Four caliphs had been murdered in nine years (861-9), and the incessant civil war which raged at Bagdad stripped the Saracen frontier of most of its defenders. The Christian arms, therefore, did not fare badly during the reign of Basil and his son Leo, and for the first time the East Roman boundary began to move eastward, and new themes were carved out of the captured territory. The Byzantine armies ravaged northern Syria and Mesopotamia as far as Amida and Aleppo. Cyprus was recovered, though only for a time, and the rebellion of the Paulician heretics on the Armenian frontier was suppressed. At the same time Basil's fleets won victories in the Aegean and the Ionian sea over the corsairs of Crete and Africa. We have already mentioned, in another place, how the admiral Oriphas aided Lewis II. to reconquer Bari, and how Nicephorus Phocas drove out the Saracens from Lucania and Bruttium, and added the southern peninsula of Italy to his master's realm. In Sicily alone was disaster met; the fall of Syracuse in 878 marks the practical extinction of the East Roman power in that island. But success elsewhere atoned for this single loss.

If Basil had been succeeded by a strong and energetic ruler, the East Roman empire might have had an opportunity of extending its sway over almost all the provinces that had obeyed Justinian three centuries before. The caliphate grew more and more decrepit: Italy was, as we have already seen, a prey to anarchy for more than half a century, and the Slavs of Eastern Europe were being crushed by the newly arrived horde of the Magyars. None of them could have opposed any strong defence against a capable commander heading the well-armed and well-disciplined host that the Eastern empire could send out. But the son and grandson of Basil, whose long reigns occupied the next eighty years, were a couple of narrow-minded and pedantic men of letters, equally destitute of taste and of ability for engaging in schemes of conquest. Leo VI., whom after generations called Leo the Wise, not for his practical cleverness, but because he had a taste for the occult sciences and wrote obscure prophecies, was the immediate successor of Basil. By some strange freak of nature the hard-drinking, unscrupulous, energetic Macedonian usurper was the father of a laborious compiler of books, the mildest and least stirring of men. Leo's prophetic oracles and his ecclesiastical writings are of small profit to the reader. but posterity must acknowledge that it owes him a considerable debt for publishing his Tactica, a military manual giving an excellent account of the organisation, strategy, and tactics of the Byzantine armies, with useful notes as to the habits and manners of the enemies whom the army was called upon to face. It was probably fortunate for the empire that he never tried to put his book-knowledge of things military to practical use in the field.

In spite of Leo's feeble personality, and of the fact that his negligence occasionally allowed the foes of the empire to snatch unexpected advantages, this reign was a time of growth for the imperial borders. The new themes of 'Lycandus' and 'Mesopotamia' were won from the enfeebled caliphate; Apulia was conquered from the dukes of Benevento and the Italian Saracens, and formed into the theme of 'Langobardia.'

Benevento itself was for some years in Leo's hands, and if he had shown a little more energy he might have pushed his army up to the gates of Rome, while the counts of central Italy were engaged in their endless bickerings with king Berengar. But the emperor neglected to support his generals, and with a tranquil mind let them fail for want of resources.

Leo died in 912, leaving the throne to his only son Constantine VII., better known as Constantine Porphyrogenitus, a weak literary man of the same type as himself. The new emperor was a boy of only five, and his whole reign was one long minority, for after he reached manhood he allowed others to govern for him, and remained buried in his books.

But in spite of the feebleness of Leo and Constantine, the empire was faring well. Its neighbours were too weak to trouble it with serious wars, though now and then a disaster occurred, such as the surprise of Thessalonica by the African pirates in 904. Such misfortunes were due to the misdirection of the empire's resources, not to their inadequacy for defence. The realm was never richer nor stronger since the days of Justinian; Constantinople had become the sole centre of the commerce of the Christian world, the one place where East and West could freely exchange their commodities. The revenue was abundant and easily raised, the army well paid and efficient, and only needed adequate generals to enable it to set out on a wide career of conquest. But the empire was not to obtain a capable ruler for many years; the days of John Zimisces and Basil Bulgaroktonos were still far off, and meanwhile the East Romans, under the feeble leadership of Leo and Constantine, remained in a condition of stationary prosperity, due to the well-organised administration of the empire. The Byzantine civil-service was well able to carry on the business of government, unless it was handicapped by the presence on the throne of a strong-handed tyrant, and whatever were their faults the sovereigns of the Macedonian house never deserved that name. There are worse things for any realm than a series of mediocrities on the throne.

CHAPTER XXIX: THE END OF THE NINTH CENTURY IN WESTERN EUROPE. CONCLUSION

Reign of Odo in France — His Danish wars — His civil war with
Charles the Simple — Charles succeeds to the throne — He grants
Normandy to Hrolf — Lotharingia annexed to France — Robert and
Rudolf rebel against Charles the Simple — Murder of Charles at Peronne
— Spain and the Moors — Growth of the kingdom of the Asturias under
Pelagius and the three Alfonsos — Its continued progress — Summary of
the period — Feudalism, its military and political meaning — Conclusion.

We left the much-vexed Neustrian realm handed over to a king whose
title to the crown lay in his strong hand and his good sword, and not in any
hereditary right. Odo count of Paris was not sprung either on the father's or
the mother's side from the house of the Karlings. His father was Robert the
Strong, a count of Angers and Blois under Charles the Bald, one of the few
Frankish chiefs who won a reputation in the struggle with the Vikings.
When Robert fell by a Danish arrow, his son appears a few years later in
power by the middle Seine and Loire, and especially in charge of Paris,
where he won his great name and his crown by the gallant defence of the
city in 886-7.

Odo was without doubt the best candidate that could have been chosen
for the West Frankish throne. The sole legitimate heir of the Karlings —
Charles the Simple, the posthumous son of Lewis the Stammerer — was
only eight years of age, and to hand the kingdom over to a minor would
have been a piece of madness. Nevertheless the choice of Odo was a bad
alternative at the best: he was but one among a dozen personages of equal
position, each of whom believed himself to be his new-master's equal.
Between 850 and 887 all the greater counties of Neustria and Aquitaine
were becoming hereditary. Charles the Bald and his short-lived successors
had everywhere bought a temporary freedom from trouble by appointing
the son to fill the father's place, and in the next generation the rulers of the
counties and duchies looked upon their title to succeed to their ancestor's
governor-ship as fixed and absolute. In every one of these districts, which
were afterwards to be known as the 'Great Fiefs,' the first commencement

of hereditary rule dates from the fatal days between the battle of Fontenay and the deposition of Charles the Fat. The first sovereign in the county of Toulouse who passed on his dominions to his son dates from 852: in Flanders the date is 862: in Poitou 867: in Anjou 870: in Gascony 872: in Burgundy 877: in Auvergne 886. To all these rulers Odo was but a fortunate equal, whom they had consented to elevate to the throne because of the imminent danger which the kingdom was suffering from the Viking raids. In spite of the oaths that they had sworn him they could not in their own minds look upon him as a king of the same sort as the Karlings had been. In a time when hereditary right was beginning to count so highly, it was a fatal weakness in a king to owe his power to the old Teutonic right of election alone. In reading the chronicles of this period of French history we are reminded in a striking manner of the troubles of the kings of the Spanish Visigoths. We find once more the utter confusion that ensues from the elective system when the nobility is too strong, and the royal name has been lowered by a series of weak or incapable rulers.

In Odo's first year he was comparatively free from troubles within; the Vikings were spread all over the face of the land, and even the turbulent counts of Neustria refrained from rebellion in face of the danger, while Wido of Spoleto, the rival of the new king, had to quit the realm for want of followers. The election of Odo received its best justification when in June 888 he smote the great army of the Danes at Montfaucon in Champagne, and drove them from the valleys of the Meuse and Marne. The whole realm concurred willingly in his second coronation at Rheims, where he was invested with a crown, which his neighbour Arnulf had sent him, in token of friendship as well as of a claim of suzerainty.

Even the distant and ever-rebellious south bowed for a time before the sceptre of Odo: when he marched into Aquitaine Ramnulf count of Poictiers, who had thought for a moment of establishing himself as an independent duke south of the Loire, struck no blow against him, but did instant homage. But while Odo was in Poitou the Vikings had again gathered in great force on the lower Seine, under chiefs among whom we descry for the first time the name of Hrolf or Rollo, the future duke of Normandy. They laid siege for the third time to Paris: the brave town held out for many months, but Odo, less able to defend his old fief as king than he had been as count, followed the deplorable precedent of Charles the Fat, and gave them money to take themselves off to Brittany.

Of course they returned ere long, but when they once more invaded central France, Odo inflicted a crushing defeat on them at Montpensier: their chief Oskytel was captured with many of his men. Like Guthrum in England the vanquished Dane offered to become a Christian, but as he issued from the baptistery, count Ingo, the standard-bearer of Odo, cut him down. 'Never trust a Dane, baptized or unbaptized,' said the murderer, and his master left him unpunished, as if he felt that the cynical plea was sufficient justification (892).

Just when he appeared to be strongest, Odo was in truth nearing his greatest danger. The Danes being for a time driven off, the unruly counts of France, free from the impending terror, began at once to conspire against their king. He was too much one of themselves for them to regard him as their absolute master, and too strong-handed for them to feel their new hereditary fiefs safely their own. In 893 some of the great nobles sent for the boy Charles the Simple, the heir of the Karlings, from his refuge in England. Richard, duke of Burgundy, William, count of Auvergne, Heribert, count of Vermandois, and Fulco, archbishop of Rheims, were the chief of the rebels. There followed six years of desperate civil war: Odo was far too strong for the fourteen-year-old boy whom his treacherous vassals had raised up against him: again and again he drove Charles from the cities where he had fortified himself, and chastised the rebels who adhered to him. But some one of the counts of Neustria or Aquitaine was always rising in favour of the Karling. Driven from one district he reappeared in another, and the land had no rest. It was to no purpose that Odo once offered to make his rival king of Aquitaine and rule himself in Neustria alone: such a compromise would not have suited his ambitious vassals, who were inspired not by any real loyalty to the ancient house, but by a wish to gain complete local independence.

At last Odo, worn out with the struggle, died on the last day of the year 898. His brother and heir Robert refused to continue the struggle against the heir of the Karlings, and did homage to Charles the Simple, receiving from him confirmation as ruler of the 'Duchy of France' — the lands of Paris, Orleans, Tours, Chartres, Beauvais, and Le Mans. Thus the civil war ended, but at the cost of the establishment of one more great fief, and that one comprehending the whole of the heart of Neustria, a very kingdom in itself.

Charles the Simple was now undisputedly king of the whole realm of the West Franks, and was recognised as its ruler for thirty-one years, till his untimely death in 929. He had by this time reached the age of twenty, and had gained much experience in the uncertainties of war and in the bearing of adverse fortune (899). He of was a man of energy and resource, the worthy brother of the long-dead Lewis III., and his nickname 'the Simple,' given him because he was too prone to trust his treacherous vassals, and was so often deceived by them, is rather a title of honour than the reverse. From the very first his position was far weaker than that of any of his predecessors had been. The great fiefs had now become definitely hereditary: any endeavour to prevent the reversion of the father's land to the son was regarded as a usurpation on the king's part, and resented by the whole body of vassals of the realm. In every part of Neustria and Aquitaine the counts and dukes had now become semi-independent sovereigns, and it was only in the royal demesne, and in the lands of the great ecclesiastical fiefs, that the king retained monarchical power.

Charles was by no means destitute either of ambition or of energy. He did his best to assert his royal authority over his vassals, and to cope with the never-ending Danish invasions. He did not forget the traditional policy of the Neustrian Karlings, their desire to unite with their own realm the whole or part of Lotharingia, the plan that had led his grandfather Charles the Bald into so many unhappy wars. More fortunate than his ancestor, Charles succeeded in laying hands on a large portion of the disputed realm. The Austrasians had grown weary of their union with Germany while ruled by the turbulent and tyrannical Zwentibold, whom Arnulf had set over them. After Arnulf s death they cast out and slew his bastard, and adhered for a time to Lewis the Child. But when the young Lewis followed his father to the grave, the Lotharingians refused to concur with the other Teutonic races in setting Conrad the Franconian on the throne. Headed by the count of Hainault, Reginald-with-the-Long-Neck, they declared that they would have none but a Karling to reign over them, and threw themselves into the arms of Charles the Simple. From 912 onwards he reigned as their king, and found his best supporters among their warriors, for Austrasia was not yet so feudalised as Neustria, and the love of the old royal house was still strong within its borders.

The Viking raids never ceased during the reign of Charles. The civil war of 893-8 had given the Danes an opportunity of returning to Neustria, and they were not slow to take it. When the chroniclers of the time are not recounting the rebellions of Charles's undutiful subjects, they are generally occupied in detailing Danish ravages. But it is now to be observed that the inroads of the Vikings are not nearly so dangerous to the realm as they had once been: the spell of the invincibility of the Northmen had been broken, and whenever they appeared they were fiercely withstood by the local counts and dukes. The land no longer gave them such rich prey, for the open towns had now surrounded themselves with walls, and were not as formerly the defenceless victims of every raider who could muster a few hundred men at his back. Still the invaders never ceased to come, for many of their former fields of action were now closed: in England Alfred and his son were too strong for them, and in Germany they never had their old good fortune after their great defeat at Louvain. France, therefore, had now to bear the brunt of their attacks, and all their hordes concentrated themselves on the coast between the Scheldt and the Garonne.

It was in 911 that Charles the Simple took a step which was to change the aspect of the great struggle with the Danes. Their main army was now lying on the lower Seine, and their chief camp was at Rouen, a great city which they had sacked and desolated and made their own. Their war-lord was now the sea-king Hrolf, or Rollo as the Franks called him, who had asserted his power by right of superior ability above all the other jarls. Hrolf s bands ranged far and wide in the Seine valley, and had fought at Chartres a bloody but indecisive battle with the host of the Franks, headed by the king's greatest vassals, the dukes of France and Burgundy and the count of Poitou.

Despairing, as Alfred had despaired thirty years before, of ever being able to drive away the Dane, Charles took the same step that the great king of Wessex had taken. He determined to offer the Viking leader a great tract of land as a settlement for his followers, if he would consent to draw them all together and to conclude a stable peace. The experiment had been made before by the Frankish monarchs, with no encouraging results, and the tale of Charles the Fat and king Godfred must have been fresh in the minds of the Vikings. Nevertheless the offer was made once more: if Hrolf would settle down, he should have an ample Danelagh — as the English would have called it — for his men. Charles proffered him Rouen and the lower valley of the Seine, and with them the hand of his daughter Gisela. The Northman blustered and affected to despise the king's offer, but presently he began to haggle and to speak of terms. The monarch of the West Franks and the veteran sea-king met at Clair-sur-Epte, and there the bargain was concluded. Hrolf asked and received all the lands from the river Epte to the sea, a grant which the Danes interpreted as giving them all the coast-land from the mouth of the Somme to the borders of Brittany. Charles added to this the easy promise of the suzerainty of Brittany itself, when Hrolf should succeed in conquering the unruly princes of that land, who for many years had paid no allegiance to the Frankish crown.

The Viking therefore received the hand of the king's daughter, promised to submit to baptism, and 'became the man' of Charles the Simple. A well-known story tells how Hrolf refused to bow the knee himself to the Frank, when the oath of homage had to be given, and deputed one of his chiefs to be his proxy, and how the Dane, with designed clumsiness, when he bent before the king's feet, succeeded in upsetting king and throne together. But Charles overlooked the insult in return for the tangible benefits that the submission of Hrolf involved, and loaded the Danes with gifts on their departure.

The Viking chief therefore settled down to live as a Frankish duke at Rouen: he had himself baptized, according to his promise, and the majority of his warriors followed his example. Contrary to what might have been expected, the experiment of planting the Northmen on the lower Seine proved a complete success for the Frankish king. The majority of the Danish war-bands in Gaul drifted, one after the other, to join Hrolf's followers, and to receive from him a fixed settlement in his new duchy. By sacrificing a part of his realm, Charles the Simple had saved the rest. The duke of Normandy, no longer rex piratarum, but the king's trusted vassal, was on the whole very faithful to the oaths that he had sworn at Clair-sur-Epte. He adhered to king Charles in all his troubles, and sent him a contingent of Danes whenever he was asked for aid. It was only when Charles had been deposed by rebels that Hrolf again turned loose his plundering bands upon France, and became once more the scourge of Neustria.

The summer of 912 saw Charles both freed from his Viking war by the cession of Normandy, and hailed as king of Lotharingia by the Austrasians. The next eight years were the most fortunate period of his reign: he waged no important wars abroad, and had no very serious troubles at home. But his authority over the greater part of France was very limited: more especially in the lands south of the Loire nothing but lip-service was granted him: neither tribute nor military aid could be expected from the great counts of the South. Yet weak as he was, Charles the Simple was still stronger than his great vassals cared that he should be. Three of the greatest magnates of his realm resolved to compass his deposition: their chief was

Robert duke of France, who in his old age began to covet the crown that he had refused to claim in 899. His confederates were Rudolf, second duke of Burgundy, and Heribert count of Vermandois. They commenced their operations by bidding the king dismiss his chief minister and favourite, count Hagano. When he refused, they sent him a formal disavowal of their allegiance, and after a space proclaimed Robert of France king of the West Franks.

Civil war at once began: supported by the Lotharingians and the Normans king Charles made head against the rebels, though they raised against him all the warriors of France and Burgundy. The armies met at Soissons for a decisive engagement: the troops of the Karling were beaten, but in the moment of victory the rebel king was pierced by a Norman lance, and by Robert's death the rising was left without a leader (923).

The great vassals were cowed for a moment by their chiefs fall, and sorely distracted by a Danish invasion. Rollo had launched against the territories of the rebel dukes a great horde of Northmen, and the invaders were joined by a fresh army from England under Regnald, whom Edward the Elder had just deposed from the kingship of Northumbria. But in spite of the ravages of the Danes, who swarmed into Burgundy, and threatened to establish a second Danelagh in the valley of the Saone, the rebels resolved not to submit to their rightful lord. They now proclaimed as anti-king Rudolf duke of Burgundy, for Hugh, son of Robert of France, refused to take up his father's claims. Charles might have fought down the insurrection, for a great Norman army was coming to his aid, if he had not fallen by treachery. Heribert of Vermandois offered to submit to him, and begged him to come to a conference at Peronne. The simple king hastened to the meeting, and was seized and thrown into a dungeon (923). The only drop of bitterness in the cup of the rebels was that Edgiva, the English wife of Charles, escaped with her son Lewis to the court of her father king Edward the Elder. There was still an heir of the Karling house safe beyond the seas.

For four troubled years Rudolf of Burgundy reigned as king of France, and Charles the Simple lay in durance at Peronne. Rudolf was but a phantom king: Aquitaine refused to acknowledge him: the Danes ranged all over his realm and beset his native duchy of Burgundy with especial fury. His own confederates in the rebellion paid him scanty homage, and went each on his own way. After a space Heribert of Vermandois quarrelled with Rudolf, and to spite the new king drew Charles out of his dungeon and proclaimed him once more monarch of the West Franks. But Rudolf bought over the double traitor to rejoin him: and for a second time Heribert seized the person of his natural lord and master. This time Charles did not escape with mere imprisonment: the cruel and treacherous count starved him to death at Peronne. At last Rudolf the Burgundian could call himself without dispute king of France (929).

Here we must leave the history of the western realm, at a moment when it had reached much the same wretched condition that Germany attained at the time of the death of Conrad I. More unhappy than their eastern neighbours, the Franks of Neustria and Aquitaine were not yet to see any such great rulers as Henry the First and Otto the Great set over them. They were destined to drink the cup of feudal anarchy to the dregs, ere a strong monarchy was once more to arise among them. The fight between the Karlings and the dukes of France was to drag on for two generations more, ere Hugh Capet finally gained the crown that his grandfather Robert and his great-uncle Odo had worn. And when the house of the dukes of France had seized the throne, they were to be for long ages as powerless as the Karlings whom they had supplanted.

As yet the only favourable symptom in the condition of France was the comparative immunity from Viking raids that it was beginning to enjoy. Thanks to the feudal horseman and the feudal castle, thanks still more to the narrowing of Danish ambition to the Norman duchy and its neighbouring lands of Maine and Brittany, the kingdom was beginning to enjoy a certain measure of peace from the outer enemy. Unfortunately the great vassals of the crown only used their opportunity to redouble their wicked feuds, and the nation's worst foes were to be those of its own household for many a long day.

There is still one region of Europe at which we have cast no glance for a hundred years. But the fortunes of Spain lie far apart from those of the Frankish empire, and during the ninth and tenth centuries form no part of the general history of Christendom. We have had occasion to mention, however, that the Moslem conquerors of the peninsula paid for forty years a wavering allegiance to the Ommeyad caliphs, and were ruled for a time by a series of ephemeral viceroys, most of whom came to violent ends. Of the fate of those of them who ventured to attack the Frankish empire, we have spoken while dealing with the annals of Charles Martel and Pippin the Short.

In 756 Spain became separated from the caliphate of Bagdad. After the massacre of the Ommeyad house by their Abbasside successor, one member of the older family escaped to Spain. The young Abderahman, after long struggles, put down all those who opposed him, and became an independent sovereign. He ruled at Cordova for more than thirty years, and not unprosperously, though he was vexed all through his life by incessant rebellions, such as that of the chiefs who in 778 called in Charles the Great against him, and led the Franks to the gates of Saragossa.

But while Abderahman was ruling in great state at Toledo and Cordova, and winning the admiration of all the Moslem world by his courage, his wisdom, and his magnificence, a little cloud was arising in the west, which was in later days to overshadow all Mohammedan Spain.

After the destruction of the Visigothic kingdom in 711-12, the viceroys of Spain had overrun well-nigh the whole land, and planted it thickly with colonists from Arabia, Syria, and Africa. But they had never completely subdued the extreme north-west of the peninsula. The Cantabrian and Asturian highlands had always been the last refuge of broken tribes from the first dawn of Spanish history. There the Galaeci and Astures had long withstood the Roman legions: there, in a later age, the Suevi had resisted the Visigoths for more than a century. And now, in the same rugged hills, the last of the Visigoths took refuge from the advancing Saracen. The annals of this rugged region are very scanty, but we learn that a certain count Pelagius, a chief with a Roman name, and perhaps, therefore, of native Spanish rather than Gothic blood, maintained himself with success against the Moslems. The narrow rocky tract between the Bay of the Biscay and the Cantabrian mountains presented few attractions to the Saracens, who preferred to settle in the fertile plains of Andalusia and Valencia, and they paid no heed to Pelagius when he drove their scattered garrisons out of the Asturias, and built up for himself a little kingdom in the hills. He is said to have reigned for eighteen years (718-36) over the Asturians. On his death his son Favila and his son-in-law Hildefuns (Aldefonsus, Alfonso) followed him on the throne. The last-named, whose pure Visigothic name recalls that of the sainted archbishop of Toledo, was the founder of the greatness of the new kingdom. Taking advantage of the civil wars of the Saracens, he issued from his hills, and threw himself upon the neighbouring province of Galicia, where a few Berber chiefs held down a discontented population of Christians. The natives rose to aid him, and the Mohammedan settlers were driven out of the land, and chased down into the plains of northern Spain (751).

Alfonso followed the flying foe, and made himself a lodgement on the southern slope of the Cantabrian hills, occupying the towns of Astorga and Leon, and pushing his incursions as far as the north bank of the Douro. He is said to have driven the Saracens completely out of the broad Tierra de Campos, the plain of Leon, and to have left it behind him an uninhabited desert, when he drew back to his fastnesses in the mountains. He laid Oporto, Zamora, and Salamanca in ruins, but was not strong enough to occupy them and add them to his kingdom.

Alfonso died in 757, just at the moment when the peninsula was falling into the hands of Abderahman the Ommeyad. The kings of Cordova proved more formidable foes to the new Christian state than the old viceroys of Spain had been, and for some generations its growth was comparatively slow. For fifty years the kings of Asturias and Galicia are mere names to us: it would appear that they were often constrained to pay tribute to the Ommeyad princes, and that they found their chief safety in the civil wars with which the Moslems were so continually vexed.

Alfonso II. (791-842) successfully repelled the last Moslem attempt to reconquer Galicia. He appears once in Frankish history as sending ambassadors to Charles the Great, to say that he considered himself the 'man' of the great king, and to offer his homage. But the Franks did not acquire any real suzerainty over Asturias, or come into any contact with its borders. The reign of Charles, however, left its mark on Peninsular history in another quarter: it was he who conquered from the Saracen the 'march of Spain,' which, under its later name of the county of Barcelona, became the second great Christian state beyond the Pyrenees. At first the 'Spanish March' was a dependency of the duchy of Septimania, but ere long they were separated, and the count of Barcelona became as free from any active interference on the part of the Frankish kings as were his neighbours, the counts of Aquitaine.

The long reign of Alfonso II. was a period of rapid growth and extension for the kingdom of Asturias. He pushed his arms forward as far as the Tagus, and in one expedition he took and sacked Lisbon. But he drew the line of his garrisons at the Douro, which remained for some time the limit of the occupation of the Asturians. They were engaged for a whole generation in repeopling the deserted plains of Leon, which had long been a waste march between the Christian and the Moslem.

Another Alfonso, third of the name, who ascended the throne in 866, was the next prince who pushed forward the Asturian border. To the kingdom that he inherited he added Old Castille, northern Portugal, and the land beyond the Douro, the extrema Durii, which keeps its name of Estremadura till this day. Mohammed king of Cordova could make no head against him, for a rising under a chief named Omar-ben-Hafs had torn his northern dominions from his grasp, and while endeavouring to subdue the rebel, he had to leave the king of Asturias to press forward unopposed.

In Alfonso's time the county of Castille and the kingdom of Navarre took their rise. The former was a border march against the Moor, intrusted by the king to the bravest of his vassals. The latter was founded by a Gascon count Sancho, who though a vassal of the Frankish crown made conquests on his own account beyond the Pyrenees, and obtained the aid of the king of Asturias by doing him homage.

Alfonso strengthened his realm by building the great frontier fortresses of Zamora, Simancas, and Osma, to protect his new acquisitions from the raids of the Moslems. In 910 his son Garcia removed his residence from the Asturian town of Oviedo to Leon, south of the hills, as if to mark the advance of his borders into the plains of northern Spain.

The progress of the Christians southward and eastward was never to be checked, though it was often delayed for a space when strong rulers sat on the throne of Cordova. Three centuries before, it was the Goths who had been a turbulent unruly aristocracy, ruling a nation of serfs, and the Saracen had swept their monarchy off the face of the earth in two years. Now the Moslem had become even as his Gothic predecessor, luxurious, proud, untrue to his king, a hard master to the peasantry who paid him toll and tribute. Religious persecution was not rare, and Andalusia could count many martyrs; the accusation of having blasphemed the name of Mohammed always stirred the Moslem crowd to sudden cruelty, and victims of all ages and conditions, from an archbishop of Toledo down to obscure monks and trades folk, suffered on that charge. While the conquerors were losing their ancient strength, the new Christian kingdom in the north-west was breeding an iron-handed race of men in its rugged mountains, a race whose life was one constant crusade against the Infidel. They had lost in their common danger all memory of the ancient grudges that separated Visigoth and Roman, and had become a perfectly homogeneous people, welded completely together by the day of adversity. The stubborn Spanish nation, poor, proud, warlike, and fanatically orthodox, was the natural product of the time when Christianity and freedom could only be preserved by accepting exile in the Cantabrian hills, and a life of constant struggle against the Saracen. The Mohammedan aristocracy, cultured, wealthy, luxurious, turbulent, and selfish, could not in the end resist such enemies. Though brave and numerous, they were divided by countless local, family and national feuds — the Arab hated the Syrian and the Berber, while all three despised the Spanish-born Moslem. Their monarch at Cordova only existed by playing off one faction against another, and was often deprived for whole years of his control over an important town or province.

It is small wonder then that the Asturian kingdom waxed, while the caliphate of Cordova waned. Perhaps we ought rather to marvel that the Moslems ruled in Spain so long and with so much splendour, in spite of all their feuds and civil wars. It is strange that in the midst of so much turbulent disorder they should have been able to found a very flourishing literature, and to leave their mark on the face of the land in the shape of such triumphs of architecture as the great Mosque of Cordova, or the Alcazar of Seville. Certainly the Saracen was seen at his best in Spain; in the other lands that he conquered, decay and decline came on him much more rapidly. The Abbassides of Bagdad had sunk into decrepitude some time before the Ommeyads of Cordova met with their fall. Syria, Egypt, and Persia became the prey of Turk and Mameluke and Tartar long ere Andalusia yielded to the Christian. Arabia itself sunk back into torpor with astonishing rapidity and ease. It was certainly in Spain that the conquering Moslems retained longest all the best and worthiest characteristics of the days of their early greatness.

We leave Europe at the end of our period in a day of gloom and depression. The picture indeed has its bright points: in Spain the balance had definitely turned in favour of Christendom, and the crescent was already beginning to wane. At Constantinople the rule of the Basilian dynasty promised a period of stationary prosperity, even if no strong emperor should arise to lead the Byzantine armies once more to victory. But in those great lands of Central Europe which then, and always, have formed the heart of Christendom, the outlook was very black — blacker than it had been at any time since the evil days of the seventh century. If the attacks of the Vikings were visibly slackening, and if the Saracens had at last been driven out of southern Italy, so that the invaders from without were for a time checked, yet the state of affairs within showed no signs of mending. The empire was dead: the papacy was falling into premature decay and corruption.

In the midst of all the treason and selfishness, the wars, murders, and rebellions of the dismal age that lies between the battle of Fontenay and the end of the tenth century, there is one thought only that can afford the student any consolation. After the break-up of the empire of Charles the Great, while Dane, Saracen, Hungarian, and Slav were simultaneously besetting the gates of Christendom, there was a very serious danger that the fabric of civilised Europe might crumble to pieces beneath their blows. That it did not do so must be attributed to the unexpected powers of resistance developed by the disintegrated fractions of the Frankish empire under the feudal system. Disastrous as were most of the effects of that system, it at least justified its existence by saving Christendom from the foe without. What the successors of Charles the Great had failed to do when all the military force of the empire was at their backs, was accomplished by the petty counts and margraves whose power was developed on the ruins of the central authority. It was the mailed feudal horseman, and the impregnable walls of the feudal castle, that foiled the attacks of the Dane, the Saracen, and the Hungarian.

While the emperor or king was expected to protect every corner of the realm, and as a matter of fact protected none of it, the governors of the gaus and marks proved, on the whole, to be equal to the task, when once they had got their hands free and were not fettered by the close supervision of their master. Europe lapsed, indeed, into utter decentralisation, and lost for centuries the administrative unity which the reign of Charles the Great had promised. A heavy blow was dealt at the slowly developing culture and civilisation which the eighth century had produced. It was not without justice that the ninth, tenth, and eleventh centuries have been called 'the Dark Ages.' Literature and art sank back to the level from which Charles the Great had for a time raised them; history has once more to be reconstructed from the scantiest materials. Architecture was stagnant, save in the single department of castle-building — the one development that these centuries produced. The internal history of continental Europe, when it ceases to be a series of Danish, Saracen, and Magyar raids, becomes a dismal record of tiresome local feuds and private wars. The remains of the old Teutonic liberty, which had survived in slowly dwindling measure, finally disappear as feudalism is perfected, and the freeman becomes everywhere the vassal of some greater or smaller lord.

But all the details of this unhappy change must not blind us to the fact that Christendom was saved from destruction by the men of the feudal age. In spite of all the faults of their system, its selfishness, its particularism, its feuds, its degradation of the lower classes, it served the required end in producing the condition of military efficiency which was needed to beat off the invading hordes from without. The problem with which Europe had to deal was that of facing quickly-moving assailants, whose object was primarily plunder rather than fighting, and who therefore had to be caught and brought to bay if they were to be checked. The slowly-moving masses of foot-soldiery which the Frankish empire put into the field were quite unable to deal with this problem. The light cavalry of the Magyars and Saracens could ride around or away from them: the Dane took to his ships and disappeared when they tardily crept up to drive him from his prey. The local count or duke who could put a few hundred mailed horsemen of approved valour into the field, men bound to him by every tie of discipline and obedience, and trained to war from their youth up, was really a far more formidable foe to the plundering invader. Even if he could not check the raiders for want of numbers, his troop of riders hung round the intruders, cut off their stragglers, intercepted them at every defensible pass or ford where the few can withstand the many, circumvented them by cross-roads which the native must know better than the stranger.

No less important than the rise of the mailed horseman was the rise of the feudal castle. In the Frankish empire fortified places had hitherto been rare: save the towns that possessed ancient Roman walls there seem to have been none that could defend themselves: Frankish ideas of fortification went no further than heaping up a mound, surrounding it with a ditch, and crowning it with a palisade. Such temporary strongholds were inadequate, and safety from the Dane was only found by the use of permanent fortifications of firm masonry. Every town that had not perished surrounded itself with a ring-wall: fortified bridge-heads were built to shut up the rivers to the Viking ships. But most important of all were the castles, which rose up on every hand, to form safe residences for the chiefs who had once dwelt in open villas, and to serve as bases for the defence of the country-side. Few in number at first, they gradually spread over the breadth of the land, as each lord who was able reared himself a stronghold. The existence of these castles changed the whole face of war: when an enemy appeared there were now countless places of refuge to seek, and the invader, instead of sweeping easily over the district in search of plunder, found that it could for the future only be procured at the cost of a series of lengthy sieges. There was hardly any sure method known of reducing a strong place, save the expedient of starving it out: but to sit three months before a castle till famine should reduce it, was not what Dane or Magyar desired. Their booty would be limited, while the delay would allow the whole military strength of the country to be mustered against them. Hence it may be truly said that the rise of the feudal castle was the best remedy that could have been found against the pressing evils that threatened Christendom in the ninth century.

The military triumph was a political disaster. At a moment when the kingly power was shaken by the unhappy civil wars of the descendants of Charles the Great, when almost every province was disputed by two lords, it was absolutely fatal that the control of the warlike strength of Europe should pass into the hands of a crowd of petty magnates, each intent on his own aggrandisement, and caring nought for the general welfare of the kingdom so long as his own county was well guarded. The price at which Christendom bought its safety was enormous: nevertheless no price was too high when the future of Europe was at stake. Any ransom was worth paying, if thereby Rome was saved from the Saracen, Mainz from the Magyar, Paris from the heathen of the North.

Made in the USA
San Bernardino, CA
01 March 2020